INSIGHT GUIDES

OMAN & THE UAE

INSIGHT GUIDE

OMAN
& THE UAE

Editorial
Series Editor
Dorothy Stannard

Distribution

UK & Ireland
GeoCenter International Ltd
Meridian House, Churchill Way West
Basingstoke, Hampshire RG21 6YR
Fax: (44) 1256 817988

United States
Langenscheidt Publishers, Inc.
36–36 33rd Street 4th Floor
Long Island City, NY 11106
Fax: 1 (718) 784 0640

Australia
Universal Publishers
1 Waterloo Road
Macquarie Park, NSW 2113
Fax: (61) 2 9888 9074

New Zealand
Hema Maps New Zealand Ltd (HNZ)
Unit 2, 10 Cryers Road
East Tamaki, Auckland 2013
Tel: (64) 9 273 6459
Fax: (64) 9 273 6479

Worldwide
**Apa Publications GmbH & Co.
Verlag KG (Singapore branch)**
38 Joo Koon Road, Singapore 628990
Tel: (65) 6865 1600. Fax: (65) 6861 6438

Printing

Insight Print Services (Pte) Ltd
38 Joo Koon Road, Singapore 628990
Tel: (65) 6865 1600. Fax: (65) 6861 6438

©2009 Apa Publications GmbH & Co.
Verlag KG (Singapore branch)
All Rights Reserved

First Edition 1998
Updated 2009

CONTACTING THE EDITORS
We would appreciate it if readers
would alert us to errors or out-
dated information by writing to:
**Insight Guides, P.O. Box 7910,
London SE1 1WE, England.
Fax: (44) 20 7403 0290.
insight@apaguide.co.uk**

www.insightguides.com

ABOUT THIS BOOK

The first Insight Guide pioneered the use of creative full-colour photography in travel guides in 1970. Since then, we have expanded our range to cater for our readers' need not only for reliable information about their chosen destination but also for a real understanding of the culture and workings of that destination. Now, when the internet can supply inexhaustible (but not always reliable) facts, our books marry text and pictures to provide those much more elusive qualities: knowledge and discernment. To achieve this, they rely heavily on the authority of locally based writers and photographers.

How to use this book
The book is carefully structured to convey an understanding of the countries and their cultures and to guide readers through their sights and attractions:

◆ To understand the region, you need to know something of its past. The **Features** section covers the states' history and culture.

◆ The main **Places** section provides full details of all the areas worth seeing. The chief

– ∙ –	International Boundary
– – – –	Province Boundary
– ∙ – ∙ –	National Park/Reserve
– – – –	Ferry Route
⊖	Border Crossing
✈ ✈	Airport: International/Regional
🚌	Bus Station
✉	Post Office
❶	Tourist Information
∴	Archaeological Site
☾	Mosque
∩	Cave
⚊	Statue/Monument
★	Place of Interest
⌇	Beach
⌖	Lighthouse
◼ ⌂	Castle (ruins)
☀	Viewpoint

The main places of interest in the Places section are coordinated by number with a full-colour map (e.g. ❶), and a symbol at the top of every right-hand page tells you where to find the map.

places of interest are coordinated by number with full-colour maps.

◆ The **Travel Tips** is a listings section with information on travel, hotels, restaurants, shopping etc.

The contributors

Like all Insight Guides, this book is a joint effort. Covering most of Oman – the Batinah Coast, Sur and the Wahiba Sands, the Interior and Dhofar – is **Christine Osborne**, who began her long association with Oman during the Dhofari War. Writing on Muscat, Oman's capital, is the journalist **Tom Athey**, who worked as the editor of *Oman Today* until moving to Dubai. Athey also

wrote the features on forts and camel racing, and compiled the Travel Tips on Oman. Archaeologist **Carl Phillips** wrote the essay on archaeology and the chapter on Musandam, and also contributed to the chapter on Dhofar and the story on frankincense.

The UAE places chapters were tackled by two UAE residents. **Ann Verbeek** wrote on Abu Dhabi, Dubai, Ras al Khaimah and Fujairah, **Matt Jones** on Sharjah, Ajman and Umm al Qaiwain and provided the short feature on wadi-bashing.

Contributors to the history and features section include **William Facey**, a director of the London Centre of Arab Studies, who wrote The Maritime Heritage and Islam in Southeast Arabia; **Alan Keohane**, a writer and photographer, who wrote The Bedu, Falconry and All that Glisters (jewellery); **Geoffrey Weston**, for many years the *Times* correspondent in the Middle East, who wrote The UAE From Rags to Riches, The Oil Boom, and the short profile on Sheikh Zayed; racing correspondent **Jamie Reid**, who wrote Kings of the Turf; and **Michael Gallagher**, curator at Oman Natural History Museum, who wrote on Dhofar's birdlife. The history of Oman was written by **Sir Donald Hawley**, who from 1958–1961 was H.M. Political Agent in the Trucial States and from 1971–1975 British Ambassador to Oman.

Travel Tips for the UAE were provided by **Jane Matthew**, whose experience of living in Abu Dhabi and Dubai was also mined for Daily Life and Expatriates. This edition of the guide has been updated by **Sylvia Buchanan**. Many new images have been added by **Kevin Cummins**, who photographed the region in 2008.

INSIGHT GUIDE
OMAN & THE UAE

CONTENTS

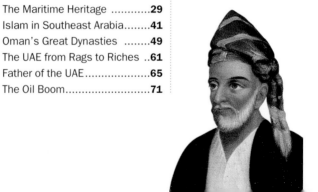

Trading anecdotes, Dubai

Travel Tips

◆Full Travel Tips index
is on page **281**

THE BEST OF OMAN

Setting priorities, unique attractions, top beaches...
here, at a glance, are our recommendations, plus some tips and tricks
even the locals won't always know

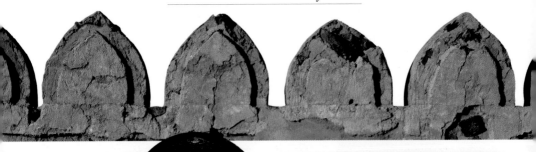

TOP ATTRACTIONS

- **Bat** These "Beehive tombs", about 20 km (12 miles) from Ibri, are representative of Oman's Early Bronze Age. *See page 163.*
- **Land of frankincense** Since antiquity, the Dhofar region has been a major producer of high-quality frankincense. *See pages 183–92.*
- **Bahla** The castle at Bahla is the largest and oldest castle in Oman. Bahla also has one of the best souqs in the country. *See page 161.*
- **Jabrin Castle** Built in the 17th century, this fortified palace is known for its painted wooden ceilings. *See page 162.*

- **Sur** This quiet little coastal city is famous for its dhow shipyards. *See page 171.*
- **The Grand Mosque, Muscat** is the only mosque in Oman that non-Muslims are allowed to visit. It can accommodate 20,000 worshippers, and has an amazing Swarovski crystal chandelier. *See page 137.*

BEST ADVENTURES

- **Al Hoota Cave** Located at the base of Jebel Shams, this cave is one of Oman's most spectacular tourist attractions. *See page 160.*
- **Desert camel trek** A trip to the desert should not be missed. Spend the night in a Bedu tent or under the stars. *See page 176.*
- **Hiking**. One of the most popular destinations for adventurous hikers is **Snake Canyon**, a trek that involves jumping into rock pools and swimming through ravines.

- **Jabal Shams** has several wonderful treks, one of which runs along the mountain rim overlooking **Wadi Nakhr**, a miniature Grand Canyon. *See page 161.*
- **Diving** The **Daymaniyat Islands** and the **Musandam Peninsula** offer the best opportunities for diving. *See pages 145 and 199.*
- **Wadi-bashing** Oman's many wadis provide adventurous opportunities for off-road enthusiasts. *See pages 148 and 165.*

ABOVE: battlements of Jabrin Castle.
ABOVE CENTRE: the chandelier in Muscat's Grand Mosque. **RIGHT:** tracks in the desert.

BEST SOUQS

Muttrah Souq
Located on the Muttrah Corniche, this is Oman's oldest souq. Under a palm frond roof, and with the scent of frankincense wafting in the air, it sells everything from Omani silver to belly dancing costumes. *See page 135.*

● **Al Husn Souq** This souq in Salalah is the focus of the old town. It specialises in gold, silver and frankincense. *See page 184.*

● **Nizwa Souq** As you pass through the souq's enormous wooden doors, you will find several traditional buildings, each labelled with the products they sell. *See page 159.*

● **Souq al Arba, Ibra** Held on Wednesday morning, this is the only souq in Oman dedicated solely to women. It allows women to haggle and barter without being observed by men. *See page 176.*

BEST THINGS TO DO IN THE OFF-SEASON

● **Visit Salalah** Thanks to an annual Indian monsoon, from early June to mid-September, Salalah is transformed into a lush blanket of green with tumbling waterfalls and meandering streams. *See page 184.*

● **Jebel Akhdar**, "Green Mountain", in Arabic, Jebel Akhdar rises to more than 3,050 metres (10,000 ft) above sea level, making it a cool retreat

for campers and hikers alike. *See page 155.*

● **Ras al Hadd** Visit the turtle sanctuary (40 km/25 miles from Sur) where temperatures are much cooler than in Muscat during the summer. *See page 173.*

● **Wadi Shab, Wadi Tiwi, and Wadi Bin Khalid** Located between Muscat and Sur, these wadis are some of the most beautiful in Oman. *See pages 170, 175.*

BEST HOTELS

● **The Chedi** An exclusive beach resort that exudes luxury and tranquillity. With its own private beach (and very few children), this is the perfect place to relax and enjoy a day at the spa. *See page 288.*

● **Al Husn Hotel at the Shangri-La Barr Al Jissah Resort & Spa** This six-star hotel near Muscat has magnificent views and ultra-luxurious rooms. You even get your own butler if so desired. *See page 289.*

● **Six Senses Hideaway, Zighy Bay** This exclusive resort is hidden away in the northernmost part of the Musandam Peninsula. Made from stone and traditional materi-

als, rooms come with their very own pool. *See page 291.*

● **Al Bustan Palace Hotel** Highlighting Arabian culture with Art Deco influences, this recently refurbished hotel now offers lagoon-side rooms. *See page 135.*

LEFT: Wadi Bin Khalid near Sur. **TOP:** go for gold in the souqs. **ABOVE:** Al Husn Hotel at Shangri-La Barr Al Jissah Resort & Spa.

THE BEST OF THE UAE

Dubai has been a top travel destination for several years, but Abu Dhabi is catching up, and the lesser known emirates – Sharjah, Ajman, Umm al Qaiwan, Ras al Khaimah and Fujairah – have their own attractions

TOP SIGHTS

- **Khor Dubai** Dividing the city, Dubai's creek is an atmospheric waterway bustling with traditional dhows, *abras* (water taxis) and other vessels. *See page 225.*
- **Souqs** Among the UAE's best souqs are Dubai's gold and spice souqs *(see page 228)*, and the massive Sharjah Souq. S*ee page 245.*
- **Hatta** A short excursion from Dubai city, Hatta offers cool pools, an historic fort and the Hatta Fort Hotel, one of Dubai's more characterful hotels. *See page 236.*
- **Beaches** Among the best beaches in the Emirates are **Jumeirah Beach** and **Mamzar Beach Park**, both in Dubai *(see pages 232 and 235)*, **Sharjah's coastline** on the road to Ajman, and **Fujairah.** *See page 274.*
- **Emirates Heritage Village, Abu Dhabi** This is one of the best places to learn about the transformation of the Emirates from a sleepy backwater to the megawealthy hub of the Middle East. *See page 214.*
- **Bastakia** Explore this district of old Dubai, with its traditional architecture and Majlis Art Gallery. *See page 231.*

TOP ACTIVITIES

- **Wadi-bashing** Four-wheel drive excursions into the often spectacular wadis (dry river beds) of the UAE make an exhilarating change from the cities. One of the best wadi trips isfrom Ras al Khaimah to Dibba via the Wadi Bih. *See page 267.*
- **A dhow cruise** At some point, preferably at sunset, be sure to take a dhow cruise. It is one of the best ways to experience old Dubai. *See page 228.*
- **Diving and snorkelling** Fujairah is the best spot in the Emirates for diving (though the Musandam Peninsula, Oman, is also good). *See pages 271–7.*
- **A night at the races** Dubai is known for its racing stables. From November–April join locals and expats for a night at Nad al Sheba racecourse. You could also join the Nad Al Sheba Club's Breakfast Stable Tour. *See pages 117 and 234.*
- **Golf** The Dubai Creek Golf & Yacht Club is the sleekest place to play golf. Afterwards, watch the sun set from the Boardwalk Restaurant. *See page 234.*

Top: traditional dhows on Dubai Creek.
Right: Dubai Creek Golf & Yacht Club.

UAE FOR FAMILIES

- **Ferrari Theme Park, Abu Dhabi** Located on Yas Island, this is the world's first Ferrari theme park. *See page 217.*
- **Wild Wadi Water Park** This state-of-the-art water-park in Dubai has 14 inter-connected rides. *See page 232.*
- **Dubailand** This theme park will be bigger than Disneyland and Disney World combined when it is finished. This won't be until 2018, but some attractions are already open. *See page 235.*
- **Dreamland Aqua Park** Located north of Umm al Qaiwain, this water park has all manner of rides, slides and wave pools. It also has an animal corner and go-karting. *See page 259.*

AMBITIOUS ARCHITECTURE

- The sail-like **Burj Al-Arab** (Tower of the Arabs), is one of Dubai's most distinctive landmarks. *See page 237.*
- **The Palms** These three man-made islands shaped like palm trees can be seen from space. *See page 237.*
- **Emirates Palace Hotel** in Abu Dhabi encapsulates the over-the-top opulence of the UAE. It has 100 decorative domes. *See page 214.*
- **Saadiyat Island Cultural District** This ambitious project in Abu Dhabi is scheduled to open in 2012. It will include a new Guggenheim Museum, a branch of the Louvre and a performing arts centre. *See page 217.*

SOMETHING DIFFERENT

- **Bird-watching** If you want to get away from the city of Dubai, visit Ras Al Khor Wildlife Sanctuary. *See page 235.*
- **Camel racing** is popular in both Oman and the UAE. It is held at the Nad Al Sheba Racecourse in Dubai and just outside Digdagga in Ras al Khaimah. *See pages 234 and 265.*
- **A bird's-eye view** Perhaps the best way of making sense of Dubai's sprawling cityscape, and spotting its famous landmarks, is by helicopter. *See page 232.*
- **Bull-fighting** is a popular sport in Fujairah. Two large and pampered bulls are pitted against each other, until one is forced to the ground. *See page 272.*
- **Motor racing** The first Formula 1 racetrack in the UAE is to open on Yas Island, Abu Dhabi. *See page 217.*

ABOVE LEFT: camel rides are popular with children. **ABOVE:** Burj Al-Arab. **BELOW:** The Palms, one of Dubai's many extravagant development projects.

A DIP INTO ARABIA

In spite of a shared culture, Oman and the UAE offer

quite different attractions for visitors

The most easy-going of the Gulf countries, Oman and the UAE are rewarding destinations for travellers. As increasing numbers of people are finding out, they are worth much more than the standard 24-hour stopover for duty-free shopping on journeys between Europe and the Far East. The two countries complement each other well. While upfront Dubai, Abu Dhabi and Sharjah offer great shopping, bustling waterfronts, dream beaches and sparkling high-rise hotels, Oman, more cautious towards tourism, offers exhilarating scenery, adventure travel and a taste of an older, pre-oil Arabia in its souqs and villages. Fujairah and Ras al Khaimah, two of the less well-known emirates, are also known for their scenic beauty.

The first section of this guide is devoted to the history and culture of southeast Arabia, with chapters on formative influences such as seafaring, Islam, and the Bedu, and features on life in the area today. This is followed by a region by region guide to Oman and an "emirate by emirate" guide to the UAE. At the back of the book, the Travel Tips section provides essential practical information, from visas and passports to recommended restaurants and hotels. ❑

PRECEDING PAGES: army band, Dubai; National Day celebrations in Oman. **LEFT:** camel and owner, Ajman.

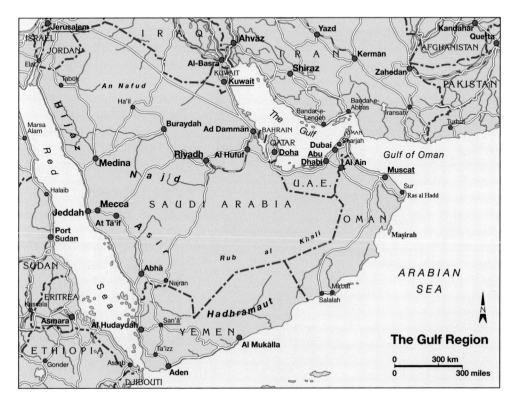

The Gulf Region

aua Oadi · Pharatha · te · Abucei · orommmus · Taxiana · Sot
Rhadi vicus · Satula · Sacor sinus · Apphana
ca ·ciuitas · A.ina · Lugana · Geesa · Adari · Sinus
Thamydeni · Leaniti · Itamos portus · E
Athritę · Salma · Arre vicus · Digima · Saphtha · Chersonesi extrema · Mallada ciuitas
Masæmanes · Læceni · Phigia · Hsbriona ciuit.
Iabri · Alata ciuitas · Magorum sinus · Themi · Ithar ciuit. · Ichara · Tharro
Salina · Vdemi · Zames mons · Asateni · Ibirtha · Bilbana ciuit. · Cora ciuitas · Atta vicus · Saxoa ciuit. · Cahana ciuit · Caplina ciuit · Sacra soli
Maliche · Gorda · Marata · Ger. · Magundana ciuit.
ithrippa · Betius fluui: · Alapeni · Biabanna · Iolisitę · Catara · rei · Sata · Aeg · Corada · ei · Anari · ti · Rho
Carna · ABIA · Giratha · gitę · Masthala · Domana · Atia · R.habana regia
Manitę · Catanitę · Malan · Marithi montes · Dacharemoizę · Tragar · L.or fluuius
Macoraba · Olaphia · Omanitę
Thumata · Jnapha · Maocosmus metrop. · Brexeum vel acipi · Omanum empo-
Smyrnophoros inte- · Tanuitę · Iritę · Labris · Latea · Eron vicus · rium
rior regio · FOE · Frala · Bliulei · Nagara metropolis · ritę
Agdami · Carman regia · Laaththa · Alumeotę · Ioba · Aula
Min · Albana · Chargata · gens magna · Marmatha · Sachalitę
iti · ei · Amara · Ango vicus
nala · Marasdi · Maraba metropolis · Sophanitę · LI · Ausara · Motaeis
dedi pagus · Doreni · Mocritę · Thumna · Vodona · X · Thabanne
cus · Mariama · montę · Gorda · Smyrnophoros regio
Sabe · Magulaba · Syleum · Citheba · Madasara- · exterior
Sabęi · Achitę · nitę · Beenum
Pudm ciuitas · Manambis · Thalba · Sabatha me- · Cathra · Mæpha · Prion flu.
Aeli vicus · regia · Climax · Araganitę · tropolis · Saruum · motrop.
Masonitę · mons · Stygis aquę fons · Araga · Maphoritę · Meibath · Fretus portus
Miba · Saphar · Areregia · Rheda · villa · Thialemath op
Elefori · Saraca · metro- · Maphoritę · Sachle · Trulla pro pidum
rgus · Sarite · polis · Mueza emporium · Sapharitę · Macala · etus · Prionotus mons · Asc
pp · Sesippi portus · Thurss · Lachchere · Hyela · Rhatinę · Sachle · Cua · Dioscori-
Pseudocelis · Sabe regia · Doua · Sochchor · Bana · Dela · Adra · Erytha · dis in
Palmdromos · Occelis emporiū · Maridache ciuit. · ri · Asabia emporiū · Mela mons · ciuitas · Trete · sula
extrema · Sarina ciuitas · Madoce ciuit. · Home · Leos vicus · te · Ammonispha · Cane empor. extremium · Dioscor
noe · vicus
Mandaith · Posidium Prom. · Cabubathra pro · Abasona · Magnum lit · Mada vicus · RVBRV
vicus · Mosylon emporium · Agathoclis
Mondi · & promontorium · Cocconata tres · RVBRVM
es empo: · Cobe empo-
um · Aualites sinus · rium
Elephas mons

CUS

Rhudiana

Sagdana
insula

Miletus

Carmaniicus
sinus

Cathrappus flu:

Thassis

Parepaphitis

Gedrosię pars

MANIA

Agde

Corius flu:

nites

Persię montes

Achindana flu:

Vorochtha

Nigista

Arę

Andanius flu:

Charadrę

Tylus

Arathos

Saganus flu:

Chodda

Armuzium
extremum

Caba

dina

Chanto

Ichthyophagorum
sinus

Taruana

Sabis
Alexandria

Throasea

Orat

nice

ciuitas

Armuza

Pas

Samydaces flu:

Cophanta

Macę

Asaborum prom:

Semiramidis mons
qui & Strongil9

argadę

Sarus flu:

Asabi

Tisa

Emandriaces flu:

Melanes montes Asaborū

Carpolla extre
mum

Cenchati

Tigris

Nonnana

Messin

Samydace

Chelono phagi

Cryptus por
ties

Appa

Rhogana

Bernobila

Badara

Libanotophoros

Bagia extre
ma

Cosude ab
as Bogara

Orbiculum
Dianę

Corodamum promonto:
rium

Gyeza portus

Alambatera
extremum

Gophanta portus

Zorumba flum:

Mulara

Abissa

Asboa vicus

Didymi montes

Organa

Polla

INDICVM   MA   RE

Sachalites sinus, in
uo Colymbetes ynici super
eribus transnauigauit

Carmina

Sarapiadis in
qua fanum

Zenobij insulę 7

Syagros extrema

Moscha portus

Medius meridianus .84.
reliqui ad hunc inclinan:
tur pro exigentia paralle:
lorum 13. 27

uitus

MARE

Decisive Dates

c5000–3000 BC Evidence of coastal and inland settlements. Discovery of Ubaid pottery at coastal sites proves contact with southern Iraq.

c3000 BC Magan, an area roughly corresponding with the UAE and northern Oman, supplies the city states of southern Mesopotamia with a range of raw materials, including copper.

c2500–2000 BC Umm an-Nar period, named after excavations on the small island of Umm an-Nar near Abu Dhabi. Period characterised by complex burials, far-reaching trade networks and sophisticated crafts.

AD 77 Pliny's *Natural History* mentions the Arabian shore of the Gulf and describes how Arab ships are sewn together.

1st century AD A Greek in the employ of the Roman navy, writes *Periplus of the Erythraean Sea*. This description of trade around the coast of the Indian Ocean describes Omana as Persian.

AD 226–640 The Sassanid period. Persian seamen control sea trade.

630 Islam is brought to Oman.

632 Death of the Prophet Mohammed.

751 Oman elects its first Imam, Julanda bin Mas'ud.

8th–9th centuries Arab seafaring and trading are at their height, with voyages as far as China.

The Bat tombs in Oman and the tombs at Hili in Abu Dhabi date from this period.

c2000 BC–1st millennium BC Arab tribes arrive from southwest and central Arabia. They find coastal communities and inland wadis inhabited by people of Persian origin.

1300–300 BC The Iron Age. The *falaj* system develops at the beginning of the first millennium BC.

563 BC Cyrus the Great from Persia conquers Oman, founding the Achaemenid Dynasty.

300 BC The region is part of a trade network involving the whole of the Arabian peninsula. Ad Door at Umm al Qaiwain is an important port. From Sumhuram in Dhofar, southern Oman, frankincense is exported across the seas and over the desert, supplying Greece and Rome.

10th century Sohar in Oman is a hub of maritime trade.

14th century Hormuz, an island off modern-day Iran, opposite the Musandam Peninsula, is at its zenith, completely controlling the mouth of the Gulf.

16th century The Portuguese dominate trade in the Gulf and the Indian Ocean. They capture Muscat in 1507 and then Hormuz.

1624–1738 Ya'ruba Dynasty rules Oman.

1650 Imam Sultan bin Saif expels the Portuguese.

1646 Commercial treaty is signed between Oman's Imam and the British East India Company. The Gulf is vital for their passage to India.

1718–28 Civil War in Oman.

1730s Saif bin Sultan II of Oman invites the Persians to help him secure his bid to be Imam.

1742 The Persians establish control of Muscat.

1747 Ahmed bin Said drives the Persians from Oman and is elected Imam. A golden age ensues.Thus begins the Al bu Said Dynasty. Meanwhile the Qawasim of Ras al Khaimah become increasingly powerful and their ports soon dominate the Gulf.

1761 Abu Dhabi is founded.

1820 A British campaign to quash the Qawasim culminates in the razing of Ras al Khaimah and other Qawasim ports, including Sharjah, Umm al Qaiwain, Ajman and Lingah. Thus begins the General Treaty of Peace and British involvement in the Emirates.

1830s The pearl trade is at its height.

1833 Dubai's Bani Yas, a sub-tribe of the Bedu Al Bu Falasah, sets up its own principality, ruled by the Al Maktoum family.

1853 The Perpetual Peace is signed. In return for ceasing hostilities at sea, the British guarantee to protect the Trucial States from external attack.

1864 The first maritime telegraph line is laid in the Gulf by the British. Telegraph stations are established on the Musandam Peninsula.

1874 The British East India Company is dissolved.

1892 The Exclusive Agreement is signed with Britain, preventing the rulers of the Trucial Coast from forming agreements with any other foreign government.

1898 Britain's Lord Curzon visits the Gulf in response to interest shown in the region by Russia and Germany.

1920s Following the defeat of Germany in World War I and the collapse of the Ottoman Empire, Britain is at its most influential in the Middle East.

1930s The pearl industry declines following the arrival of the Japanese cultured pearl.

1932 Imperial Airways (later to become British Airways) begins its air service to Sharjah.

1936–1952 The rulers of the Trucial States sign oil concessions with the Iraq Petroleum Company.

1950 Formation of the Trucial Oman Scouts, a defence force led by British officers.

1951 A causeway is built linking Abu Dhabi to the mainland. It is replaced by Al Maqta Bridge in 1968.

1952 Saudis occupy part of Buraimi, but are eventually (1955) driven out by Trucial Oman Scouts. A Trucial States Council is formed, with the aim of solving problems of common interest.

1954–59 Imamate rebellion under Ghalib ibn Ali in Oman. British help restore Said bin Taimur to power.

1959 Oil is discovered in Abu Dhabi.

PRECEDING PAGES: Ptolemy's map of Arabia, published in 1584, shows Greek placenames.
ABOVE LEFT: prehistoric rock engravings of camels at Tawi, the Musandam Peninsula.
ABOVE RIGHT: mural of Sultan Qaboos.

1965–1975 Dhofar Rebellion in Oman.

1962 The first bridge is built over Dubai's creek.

1967 Oman produces oil in commercial quantities.

1970 Accession of Sultan Qaboos bin Said in Oman.

1971 Britain withdraws from the Gulf. The United Arab Emirates is inaugurated on 2 December, with Sheikh Zayed of Abu Dhabi as President of the Federation and Sheikh Rasheed bin Said Al Maktoum as Vice-President and Prime Minister.

1973 Oman's first airport, Seeb International, opens.

1980 Iran-Iraq War.

1981 The GCC (Gulf Cooperation Council), comprising Saudi Arabia, Kuwait, the UAE, Bahrain, Qatar and Oman, is formed.

1986 Sultan Qaboos University, Oman's first university, opens.

1990 Iraq invades Kuwait. Gulf War ensues.

1991 Oman's Majlis Ash-Shura, a consultative council with 59 elected members, is inaugurated.

1995 Oman celebrates Sultan Qaboos's silver jubilee.

2004 The founder and president of the UAE, Sheikh Zayed bin Sultan Al Nahyan, dies at the age of 86.

2006 Sheikh Maktoum bin Rashid al-Maktoum, leader of Dubai, dies aged 62.

2007 Cyclone Gonu hits the Ararbian Peninsula, causing nearly 50 deaths and some $4.5 billion-worth of damage in Oman. Abu Dhabi unveils plans for a new multi-billion-dollar cultural district on Saadiyat Island. Planned features include a Guggenheim Museum and a branch of the Louvre. ❑

ARCHAEOLOGY

*Recent archaeological explorations of Oman and the UAE have revealed
a rich and varied ancient history*

If there is a general perception that the southeast corner of the Arabian Peninsula has, until recent times, been relatively isolated, nothing could be further from the truth. From as early as 5000 BC, the area played an important part in the development of the ancient civilisations of western Asia.

There are practically no historical documents originating from the UAE and Oman prior to the Islamic period, though there are references to the region by neighbouring peoples and trading partners from as early as *c.*2330 BC. Unfortunately these are few and far between, so the historical framework used by archaeologists is based primarily on the results of excavations. The names given to different periods in the development of southeast Arabia are usually derived from the names of the excavated sites.

Prehistoric prelude (5000–3000 BC)

Archaeological surveys indicate a constantly changing mosaic of coastal and inland settlements, but many of the earliest sites lie along the shores of the Arabian Gulf and the Gulf of Oman. Until about 16,000 years ago, when sea levels began to rise, the area now occupied by the Gulf would have formed a river valley extending as far as the Straits of Hormuz. The shoreline of the Gulf of Oman would have been distant from its present location and 100–150 metres (330–490 ft) lower than the present-day mean sea level. When the sea level began to rise it attained something like its present level about 8,000 years ago, creating a variety of coastal landscapes, including the sand and mud flats of the Arabian Gulf, the fjord-like coastline of the Musandam Peninsula, the plain of the Batinah and the steep cliffs extending from north of Muscat south past Ras al Hadd. Coastal lagoons, rich in mangroves, also became a significant feature and can still be seen near the

coast of Umm al Qaiwain, at Khor Kalba and at Qurm near Muscat. These varied marine habitats afforded a glut of easily obtained food such as shellfish, fish, turtle and dugong. Mangroves attracted birdlife which could be hunted, and adjacent inland areas supported gazelle and, later on, grazing for sheep, goats and cattle.

The archaeological remains left by these early communities are distinguished by large accumulations of shells that were collected for food and then discarded. Excavation of "shell middens" at Ras al Hamra near Qurm has revealed the ground plan of small groups of circular buildings, indicated by stone foundations or arrangements of post-holes. Other finds show that the inhabitants were adept at making stone tools and shell artefacts, including personal jewellery and functional but nevertheless aesthetically pleasing objects such as large shell hooks.

Such items were often found amongst burials, which form large cemeteries and hint at the social complexity of the fishing communities.

LEFT: Great Hili Tomb near Al Ain (3rd millennium BC).
ABOVE RIGHT: finds from Shimmel, displayed in Ras al Khaimah's museum.

On the Gulf coast similar shell middens are found along the margins of former lagoons, for example at Umm al Qaiwain and the Hamriyah area of Sharjah. Some of the Gulf coast middens have also provided evidence of contact with southern Iraq from 5000–4000 BC, in particular a type of pottery called Ubaid pottery, named after a site in southern Iraq. The pottery was clearly imported at this early date, though whether directly or indirectly has not been confirmed. However, similar finds on the island of Dalma (Abu Dhabi) suggest that the inhabitants were already accomplished sailors by this time.

Coastal midden sites were occupied up to and

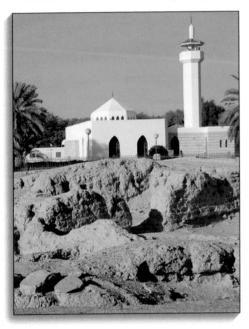

beyond 3000 BC. Prior to this it is probable that the arid conditions of Arabia today were not so harsh and that open grassland was available. Many of the stone tools, including finely crafted arrowheads, found in desert areas probably date from 5000–3000 BC and represent inland hunting and herding communities contemporary with the coastal communities.

The Hafit, Umm an-Nar and Wadi Suq periods (3000–1300 BC)

At around 3000 BC there was a dramatic transformation of the way people lived in southeast Arabia. Contact with southern Iraq, indicated by the presence of Ubaid pottery, ended by around 4 000 BC. Whilst the local communities of southeast Arabia continued to flourish beyond this time, at around 3000 BC there is evidence of renewed contact with southern Mesopotamia. In the late 4th millennium BC there are references in Mesopotamian texts to a place named Dilmun (now Bahrain), and towards the end of the 3rd millennium, c.2330 BC Dilmun is mentioned along with Magan and Meluhha.

Between them, these three places supplied the city states of southern Mesopotamia with a range of raw materials and exotic goods, including timber, stone and, above all, copper. On the basis of the abundance of copper deposits, and archaeological evidence that they were being exploited as early as the 3rd millennium BC, Magan, sometimes referred to in texts as "the Copper Mountain of Magan", is recognised as the area of southeast Arabia which corresponds with the UAE and Oman. Meluhha is generally identified as the Indus Valley.

COPPER MINING

Ancient Magan was an important supplier of stone and copper. Sites in Oman such as Maysar, in the Wadi Samad area near Nizwa, have produced clear evidence for the mining, processing and export of copper on a large scale during the 3rd millennium BC, including anvil and crushing stones, a smelting oven and copper beads and rings, chisels, knives and axes. It has been estimated that up to 4,000 tonnes/tons of copper were produced in the region in the Umm an-Nar period.

Copper was still being mined in the late Middle Ages with travellers to the region reporting on copper mines. However, by the late 19th century copper sheeting was being imported from Bombay.

Both stone and copper are still readily obtained in the UAE and Oman, and though oil and natural gas have dominated the economy for decades, recent attempts to reduce dependence on oil in Oman have seen a regeneration of the copper-mining industry. In 1983 a mine at Lasail, in Wadi al Jizzi near Sohar, was reworked for the first time since antiquity and new deposits have been found in Yanqul, north of Ibri, and on the Batinah Coast. A bonus of the refining process are small quantities of gold and silver.

Renewed contacts with Mesopotamia from the end of the 4th millennium are an indication of Magan's developing trading relations with surrounding countries, as described some 700 years later in Mesopotamian texts. Evidence includes pottery of Mesopotamian import found in tombs.

These tombs are of a type unique to the UAE and Oman at this time, when they became a conspicuous feature of the landscape – large, stone cairns, often placed at the entrance to wadis and in clearly visible groups, or along the ridges or summit of a mountain to form a dramatic skyline. Tombs of this type were first

wheat, barley and dates being cultivated. Crops and the herding of sheep, goats and cattle, introduced at an earlier date, as shown by some of the coastal midden sites, led to settlement in inland areas where there was sufficient water for irrigation. A settlement pattern similar to that of more recent times began to emerge and from 2500 BC there is a clear picture of what these early settlements were like.

The period from 2500–2000 BC is referred to as the Umm an-Nar period, named after the small island near Abu Dhabi where excavations by Danish archaeologists first produced evidence for this period. During this period a new

excavated at Jebel Hafit near Al Ain and are often called "Hafit tombs". Others have a characteristic beehive-shape and are consequently called "beehive tombs". Both the Hafit and beehive tombs date from the end of the 4th millennium to c.2500 BC.

These tombs indicate the probable distribution of settlement and there is evidence that a farming, oasis-based economy had been introduced by this time. Excavations at the important site of Hili 8, near Al Ain, show that by 3000 BC agriculture was established, with

LEFT: Hili Archaeological Park in Al Ain, Abu Dhabi.
ABOVE: beehive tombs (2500 BC), near Al Ain.

type of tomb was introduced. Circular and averaging about 9 metres (30 ft) in diameter, it stands above ground and has a smooth exterior wall built of finely worked masonry. Some of the tombs on the island of Umm an-Nar also had relief carvings on the outer wall, depicting wild animals such as gazelles and snakes as well as domesticated animals like cattle. There are also depictions of camels, which were probably domesticated by this time.

Excavation has shown that the tombs were used for multiple burials with a range of grave goods, including pottery (some imported from Mesopotamia, Iran or the Indus), stone vessels, bronze weapons, shell rings and shell and stone beads. The most spectacular Umm an-Nar tomb excavated so far is displayed in Hili Archaeological Park, near Al Ain*(see page 217)*. It has carvings on the outer wall of humans as well as animals.

The excavations at Hili 8, near Hili Archaeological Park, show that settlements from this period included large defensive towers. It is probable that similar towers were also built from the beginning of the 3rd millennium, and thus represent an established local tradition. The towers were probably surrounded by smaller buildings made from mud bricks and date palm wood. At Hili, Bat and Wadi Bahla such towers are distributed over a large area. They probably defined and defended the area of habitation and cultivation.

From the beginning of the 3rd millennium local pottery had been produced, and during the Umm an-Nar period pottery and other craft industries flourished. Distinctive stone vessels were manufactured and widely distributed, not only locally, but also to places in southern Iraq, Bahrain, Iran and the Indus. Likewise, imported items continued to arrive in southeast Arabia and the resulting distribution of exported and imported goods reflects the network of trading relations described in the Mesopotamian texts of the later 3rd millennium.

At the end of the 3rd millennium Magan ceased to be mentioned in Mesopotamian texts and Dilmun appears to have had a monopoly over the supply of goods to Mesopotamia. However, the range of exports remained much the same, with a large demand for copper, and since Dilmun had no copper sources of its own Magan probably remained the main supplier.

Recent excavations suggest that many of the 3rd millennium settlements continued to be occupied during the 2nd millennium. However, there are radical changes in the architecture of tombs and the range of pottery and other objects produced.

At the beginning of the 2nd millennium at least two types of tomb are characteristic. The first is circular, 3–4 metres (10–13 ft) in diameter, with a central, below ground, stone-lined burial chamber. Such tombs were first excavated in Wadi Suq, at the east end of Wadi al Jizzi which links the inland area of Al Ain with Sohar on the Gulf of Oman. Subsequently Wadi

Suq was adopted to describe the period from around 2000 to *c*.1300 BC.

The second type of tomb characteristic of the early Wadi Suq period was first recorded at Shimmel, near Ras al Khaimah. The Shimmel-type tombs are rectangular, a few metres wide but several metres long, and stand above ground. Grave goods included new types of pottery and stone vessels introduced at the start of the Wadi Suq period.

Imported items continue to show on-going trading links with surrounding countries, and

ANCIENT EXPORTS

Distinctive stone vessels were distributed to places in southern Iraq, Bahrain, Iran and the Indus Valley.

coastal settlements, particularly Ras al Jins near Ras al Hadd in Oman, which appears to have flourished during the Umm an-Nar and Wadi Suq periods, provide evidence for the highly developed maritime trade of this period.

In the past it was thought that the Wadi Suq period came to an end around 1700 BC and was followed by a "Dark Age" until the Iron Age at the beginning of the 1st millennium BC. This theory resulted from the lack of Wadi Suq period settlements showing a prolonged period of occupation. More recently, however, excavations, notably at Tell Abraq on the Gulf coast, have shown that the Wadi Suq period persisted until the start of the Iron Age (*c*.1300 BC).

The Iron Age (c.1300–300 BC)

In the Iron Age period there was an increase in the number and variety of settlements, which may have been due to the development of the *falaj* system of irrigation *(see page 156)*. Coastal middens continued to be occupied, villages evolved along the courses of wadis in mountainous areas, and there is evidence for larger villages of mud-brick houses, as excavated at Rumeilah and Hili 2 near Al Ain. There is also evidence of fortified hill-top settlements, such as at Lizq in Wadi Samad, Oman.

As in previous periods, changes are evident in the pottery and soft stone vessels manufac-

important for the supply of frankincense and whilst most of this was transported north through western Arabia southeast Arabia did not become marginalised. By the 1st century AD maritime trade was conducted around the entire Arabian Peninsula.

One of the main sites of the period is Mileiha, south of Dhaid. Occupation here dates from the end of the Iron Age when a large area became occupied for the next 700 years. From the earliest phases of occupation there are amphorae from Rhodes, alabaster vessels from the Yemen, and other imported goods. The town had a necropolis of monumental tombs. From the later

tured. The discovery of distinctive vessels in neighbouring countries such as Bahrain indicates that maritime trade had become an important part of the regional economy.

The post-Iron Age Period

From *c.*300 BC, in the period following the death of Alexander the Great, the UAE and Oman were part of a network of trade that involved the whole of the Arabian Peninsula and linked the countries of the Mediterranean with those of the Indian Ocean. Yemen and Dhofar became

phases of occupation are traces of a fort, graves with sacrificed camels and horses, and evidence that the town was minting its own coinage.

Contemporary with this phase of occupation (the first centuries AD) is Ad Door near Umm al Qaiwain, which was probably the port for inland Mileiha. Coins of the type minted at Mileiha have been found there as well as similar graves with sacrificed camels, pottery from the eastern Mediterranean, and items from neighbouring parts of Arabia, Iraq and Iran.

In Wadi Samad there is evidence of occupation of the same date as Mileiha and Ad Door and a wide range of items, some similar to finds at Mileiha and Ad Door, have been excavated. ❑

LEFT: Tower Tomb, Eastern Hajar.
ABOVE: Ad Door, post-Iron Age site.

Muskat &
from the Fisher-m

THE MARITIME HERITAGE

The UAE and Oman share an illustrious seafaring history. As early as the 8th century, trade vessels from the Gulf were sailing all the way to China

Dubai can come as a surprise to first-time visitors. Its modern buildings are imposing but are not distinctively Arabian. One hears a myriad of languages in addition to Arabic (75 percent of the population is expatriate) and the goods for sale seem to come from everywhere except Arabia. It all seems so cosmopolitan.

Yet, paradoxically, these very qualities are what make it typical of Gulf ports throughout history. Walk along the quaysides of the creeks at Dubai and Sharjah and you will be transported back in time, to an earlier kind of cosmopolitanism. Wooden dhows from Iran, Pakistan and India, as well as from other Gulf ports, line the quays up to five deep, while sons of Sindbad unload cargoes ranging from fridges, televisions and building materials to fabrics, spices and aromatics.

The pattern of trade

A casual glance at a map will show that the Arabian Peninsula stands between the Indian Ocean and the Mediterranean, and that this land mass is penetrated by two long seas, the Gulf of Arabia (also known as the Persian Gulf) and the Red Sea, channels for the westward flow of Indian Ocean goods to the centres of civilisation in the Near East and Mediterranean.

Alexandria's foundation and prosperity in the 4th century BC owed everything to the Red Sea trade from Africa and the Indian Ocean. With the coming of Islam in the 7th century AD, both the Gulf and Red Sea were crucial to the eastern trade of the Islamic world. But it is perhaps the Gulf which has the most glorious commercial history of the two, and Oman commands the Straits of Hormuz, which joins it to the Indian Ocean. As the centuries wore on, many commodities were passed on to Europe, first through the medium of Genoa and then Venice.

But not all the Indian Ocean trade was long-

PRECEDING PAGES: *Muscat Harbour*, from "16 Views of Places in the Persian Gulf 1809–10" by R. Temple.
LEFT: a *ghanjah*, used for cargo off Dubai in 1950.
ABOVE RIGHT: Arab passenger boat in the 13th century.

distance. Much of it was within the Indian Ocean itself. Over the millennia, this trading activity brought about a tremendous mixing of peoples around the coasts of the entire ocean and a lot of cultural as well as commercial exchange. The coves at Muscat and Muttrah, and the beach at Sohar, have witnessed the com-

ings and goings of Mesopotamians, Persians, Arabs, Indians, Africans, Greeks, Jews, Turks, Italians, Portuguese and northern Europeans.

The antiquity of the sea route

By the time of the Greek and Roman empires, trade from Ethiopia, southwest Arabia and India into the Near East and Mediterranean was in full swing, much of it by camel caravan along the land routes of the Arabian Peninsula. Gradually this trade transferred from the land routes to the Red Sea, as seafarers from Egypt, with Mediterranean ships, began to master the monsoon routes. By *c*.100 BC these interlopers had discovered that in their strongly built, square-rigged ships they could sail direct from Aden to India using the southwest monsoon, something which the Indian Ocean ships with their stitched construction were too fragile to do.

A vigorous trade developed, with merchants reaching India and China, and paying for luxury goods with Roman coin. This eventually caused a serious drain of precious metals in the Roman Empire, leading to devaluation and a slump in trade in the 3rd century BC.

When the sea trade revived, during Sassanid rule of Persia in the 5th century, it was in the hands of Persian seamen. They controlled trade between Ceylon and the Gulf, to the detriment

African explorer Ibn Battuta who had first-hand experience of them.

Hull planks were stitched together edge-to-edge with coconut twine, and the ribs were fitted later – the exact opposite of European boats. Gaps were caulked with a mixture of coir and fish oil being rammed into them. Except in larger vessels even a partial deck or a cabin was a luxury. Ships were still pointed at both ends, and used steering oars, one on each side. The square sail had evolved into something more triangular, enabling ships to sail close to the wind though not to tack in a modern sense.

The boat was essentially a cargo-carrying tub

of the Red Sea. It was this tradition that the Arabs took over after the spread of Islam in the 7th century. The first named Arab to make the voyage to China was an Omani in AD 750.

Medieval ships

The average Arabian seaman in pre-modern times spent his days and nights exposed to the elements, in conditions of hardship and hard work. First of all, he would have made a voyage in a smallish vessel, the planks of which were not nailed but stitched together, a mode of ship-building that came as a constant surprise to Europeans and Arabs from the Mediterranean, such as Marco Polo and the North

which needed constant maintenance. Crew and passengers accommodated themselves as best they could on top of the cargo, and ablutions were carried out in a precarious box slung out

THE ARABIAN NIGHTS

The coming of Islam, and the move of the Muslim capital from Damascus to Baghdad in AD 751, ushered in a Golden Age of Gulf trade. This period of Arab trade with China is associated with the court of the Caliph Harun al Rashid at Baghdad. The sailors and merchants inspired the stories of Sindbad the Sailor and the Arabian Nights.

over the side of the boat. The main advantage of such a craft was that it was flexible in heavy surf, and therefore less likely than more robustly built ships to be smashed while coming inshore. These fragile craft could be quite large, some carrying up to 400 men.

At the height of Gulf trade, in the 9th century, Gulf and Omani seamen were sailing all the way to China in such ships, and there was a huge colony of Arab merchants at Canton. By sailing all the way like this Arab merchants could cut out the middle man and make massive profits.

HIGH REWARDS

In a single successful voyage a merchant could make his fortune for life.

early December and make the round trip to China in 18 months, returning with the end of the northeast monsoon in April or May. Ships sailing to India and East Africa also made use of the northeast monsoon season. The breezes of the southwest monsoon in April to May were handy on the return from East Africa, blowing the ships back to the Omani coast.

By the 13th century the stern rudder was invented, but not the tiller: it was operated by a system of ropes, which allowed the rudder to be unshipped easily when the boat was beached.

Gulf merchants' tales of the 8th–10th centuries describe hair-raising shipwrecks and adventures, and enormous mercantile risks. The loss of a single cargo could ruin a group of merchants and even contribute to the decline of a port. The rewards of a single successful voyage were correspondingly prodigious: a merchant could make his fortune for life. They would set out from the Omani coast in late November or

ABOVE LEFT: *A View of Muttrah from the East* by R. Temple 1809–10.
ABOVE: *European Trading Galleons in Muttrah's Harbour,* an oil painting attributed to the Dutch painter Jan Peeters (1642–80).

By now Arab merchants were no longer sailing direct to China. Instead, the Chinese were sailing to the Malabar coast and the Palk Strait between Ceylon and India, where goods were transhipped to Indian and Arab vessels. By the 13th century large junks could be seen in Malabar ports, and the 14th century saw the extraordinary Ming Voyages, when the Chinese in fleets of vast junks sailed around the shores of the Indian Ocean, reaching East Africa and the Omani coast at Dhofar.

These voyages stopped abruptly in the 1430s and the Chinese left the Indian ports. By the time of the European discovery of the East in 1498 their voyages were a distant memory.

The great ports

Medieval merchants set out from the great Islamic port of Basra on the Shatt al Arab in Iraq. But the large ships required to make the China run could not anchor off Basra, and so ports further down the Gulf became important points of transshipment – first Siraf in Persia, and then Sohar on the Omani coast.

Sohar flourished. It was at the point where trade from Aden and East Africa met the trade coming and going to India and China. Sohar was, as the 10th-cat, with its natural harbour, had supplanted Sohar and Qalhat on the Omani coast.

Cargoes combined high-value commodities with bulk goods, because all ships need ballast. From Iraq these bulk goods were mainly dates, while the Arabian ports of the Gulf and Oman supplied dates, leather and dried fish. From East Africa the bulk goods were timber; from India, rice, dried foods, teak and other ship-building timber; and from China, copper cash, other metals and sugar.

PRECIOUS CARGOES

The glamour and profit were in high-value goods, which increased in value with every merchant and port they passed through.

century Arab geographer Muqaddasi observed, "the hallway to China, the storehouse of the East and Iraq, and the stay of the Yemen... There is no city bigger than this on the China Sea. It is a populous and beautiful spot, where wealth and fruits are in abundance... There are wonderful markets all along the coast. Houses are high and built of teak wood and mud bricks, and there is a canal of fresh water."

Eventually Qais Island supplanted Siraf and Sohar, and by the 14th century Qais was ousted by the island of Hormuz. With its satellite ports at Qalhat in eastern Oman and Julfar near present-day Ras al Khaimah, Hormuz completely controlled the mouth of the Gulf. By 1500 Mus-

But the glamour and profit were in the high-value goods, which increased in value with every merchant and port they passed through. Oman and the Arabian shore of the Gulf provided horses, frankincense and pearls. From India and Ceylon came gemstones, glass, ironware, swords, cotton cloth, spices and aromatics such as sandalwood and incense. China's silk, porcelain, lacquerwork, metalwork and other manufactures were in big demand. In exchange, the Islamic lands sent glassware, carpets, muslin, brocade, perfumes, incense, weapons and armour – but also money too.

Perhaps the most valuable raw commodities came from East Africa: gold, slaves, ivory, rhino horn and leopard skins. Of all the seafaring Arabs, it was the Omanis who dominated the rich East African trade, introducing its hugely prized products into the economies of the Islamic Near East.

Portuguese power

It was into East Africa, in 1498, that the first Western threat to local control of maritime trade since Greco-Roman times arrived: the Portuguese. Under Vasco da Gama the Portuguese rounded the Cape of Good Hope into the Indian Ocean in 1498, and proceeded to dominate the international trade of the Gulf and Indian Ocean

LEFT: Portuguese carracks.
ABOVE: Vasco da Gama's voyage around the Cape of Good Hope in 1498 changed the face of seafaring in the Gulf.

for over a century. Portuguese trade was a royal monopoly carried forward by gunpowder and force of arms, and the small Portuguese fleets had an impact on the people of the Indian Ocean shores out of all proportion to their numbers. They came in search of Indian spices and the spice islands of Indonesia, and of other luxury goods which the Venetian monopoly had made so costly in Europe. Their greatest colonial visionary, Affonso D'Albuquerque, quickly

realised the strategic importance of Aden, Hormuz and Malacca in the trade.

Hormuz, whose inhabitants were a mixture of Arabs and Persians, commanded the Musandam Strait, and in spite of being a waterless island had grown immensely wealthy by raising customs dues on all cargoes passing up the Gulf.

The Portuguese took Hormuz after their capture of Muscat in 1507. While they diverted some of the trade from the Far East around the Cape of Good Hope, they profited from the rest by levying customs dues on the Gulf route just as the Hormuzis had done before them. They built a line of forts along the Omani, African and

EUROPEAN INFLUENCES

The incursion of the Portuguese and the proliferation of Portuguese ships off the western coasts of the Indian Ocean introduced profound changes to Arab shipbuilding, including nailed instead of stitched construction, transom sterns, tiller-operated rudders, and raised and often decorated poop decks. But shipbuilding in the Gulf continued to be carried out in the time-honoured way, entirely by eye.

By the early 1800s British ships were being built in the yards of Bombay, and local rulers such as the Sultan of Muscat owned European-style vessels. This resulted in greater European influences in Arab boatyards and a mixing of local and European styles.

When metal ships eventually took over long-distance trade, the old styles survived in smaller local craft. The last stitched boat in Oman was built in Dhofar as late as the 1970s.

Indian coasts and farther east, with Goa as their capital. Muscat, Sohar and Hormuz were key to their control of the Gulf. The twin Portuguese forts dominating Muscat's old harbour were built at this time.

The Omani Empire

The Portuguese saw off Ottoman Turkish attacks in the 16th century, but others were to come early in the 17th century from Persia, Holland, England and Oman. Unlike the Portuguese, the other European nations arrived as merchant companies wishing to trade in peace.

During the 1630s and 1640s a renascent Omani Imamate succeeded in ejecting the Portuguese from Muscat and their coastal forts. The Omanis captured Portuguese ships, and went on to establish a maritime empire. Their ships and seamen, who often included European renegades, were an equal match for those of the Portuguese, English, Dutch and French. By the end of the 17th century they had taken control of a stretch of the East African coast down to Zanzibar and Mombasa, expelling the Portuguese. Oman became a power on parts of the Persian coast, and even at times up the Gulf as far as Bahrain.

PASSAGE TO INDIA

The Gulf was increasingly vital to communications between London and the East India Company's possessions in India.

It brought them into conflict with the imams of Muscat and Omani maritime ambitions.

By 1780 the Qawasim were firmly established on the Persian side of the southern Gulf too. Very soon they began to threaten Muscat's control of the trade from India and East Africa into the Gulf.

By now the British East India Company was set to become involved. The Gulf was becoming more and more vital to communications between London and the Company's growing possessions in India. When

In the mid-18th century Oman fell victim to civil war and a revived Persia under Nadir Shah, who took Muscat in 1742. But after 1744 the reunited Omanis drove out the Persians. Omani fortunes began to revive again, just as a rival sea power, the Qawasim of Sharjah and Ras al Khaimah, rose up in the southern Gulf.

The Qasimi "pirates", 1722–1820

The Qawasim of Ras al Khaimah seized Lingah on the Persian shore following the death of Nadir Shah in 1747. The rise of their ports at Sharjah and at Ras al Khaimah, which had replaced ancient Julfar just to the north, where they built up their fleets, was remarkably rapid.

Napoleon's occupation of Egypt in 1798 blocked the Red Sea route one British response was to enter into treaty relations with the Imam of Muscat, a move which inevitably placed them in opposition to the Qawasim. At the same time, the British blamed the Qawasim for the piracy that then plagued the Gulf and led a series of seaborne campaigns against the so-called "Pirate Coast". These climaxed in 1820 in the destruction of the Qasimi fleets and the first of the Maritime Truces.

British officials almost certainly exaggerated the Qawasim's involvement in piracy, but their campaign against them was determined. In 1806 the British attacked Ras al Khaimah. In 1809

Ras al Khaimah, Lingah, Luft and Shinas were burnt and ships destroyed, and Ras al Khaimah was bombarded again in 1816. Finally between 1819 and 1820, a large naval and military operation was mounted which razed Ras al Khaimah. Its ships were destroyed along with those of Sharjah, Umm al Qaiwain, Ajman, Lingah and other Qasimi ports.

The Maritime Peace, 1820–53

It was only after this expedition that maritime peace became a real prospect, and Britain's continuous and official involvement began in what are now the Emirates. The destruction of Qasimi real emergence as the chief trading port on the southern Gulf was due to the migration there in 1833 of the Al bu Falasah, a clan of the Bani Yas from Abu Dhabi. Its leading family Al Maktoum set about turning themselves into the merchant princes of the Gulf Coast, a position they have held ever since.

One long-term result of the peace was an expanding pearl trade. An ancient Gulf industry, pearling was recorded by Greek and Roman writers and probably traces its origin to the late Stone Age. Pearls are not found in abundance in Omani waters outside the Gulf, but the shallow southern Gulf off the Trucial Coast was rich

ports and ships was followed by a "General Treaty of Peace with the Arab Tribes" in 1820. Britain's primary aim was to pacify the seas and so secure its route to India.

The decline of the Qawasim was hastened by the growth of Abu Dhabi and Dubai as competitors on the pearl banks. Abu Dhabi had emerged only in the late 18th century and its sheikh had signed the General Treaty of Peace in 1820. Dubai too was included, but Dubai's

LEFT: fanciful depiction of a pirate raid.
ABOVE: a pearling boat heading into Dubai in 1949, by which time the pearl trade was in decline thanks to the Japanese cultured pearl.

PEARLING

By 1900 Abu Dhabi's had become the largest of the sheikhdoms' pearling fleets, numbering some 410 boats, about one-third of the total. In all, more than 22,000 men were employed on the pearl banks – a very considerable proportion of the population at that time. The life of the pearl diver was grindingly hard. Diving took place in the hot summer months and boats were out at sea for up to four months at a time. The men would dive on empty stomachs (to avoid getting cramp) to depths of over 20 metres (65 ft). They were vulnerable to attacks by jellyfish and sharks.

in pearl oysters and the warm sea shallow enough to make diving feasible.

In 1835, the rulers of Sharjah, Dubai, Ajman and Abu Dhabi signed an inviolable truce under British pressure, outlawing acts of war at sea during the pearling season. Made year-round for 10 years in 1843, it became the Perpetual Treaty in 1853.

Perpetual Peace

With the Perpetual Treaty of Peace of 1853, the rulers of the Gulf Coast agreed to cease hostilities at sea, and in return the British undertook to protect them against external attack. The British were determined not to become involved in disputes on land. However, as the 1860s wore into the 1870s, the line between peace at sea and peace on land became more and more difficult to discern.

By then the Gulf's importance as a channel for imperial communications had greatly increased. In 1862 the British started a fortnightly steamer service from Bombay to Muscat and some of the Gulf ports. Equally significantly, in 1864 they laid the first submarine telegraph cable in the Gulf, running from Karachi to Bushire and Fao via the Musandam Peninsula in Oman.

LAST VESTIGES OF A WAY OF LIFE

A good example of Arabian seafaring success was Sur in eastern Oman. Here Omani tribesmen turned themselves into great shipbuilders using timber imported from India and East Africa. They were supremely placed to control the trade to East Africa, and did so during the latter part of the 19th century, following in the tradition of the great medieval Hormuzi port of Qalhat nearby.

It is at Sur today that one can see the last traditional boatyard in Oman *(see page 171)*, although the work is now carried out by Indian craftsmen. Elsewhere you can look almost in vain for vestiges of the great maritime heritage of the region, but just occasionally, on a long sandy beach or in a secluded cove, one comes across a rotting hulk of an abandoned *badan* or *baqqarah*. Look carefully and you may see that part of its hull still shows some stitching.

In the 1970s the last big *ghanjah*, a ship with more than a touch of the Portuguese galleon about it, still lay beached in Muttrah harbour, but it is long gone now. Another lay below the tideline at Sur. These few relics, all of them built by hand and eye, without the help of drawings or specifications, are the last evidence of a 5,000-year tradition of seafaring.

Oman's decline

British support to Muscat continued throughout the 19th century and into the 20th. Sultan Said (ruled 1807–56), maintained a fleet of warships and merchantmen which included European ships, and even sent one of them to New York and London in 1840 and 1842.

By the time he died in 1856 the Omani maritime realm extended once again from enclaves on the Persian coast to large stretches of the East African coast. Although hampered by Britain's anti-slaving policy, Sultan Said developed the economy of Zanzibar, which became almost a second Omani capital. After

merchants and rulers in Muscat, Sur and Dubai.

Oman then began a long period of economic decline which lasted right up until the 1960s, and its role in the international sea trade of the Indian Ocean all but vanished.

Great power rivalry

After 1869, rivalry among the Great Powers began to threaten Britain's position in the Gulf. The Ottomans occupied Al Hasa and Qatar in 1871, and claimed eight Trucial Coast settlements, and in 1887 a resurgent Persia took over some Qasimi territory on the Persian shore. This prompted Britain to obtain from the sheikhs of

his death, the Omani Empire was split between his two sons, Thuwaini and Majid, into Oman and Zanzibar.

This split was damaging to Oman economically. Other blows to its maritime prosperity followed in quick succession. Steamships were bad enough, but the Suez Canal was opened in 1869, making the Red Sea much more important than the Gulf. In addition, the British had set about suppressing the slave and arms trades, which were lucrative sources of income for

the Trucial Coast a written assurance not to correspond or agree with any other government, or to allow agents of other governments to reside in their territories.

By the early 1890s both France and Germany were trying to establish a presence in the region. In March 1892, therefore, Britain developed the 1887 assurance into an Exclusive Agreement, the basis of her relations with the Trucial States until 1971. Nonetheless in the 1890s Russia also joined the race to seek a foothold in the Gulf.

By the end of World War I all these threats had evaporated, and Britain found itself in a position of unprecedented power in the Gulf.   ❏

LEFT: life on Dubai's creek before the bridges were built across it. **ABOVE:** the boat-building yard in Sur, the last traditional boatyard in Oman.

ISLAM IN SOUTHEAST ARABIA

Islam shapes the principles of government as well as private lives. And in Oman a particular brand of Islam, Ibadism, has played a crucial role in the country's history

It is tempting to regard oil-rich Arabian rulers, coming as they do from an authoritarian and paternalist tribal background, as dynastic despots mainly out for themselves and their families. But Sheikh Zayed, President of the UAE, is frequently heard to express the view that "oil is useless if it is not exploited for the welfare of the citizen", or that "the main function of our wealth should be the greatest happiness for the greatest number of people" – sentiments which Oman's Sultan Qaboos would wholeheartedly endorse.

This principle sounds utilitarian, unexpectedly so in its Arabian context. For Muslims, however, who know little of the social philosophy of the 19th-century British expounder of utilitarianism, Jeremy Bentham, it simply encapsulates the Islamic basis of the comprehensive social welfare policies which the Arabian oil states espouse.

Islam revealed

Islam was revealed to the Prophet Mohammed, a native of Mecca in western Arabia, in a series of revelations beginning in AD 610 and continuing until his death in AD 632. Muslims believe that God vouchsafed these utterances, of which the Qur'an is held to be a verbatim record, as the final and perfected revelation of Islam.

Islam, as the religion of Allah, is believed to have existed unchanged for all time, and to have been the religion of the patriarch Abraham. Subsequent prophets, such as Moses and Jesus, are revered but regarded as not having been in complete possession of the divine Message. Muslims do not believe that Allah is distinct from the God of the Bible and the Torah.

Islam, meaning "submission", permeates all aspects of the believer's public and private lives, laying down rules for everyday conduct and social relationships. Distinctions between religion, morality, legal affairs and politics do not exist, for they are judged to be subsumed under God's indivisible law. The faithful express their belief without self-consciousness wherever they happen to be, whether at home, in the street or in the mosque, in the five daily prayers.

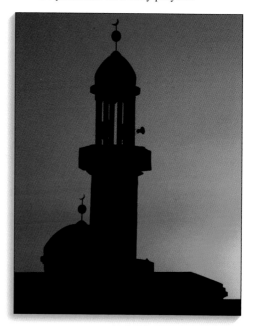

THE FIVE PILLARS OF ISLAM

The Five Pillars of Islam are public acts which make all Muslims known to each other and create solidarity in their faith. These acts are:
- the declaration of faith
- the five daily prayers
- payment of the alms tax *(zakat)*
- fasting during daylight hours during the holy month of Ramadan
- the pilgrimage to Mecca (the *haj*) once in a lifetime.

The obligation to fulfil the *haj* is only applicable if one has the means to make the journey.

PRECEDING PAGES: Islamic ideal depicted in tiles on a fountain at the Clocktower in Muscat, Oman.
LEFT: Sultan Qaboos Grand Mosque, the only mosque in Oman that is open to non-Muslims.
ABOVE RIGHT: minaret, Bahla, Oman.

The Arab tribes

To find the origins of this mentality, it is necessary to probe back before the Islamic era (calculated from the year AD 622). Perhaps as early as the middle of the 1st millennium BC, Arab tribes arrived from southwest and central Arabia. The newcomers found the inland oases and mountain wadis already peopled by settled farming communities of Persian origin which were not tribally organised but had a highly centralised, feudal kind of organisation which had enabled them to build the enormous *falaj* systems *(see page 156)*.

The incoming Arabs at first fought these people and established control over some areas. As time passed by, however, and especially following the coming of Islam in the 7th century AD, the two peoples began to merge: the Arabs settled and became farmers, while the old settlers were absorbed into the tribal structure of Arab society.

The coming of Islam

Islam arrived in Oman in AD 630 – an historically attested event which formed part of the early spread of the new religion within Arabia during the lifetime of the Prophet Mohammed. The Prophet sent emissaries from Medina, as he did to all the tribes and settlements of Arabia, calling them to Islam. The one he sent to Oman was the general 'Amr bin al-'As, later in the 640s to be the Muslim conqueror of Egypt.

Though 'Amr targeted the flourishing Persian port and capital of Sohar on the Omani coast it was the Arab tribal ruling family, the Julanda, and not the Persian governor, who accepted his message. For the Arabs the call to Islam was the call to eject the ruling Persian colonisers of Oman out of the province of Mazun – the Batinah coastal plain of Oman.

On the death of the Prophet in AD 632 much of Arabia apostatised from the new religion, including many Omani converts. However, the Julanda stood firm, supported by three armies sent from Medina by the Caliph Abu Bakr. There followed a great battle at the Arab port of Dibba, in the north, which proved a decisive victory for the Muslims, and Islam quickly took hold among Oman's tribespeople.

Ibadism in Oman

The Islamic conquest of the empire of the Sassanid Persians in Iran and further east drew many tribesmen from Oman to the great Muslim foundation at Basra, the springboard for the campaigns. Here they were drawn into the political and ideological conflicts which nearly succeeded in bringing down the Omayyad Caliphate, creating enormous disorder in the early Islamic state and producing the rebel *Khawarij* or "Outsiders" movement. Oman's distinctive brand of Islam, Ibadism, began as part of this doctrinal struggle.

Tribesmen returning to Oman over the next two centuries introduced Ibadism into the tribal areas of Oman. In common with other movements which today would be called fundamen-

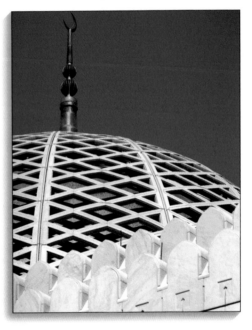

talist, it was their aim to restore the pure Islamic state according to the teaching of the Prophet, before it had been corrupted by the third Caliph 'Uthman. As in much of the Islamic world, Islam introduced a new and fervent intellectual debate into people's lives, centring on God's law and the organisation of society. This was especially true of Ibadism in Oman, and it was to produce an extensive Omani literature, particularly rich in law and history.

Though there were several other centres of Ibadism in early Islam, notably in Yemen and Hadhramaut, today Inner Oman is the chief survivor, and the Omani national character is indelibly coloured by it.

True Ibadism is distinguished from orthodox Sunni Islam at the political level, in two ways. First, the hereditary principle is anathema. Ibadis believe their ruler should be elected by an electoral college of good and learned men and proposed to the community. This Imam can be drawn from any family, for the first condition an aspiring Imam must fulfil is that of piety and learning. Second, Ibadis do not believe it is necessary to have an Imam at all times. During periods of political upheaval the Imamate can lapse and go into a state of secrecy, abeyance or latency known as *kitman*. This has occurred in Oman's history, sometimes for centuries.

This kind of consultative system works well when everyone is in agreement, but immediately falls apart when they are not. Only rarely, therefore, has the Imamate succeeded in genuinely uniting the tribes of Inner Oman. More usually the Imamate has been the political prize sought by rival tribal groupings.

While the Imamate sometimes succeeded in harnessing and harmonising tribalism, it never eradicated it: the Imam was simply a kind of supra-tribal leader, his office modelled on that of a tribal chief. Nor has Ibadism been able to tolerate pluralism in its midst – it has remained essentially inward-looking, surviving in its

Of all doctrines of sovereignty, this is a rather minimal one and one likely to appeal to a tribal mentality. In common with other Muslim attempts to reflect the rule of God upon earth, the ideal of the good ruler included the condition that allegiance to him should be withdrawn if, when God's law was transgressed, he showed no sign of repentance. There was no standing army under central command to enforce sovereignty, and no elaborate bodyguard: militias were raised by the Imam calling up tribal levies.

LEFT: dome of the Sultan Qaboos Mosque in Muscat.
ABOVE: Friday prayers in Dubai.

IMAMATE RULE

There have been two exceptional periods of Imamate rule in Oman, when Imams have managed to overcome the limitations of the Ibadi system by the force of their personalities and their political acumen. When an Imam's power has been such that he can transcend tribalism and exercise control over the coastal ports, then a golden age of prosperity, learning trade, and architectural achievments has generally ensued. This is what the Imams of the First Imamate in the 9th century, based at Nizwa, and the Ya'ruba Imams of the 17th century, operating from Rustaq, achieved.

inaccessible mountain retreat. With the xenophobia typical of many devout religious movements, it shrank from contact with foreigners and other creeds, which involvement on Oman's outward-looking coastline inevitably brought. The result has been that until the modernisation of recent decades Oman's history has tended to repeat itself in a well-worn cycle.

The cycle begins with the country united under a strong Imamate. With coast and interior united, wealth increases. As prosperity increases, and in some later instances the Imam himself indulges in commerce, encouraging contact with foreigners, the religious ideal

weakens. The Imamate then becomes the prerogative of a single tribal group, and degenerates into secular, tribal power. Pietists are aroused, and civil war ensues, normally resolved by one or both of the sides calling in an outside power, usually with catastrophic results for Oman's autonomy. The resulting disorders await the arrival of a strong new Imam who can unite the people.

Oil wealth has broken the cycle and reconciled Omanis to being united under an enlightened and benevolent Al bu Said ruler. In the modern era, the ruling family has founded its legitimacy not just on piety, but on the sharing of prosperity too.

Sunni Islam on the Gulf coast

Ibadism remained a phenomenon of the fastnesses of the Omani interior. Along the Gulf coast and in northern Oman things were different again. Here the Arab tribespeople were orthodox Sunnis, as were the closely related seafaring Arabs in the ports and villages on the Persian coast of the southern Gulf. There was much mixing with Shiite Persians, and it was a mixture of Arabs and Persians who populated Hormuz in the late Middle Ages and made Julfar, near present-day Ras al Khaimah, prosperous. In the 18th century settlement along the coast of the Emirates took on something like its present configuration as the Qasimi clan turned Sharjah and Ras al Khaimah into flourishing ports, and the Bani Yas made Abu Dhabi their chief settlement.

The people of the coast of Oman and the Emirates have thus been exposed to a great deal of foreign influence, whether as seafarers along the coasts of India and East Africa, or at home where foreign trading communities have grown up. This has led them to tolerate differences, but without abandoning their own traditions and beliefs.

The way in which the legal system has evolved in the Emirates is a good example of this. Before the onset of modernisation, the judicial system relied on the traditional *qadi* to judge cases of law and order, based on his interpretation of the Shari'ah. This included the settlement of disputes arising out of the conduct of business and commerce. However, the ruler exercised the ultimate powers of discretion.

The discovery of oil and the establishment of Federation in 1971 brought an influx of foreign workers and changed the structure of society in the Emirates. The population, indigenous and numbering only around 180,000 in 1968, grew within a few years into a much larger multicultural society.

This necessitated the modernisation of the country's judicial system. New laws were framed to assist the smooth functioning of a pluralistic society while at the same time protecting the interests of the local people. The result is that statutes now not only enforce the criminal justice system based on the Shari'ah, but also

ABOVE LEFT: religious reminder on a road near Quriyat in Oman. Such signs are common in the region.
ABOVE RIGHT: shoes must be removed before prayer.

Federal civil and criminal codes, and regulate economic and commercial practice.

In a landmark decision by the Federal Supreme Court in 1993, it was laid down that punishments prescribed under Islamic Law and handed down by Shari'ah courts, could no longer be applied to non-Muslims, who would from then on be dealt with under the civil and criminal codes. In Oman too, which sets great store by the Shari'ah as the law of Oman, there is an additional body of law to deal with administrative, civil and commercial practice.

Despite their new wealth, there is an engaging openness and lack of pretentiousness about Oman and the Emirates and their people. This has much to do with their exposure to the outside world, their seafaring history, and the egalitarianism of their tribal background. They provide business opportunities and employment for millions of foreigners with a good grace. Both countries welcome responsible tourism, and the Emirates host numerous international events, particularly sports, such as Dubai's world-famous horse racing season, tennis and golf tournaments. They quite naturally cling to their traditions and beliefs, but are confident enough in them to keep an open door to the outside world.   ❑

SHARI'AH LAW

Shari'ah law, or Islamic law, is derived from the Qur'an and the Sunnah (Way of the Prophet, based on actions and utterances of the Prophet in his lifetime which have been passed down the generations). It deals with every aspect of social behaviour and sets out rules for the conduct of life, including some specific rules and penalties for certain types of criminal acts, as well as for civil liability between individuals. As time has gone by, the body of law has developed through consensus of jurists and through reasoning, the chief concern being that any new formulation should be at least consistent with the Shari'ah.

Some of the more severe sentences under the Shari'ah include amputation for theft and stoning for sexual offences. In the case of adultery, stoning to death may be inflicted only in cases where there are four male witnesses and the accused admits guilt.

Such punishments can be inflicted only with the approval of the ruler of the emirate where the case is brought. A death sentence by firing squad or hanging is the usual penalty for murder and rape, both very rare in Oman and the UAE. In the case of murder a death sentence may be commuted if the family of the victim grants a personal pardon.

OMAN'S GREAT DYNASTIES

The Ya'ruba dynasty succeeded in uniting Oman and turning it into a place of learning and elegance. The Al bu Said turned it into an imperial power

Throughout the greater part of its history since the arrival of Islam, Oman was ruled by Imams, the first of whom, Julanda bin Mas'ud, was elected in AD 751. Some were stronger than others and held dominion over large areas of the country. Others were not able to exercise such central control. Nevertheless there was a fairly constant line of Imams, who followed the Ibadi precept of Islam *(see page 42–3)* from AD 751–1154 when there followed a series of Meliks or Kings of the Nabhan. The Imamate was then resumed but it reached its zenith with the Ya'ruba Dynasty which ruled Oman from 1624–1738, and began and ended in tragedy.

The Ya'ruba Dynasty

According to Omani chroniclers the first Imam of the Ya'ruba Dynasty, Nasir bin Murshid, made the "sun of salvation" shine on the long-afflicted people of Oman. His reputation rested on unifying the country and capturing Sur and Quriyat from the Portuguese and weakening their hold on the Omani coast.

On Nasir's death in 1649 his cousin Sultan bin Saif was elected Imam and it was he who ousted the Portuguese from Muscat, where they had been entrenched since the arrival of Affonso d'Albuquerque in 1507. He continued the unification of the country and built the great round fort at Nizwa *(see page 157)* At this time Oman had considerable seapower, which was used to attack the Portuguese in India.

Sultan's son Bil'arub succeeded him in 1688 though the new Imam's brother, Saif bin Sultan, eventually becoming stronger, was elected Imam and succeeded his brother. Saif had a large fleet, including one ship of 74 guns and one of 60. During his reign the Omanis succeeded in considerably weakening Portuguese

power in East Africa, where they had been strong since 1503, and also on the island of Salsette off Bombay. When Saif died in 1711 his son Sultan bin Saif II became Imam and was another strong ruler.

The unification of the country under these five rulers led not only to the revitalisation of

Salsette off Bombay and military prowess but also to commercial prosperity, the encouragement of learning, and buildings of strength, beauty and elegance such as the magnificent castle at Jabrin *(see page 161)*, built by Bil'arub. The first trading agreements without the British were made during the Ya'ruba period, in 1646 and 1659.

On Sultan's death in 1718, the unity which Oman had known for nearly a century came to an end and civil war ensued. Fighting over the succession led to tribal animosity and the whole of Oman became embroiled in desultory warfare between the two traditional factions of the Ghafiri and the Hinawi. In the late 1730s Saif

---

PRECEDING PAGES: National Day celebrations, Oman.
LEFT: the Sultanate's emblem of two crossed swords with a *khanjar* and belt on the palace gates, Muscat.
ABOVE RIGHT: Oman's current Sultan Qaboos belongs to the Al bu Said dynasty, in power since 1747.

bin Sultan II – one of the rival claimants to the Imamate, the other being Muhanna bin Sultan – invited the Persians under Nadir Shah to intervene on his behalf, a decision he came to regret as the Persians refused to give up their conquest.

The two rival Imams had died by 1745 and no Ya'rubi claimant came forward. Meanwhile Ahmed bin Said, who held the fort at Sohar, continued to fight the Persians, becoming both a hero and the elected Imam. In 1747 he succeeded in driving the Persians out.

The Al bu Said

Thus began the Al bu Said Dynasty, which has held the Imamate or Sultanate ever since.

Ahmed himself was a man of outstanding courage, vigour, enterprise, generosity and personality. These qualities were sorely needed at the time. At home he was a good administrator of a fairly strong centralised government and he had a liberal reputation. He had in his retinue scholars, Islamic judges and notables. His bodyguard consisted of some 1,000 freemen, 1,000 Zanzibaris and 100 Nubian slaves. Abroad he led an expedition against the Persians at the request of the people of Basrah in southern Iraq, and the Mogul Emperor Sha Alam sent an embassy to make a treaty to assist Ahmed against his enemies and to establish in Muscat a resident mission in what came to be known as the "Nabob's house".

Ahmed died in 1783 and his grandson Hamad became the *de facto* ruler, though his father, Said, had been elected Imam. On Hamad's death in 1788, Sultan – another son of Imam Ahmed bin Said – took the reins of government, though Said remained nominally Imam. Sultan was brave and of noble countenance and both the British and the French, whose interests were in conflict in the east as well as in Europe, treated him and addressed him as if he were the Imam. He was, however, killed at Lingeh in southern Persia in 1804 by the Qawasim of Ras al Khaimah who were at war with the Omanis over trade.

Said bin Sultan succeeded his father, Sultan, and reigned for 52 years until 1856. Although some of the nobles who held the great castles were often in rebellion and there were incursions by the Wahhabis from what is now Saudi Arabia, his internal authority was in no real doubt. Europeans who met him were impressed by his commanding figure, his courtly, dignified and affable manner and his kindness both to his own people and to foreign visitors.

Said's influence in the Arabian Seas was considerable. Like his father he sought to control the trade passing through the Strait of Hormuz and to this end he retained control of places on the north of the Gulf which had been acquired by Sultan. These were Hormuz, Qishm and Henjam islands together with Gwadar on the coast of Makran, which remained a part of Oman until 1958, and Chahbar.

It was, however, in Africa that he made his deepest impression and from 1829 his heart and main interests lay there. This was to have

profound results later for the sultanate. He sought alliances with local queens in Madagascar and Mozambique and controlled the main Arab settlements on the east coast of Africa, making Zanzibar his second capital and transferring the Omani state archives there. He was very much the "Sailor Sayyid" and had 20 ships of his own for private trade – which he delighted in commanding himself – and paid much attention to the Omani navy. He presented King William IV of England with a fine warship, later called the Liverpool and received in return a handsome yacht, *The Prince Regent*. He also presented King William and Queen Victoria with fine Arab stallions and mares. Britain and Oman had been in treaty alliance since 1800, but Said also negotiated a Treaty of Amity and Commerce with the USA in 1834.

He gave fresh life to interests in East Africa, particularly by introducing cloves as a cash crop in Zanzibar and establishing rice plantations. Many European travellers have left accounts of him and Burton, Speke, Livingstone, Grant and Stanley all had good reason to thank the Al bu Said rulers of Zanzibar for assistance in their

SAYYID THE SAILOR

Said bin Sultan was very much the "Sailor Sayyid". He had 20 ships of his own for private trade – which he delighted in commanding.

a year to the ruler in Muscat to adjust the inequality in the inheritance, as Zanzibar was at this time by far the richer part. From then on the two parts remained separate, though governed by members of the same family until 1964, when Zanzibar was incorporated into Tanzania.

Thereafter the fortunes of Oman as a maritime power declined, accelerated by the introduction of steamers by the British India Steam Navigation Company in 1862. This put the Omanis at a disadvantage

African explorations. He had 36 children, but a problem arose between two of his sons after his death in 1856 on a voyage to Zanzibar. Thuwaini in Muscat claimed the whole Sultanate but Majid in Zanzibar also claimed it.

The matter was referred to Lord Canning, the Viceroy and Governor-General of India – though the Sultanate had always been regarded as an independent state. With British pragmatism Lord Canning decided that Majid should rule Zanzibar and pay 40,000 crowns

FAR LEFT: portrait of Sayyid Said bin Sultan Al bu Said.
ABOVE LEFT: Feisal bin Turki.
ABOVE RIGHT: Taimur bin Feisal.

since their ships ceased to be competitive in the carrying trade.

Thuwaini was killed by his son Salim in 1866. A struggle for control of the Sultanate ensued between Azzan bin Qais, based in Rustaq, who headed the tribes of the Interior, and Turki, who had been Governor of Sohar and was another son of Said bin Sultan. Turki won the day in a battle in Wadi Dhank in 1870 and was recognised by the British. This event has present-day significance, as the Basic Law of the State issued in 1996 specifies that the Sultan of Oman "shall be a male descendant of Sayyid Turki bin Said bin Sultan", who is also "a legitimate son of Omani Muslim parents."

Turki was sultan until 1888, although he had to cope with rivalries. He was then succeeded by his son, Feisal, who took over at the age of 23 and ruled until his death in 1913. Taimur bin Feisal followed him until 1932, when he abdicated in favour of his son Said bin Taimur.

During these reigns the Interior of the country was not always at one with the sultans and their jurisdiction on the coast. The strong sheikhs of the Harth tribe in the Sharqiyah posed a particular problem and

HABIT OF A LIFETIME

Even when oil revenues began to accrue in 1967 Said was unable to abandon the frugal habits of careful husbandry.

when the Imam Mohammed bin Abdulla al Kharusi died and the new Imam Ghalib, with his brother Talib, tried to establish central Oman as a separate principality. This matter was not settled on the ground until 1959 and even then the problem was of such a proportion that "The Question of Oman" came up every year at the General Assembly of the United Nations until 1971.

Sultan Said bin Taimur took over a country which was still in debt, the economic situation being exacerbated by the gen-

the very name of the country, Muscat and Oman, reflected this dichotomy.

In 1913 the tribes of the Interior elected Salim bin Rashid al Kaharusi as Imam. Eventually accommodation was reached with an agreement – sometimes called (erroneously) "The Treaty of Seeb" – under which Taimur bin Feisal agreed not to interfere in the affairs of the Interior, not to impose taxation in excess of 5 percent and to allow the tribes of the Interior to enter Muscat and the coastal towns in safety and freedom. This administrative *modus vivendi* – although in a sense it re-emphasised the historical differences between coast and Interior – worked satisfactorily until 1954,

eral depression of the late 1920s and early 1930s. By his own sustained and patient efforts he largely restored the situation. His stewardship ensured that when Sultan Qaboos took over in 1970 the state's finances were in a relatively flourishing state. A man of great charm and ability, Said was unable to abandon the habits of economy and careful husbandry, which had become ingrained after many years of hardship, even when oil revenues began to accrue to Oman after 1967.

In 1967 a local rebellion of the Dhofar Liberation Front in the south of the country grew into something more serious, when it received support from the Marxist People's Democractic

Republic of Yemen. The intentions of the main revolutionary body were made clear in their name: "The People's Front for the Liberation of Oman and the Arabian Gulf". The situation reached such a point that Said was displaced by his son Qaboos on 23 July 1970.

The reign of Sultan Qaboos

Sultan Qaboos, the 12th member of the Al bu Said Dynasty, was 30 on his accession and he proclaimed his faith in the future by announcing that his country would be known as "The Sultanate of Oman" instead of "Muscat and Oman". He also said in his first speech that

ber of Arab states, leading to "Imamate Offices" in Cairo, Damascus, Riyadh and Beirut.

Apart from the Omanis associated with the Imamate and those in rebellion in Dhofar, there were many other Omanis in opposition to Sultan Said, and young men, despairing about the limited educational facilities offered by the only three schools in the country, had sought education abroad – especially in Egypt and the Soviet Union. Thus at home the young Sultan found a country severely affected by the brain drain as well as lacking the infrastructure and services of a modern state. Abroad he yet had to acquire new friends. Only Britain and India were

under a new flag people would no longer distinguish between the coast and the Interior and the southern province of Dhofar. Oman was to be a single country. The auguries were, however, not auspicious. Sultan Said had made no effort to seek international recognition, though his country was and had always been regarded as independent. He remained happy under the penumbra of the British, making it easier for the Imam Ghalib to establish relations with a num-

LEFT: Oman's flag: white represents peace and prosperity, red for the struggle to liberate and unify Oman, and green for Islam. **ABOVE:** military bands at the Omani National Day celebrations, Muscat.

A WORLD OF DIFFERENCE

When Sultan Qaboos came to power in 1970 Oman had become an inward-looking backwater that lagged centuries behind the modern world. There were only three schools in the whole country (in Muscat, Muttrah and Salalah), no newspapers, radio or television, no civil service and only one hospital (with just 23 beds). The average life expectancy of an Omani was 47. Muscat still closed its gates at night and, apart from the road to the little airport at Bait al Falaj, there were only two graded roads in the whole country – from Muscat to Sohar and from Muscat to Fahud.

represented diplomatically in Muscat, each with a Consul-General.

There was a shortage of Omanis with the training to bring Oman into the modern world. But the Sultan and the Omanis themselves were undaunted and with the help of Britain and others began the process. Ministers were appointed and the governments structured to enable Oman to become a modern state using the gradually increasing oil revenues. The objects were to establish internal peace and security; to frustrate attacks inspired from abroad; to attract back talented but disaffected Omanis; and to gain international recognition.

and rebels were able to see for themselves that a new era had indeed begun. The growing physical signs of development brought an increasing number of rebels over to the government side. Thus, as a result of a hard military campaign – fought with the help of Britain, Iran and Jordan in particular – combined with civil measures, the Sultan was able, on 1 December 1975, to announce the end of the war.

A nation transformed

After that the government, which had become increasingly sophisticated, was able to concentrate more closely on development and laying

Goodwill missions were despatched to Arab countries and in 1971 applications were lodged to join the Arab League and the UN. That both were successful, show that the international community accepted that genuine change had taken place and the "Question of Oman" was removed from the agenda of the UN.

However, the main challenge to Oman's future in 1971 lay in Dhofar. Although Sultan Qaboos had offered a general amnesty immediately on his accession, the initial effect on the rebels was minimal. Between 1972 and 1975, however, the military balance began to shift in the Sultan's favour, especially as the "hearts and minds" campaign began to carry conviction,

down a countrywide infrastructure. Thus a country without any basic services outside Muscat itself has been transformed since 1970 into a land with a fine road system, public electricity and water even in remote villages, and schools and hospitals spread all over the country.

One of the Sultan's first acts was to encourage general education, and schools in makeshift tents were immediately opened in many places. From this small beginning the Omani educational system has reached standards unimaginable earlier. At its apex is the Sultan Qaboos University, which opened to students in 1986 and now has seven faculties (Science, Agriculture, Medicine, Engineering, Arts, Commerce and Economics, and Education and Islamic Sciences). The Medical School's degrees are recognised in Britain, the US and Western countries generally, and Omani hospitals are recognised by the Royal Colleges in Britain and by similar bodies elsewhere.

The educational system now embraces nearly 1,000 schools with free state education provided to secondary level. There are also teacher training institutions. The scale of provision necessary may be judged from the fact that the average number of children in an Omani family

A LONGER LIFE

The average life expectancy of Omanis in 1970 was just 47. It has since risen to 68.

average life expectancy in 1970 was 47 whereas it is now over 70. There are now 50 hospitals, including the excellent Royal Hospital in Muscat, and some 120 clinics all over the country.

Sultan Qaboos has encouraged music of all sorts since his accession, when there was virtually no-one in Oman who could blow a note. Now Oman has very fine military bands, which have even taken the Edinburgh Tattoo by storm. The bands include bagpipers – a form of bagpipe having long been known in the Gulf area. There

is now 7.4. Indeed, Oman has the world's highest birthrate.

This statistic also underlines the scale of the necessary commitment to public health. There has been a dramatic change in the general health of the Omani people since 1970 – so much so that it is no longer complaints common to the Third World that are of most concern to Omani doctors, but diseases of the First World, such as heart disease and cancer. The

LEFT: boys board a school bus: schoolchildren were among the first to benefit from the influx of riches.
ABOVE: Omani school girls. Until the 1960s girls received no official education.

is also a Royal Oman Symphony Orchestra, which frequently plays with well-known soloists and conductors.

None of these developments would have been possible had it not been for a healthy economy and this depends primarily, despite attempts at diversification, on oil and gas. The export of Liquefied Natural Gas (LNG), of which Oman has considerable reserves, has added an important element from 1999.

What the future holds

The Omanis have an economic vision of Oman 2020 and manage their development through a series of Five Year Plans. Emphasis is placed on encouraging a competitive private sector and diversification. Agriculture and fisheries are important but industrialisation is also envisaged and already a variety of factories is making an impact on Oman's economy and social life.

The country's geographical location on the Indian Ocean and the south side of the Strait of Hormuz gives it a strategic importance beyond its size and wealth. For this as well as historical reasons the Omani Armed Forces have benefited from a large proportion of the Omani budget. The Sultan's own training at Sandhurst in England gave him both a good knowledge

weapons – are equipped inter alia with Hawk, F3, Jaguar and Hunter aircraft supported by an integrated air defence.

In Foreign Affairs there has been an extraordinary change since 1970. After admission to the Arab League and United Nations, Omani Foreign policy – which was very much that of the Sultan personally – was to reinforce its age-long connections with India and Pakistan and to develop relations with other Arab and neighbouring and friendly states, notably with the moderate states of Egypt and Jordan.

By the 1990s Oman had diplomatic relations with 135 countries. Oman's foreign policy has

and a deep interest in military matters. The Sultan's Armed Forces (SAF) now consist of an Army of infantry brigades, each with four battalions, together with armoured, artillery, parachute, reconnaissance and training troops; a special commando unit; and tribal militia, in addition to the Royal Guard.

The Royal Navy of Oman has eight fast patrol boats – necessary for Oman's long coastline of 1,700 km (1,000 miles) and four Province Class fast-attack craft armed with Excocet missiles. The Royal Air Force of Oman – the men of which, like the other Armed Forces, are Omanis who have been educated and trained to handle the most sophisticated

been empirical and pragmatic and is based on good neighbourliness, non-alignment and the encouragement of co-operation between the Gulf states and particularly those of the GCC (Gulf Co-operation Council). Oman's pragmatic policies often appeared in the past to run counter to the political wisdom of the day but have been subsequently applauded as far-sighted.

East African links

Early in Sultan Qaboos's reign, Oman revived its interest in East Africa and many Zanzibaris and Kenyans of Omani origin were welcomed to Oman, and subsequently play important roles in its continuing development.

Participation of the people in government has grown steadily. People were always able to appear before the walis, the governors of regions, and participate in their *majlis* (councils), but they are now able to share in more modern institutions. In 1981 a state Consultative Council was formed consisting of 55 members including government officials. In 1991 this was replaced by the Majlis Ash'Shura consisting of 59 members selected from citizens nominated by the people of each *wilaya*, or governorate. There are no official

WOMEN FIRST

Oman was the first Arab country to have women police officers.

was also the first Arab country to appoint women police officers. Women now hold high rank not only in the Royal Oman Police, but the armed forces and in government. They are also represented in the Majlis Ash'Shura.

Generally the Omanis retain the courtesy and charm for which they are renowned. They still justify the words of the 19th-century traveller, J.S. Buckingham: "The people seemed to me to be the cleanest, neatest, best dressed, and most gentlemanly… and inspired a feeling of confidence, goodwill and respect."

members and the Majlis Ash'Shura is more directly involved than the earlier assembly in considering and questioning the process of government. The Basic Law promulgated in November 1996 not only deals with the royal succession, but also political, economic and social principles, public rights and duties, the organs of government and the judiciary.

In 1994, Omani women were among the first in the Arabian Gulf to be enfranchised. Oman

Thus, from somewhat unpromising beginnings, Oman has been transformed into a modern country, strong and respected by its neighbours with defined and agreed frontiers, all the earlier boundary disputes having been settled amicably – most significantly with Yemen.

Sultan Qaboos's achievement in building Oman into a modern state is illustrated by the many beautiful buildings which have been erected – mosques, government buildings, palaces and private houses. Many are based on traditional buildings, which the government has done much to restore all over the country. They testify to the general harmony which has been created in a state once riven with faction. ❏

LEFT: Sultan Qaboos at the three-day Gulf Co-operation Council held in Oman in 1995.
ABOVE: street decoration at Sultan Qaboos's silver jubilee held in 1995.

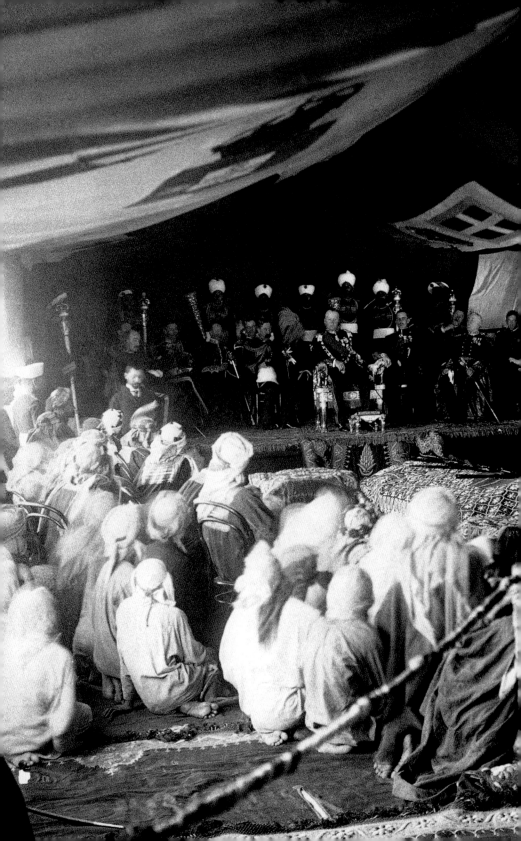

THE UAE FROM RAGS TO RICHES

How the discovery of oil and an urgent need for security persuaded seven
of the Trucial sheikhdoms to put aside local rivalries and form a federation

After more than a quarter of a century of existence, the United Arab Emirates has proved to be the Arab world's most successful attempt at unity despite widespread scepticism at its formation in 1971. Attempts by Egypt under Gamal Abdel Nasser and later by Libya under Muammar Gaddafi to merge with other states were short-lived, and the squabbles surrounding such moves made the emotive concept of "the Arab nation" something of a laughing stock among commentators outside the region. The UAE was one of the most unlikely bids for unity but has shown itself to be the exception to the rule.

Old roots

The well-known rags to riches story of the Gulf states of Arabia created by the oil boom of the 1970s and 1980s caused many commentators to look upon the peoples of the region as upstarts. The UAE is quite new as a state – and its inhabitants are rather proud to be *nouveaux riches* – but these once largely maritime peoples can trace their roots back to prehistoric times. Excavations at Umm an-Nar (now in the shadow of an oil refinery), an island off Abu Dhabi, and elsewhere show that in these early times the Gulf Arabs were under two influences – those of Mesopotamia and of the Indus civilisation in India *(see page 22).*

The coastal dwellers were the first to deal with European travellers, but inland the Bedu *(see page 93)* continued their timeless nomadic existence or settled in places where they could grow a few crops, such as dates, or graze small numbers of livestock. The latter in particular achieved their sense of belonging not in terms of the districts or fixed borders within which they conducted their spartan lives but through

their tribal allegiances to a local sheikh. Long before the rise of Islam in the 7th century, the land that is now the UAE and the other Gulf states of eastern Arabia – Kuwait, Bahrain, Qatar, Saudi Arabia and Oman – had a tightly structured Arab society that was divided into tribes, sub-tribes and clans.

Key tribes

The Bani Yas, who had become a powerful federation of clans, were described as "land-faring Bedouin", wandering great distances in search of grazing for their camels and then returning to their date gardens around the Liwa oases on the edge of the Empty Quarter, the vast unbroken sand desert immortalised by the explorer Wilfred Thesiger in *Arabian Sands.*

As long as anyone can remember, the leader of the Bani Yas has always come from the sheikhs of the Al bu Falasah sub-tribe. One of them, called Nahyan, was the ancestor of the present ruling family of Abu Dhabi. As pearls became increasingly popular in India and then

---

PRECEDING PAGES: Britain's Lord Curzon visits the sheikhs from Abu Dhabi, Sharjah, Dubai, Ajman and Umm al Qaiwain in 1903.
LEFT: former UAE President Sheikh Zayed bin Sultan Al Nahyan celebrates the end of Ramadan, 1962.
ABOVE RIGHT: aerial view of Abu Dhabi town 1962.

among European women in the 19th century, the Bani Yas gravitated towards the rich pearl banks of the Trucial Coast.

The town of Abu Dhabi was founded as early as 1761 after a good supply of water had been found there. In Dubai, fresh water flowed abundantly into aquifers from the Hajar Mountains, and a settlement that grew up there was a dependency of Abu Dhabi. In 1833, Dubai's Bani Yas set up its own principality, which has been ruled by the Al Maktoum family ever since.

By 1900 the pearling industry was enjoying such a boom that not enough men could be found to man the 1,200 boats engaged in the

tional consortium. But oil exploration only really began in earnest after World War II.

The decline of the British Empire after the war, especially the granting of independence to India in 1947, helped to speed changes in the Gulf. The British presence in the region was to linger a few more years. With British help the Trucial Oman Scouts (a defence force) was set up in 1951, while the following year a Trucial States Council was formed to bring a kind of unity to the coastal region through twice-yearly discussions on common problems and interests. The rulers of what became the United Arab Emirates had not met all together since 1905.

trade. Control passed irrevocably to the sheikhs who ruled the coastal areas, and this power was further reinforced when the British made it clear they were only interested in the coastal areas and effectively endorsed only their rulers.

The pearl boom collapsed in the 1930s with the arrival of the Japanese cultured pearl. The ensuing depression caused some pearl boatmen to burn their boats in desperation for fuel. But the search for a new fuel had begun.

Oil concessions

Between 1936 and 1952 the rulers of the seven Trucial States signed oil concession agreements with the Iraq Petroleum Company, an interna-

The British withdraw

The big bombshell came when Britain's cash-strapped Labour Government decided that big savings must be made in defence. In February 1967 the Prime Minister, Harold Wilson, announced that Britain's military presence east of Suez was to be scrapped by the end of 1971. It spelt the end of British protection in the Gulf and was in breach of written agreements between Britain and the Trucial States, as well as the unwritten Arab law of trust and friendship. The British decision led directly to the formation of the UAE and speeded the process of modernisation in the region, which had already been accelerated by the discovery of massive oil deposits. But the emirates were ill-prepared for sudden independence and had few qualified people, particularly in the spheres of defence and foreign affairs, which the British had long taken care of.

The UAE is formed

Shortly after the British decision to withdraw from the Gulf, the rulers of Abu Dhabi and Dubai announced that they would form a federation and reached an agreement over offshore oil rights. The speed of their action helped to settle frontiers, even though the UAE is now

ABUNDANCE OF RICHES

In a few years Abu Dhabi's resources were to carry the emirate's income to the highest in the world.

between any opposing views. Sheikh Zayed bin Sultan Al Nahyan, Abu Dhabi's ruler, repeatedly said that the resources of Abu Dhabi – which in a few years were to carry the emirate's income to the highest in the world – were "at the service of all the emirates".

Dubai and Abu Dhabi invited the other Trucial States – Sharjah, Ajman, Umm al Qaiwain, Ras al Khaimah and Fujairah – to join them in the federation, together with Qatar and Bahrain. There was clearly a strong mutual desire for security, modified by a wish

a patchwork of subdivisions making up the seven emirates that form the federation – a process that had never been formalised before because of the changing tribal allegiances.

Abu Dhabi, well aware by 1970 that it was the richest oil emirate, was especially anxious to reach an overall agreement on a federation and clearly demarcated borders because of the mounting importance of oil revenues and the oil rights that would be granted once land divisions had been agreed. From the outset it adopted a policy aimed at finding a middle ground

for a degree of independence in each emirate, as the departure of the British drew near.

By June 1971, Bahrain had decided it was secure enough on its own and announced in August it would not join the federation, while Qatar followed suit less than three weeks later. Six of the remaining sheikhdoms had reached agreement on a federal constitution by July, and the UAE formally came into being on 2 December. In Ras al Khaimah, Ruler Sheikh Saqr bin Mohammed al Qasimi – hoping that he would find oil on Qatar's scale – held out for another two months before swallowing his pride at the prospect of massive largesse from Abu Dhabi and joined the federation too. Sheikh Zayed of Abu

ABOVE LEFT: Abu Dhabi in 1954.
ABOVE: the Ruler's Palace, Abu Dhabi, also in 1954.

Dhabi became President of the Federation, with Sheikh Rashid bin Saeed Al Maktoum, Ruler of Dubai, as Vice-President and Prime Minister.

Security was a major motive for forming the UAE, and such concern was justified in view of the massive oil deposits later discovered in the region. The possibility of a threat from the Soviet Union (particularly after its invasion of Afghanistan) always existed in the minds of the Gulf leaders and of the Western politicians whose countries depended on the Gulf's oil.

SAFETY FIRST

Security was a major motivation for forming the UAE, a concern fully justified in view of the massive oil deposits discovered since the 1930s.

dad was a threat to all six GCC countries. It was launched on the pretext that Kuwait and the UAE had allegedly exceeded their oil export quotas set under the Organisation of the Oil Exporting Countries (OPEC) agreement. Luckily for the UAE, Kuwait was the nearer country to Iraq and thus was the first in what might have been a series of domino-style collapses, including the UAE, if the international community had not acted swiftly to check Saddam. Following the US invasion of Iraq in 2003 and the subsequent

The volatility of the region was underlined by the Iran-Iraq War, which broke out in 1980, as well as the Arab-Israeli conflict. With the strategic giants of the Gulf – Iran and Iraq – busy fighting each other, the six oil-rich Gulf monarchies (Saudi Arabia, Kuwait, the UAE, Bahrain, Qatar and Oman) seized the chance to set up their own organisation – the Arabian Gulf Co-operation Council. It was conceived on the lines of the European Economic Community but with defence interests hidden under the surface. The AGCC formally came into being in 1981.

Iraq's invasion of Kuwait in 1990 sharpened the focus on a number of needs. Above all, it was instantly recognised that the threat from Bagh-

downfall of Saddam, the UAE embarked on a new era of prosperity.

Since the turn of the millennium Dubai in particular has gone from strength to strength, with ever-more audacious building projects such as the The Palm and The World *(see page 237)* attracting worldwide attention. Meanwhile Abu Dhabi, awash with oil money, is planning a new role for itself as the cultural capital of the Gulf. Its new Saadiyat Island Cultural District, scheduled to open in 2012, will have a Guggenheim Museum, a branch of the Louvre and a world-class performing arts centre. ❑

ABOVE: Dubai Creekside, viewed from Bur Dubai.

Father of the UAE

From the formation of the United Arab Emirates in 1971 until his death in November 2004, the Federation was led by Sheikh Zayed bin Sultan Al Nahyan, but he was much more than head of state. Not only was he the father figure of the nation but he also spanned two eras – the one of near-starvation and the current one of astonishing wealth.

Born in 1918 in the picturesque Al Hisn Fort in Al Ain, where he grew up, Sheikh Zayed never lost his love for his birthplace, where he became Governor in 1946. The explorer Wilfred Thesiger met him in the 1940s and described him in his classic book *Arabian Sands* as "a powerfully built man of about 30 with a brown beard. He had a strong intelligent face, with steady observant eyes, and his manner was quiet but masterful. He was dressed very simply, in a beige coloured shirt of Omani cloth and a waistcoat which he wore unbuttoned...He wore a dagger and cartridge belt; his rifle lay on the sand beside him.

"He had a great reputation among the Bedu," Thesiger went on. "They liked him for his easy informal ways and his friendliness, and they respected his force of character, his shrewdness and his physical strength. They said admiringly, 'Zayed is a Bedu. He knows about camels, can ride like one of us, can shoot and knows how to fight.'"

In old age Zayed's hands were still calloused from the days when he used to dig, move stones and plant trees while working on restoration of the ancient *falaj* system of canals needed to irrigate the date groves of the Buraimi oasis near Al Ain.

It was in 1966 that his brother Shakhbut, who had ruled the emirate since 1928, abdicated, and Zayed replaced him. The first oil exports had begun only four years before and two years later the British Government was to announce its withdrawal from the Gulf, so that Abu Dhabi and the other Trucial States were free to manage their own affairs.

The new ruler thus took over in stirring times and quickly joined forces with the late Sheikh Rashid bin Said Al-Maktoum of Dubai in laying the foundation stones of a new federal state. The two were elected President and Vice-President respectively *(see page 64)*.

President Zayed's considerable skill in achieving lasting harmony between the traditionally rival inter-

ests of the UAE's seven emirates, each with its own ruler, was well-established – particularly in the face of a chorus of scepticism at the outset from commentators who claimed it would never work. There is no doubt that Abu Dhabi's soaring wealth helped. Zayed was always quick to help the poorer emirates financially and to spend money on vast public works throughout the country, including a welfare state that is second to none worldwide.

One of the most impressive sights for any visitor to the UAE is the landscaping and planting in a country that is still 70 percent desert. The dream of the poor Bedu to make the desert bloom has come true in Abu Dhabi, as nowhere else. "Greening" the

desert was a vision that was always dear to Sheikh Zayed's heart. Outdoor plants and trees are given away free on demand to all UAE householders.

Abu Dhabi city now boasts some two dozen parks and nearly 1,500 hectares (3,700 acres) of grass. They are watered by electronically controlled sprinkler systems and decorated with spectacular fountains. Zayed's beloved Al Ain has some 40 parks and is connected to Abu Dhabi City, 160 km (100 miles) away, by a six-lane highway divided by a constantly watered grassed reservation, planted with palm trees, bougainvillea, oleanders and other flowering plants, while a thick belt of trees on either side keeps the desert at bay. It is a far cry from the sandy track that was all that connected the two places in his youth. ❏

ABOVE RIGHT: Sheikh Zayed bin Sultan Al Nahyan, the leading light in the transformation of the UAE and father of the current ruler, Sheikh Khalifa bin Zayed al Nahyan.

FOOTPRINTS IN THE SAND

Oman and the UAE are on the rim of the Empty Quarter, a vast wilderness of dunes impenetrable to any but a few Bedu until as late as the 1930s

Arabia has attracted some of the world's best-known explorers, from Charles Montague Doughty to Richard Burton. Names associated with Oman and the UAE in particular include Ibn Battuta, Marco Polo, the 18th-century Danish explorer Carsten Niebuhr (left), whom William Gifford Palgrave called "the intelligence and courage that first opened Arabia to Europe" and, in the 20th century, Bertram Thomas, Wilfred Thesiger and Sir Ranulph Fiennes, who attempted to find the lost city of Ubar (*see page 192*) as recently as 1991. In addition to such well-known names there were British political agents and Western officials in the employ of the sheikhs who by the very nature of the territory – tribal and inaccessible – were often the first foreigners to set foot in a place.

△ **PERCY COX**
When Percy Cox, British Agent in Muscat from 1899–1904, visited Tanuf, he was told that no rain had fallen since the last British agent to visit had taken photographs there 25 years before. The sheikh demanded compensation for the crops that had perished as a result.

WILFRED THESIGER

The explorer most fondly remembered in Oman and the UAE today is undoubtedly Wilfred Thesiger, whose two great crossings of the Rub al Khali (Empty Quarter) are documented in his book *Arabian Sands*. Thesiger seized the opportunity to cross the Great Sands when he was offered a job in the region by the Anti-Locust Research Centre. To make himself less conspicuous in hostile country he pretended to be a Bedu from Syria, a disguise that could explain his strange looks and accent. His disguise was generally successful, and often only his closest Bedu companions knew the truth. The one thing that gave him away, they said, were his unusually large feet. They advised him never to leave footprints in the sand.

▷ **DRESSED FOR THE PART**
Thesiger in Bedu dress.

THE FIRST TO CROSS THE SANDS

Though Wilfred Thesiger's crossings of the Rub al Khali are probably the most famous, the first Western person to cross the Great Sands was Bertram Thomas in 1931, who trekked from Salalah to Doha in 55 days. He was followed later that year by Harry St John Philby, who took a more difficult route through Saudi Arabia.

Thomas described his journey in his book *Arabia Felix*. He said of the Sands, "a vast ocean of billowing sands, here tilted into sudden frowning heights, and there falling into gentle valleys…without a scrap of verdure in view. Dunes of all sizes, unsymmetrical in relation to one another, but with the exquisite roundness of a girl's breasts, rise tier upon tier like a mighty mountain system."

He also talked of the "roaring of the sands" which, he said, resembled a ship's foghorn.

Thomas was in Oman as Financial Adviser and Wazir to the Sultan of Muscat and Oman, a post he took up in 1924 after serving as Political Officer in Iraq. Through his position he gained the respect of unpredictable tribal leaders who usually scorned, even murdered, infidels.

This proved invaluable on his journey through the Sands. Thomas claimed the Rub al Khali "obsesses every white man whose life is cast in Arabia".

◁ **MARCO POLO**
Another famous visitor to the region was Marco Polo (1254–1324). He visited Dhofar – "a great and noble and fine city" and then sailed up the Omani coast to Qalhat.

◁ **IBN BATTUTA**
The 11th-century North African geographer Ibn Battuta visited southeast Arabia when he was just 21. His original six-month *Haj* extended to a 24-year trip taking him as far as China.

△ **CROSSING THE RUB AL KHALI**
This map shows Thomas's journey in 1930–31 (orange) and Thesiger's crossings in 1946–47 (green) and 1947–48 (purple).

THE OIL BOOM

The speed and scale of change brought by the discovery of oil in the Arabian Gulf was unprecedented in world history

If you had tried to travel to Abu Dhabi by air in 1959, you would have found there was no regular air service and, if you had managed to find a charter plane, you would have touched down on a bumpy airstrip on Abu Dhabi Island – or you might have had to land at Britain's Royal Air Force base in Sharjah, which accepted a few commercial flights. Once on the ground, you would have had a bumpy ride by Land Rover over the sand dunes until you reached a single line of palm trees, a white-washed fort and a cluster of buildings that marked Abu Dhabi town. Hens, goats, donkeys and camels wandered then between the houses and their fences of woven palm leaves. Two other white buildings dominated the sea front – the police headquarters and the oil company, and the odd fishing boat might have been drawn up on the beach.

It was in that year that oil was first discovered in commercial quantities in Abu Dhabi – in the offshore Umm Shaif field. The following year it was found on shore in the Murban field. Two more years were to pass before the first oil exports left Abu Dhabi via Das Island. Dubai first exported oil only in 1969, but Dubai had long been the bustling centre of the entrepot trade for the entire Gulf region, centred on its famous creek. Abu Dhabi, although much bigger in territorial terms, was the poor unsophisticated rival down the coast – a relationship that was to be revolutionised almost overnight.

In reserve

Today, the UAE's proven hydrocarbon reserves amount to 98 billion barrels of oil – enough to last well into the 22nd century at present extraction rates – and 5.8 trillion cubic metres of gas, estimated to be enough for at least 150 years. The oil reserves alone represent 9.8 percent of the world's total, the third largest after those of Saudi Arabia and Iraq, while gas reserves (4.6 percent of the

world's total) are the fourth largest after those of Russia, Iran and Qatar. This wealth is staggering for such a small country with a population of only 5 million. The speed and scale of change it was to bring in its wake has never been approached in world history and would certainly have been totally incomprehensible to the poor fishermen

and pearl divers of Abu Dhabi in the 1950s. This was the archetypal rags to riches story.

Of these massive reserves, no less than 92 billion barrels of oil are to be found in Abu Dhabi, with 4 billion in Dubai, 1.5 billion in Sharjah, 0.5 billion in Ras al Khaimah, but none so far in the other three emirates. Abu Dhabi's reserves are forecast to be enough for another 130 years, Dubai's for 15–20 years, while the other fields in Sharjah and Ras Al-Khaimah will be exhausted much earlier. These figures give a fairly accurate impression of the relative prosperity and economic power of the seven emirates, although Dubai depends more than the others on its trade and entrepreneurial skills.

PRECEDING PAGES: oil tanker being filled at the port of Dubai. **LEFT:** an oil jetty at a Fujairah terminal. **RIGHT:** keeping the oil industry rolling.

Prospectors toiled for 39 years in the Sultanate of Oman before discovering commercial quantities of oil in 1964, and exports followed three years later. Although the Sultanate has also enjoyed the fruits of modern development, the effects were delayed a few years until Qaboos bin Said acceded in 1970.

Oman is not quite as well endowed with oil and gas as the other Gulf countries. Its known reserves of 5 billion barrels of oil are likely to be

SPEND, SPEND, SPEND

When the oil money first flowed out to the people, shoppers would go out and buy 15 loaves of bread at a time – not because they needed so many but because they had never been able to afford to buy so much in their lives.

tries of the Organisation of the Petroleum Exporting Countries (OPEC), of which the UAE is a prominent member, quadrupled crude oil prices and then increased them massively again in 1979. From around $5 for a standard barrel of crude oil in 1972, oil reached a peak of $34 in 1979.

In Abu Dhabi in particular, money is no object. When the oil money first flowed out to the people, as it did quite quickly, shoppers would go out and

exhausted in less than 20 years, although its gas reserves are rather healthier at 2.7 trillion cubic metres.

Although the UAE is in most ways a model of a free-market economy, oil and gas reserves and production – as in the other Gulf states – stay firmly in state hands, each emirate controlling its own. Without the poorer emirates in the UAE to look after, Abu Dhabi would, it has been argued, be able to claim the highest per capita income in the world if it were an independent state on its own.

Discovering so much oil and gas by the 1960s was not alone the key to all this prosperity. It was the oil-price shock of 1973, when the 13 coun-

buy 15 loaves of bread at a time – not because they needed so many but because they had never been able to afford to buy so much in their lives. Looking back, the locals now smile sheepishly at what had seemed at the time outrageous extravagance. Cynical Western expatriates today may remark that, in the richest Gulf states (the UAE rather than Oman), belt-tightening for the average local means thinking twice about replacing the Rolls-Royce when the ash trays are full or sighing at the unaccustomed prospect of turning down the air-conditioning in their luxurious homes when they leave for one of their many globe-trotting vacations.

The two oil shocks benefited all the countries around the Gulf, which, through a geological freak of nature, contain more than half of the world's oil reserves, 45 percent concentrated in the hands of Saudi Arabia, the UAE, Kuwait and Qatar. Iran and Iraq have vastly bigger populations than the six monarchies of Arabia and so the new oil money did not go so far there. Less well endowed Bahrain – the first country in the region to export oil (in 1934), which is now almost exhausted – and Oman are not OPEC members.

WELL ENDOWED

Through a geological freak of nature, the countries around the Arabian Gulf are known to contain more than half of the world's oil reserves.

private sandy beaches along a superb winding corniche. Luxury is the norm. Dubai's creek, Sheikh Zayed Road and Jumeira Coast offers more of the same, while some of the wealth has spilled over into the much poorer emirates. In Oman, trade was limited to dates, limes and animal skins in the pre-oil 1960s, but in tourism Oman is now second only to the UAE.

Most Europeans who came to the UAE during the oil boom recall gigantic dusty construction sites in Abu Dhabi and Dubai, as this once barren

The 1970s and 1980s saw businessmen, particularly from the West, rushing to the Gulf like bees to a honey pot. Many made a lot of money. The UAE, for its size, absorbed a lot of them and like its neighbouring states at first paid gullibly through the nose for modern development, before its sharp trading instincts reasserted themselves.

Changing landscapes

Abu Dhabi's capital today is an extraordinary modern city of tower blocks, some of the world's most lavish hotels, set on immaculate

FAR LEFT: Abu Dhabi's first refinery at Umm an-Nar.
ABOVE: a barrel bears the logo of a familiar brand.

REAPING THE BENEFITS

Not least among the investments was social security, all of it free to locals (though not to expatriates, whose companies footed the bill). Citizens enjoyed the last word in schools and universities, while new hospitals resembled 5-star hotels with the finest medical personnel and the best equipment that money can buy. Any cases that required overseas treatment were granted it at government expense. There was no need for taxes, and essential utilities such as water, electricity and, of course oil, were so heavily subsidised that their consumer prices were derisory.

desert territory turned itself into a modern state. Even those who returned after an absence of a decade were astonished at the scale of change. Indeed, Dubai continues to grow at an astonishing rate. Its skyline is dotted with cranes – the largest number of any city in the world by one estimate – used to build towering concrete and glass blocks for residential, hotel or office use. Along its coast, not one, not two, but three palm-shaped islands and a man-made archipelago resembling a map of the world are being reclaimed from the sea, significantly expanding the emirate's waterfront amenities *(see page 237).*

ate bids to beat the shipping queue but then changed hands for 30 times the price they had fetched only months before. Oil revenue accumulated so fast that government departments could not spend it fast enough.

In 1971 the city of Jeddah had a budget of less than £850,000. Six years later it had leapt to £225 million. The Mayor had streets of compacted sand simply covered with asphalt so that people could see money was being spent, but it lasted only a matter of weeks and in places the blistering heat caused the roads to expand into waves that rose 2 metres (6 ft) into the air.

Too much too soon

The problems of rapid development have been experienced by all the countries of the Gulf, and often more acutely than in the UAE and Oman. Saudi Arabia, richest of all the Gulf states by far, with more than a quarter of global reserves of oil and the world's biggest oil fields, on shore and off shore, saw even more astonishing changes.

By the mid-1970s, the port of Jeddah, through which nearly all Saudi imports passed, was such a bottleneck that ships were queueing outside for six months to unload their merchandise. Cement bags were being winched to the shore by helicopter in desper-

NATURAL GAS

The UAE has led attempts to recover the enormous quantities of natural gas extracted automatically with oil but previously wasted by flaring. It now recovers virtually all of it, with 92 percent coming from Abu Dhabi, 5 percent from Sharjah, 2 percent from Dubai and 1 percent from Ras al Khaimah. The UAE is the world's seventh largest exporter of natural gas, and Oman, too, has considerable reserves. Since 1999 a huge new development by LNG (Liquefied Natural Gas) has been piping gas from central Oman to Sur for export, increasing revenues by 20 percent.

And in Qatar, where in living memory people had been starving, the government gave everyone a free house and the money to furnish it and buy a luxury car. They also had the right to a government job at a handsome salary: if there was no job available, the salary was still guaranteed. Many Qataris took up the right to lease their car back to the Government and then earned a further salary for driving it on official duties. As one ageing driver put the situation laconically, "God decided it was our turn".

> **GREEN DREAMS**
>
> Greening the desert came to be regarded not just as a dream but as an extremely practical need.

The chance to take stock

As money was the last commodity that was in short supply, it did not take many years before all the highways and houses, the hospitals and schools, the government buildings, airports and defence establishments had been put into place.

But wealth bred all kinds of fears for security. Up and down the Gulf there was an uneasy feeling that one day the Western and other developed countries that imported so much oil from the Gulf might hit back in the face of oil

Kuwait invested a lot of its oil revenues wisely, and by law 10 percent had to be put into the Fund for Future Generations. After the second oil price shock of 1979, it was calculated that the Kuwaitis could all sell off their valuable piece of real estate called Kuwait, invest the proceeds and then retire to the south of France on an income of not less than £50,000 a year – every man, woman and child. Kuwait became the first nation of independent means in history. National pride stopped this happening, but some doubtless regretted it had not been done when Iraq invaded Kuwait in 1990.

LEFT: natural gas plant, Dubai.
ABOVE: irrigation aids agriculture in the Salalah region.

price rises by refusing to supply the Gulf states with food, and so food security, as much as military protection (on which huge sums were already being spent), became a new sphere of investment.

Despite the inhospitable climate and the lack of water, massive resources were channelled into agriculture, and greening the desert came to be regarded not just as a dream but as an extremely practical need. Incredibly, Saudi Arabia became the world's sixth largest producer of wheat, far more than the population could consume, while Dubai was able to export surplus strawberries to Europe in the winter months.

Forward planning

Despite the unprecedented cornucopia, the shrewdness of the Gulf Arabs quickly showed behind their spending sprees. Even the Saudis, whose oil could last until the end of the 21st century, planned for the days when the oil runs out or is superceded by some as yet unknown source of energy. Diversification away from oil was planned as soon as the bonanza began.

Extracting the oil was so easy and cheap that the prospect of very low-cost energy to fuel local industry soon became a reality. Steel and petrochemical industries sprang up, eventually reaching world-class, as well as cement works,

construction firms and food processing. Then came furniture and pharmaceutical factories. Imports of many commodities were cut dramatically. Exports have grown steadily.

The headlong rush to spend was bound to ease up eventually. In 1982, the Kuwaiti Government, one of the most cautious in the region, put its foot down, doubling the local price of petrol (the first rise in 12 years) and raising diesel prices 700 percent. Filling up the tank of your Cadillac for $3 was no longer on. The days of wanton profligacy were over.

A global oil glut was already building up, caused partly by new sources of non-OPEC oil from regions like the North Sea, Mexico and China. Prices on the open market began to fall, and the following spring the official price of oil fell – for the first time since the boom – by $7 to $27 a barrel. Two years later prices collapsed, at one stage edging below $10 a barrel and in subsequent years have mostly hovered at around $15–20 a barrel, while quotas agreed between OPEC members became necessary.

But by then huge financial reserves had been built up in the Gulf monarchies, and although they suffered relative recessions, there was a reluctance to make unpopular economies although some cutbacks were made. Budget deficits became the norm, although not in the UAE, but there was no question of bankruptcy. The Gulf economies had simply settled down to the kind of level that Western countries were used to, which meant borrowing on the international markets.

Regional conflicts

Western intervention in the Arabian Gulf during the last two decades has revolved around war with Iraq, first in 1990 to repel Saddam Hussein's invasion of Kuwait, and again in 2003 when US and British forces overthrew the Iraqi dictator. The West is determined to defend the status quo in the Gulf and safeguard the supplies of oil on which it depends.

In OPEC negotiations, Kuwait, the UAE and Qatar have not necessarily sided with the Saudis, although the four have rarely been in direct conflict. They compete against each other but cannot afford to differ over oil policies as much as they can with other members of OPEC.

Sooner or later the countries with smaller oil reserves will run out, and oil in the Gulf will be the preserve of Saudi Arabia, Iraq, the UAE and Kuwait, but new oil discoveries continue to push that scenario further into the future. Will that mean an oil shortage and another oil price shock? The experts, who have often been wildly wrong, say this would harm oil producers as well as importers. But expanding production is costly and time-consuming. If the Gulf Arabs act too soon they will be left with white elephants – too late, and there will be another oil price explosion that will damage their investments overseas. Whatever the answer, the UAE Government is determined that the last barrel of oil ever sold will come from their country. ❏

ABOVE LEFT: buying at source.
RIGHT: sooner or later the sun will set on oil.

DAILY LIFE

*In spite of the massive changes that have taken place in Oman and the UAE,
everyday life is still very traditional in many respects*

The UAE and Oman are frequently misunderstood by outsiders. People imagine them to be traditional Muslim countries with many restrictions for everyone. In fact, both countries succeed in mixing modern life with established social traditions. They combine a delight in their culture and heritage with a sense of their place in the modern world.

Another common misconception is that women in the UAE and Oman are compelled to lead very restricted lives, barred from working outside the home or driving. In fact, in the cities women are increasingly strong in the workplace and although home is central to their lives, education and work are also important.

Family values

Life tends to revolve around the family home, in cities and rural areas alike. Family life is important for both men and women, though the roles of the sexes are different. Broadly, it is the men who go out to work and finance the home, and the wives and other women of the family that organise and run the house and children. However, there are plenty of exceptions to this stereotype. Many richer women own and run businesses, in some cases performing roles that shield them from the public. And less well-off women often work for large institutions such as banks and public utilities, doing office work and dealing directly with customers. Some work at women-only branches.

That said, expectations for girls are fairly well established – to grow up, marry and have children – although nowadays many are well educated and have often travelled abroad. Many young women will work prior to marriage, and even continue working afterwards, although this is mainly in the cities where there tends to be larger networks of female relatives to look after the children.

PRECEDING PAGES: men in the souq at Nizwa; a woman passes before a typical wrought-iron gate in Ras al Hadd. **LEFT:** the army band plays on, Dubai.
ABOVE RIGHT: something for the wedding album, Oman.

Eighty percent of girls have an arranged marriage with a partner from a suitable family known to her own family. Often a girl will marry a first cousin or man from the same tribe. Girls often marry young, sometimes soon after puberty, and Muslim women always marry a Muslim, although the same is not true of men.

Muslim men socialise regularly outside their homes, whereas until recently women mainly socialised in one another's houses. Men are not usually involved in the daily routines of childcare, but families do go out together as groups. Increasingly fathers are seen in public in domestic family scenes, playing with their children in the park, shopping with their wives, or going out to dinner with their family.

Bride to be

Marriage is a major milestone in a woman's life and this important event is governed by strict traditions. First, the woman's family receives a marriage proposal from the would-be groom's family, who will then pay them a social visit. If all goes well, formal arrangements commence. According to custom, the male members of the two families meet to discuss the bride money and set the date for the wedding. Money and jewellery given to the bride remain her own throughout marriage, and in the event of a divorce she has these to fall back on.

Once the marriage licence has been arranged and recorded in the courts, preparations are made for the preliminary and wedding-night celebrations, usually held at the

ANOINTED

The evening before her wedding the bride will be massaged all over with perfumed oil and will hold her "henna night".

The bride is kept in seclusion for three days (formerly seven) before her wedding day. During this time she is pampered by a beautician, who is hired for the duration of the festivities, and surrounded by her closest female friends and family members. On the evening before her wedding the bride will hold her henna night *(laylat al henna)*, when she will be massaged with perfumed oil and decorated with henna. For this she wears a traditional gold-embroidered green dress and elaborate gold jewellery, often part of her

bride's house. Invitations are issued verbally between the women, while the men announce the occasion at the mosque. These days printed invitation cards may be sent out.

On the day of the wedding the bride's house is decked out in hundreds of lights strung around trees and the garden walls. Huge, colourful tents are erected for the guests, and tables are laid with many different dishes. Food is served in separate areas for the men and women, and it is usual for guests to take away small parcels of food to give to friends and relatives unable to attend the festivities. To cope with this mass catering, a special kitchen is usually set up within the wedding area.

wedding gift. She sits on traditional cushions – *te-keyya* – and henna is applied to her feet and hands in intricate patterns.

The henna, a powder made from the leaves of an Egyptian tree, is mixed into a paste with water and then squeezed like icing through a cone of paper and left to dry overnight. When the dried crust drops off the next morning it leaves a lacy stain on the skin which lasts for several weeks. The best henna artists command high fees for their work.

Entertainment is an important component of any wedding. At city weddings, which now tend to be modern affairs in large hotels, the highlight is usually a singer and a band. In rural areas dancing is an important part of the festivities. In the popular "hair dance" *(ayala)* girls swing their long hair as they dance in a circle. Singing often accompanies the dancing and loud clapping beats out the rhythm. This can go on for hours to noisy and exciting effect.

Men are allowed to marry a non-Muslim, although in many cases their wife will convert to Islam at some time during their marriage. Islam allows a Muslim man to have up to four wives, providing he can afford to treat them equally, but polygamy is not widespread.

BABY CARE

A newborn baby's eyes are lined with *kohl* to cleanse and protect them from infection.

In general it occurs only when a first wife is unable to bear children, or is a non-Muslim.

Divorce is relatively uncommon, and is usually instigated by the husband in the event that his wife is sterile or has not borne a son. Women can also divorce a man, although this is seldom done as the stigma of divorce is considerable for a woman. A divorced woman will normally return to live with her family, taking with her the money she took into the marriage as her means of support.

ABOVE LEFT: a bride displays her hennaed hands, decorated the night before her wedding.
ABOVE: mother and toddler, Oman.

The blessing of children

Married women are expected to bear children, and the birth of a child of either sex is considered a very happy occasion. These days most women give birth in modern hospitals, a development that has slashed the previously high mortality rate. Despite the clinical surroundings, the atmosphere is festive with many visitors, all bearing presents and offering special foods for the new mother and baby. Huge bouquets of flowers line hospital corridors, and all the new mums on a ward are congratulated by all the visitors, even though they have probably never met before.

As with marriage, the birth of a child is attended by many traditions. The mother is given specially prepared food and drink, including camel and goat's milk, and the baby's eyes are lined with *kohl*, believed to cleanse and protect the eyes from infection.

The way of death

In Islam mourning is not an important part of death. The deceased will be washed and anointed with perfumed oils and then wrapped in a white cloth and borne on a simple bier to the cemetery. The body is always buried (on its side facing Mecca) and if possible burial should take place on the day of death. Forty days after death, the close relatives of the deceased will hold a feast to mark the ascent to heaven, believed to occur after this 40-day period.

National dress

All over the Gulf region, one of the most striking features for the visitor is the very noticeable national dress of both men and women. Virtually everyone wears it, and in Oman national dress is mandatory for anyone working in the public services. In the Gulf areas men wear a *dishdash*, a white or pastel-coloured ankle-length robe, with a headdress *(ghutra)*, held in place by black ropes *(iqal)*. On formal occasions, men sometimes wear an over-garment, a gauzy black or brown robe *(bisht)* edged in woven gold thread. In Oman men favour headresses wrapped like turbans without the black ropes used in the Gulf. One of the most distinctive accessories worn by Omani men on special occasions is the *khanjar* (silver dagger) tucked into the belt.

Women cover their heads and bodies with a voluminous black overdress *(abbaya)*, under which is worn a black head scarf to cover the hair. These garments often hide brightly coloured dresses which are long-sleeved with very elaborately embroidered necklines and wrist to elbow decoration, sometimes embellished with crystal beading and sequins. Wealthier women may wear French designer clothes under their plain black *abbaya*.

The *abbaya* may also be edged in beads or sequins and the under scarf is sometimes also very beautifully decorated. The result is that a sense of style is not lost by these black robes.

headdress may be drawn across the face as a veil. To wear the *burqa* or not is a matter of personal choice, and can be dependent on the situation. City women often wear this mask in very public places such as supermarkets and shopping malls, yet may not wear it when driving their cars. In Dubai many women do not wear it in the streets at all. In Oman and in the more conservative, rural areas of the UAE it is still very common.

The social round

Social visiting is an important part of daily life and a favourite form of relaxation. Men

Make-up, too, is important, and used to alluring effect.

The traditional face mask *(burqa)* worn in Oman and the UAE is a light and simple structure semi-covering the face, with a thin strip across the forehead and over the nose, leaving the eyes and cheek areas free. The mask stops under the nose, covering the top lip but leaving the chin free. It is made from black cotton, the front covered with a gold, purple or red dye with a blueish sheen. There are several designs and women may wear a gold one for special occasions.

The mask is worn by many married women, though not by all women in public. Instead the

THE COFFEE CEREMONY

Every visitor to a UAE or Omani home will be offered coffee or tea. The traditional Gulf coffee – *kahwa* – is made from green coffee beans, is very strong and sometimes flavoured with cardamom or saffron. Poured from a distinctive coffee pot, it is served in tiny cups without handles, which are refilled several times until a guest "wobbles" the cup from side to side, indicating sufficiency. Three cups is considered the polite number to drink, indicating pleasure at the coffee, but not drinking to excess. The social custom of drinking coffee is also important in business.

and women usually socialise separately, with men visiting one another in the *majlis,* the public part of the home, to sit together, drink coffee, talk and exchange news, and eat sweetmeats. The entrance to the *majlis* is always separate from the main door into the domestic sections of the house, where the women frequently hold their own, all-female social gatherings for family members, friends and neighbours.

It is customary for all guests to remove their shoes when entering the sitting areas of a home

UP IN SMOKE

The appearance of the incense burner marks the end of a social occasion.

offered *seh,* a preserve made from mashed ripened dates.

At female gatherings similar customs are followed, but with the additional offering of perfumes, a selection of which will be passed around on a tray. Each women will removed the stopper of the scent she prefers and anoint her face and clothes.

Afterwards the incense burner is filled and passed around, so that each guest can fan scented smoke onto her face. Men may also use incense. These ceremonies signify the end of the occasion.

– a measure originally adopted for reasons of hygiene when streets were considerably dustier than they are today but now simply a matter of polite behaviour.

Food is a key ingredient of any social meeting. Coffee or tea is always offered as a symbol of hospitality even during quite brief encounters, as are dates and sweetmeats. In Oman one might be offered *dibis,* a date syrup derived from pressed dates, mixed with *tahineh* and spread on bread. In the UAE it is common to be

LEFT: wearing a traditional face mask or *burqa.*
ABOVE: young men watch the world go by on a corner in Ajman.

High days and holidays

Other important social occasions are the main religious festivals. The *majlis* is particularly important during these holidays and during the evenings of the month of Ramadan. This is the month (a moveable period governed by the Hejira calendar) when Muslims fast during daylight hours. After sunset, there is a busy round of dinners and social visits.

Ramadan is followed by the holiday celebrations of Eid, when gifts are exchanged and important meetings take place in both business and social spheres. This is an important time for tribal leaders and businessmen to visit and reinforce ties.

Education and work

Employment of nationals in the local workforce, filling jobs previously occupied by immigrant expatriates, is increasing in both Oman and the UAE. Many young nationals are now well educated, and qualified to fill jobs in industry, banking and other main sectors of the economy. More and more international companies are starting training schemes for these young men and women, enabling them rather than the vast army of expats to run the country.

THE HOODED CLAW

It has been known for falcons to be carried into city offices, and placed, hooded, on perches next to their owner's desk.

Education is the key to the future of both countries. Women have grasped this fact with great success, and are forging ahead in education and employment. Their results at university are impressive, and they are fast becoming a skilled force to be reckoned with. Middle or higher income women are often sent abroad to be educated, although with the growth of first-class universities in the region this is no longer necessary.

Even in rural Oman women are being encouraged to attend local women's centres where, among other things such as learning about birth spacing and family health matters, they can receive training in needlework. The aim of this programme is for Omani women to be able to replace expatriate tailors in rural areas over the next few years. Such centres include a creche.

Sporting passions

In both the UAE and Oman there are plenty of leisure activities for the younger generation. Cinemas, bowling alleys and indoor sports abound, and thanks to a good climate for much of the year outdoor sports are popular. Many nationals are passionate followers of their football teams in the national leagues.

But traditional sports are still enjoyed, including horse racing, camel racing, and falconry. Horse racing, particularly in the UAE, has become a world class event *(see pages 115–19)*. Camel racing is an old traditional sport, though these days the owner usually follows his camel around the inside of the track in a four-wheel drive, while the spectators watch the action on enormous television screens from the comfort of an armchair in the lounge. The ancient sport of falconry continues and it is not unknown to see falcons being carried into city offices, where they are placed, hooded, on perches next to their owner's desk.

Other forms of game hunting are not widespread, although many wealthy Omanis and UAE citizens pursue the sport abroad. Modern substitutes are clay pigeon shooting and rifle clubs. Water sports are also extremely popular thanks to the combination of superb beaches and climate. Traditional dhow races are held annually, as are world-class events in power boat racing, in which UAE competitors have excelled. Water skiing, jet skiing and windsurfing are also popular. Sand-surfing is a variation on a theme.

Woman are generally less active, and tend to visit parks and beaches, some of which are built specifically for women and children.

These aspects of life and the ever-changing attitudes of society as the possibilities and needs of modern life are absorbed, create an exciting and interesting place to live. Each generation makes its own small changes to a culture living in a traditional way. ❏

ABOVE LEFT: the traditional sport of falconry remains a very popular pastime in Oman and the UAE.
RIGHT: a game of football on the beach in Dubai.

THE BEDU

The life of the Bedu used to be one of thirst and hunger, and of great journeys to find water. The lack of such hardships today is testing the strength of their culture

The Bedu of Oman and the Emirates are among the oldest tribal peoples of the world. Tracing their ancestry from a mythical hero called Kahtan in the Yemen, these southern Arabian tribesmen are sometimes referred to as the "Pure Arabs". Kahtan has been identified with Yoktan, listed in the Old Testament as a descendant of Shem, a son of Noah, making these tribes of older, purer Arab stock than the younger northern tribes that trace their ancestry from Ishmael. Of these southern tribes the Bait Kathir and Rashid are the most famous, having been Wilfred Thesiger's companions on his exploration of the Empty Quarter in the second half of the 1940s. Other tribes in the region include the Harasis, Al Wahiba, Ajman and Jenuba. Bedu is the Arabic word for nomadic tribespeople. The singular is *Badawi*, but as this word is little known in the West, Bedu is used throughout this book. The more common Western version, *Bedouin*, is a strange double plural which does not exist in Arabic.

For modern Westerners concepts of tribal descent and purity of blood lines may appear somewhat irrelevant. In Arabia, family ties and tribal identity are the building blocks of society, modern as well as traditional. A citizen of any Arabian Gulf state is identified by a personal name, then as the child of a father and grandfather, and then by their clan and tribal name.

This sense of being from a line of descent, of belonging to a family grouping that extends through a clan and a tribe to a wider society is fundamental to Bedu life and is probably the single most important influence within the relatively young states of the Arabian Peninsula.

Adapt or die

The Bedu evolved as nomadic herdsmen, living off the products of their animals, drinking their milk, weaving their hair, making leather from

PRECEDING PAGES: men making *halwa*, a sticky sweet made with honey and sometimes almonds.
LEFT: Bait Kathir Bedu in Rub al Khali, Oman.
ABOVE RIGHT: a young Harasis Bedu woman.

their skins and eating their flesh. Their lifestyle was the supreme adaptation of man to the hostile environment of some of the hottest, driest areas on earth. The land is too sterile for them to stay long in any one place. The vegetation is too thin and grows too slowly. Instead the Bedu have learnt to move, following the limited rains,

grazing their animals on small patches of grass wherever they can be found. It was not an easy life but it was survival. T.E. Lawrence wrote that "the Bedouin ways were hard even for those brought up in them", that they were "a death in life". If one asks the Bedu today what life was like in the old days, their tales are of constant thirst and hunger, of great journeys to bring water from wells or to look for areas that had received some rain.

Whenever one thinks of the Bedu one imagines them with their camels and their goat hair tents. The *bait sharar* ("house of hair") is synonymous with the Bedu. The reality is slightly different. There are tribes who have never lived in tents and those who have traditionally only used tents during winter when a shelter from the cold, wind and occasional rain has been a necessity. In Oman it is only the tribes of the Empty Quarter, the Bait Kathir and Rashid that have used tents. Previously the tribes of the stony plains, where trees are more plentiful, built their camps around the shade of these natural shelters, often covering them with blankets or cloth to improve them. Other tribes, especially on the coast, used palm fronds to build easily assembled and dismantled shelters called *barasti*. These are still a common sight around the Wahiba Sands in Oman and along the coasts of

the Arabian Gulf. More recently the Bedu have started to use metal grills to form temporary shelters. These are common among the Bedu on the Jiddat al Harasis in Oman, where they resemble metal bedsteads up-ended and joined together to form small cabins.

Tent life

But the goat-hair tent remains a potent symbol of the nomadic way of life. It is easily pitched and taken down – customarily the work of women, although usually helped by men. The main division within is between the men's section and the women's side where the family's possessions are stored and food is prepared. The sides are usu-

ally separated by a decorated woven curtain. In a large tent a third division may be used for storage or cooking. The divisions effectively create a public and private space, all male visitors being entertained in the men's section. It is here that the coffee and tea utensils and fire are placed. Essential for entertaining, the coffee hearth comprises a fire on which the coffee beans are roasted using a ladle and stirring rod, plus coffee pots of various sizes, and bags of wool or animal skin containing the coffee, tea and sugar. Added to this is a mortar either of brass or wood, the kettle and tea utensils. Other articles might include a camel saddle and, once guests have arrived, rugs and cushions for them to sit on.

The kindness of strangers

Hospitality is an essential part of Bedu life. All passers-by are welcomed by a set exchange of greetings and the asking of news, to which the reply is always that there is no news or only good news. Guests are then refreshed with tiny cups of coffee and glasses of sweet black tea of which it is polite to drink three cups before refusing more by wobbling the empty glass.

In a land where people are few and far between and there is little to sustain life, hospitality becomes a means of survival. In the past any traveller seeing a tent would immediately travel towards it, sure of receiving a friendly welcome. In exchange for his news he would be greeted with tea and coffee and be invited to share a meal. According to custom, he would be assured of food and shelter for a period of three and a third days. It was, and still is today, a system of mutual support. In the desert, today's guest may well be tomorrow's host. In the absence of men, women and even small children are also bound by this code of generosity. It is not unusual to be invited into a camp by a young boy who will make coffee with great dignity, following the Bedu code with care and concentration, knowing that in the absence of his father, the family's honour is in his hands.

NO NEWS, GOOD NEWS

Passers-by are welcomed by a set exchange of greetings and the asking of news, to which the reply is always that there is no news or only good news.

Hospitality is part of a strict code of honour and protection in a world fraught with danger. Visitors knew that they would not only receive food and shelter, but also the protection of their host for the duration of their stay and for another three days after – this being the time it takes for all traces of his host's food to pass through his body. The code tying the host to his guest is called the bond of salt. Even if a visitor carried only the salt of his host in his stomach, he could call on his protection.

HONOUR MATTERS

Honour is held not just by the individual but by the family and tribe as a whole. It is passed on from generation to generation. It can be lost as well as won.

important role in the family *sharaf*. As it can only be lost through shameful conduct women are a protected part of Bedu society, and the tribes' women are kept well away from the opportunity to bring shame on the the family.

In the past when a family's fortunes were uncertain, governed by acts of nature and the fortunes of inter-tribal raiding, the Bedu developed a fatalism whereby everything lay in God's hands. The only things a person could be sure to control were his dignity and honour. This meant that

In fact a traveller need not even reach the tent but simply receive a response to his greeting of "*As-salaam aleykum*" (peace be with you) for this code to operate. With the reply "*Waleykum as salaam*" (with you be peace) came the protection of the speaker and all his or her kinfolk, even if the words were spoken by a child.

The code of honour called *sharaf* is extremely strict, honour not just being held by the individual but by the family and tribe as a whole. It is passed on from generation to generation, and lost as well as won. *Ird*, the honour of a woman, plays an

ABOVE LEFT: a Bedu woman in Nizwa.
ABOVE: making rope and camel harnesses.

even if circumstances left a man destitute he could still be proud in more wealthy company, knowing that he would be judged primarily on his reputation and conduct.

Camels, a crucial commodity

Up until the adoption of motor vehicles, the entire lifestyle of the Bedu relied on the camel. It was the beast of burden by which they moved their tents and possessions as well as the mode of personal transport. The camel is still a source of milk, meat and wool. The wool, prized for its strength and warmth, is used to make cloaks and equipment such as udder bags, as well as the detailing on the tent curtain.

Under hot summer conditions the Bedu try to water their camels every day or two days, but in winter the period can be weekly or, if the grazing is good, the herds will not be watered at all. If need be, the camel can show incredible stamina. H.R.P. Dickson, a British political agent in Kuwait between 1929 and 1936, and author of *The Arab Of The Desert*, reported how one Bedu sheikh, in about 1925, rode a camel between Riyadh and Nasriyah, in Iraq, in eight days, covering a distance of about 1,287 km (800 miles). On Wilfred Thesiger's first crossing of the Empty Quarter in the winter of 1946–7, his party travelled for two weeks across the sands without finding a well where it could water its animals.

Different tribes have developed their own thoroughbred strains that are valued for particular characteristics. Thus the Omanis breed tall, long-legged camels famous for their speed and stamina. Camel racing has become the main way in which the Bedu can show off their skills as breeders and trainers. Race meetings in both Oman and the UAE attract enormous crowds with winning camels being exchanged for vast sums of money in much the same way as race horses in the West.

All camels in the Middle East and Arabia are domesticated and the work of herding, breeding and milking them is traditionally the task of men. Each camel will be branded with the mark, called a *wasm*, of its owner and tribe, on its neck, shoulder or hind-quarters. However even a man with over 100 animals will commonly know his own camels individually and will usually have given names to each of them.

Camels are kept by the Bedu primarily as a source of milk. Thus the majority of animals are female. The Bedu will rarely kill an adult camel, unless it is obviously sick and dying. However, they will slaughter the occasional calf, especially a male. The only time that adult camels are normally killed for food is in order to feast a large number of guests such as for a marriage or to honour a visiting sheikh.

The Bedu's diet consists primarily of camel milk drunk cold or hot or boiled with bread (a mix called *threat* by the Bait Kathir in Oman), or cooked with rice. Meat is an occasional luxury and more often than not is goat's meat bought in the market. Along the coasts fresh and salted fish is an important staple for people and animals, and sun-dried sardines are a traditional supplementary feed for camels.

The role of Bedu women

Whatever the impression of women in Muslim society in general, Bedu women enjoy a great deal of freedom and play an important role. In such a harsh environment, and with the heavy demands of a nomadic existence, it would be impossible for the family to survive without the women taking their share of responsibility. What segregation exists is not a reflection of lack of status. Women's separation from strangers and the use of veils is due more to a sense of modesty and the protective concern of the menfolk. It is a custom more akin to a code of chivalry than a regime of repression.

THE WAY THE BEDU RIDE

Camel saddles vary between southern Arabia and the north. In Oman and the UAE the frame of the saddle *(shedad)* is no more than an anchor that sits over the hump and holds in place a cushioned strap that runs over the camel's hindquarters. The rider then sits or kneels behind the hump, supported by the cushioned pad of the strap. This requires a great sense of balance which the Bedu like to display by standing up on their camels. Instead of bits, a loop halter is placed around the animal's muzzle or a rope is simply attached to a ring through its nostrils.

As children, brothers and sisters are taught to have a special sense of closeness. A young boy is encouraged to see himself as his sister's protector, to bring presents to his female siblings. He is their chaperone in public and champion of their honour. A Bedu male would not tolerate any person harming his sister's reputation, verbally or otherwise, and until his sister is married he will act as a surrogate husband. Even after her marriage he is responsible for the protection of her honour (more so than her husband) as her

WOMEN'S WORK

Where families have no sons, the daughters will often be found herding all the animals, entertaining guests and driving the family vehicles.

camel herds. Where families have no sons, the daughters will often be found herding all the animals and entertaining guests, as well as driving the family vehicles.

Under normal circumstances, the segregation of the sexes so obvious to the stranger hardly exists. When staying with families, foreign visitors may be surprised by how quickly barriers are broken down. After a few days, Bedu women often start to relax as they see their men accept a visitor. They may even dispense with wearing their face

reputation is that of his family's, thus her honour is his honour.

Similarly young girls are their brothers closest confidantes and are encouraged to contribute to their brother's comfort and public image. Sisters will sew and weave their brothers' clothes and camel trappings, as well as cook their favourite foods for them. From a very early age a girl takes an active part in the daily work of the family. She will herd the sheep or goats if they have any, and a teenage unmarried girl will typically be left to pasture one of the family's

ABOVE LEFT: Al Wahiba Bedu astride his camel.
ABOVE: Bait Kathir with his *khanjar* in his belt.

masks if the guest comes to be regarded as an honorary member of the family.

Dress code

The costumes for both men and women are similar in basic outline among all Bedu and practically common to all Arabs. Both sexes wear a long garment that covers the body from the base of the neck to the ankles, with long sleeves, that adheres to the Islamic demand for modesty. However details of cut, material and colour are variable particularly among women. This basic dress, called a *dishdashah* or *dish-dash*, is traditionally made of cotton, but can also be made from silk, wool or commonly from nylon or a cotton mix. Traditionally the cut of a Bedu woman's dress was larger and looser than her settled sister. The sleeves were longer with trailing cuffs. When working the women would often roll up the sleeves to the shoulder and tuck the front of the skirt into their belts.

When visiting each other or going to a market, the Bedu men of Arabia also like to wear silver or gold belts fitted with highly decorated curved daggers called *khanjar*. These have much more than a decorative value, being a daily tool for cutting

BEHIND THE MASK

Young Bedu in search of an eligible wife can be driven to distraction by skilful flirting.

ropes and killing and skinning animals. Further north the Bedu use straight bladed knives.

Belts designed for carrying bullets are *de rigeur* for men, as are rifles and pistols. It is a common sight in any gathering of Bedu to see the men fully armed as if the desert was on the verge of a war. Firearms and knives are still very much a part of a man's costume and are integral to his sense of manhood and independence.

All Bedu girls cover their hair once they reach puberty. Head scarves are often lacy and semi-transparent showing off any earrings or necklaces the girl is wearing. Among virtually all tribes in the region it is the custom for a girl to veil her face covering it with a *burqa*, a striking mask, made of cotton and dyed with indigo, more like an ancient Greek's visor than a veil. Details of design vary a great deal. Within the general custom of her tribe, a woman has the freedom to make her own mask how she likes. If a girl wishes to be more revealing she can cut the shape slightly smaller, especially around her chin, and cut larger eye holes.

Some young Bedu girls use this freedom to create their own fashions. Al Wahibi girls sometimes wear gold-coloured *burqas* which they style by bending the bottom half outwards. The result is that their masks are not only very eye-catching, but also reveal tantalising glimpses of the line of the jaw and the girl's typically high cheekbones, especially when their head is held in certain positions. Young Bedu men, in search of an eligible wife, can be driven to distraction by this skilful flirting. Young girls think of the

WOMEN'S WORK – WEAVING

Weaving, almost entirely in the hands of women, is one of the oldest crafts of the Arabian Peninsula, and the earliest illustration of the ground loom used by the Bedu is in an Egyptian fresco dating back to over 2000 BC.

Women spin using a stick with a cross head whorl and hook before dyeing the wool and then respinning the material, producing a double strand of yarn. In the past, natural dyes from plants were used; modern synthetic dyes give access to brighter and more varied colours.

Most decorative motifs are geometric but the repertoire also include stylised representations of familiar objects and animals, such as coffee pots, scissors and

camels. The patterns are repeated to the edge of the piece, reflecting the infinite horizon of the desert.

The tent curtain, the largest decorated piece of textile made by the Bedu, is usually in black and white. The white is commonly cotton yarn but can be white camel hair. A narrow pattern, it runs the length of the textile and uses symbols and designs including geometric representations of household objects. Designed to run from the back wall to the front, it is made extra long so that it can be extended into the open space at the entrance of the tent, creating a private space for the women. The curtain is hung with the good side facing into the men's half of the tent.

veil not as a form of repression, but as a sign of their coming to maturity. They look forward to covering their faces in the same way as Western girls long to wear make up.

Changing times

Today the Bedu are facing a challenge that is testing the strength of their culture. Throughout the Middle East the life of the desert is in a state of transition. Mass production of the motor vehicle and the birth of nation states with political identities have irrevocably changed the Bedu lifestyle. Modern employment, schools, hospitals and industry are not designed for a

from his view across the desert – have alienated him from the environment and deprived him of the roots that give meaning to his sense of hospitality and honour.

The governments of the Emirates and Oman are not blind to the special needs of their nomadic peoples, but finding a meaningful alternative for them, without destroying their culture, is not easy. So much of the Bedu traditions is about surviving in a harsh world where starvation and thirst were constant threats. The oil companies and governments have dug new wells and helped the nomads make the transition to motor vehicles by providing grants and

nomadic population. To find jobs and take advantage of schools, the Bedu have had to give up their migrations and adapt traditions never designed for a sedentary lifestyle.

One old Bedu sheikh explains this with the example of a man in his house who, on hearing a knock at his door, calls out, "Who is there?" In the old days, seeing a traveller from afar, the man would prepare fresh coffee and go out to meet his visitor with words of welcome. For him, the car – that makes travel too quick and easy – and the house – cutting the Bedu off

ABOVE LEFT: a Harasis Bedu girl.
ABOVE: preparing a feast in the Wahiba Sands.

simple employment. Deep bore holes provide reliable water where previously there was none. Tanker trucks can now deliver water to the herds, cutting out days of travelling to water sources. Animal feed, bought in town and trucked out to the camps, reduces dependence on pastures. Modern communications and four-wheel drive vehicles make weather forecasting and the search for pasture quicker and more reliable. Once the Bedu were fighters protecting their herds from theft; peace has left them without a role. Lack of demand for their camels has reduced the size of their herds.

The Bedu, without a role that gives value to their traditions, are doomed to disappear. ❏

FALCONRY

Hawking is an old and much-loved pastime in the Gulf. Falconers pay huge sums of money for the very best birds and pamper them accordingly

Falconry is a passionate sport in the Gulf. It has its origins as the hunting technique par excellence of the Bedu, who admired the birds' courage, cunning and proud appearance and took pleasure in their skills at training them. During winter, on the edge of any major town, it is common to see members of the local falconry club exercising and training their birds in the cool of the evening.

The main source of falcons in the Emirates is the livestock market in Sharjah, where three or four dealers import birds from Iran and Pakistan. Aged between six months and three years, a bird can be worth anything between US$240 and US$32,000 depending on its species, age, general health and looks. Females are preferred over males as they are on average one-third larger.

Although it is illegal to trade in wild birds, they are favoured over more docile captive-bred falcons, which were thought to lack the natural instinct to hunt. Happily, captive-bred falcons are now becoming more popular. Fledglings, taken from the nest in the wild, are also less sought after for similar reasons. By contrast, mature wild birds, used to their freedom, are hard to train but are exceptional hunters. These attract more experienced falconers.

The best time to capture a bird is on its first autumn migration as it passes over the desert on its way south. These immature wild birds are relatively easy to train, but already have a developed hunting instinct.

The saker, from the Arabic *saqr*, is the most popular bird on account of its size, toughness and versatility. Known for its intelligent hunting tactics, it predicts the movements of its prey and uses the landscape to hide its attacks.

Smaller and more fragile than the saker is the peregrine falcon *(shahin)*. Built for speed, it is designed to kill on the wing and is vulnerable on the ground. Difficult to keep in captivity, peregrines have become rare and valuable. The lanner, or *shahin wakri*, is a small falcon, like the peregrine, but with the qualities of the saker. Gyrfalcons have also appeared in Arabia in recent years. Mostly captive-bred, they are exotics, not desert falcons, adapted to to live in the Arctic, and desired for their size (twice that of a peregrine) and good looks.

The season for hawking is very short, lasting from October to January and coinciding with the autumn migration of the game birds, mostly houbara. The traditional falcon species are also migratory and cannot stand the desert summer. It was once common for falconers to release their birds at the end of each hunting season. Now owners hang onto favourite or valuable birds throughout the year, caging them in air-conditioned environments.

Falconry has become a sophisticated pastime of the wealthy. All the Gulf sheikhs engage vets to staff private falcon hospitals in an effort to improve the captive conditions of these essentially wild creatures. ❏

PRECEDING PAGES: falconry as a tourist attraction in a Dubai hotel. **LEFT:** falconry as sport.
ABOVE RIGHT: a fine specimen.

ALL THAT GLISTERS – JEWELLERY

Jewellery performs much more than a decorative purpose among the Bedu of the Middle East – it can be a talisman or even the family safe deposit

Oman is particularly rich in silver jewellery which the Bedu, notably the Al Wahiba, still wear in great quantities. The jewellery of the Bedu is not very different in style from that of the towns-people of the region. Never having their own silver or goldsmiths, the Bedu would buy or commission pieces from village jewellers during visits to markets. At other times, travelling traders of *Haj* pilgrims passing through tribal areas would sell their jewellery as well as wares, carpets and firearms to fund their journey.

Jewellery is worn almost exclusively by women and children (though men use silver accessories such as toothpicks, tweezers and ear spoons). Women make up their own pieces with beads and chains bought individually, adding coins, amulets and pendants either received as gifts, earned through the sale of produce, or found and kept for their magical powers. A woman's jewellery is technically her own, but she often also acts as the family bank, a custom dating from the days of raiding when women were immune from robbery. Even today, silver and gold provide a more trusted way of hoarding wealth than putting money into a bank.

PROTECTIVE PROPERTIES

A woman's wealth, worn as necklaces, bracelets, anklets and decorated veils, is much more than a financial reserve. Silver amulets, boxes and cylinders contain fragments of Qur'anic verse to protect the wearer against accidents, snake bites and scorpion stings. In Oman large round silver pendants called *sumt*, believed to contain an imprisoned *djinn* (demon), are popular.

△ **A FAMILY AFFAIR**
The combination of adornment and costume allows women to create tribal identities recognisable by their neighbours. Children, especially male babies, are protected from the evil eye by charms hung around their necks or anklets.

◁ **IN THE MAKING** Muttrah, Bahla, Rustaq, Nizwa and Sur are traditional centres of silver jewellery production in Oman. Each of these centres has its own distinctive style. Sur, for example, favours flower or geometric patterns, Nizwa produces etched lines and Nizwa appliqué.

△ **RINGS ON HER FINGERS**
Rings are commonly engraved with religious dedications, verse or even moons and stars representin the planets, symbols of pre-Islamic beliefs. First finger rings are normally pointed, second finger rings round or rhomboid, third finger ones square, and little finger rings the only ones with a stone.

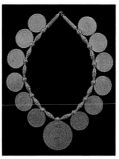

Originally silver was the main metal used in jewellery, with heavy gold pieces such as the necklace above belonging to people of importance (the piece above, now in the TSR Museum in Kuwait, belonged to an Omani princess). But now gold jewellery, largely produced by Asian craftsmen, is replacing silver as a means of hoarding and displaying wealth.

This is as true amongst the Bedu as it is townsfolk. A Bedu woman may walk barefoot and live under a tree, but around her neck she wears several hundred dollars' worth of gold and has earrings to match.

Urban centres like Abu Dhabi, Dubai, Sharjah, Muscat and Salalah are the best places to buy gold (usually 22-carat). Price tags are governed by current gold prices: workmanship is surprisingly not a factor.

Gold is an essential component of the bride's price. Most brides expect to receive a full complement of gold jewellery – headdress, rings, necklaces and bracelets. Often this will be specially commissioned.

▽ **THE ROLE OF COINS**
Coins are often incorporated into jewellery. Among the old silver coins used are the Marie Theresa thaller (originally called riyals by the Bedu), which has an 80 percent silver content.

△ **COMMON TALISMAN**
A selection on *hirz*, worn for protection against the evil eye. Sometimes a *hirz* will include a compartment containing fragments of paper on which verses from the Qur'an have been written.

THE EXPATRIATES

For years the Gulf was run by expats who came in search of tax-free salaries and first-class benefits. Times are now changing as nationals reclaim the plum jobs

Expatriate foreign workers are a long-established feature of the oil-rich Gulf countries. In most people's imagination the archetypal members of the species are oil industry workers brought to the country for their technical skill and valued for that but isolated from the mainstream of life. But in reality there is a huge range of expats in both the UAE and Oman and the result is a rich mix of different, interacting nationalities, each making its own contribution to society.

Both the UAE and Oman have had non-nationals living in the countries for centuries, but after the oil boom of the early 1970s expatriate labour became essential if the Gulf countries were to become the effective economies they wanted to be. They needed the outside labour to make their national dreams happen.

This was particularly the case in the UAE, where populations were made up of small communities of Bedu or traders, plus some modest farmers in the northern emirates. In Oman there were sufficient numbers of people, but their education and training levels were poor.

Situations vacant

The UAE, in particular, actively cultivated its open image and marketed its attractions to foreigners. Both the UAE and Oman, for example, allow relatively free access to alcohol. Though purchase for home consumption is limited to residents with licences and forbidden to Muslims, alcohol can be bought by anyone in larger hotel bars and restaurants, unlike in some other countries in the region where alcohol is prohibited or only allowed in expatriate compounds.

But this deluge of people with very different lifestyles and customs has not been without cost for the local populations. Many nationals have felt their values and society to be under threat. This issue has been particularly crucial in the UAE, where over 75 percent of the population is

PRECEDING PAGES: expats get set for a game of polo, Dubai. **LEFT:** Asian dockers pass time on Dubai Creek. **ABOVE RIGHT:** dune-bashing, a favourite with expats.

now expatriate. Such a huge number of non-national residents tends to set the tone of the country, and the nationals are conscious that they are a minority in their own state. In Oman, the situation is almost the reverse, where 72 percent of the population is Omani, but the very high level of economic and technical influence of the

28 percent of expatriates has triggered a drive in Omanis to take control of their own economy.

Who are the expats?

The most established expatriate communities in the UAE and Oman are the Indians, Pakistanis, and Iranians. A reciprocal pattern of settlement has gone on for generations. There are Omanis in Pakistan, Indians in the UAE and Oman, and Iranians in the UAE. To the outsider many Indians, Pakistanis and Iranians are indistinguishable from true nationals: they talk in Arabic, have friends in the national community, and are part of the social and business scene.

Another wave of expatriates to come to the

UAE during the 1960s and 1970s comprised other Arabs, who found that just as the oil boom was creating a need for skilled technicians, businessmen and managers in the Gulf, their home countries of Palestine, Jordan, and Lebanon were going through terrible political convulsions with war and civil strife. At the same time, Egypt's massive population was looking for profitable work as the grim impact of Arab Socialism under Gamel Abdel Nasser began to be felt by the Egyptian population.

IN LIMBO LAND

In theory it is legally possible for an expatriate to obtain nationality, but in practice this is rare.

Many families simply packed their bags and sought security and good salaries in the Gulf rather than try to live in the middle of a war zone or in Egypt. To this day, the Lebanese and Egyptian communities are large and important in the UAE.

Westerners make up the third major category of expatriate. In both countries, Britain played an important role as the imperial power until 1971 when it stopped many of its active political involvements east of Suez. The important legacy of British involvement in the machinery of state in Oman and the UAE gave the British community a standing way above that justified by their numbers. However, in recent years British sway has receded and the Americans have taken over as the dominant foreign influence in the region.

The right to nationality

However important the expatriates are to the economy, they remain expatriate. They are not, for example, entitled to the many state benefits enjoyed by nationals. UAE nationals can claim free education, free health care, and grants of free land available for commercial exploitation from which to derive an income, as well as free electricity and water. Oman has similar benefits, but since the population is larger and the government revenues smaller, the scale of the benefits is more modest.

Most importantly, however, expatriates do not have any automatic right to residency, nor are they allowed to claim nationality, though since 2002 in Dubai they have been allowed to own freehold property in designated developments – an initiative that has since spread to other emirates and Gulf states. In theory it is legally possible in both Oman and the UAE for an expatriate to obtain nationality, but in practice this is rare. Any implication that there should be a right to nationality is

a very sensitive issue, since any legally defined access to nationality would mean that many long-term expatriates would find grounds to claim it.

However, in the UAE many expatriates who came in the early oil boom days of the 1970s are still there and their children are growing up in the Gulf. As a result, the UAE is developing twin societies of nationals and expatriates who grew up together and are used to interacting, yet remain separate.

However, some have married into other cultures. Young women from many different coun-

tries have come to the region for work, but ended up marrying into a large Arab or Indian family.

This social dynamic has yet to unfold to its full potential, as members of the second generation of expats have only recently come onto the job market. But it does mark the start of a population which includes expatriates who were brought up in the UAE and know no other country.

The good life

Expatriates have a high standard of living. The cities are clean, with little crime, and the infrastructure is excellent. Company benefits often include accommodation, health care and plane tickets for annual leave home. Salaries are tax-free and opportunities for promotion more forthcoming than in countries with tighter management and union practices. Many individuals come to the Gulf to do one job, find an opportunity to move up the ladder quickly, or to move to a totally different field, and prosper, all within a few years. Similar achievements elsewhere might have taken decades.

As a result, people want to stay in the Gulf even though the very high salaries of the 1970s have dropped away. They commit to large mortgages, heavy school fees, and a lifestyle

TRAPPED BY SUCCESS

Some become prisoners of their expatriate packages of salaries and benefits and cannot return home.

behaviour of expats is regarded with a certain degree of leniency, there are boundaries, and woe betide those who cross them, such as a British couple imprisoned and then expelled for public indecency on a beach in Dubai in 2008.

But there are many positive aspects to the expat life, including the excitement of absorbing the cultures of many different people in one place. The bond of expatriatism allows all sorts of people to mingle, people who might never get near one another in any other context. ❑

they would not be able to afford at home. They can become a prisoner of their package of salaries and benefits, unable to return home without a drastic loss of income. While this phenomenon is common among Europeans, it is more intense among Asians, whose home economies cannot offer anything like the savings potential of the Gulf. Many will do any job, and suffer any conditions, in order to remain.

There is also another price to pay. Criticism of the ruling regimes is unthinkable, and likely to lead to expulsion. Similarly, although the

TIME OFF

The only gap in many Western expats' lives is the lack of a Western cultural life. This is compensated by excellent recreation facilities. Fabulous beaches and watersports are features of both the UAE and Oman, and the desert interiors of both countries offer opportunities for overnight expeditions, camping, or simply picnic lunches in the sand dunes or wadis. There are also some great holiday destinations in easy reach. Jordan, Lebanon and Egypt are only a short flight away, India only two hours, and even the Maldives and Seychelles are within range for a long weekend.

ABOVE LEFT: working on the expat tan, Dubai.
ABOVE: conspicuous wealth, the Gold Souq, Dubai.

KINGS OF THE TURF

How the Maktoum family of Dubai transformed international flat racing and made
Dubai the setting for the richest horse race of all time, the Dubai World Cup

In Britain it's long been customary to talk about horse racing as the Sport of Kings. The present Queen Elizabeth, like the late Queen Mother before her, is both a knowledgeable and enthusiastic student of bloodstock and racing form. No Derby or Royal Ascot meeting would be complete without her avid attendance in the royal box. But considering the Queen's resources and the number of horses she has had in training, her big race successes have been surprisingly few. And you have to go back to her Silver Jubilee year in 1977 to find the last occasion on which she won a classic horse race in England.

Royalty's influence on the Turf may have waned but its continuing association with the sport has acted as a magnet for other wealthy and ambitious individuals from all corners of the world. American industrialists, Japanese tycoons and international aristocrats like the Aga Khan continue to duel regularly on the racetracks of Britain, Ireland and France.

Yet however important and influential these figures may be, their activities still pale into insignificance when compared with the phenomenal investment in bloodstock that has been undertaken by a small group of powerful men from the Middle East. Racing may no longer be the sport of European kings but it is emphatically the sport of Arab sheikhs and princes. And within those heady circles not even such stellar figures as Saudi Arabia's Prince Khaled Abdullah, owner of the great 1986 champion racehorse Dancing Brave, can match the scale of influence now exerted over the Turf worldwide by the Maktoum family from Dubai.

The Maktoums

There are three remaining Maktoum brothers (the fourth and the eldest, Sheikh Maktoum bin

Rashid Al Maktoum, died in 2006). Sheikh Hamdan, the second eldest and known to British racing lovers as the owner of the 1989 and 1994 Derby winners Nashwan and Erhaab, has studs in the UK and Ireland, including the Shadwell Estate in Norfolk. The youngest brother, Sheikh Ahmed, also shares his brothers' enthusiasm for

horses. But it's the third brother, His Highness Sheikh Mohammed bin Rashid Al Maktoum, ruler of Dubai and Vice President and Prime Minister of the UAE, who is the most dominant figure in international racing.

Sheikh Mohammed is an imposing man in every way and he has brought his formidable reputation to bear in pursuit of a lifetime's dream: to focus the world's attention on the Middle East through the thoroughbred, the beautiful and capricious creature that owes its very origins to this region. Every thoroughbred racehorse competing in the world today can trace its lineage back to three Arab stallions – the Godolphin and Darley Arabian and the

PRECEDING PAGES: late-night line-up of competitors.
LEFT: Sheikh Hamdan Al Maktoum (left) at the races.
ABOVE RIGHT: Sheikh Mohammed bin Rashid
Al Maktoum, the driving force behind Godolphin.

Byerley Turk – that were "imported" into Britain more than three centuries ago to improve the speed and stamina of the domestic breed. The Sheikh's ambition to see the thoroughbred return in glory to its desert roots enjoyed its defining moment at Dubai's Nad Al Sheba racetrack in March 1996. The occasion was the first-ever running of the Dubai World Cup, now worth US $6 million and the richest horse race in the world. But the journey to that star-studded event began more modestly in England nearly 30 years ago.

A dream in the making

It was while he was studying at Cambridge University in England in the late 1960s that Sheikh Mohammed first became attracted to the flavour and atmosphere of nearby Newmarket racecourse. The history and traditions of British racing so appealed to him that within 10 years he and his brothers all had horses in training there. Their first big classic win came when a horse of Hamdan's called Touching Wood won the 1982 St Leger at Doncaster.

The Maktoums' investment in bloodstock was soon flowing on a massive scale, though some outside observers felt that the family were spending their money not wisely but too well. One or two English trainers and bloodstock agents were talking openly about Arab patronage being the racing equivalent of a "magic carpet ride" to the bank. The Sheikhs duly wised up to the people who were trying to take advantage of them and adjustments were made. But not to the spending spree. By the end of the 1980s the Maktoums' involvement in racing had spread to unprecedented levels. Today, the family has more than 1,500 racehorses in training, at home in Dubai, in Europe and North America; treble that number in broodmares, their foals, weanlings and yearlings; and vast property interests in thoroughbred stud farms in England, Ireland and the USA.

At the time of Sheikh Mohammed's entry onto the English racing stage, the top man on the owners' list was the Vernons Pools heir, Robert Sangster. In alliance with the distinguished Irish trainer Vincent O'Brien he had built up a smoothly professional syndicate based around his Swettenham Stud breeding operation in England and the Coolmore Stud stallion station in Tipperary. But once Sheikh

Mohammed developed a taste for buying the best-bred yearlings on the market, he left Sangster and his partners trailing in his wake.

The American trade magazine *The Blood-Horse* has documented the Maktoum influence at the Keeneland Select Sales in Kentucky, the world's premier showcase sale of thoroughbred yearlings. Between 1980 and 1995, it says, the brothers spent a staggering US$402.9 million on 593 yearlings, averaging US$679,500 a horse. During that period they also featured prominently at the Tattersalls sales in Newmarket, at Goffs

in Ireland and at Deauville in France. Not all of their purchases were successful ones. In 1982 Sheikh Mohammed spent US$10.2 million on an American-bred yearling called Snaafi Dancer who turned out to be so useless that he never even set foot on a racecourse. But there were still enough good buys for the Sheikh to finish top of the owners' table regularly in England, Ireland and France.

Dubai becomes the hub

The Maktoums' love affair with the big US breeding farms is over. The brothers' own breeding operations, stocked with broodmares bought as yearling fillies at Keeneland, are now self-sufficient. As buying scaled-down so the family in general and Sheikh Mohammed in particular began to focus their operations on Dubai. Vital to restructuring the brothers' largely English-based racing concerns was the Emirates' success in securing in 1991 a disease-free status for livestock movement, allowing rapid transport of horses in and out of Dubai.

Plans to develop Dubai as the family's main racing base have now intensified to the point where a thoroughbred revolution is underway there, unmatched by anything else in the world. Major developments include Nad Al Sheba Club. Built in 1986 as a modest training facility,

built on bare desert next to Nad Al Sheba. This complex complements the Zabeel stables and training centre, built more than 25 years ago by Sheikh Rashid on grounds neighbouring his Zabeel Palace and designed for the use of a small team of Arab-breds.

Al Quoz and Zabeel are the launching pad for Godolphin Racing Stables, the audacious – and audaciously entitled – operation to ship mainly Maktoum-owned horses to all points of the globe in search of big race victories. Godolphin has enjoyed quite stunning results since its inception, especially in 1995 when it carried off classic and grade one prizes in England, Ireland,

it has had a complete facelift. The sand track has been upgraded for racing and a grass track added inside it, floodlights have been installed around its 2,200-metre (2,405-yd) circumference and the grandstand has been refurbished on opulent Euro-Arabic lines. A second grandstand, the futuristic Millennium Grandstand, was completed in time for the 2001 World Cup and is a popular venue for Friday brunches. The complex contains restaurants and bars, and a flood-lit 18-hole green golf course (see page 234).

In addition, the royal Al Quoz stables were

ABOVE LEFT: spectators at the races.
ABOVE: on the way to the finish, Nad Al Sheba.

ALL MOD CONS

The Maktoums' expenditure on racing is estimated at around US$2.4 billion. No expense was spared in setting up the Al Quoz stables in Dubai or on improving Nad Al Sheba Club and Zabeel training facilities. Each horse has two men looking after it, and the facilities include an equine veterinary clinic that apparently leaves visiting leaders of the profession in awe, and a feed mill that custom mixes more than 8,000 kg (17,600 lb) of food daily for the royal family's menagerie of falcons, racing and breeding camels, livestock and, of course, Arab and thoroughbred horses.

France, Italy, Hong Kong, Japan and the USA. Supreme among those triumphs was the hat-trick recorded by the blue-blooded colt Lammtarra, a son of the 1970 Derby winner Nijinsky and foaled by an English Oaks winner, Snow Bride. As a two-year-old Lammtarra had been trained in Newmarket, where he ran and won once. But he was then shipped out to Dubai during the northern hemisphere winter. He showed the positive effects of the warm Gulf climate and the innovative Godolphin training

GAMBLERS ANONYMOUS

Dubaians have no need to bring money with them as Islamic law forbids gambling. You certainly won't see a Tote kiosk or a bookie's pitch at Nad Al Sheba Club racecourse.

and the Jebel Ali sand-oil mix track built in 1990 and noted for its steep incline 200 metres/yds from the winning post). Nad Al Sheba is the busiest centre, staging 37 racing days in the November to April season. About 20 meetings are spread between the three other tracks. A typical meeting offers a programme of six races, four of them for thoroughbreds and two for Arab-breds. Prestige outweighs prize money, with purses scarcely relative to the cost of training and feeding a racehorse. The six races

regime, by arriving back ready to race off the plane the following May. He only ran three times as a three-year-old but achieved the historic and prestigious treble of the Derby at Epsom in June, the King George VI and Queen Elizabeth Stakes at Ascot in July and then the Prix de l'Arc de Triomphe at Longchamps in Paris in October. It was a feat only managed once before by the immortal Mill Reef in 1971.

Race meetings

Racing in the UAE takes place in Abu Dhabi (one grass track, one sand), Sharjah (a 1,380-metre/1,500-yd sand track within the Sharjah Equestrian complex) and Dubai (Nad Al Sheba

in the International Jockeys Challenge are valued at 8,000Dhs (dirhams) each, roughly US$2,220, provided through sponsorship or heavy subsidies from the ruling family.

Attendances vary, with an average of 3,000 at a normal meeting, 9–10,000 at a feature event such as the Jockeys Challenge series and up to 15,000 for one of the handful of meetings at which a prestige international race has been scheduled. Dubaians have free entry to the car park and the race track and have no need to bring money with them as Islamic law forbids gambling altogether. You certainly won't see a Tote kiosk or a bookie's pitch at Nad Al Sheba. However, to add to the spectators' entertainment, the race club officials provide in the complimentary racecard an entry form for a "Pick Six" competition; entry is free and a prize of about 20,000 dirhams (US$5,500) is awarded to the entry that names the six winners of the meeting.

The Dubai World Cup

This kind of diversion would normally be regarded as strictly small beer by hardened British and US racing types, as attracted to their daily doubles and trebles as to their frequent visits to the bar between races. Sheikh Mohammed knew that in the early stages of his Dubai experiment, some visiting racing figures were happy

enough to accept his hospitality while sniggering behind their hands about the whole thing being just another case of a rich man wanting to play with his toys in his own backyard. To legitimise the operation in the eyes of the international racing community, he knew that he had to think up a contest so big and so spectacular and challenging that his international rivals would find it impossible to stay away. So he came up with the Dubai World Cup.

The inaugural running of the cup on 27 March 1996 offered total prize money of US$4 million,

the winner alone taking home US$2.4 million which is more than the total winning prize for the Derby and the Prix de l'Arc de Triomphe combined. When entries for the very first race closed in mid-October 1995, 48 of the world's best performing racehorses were eligible via a US$5,000 nomination fee, while another 20-odd were added at the second entry stage in January 1996 at double the original fee. Later that month, an international panel of handicappers determined the composition of the 14-strong field, at the same time drawing up a lengthy list of reserves.

To ensure a truly World Cup flavour, they had to choose four starters from the UAE, three from the Americas, three from Europe and two each from Asia and Australasia. Britain was represented by Pentire, second only to Lammtarra in the previous year's King George VI and Queen Elizabeth Stakes. Godolphin's principal representative was Halling. And from America came the mighty Cigar, the raw-powered six-year-old bay horse, owned by aerospace tycoon Allen Paulson and coming into the Cup on a roll of 13 consecutive victories spaced over 14 months. It was a brave decision by Paulson, who didn't need the money, to risk his champion in a distant arena and on an alien sand surface far away from home.

In the end almost everyone got the result they wanted. Halling may have flopped and Pentire could get no closer than fourth place. But Cigar maintained his proud record in heroic fashion, fighting back in the dying stages of the race to outpoint fellow American challenger Soul of the Matter (owned by songwriter Burt Bacharach), by half a length, with the other American runner in third. Intense American media interest in future runnings of the Cup was guaranteed.

There was fulsome praise afterwards for the courage and class of Cigar and for the skill of his trainer Billy Mott. And even the most cynical observer was forced to admit that Sheikh Mohammed's race across the sand, beneath floodlights and against the darkening desert sky, had raised the princely sport of horse racing to new and previously unimagined levels. ❏

ABOVE LEFT: in training for the big race.
ABOVE: the green and pleasant Zabeel Stables.

PRIZE GIVING

Sheikh Mohammed had to think up a contest so big and so challenging that his rivals would find it impossible to stay away. He came up with the Dubai World Cup.

CAMEL RACING

This unusual sport provides great entertainment for participants and spectators alike. But it is also a serious business

If you are looking for an indication of how seriously Arabs take their camels then you need look no further than Oman where the government actually has a department for camel affairs. Back this up with the fact that top racing camels often change hands for over US$160,000 and you'll realise that training these strange-looking creatures can be a worthwhile investment.

The sport is still strongly influenced by the Bedu, who train the majority of racing camels and prepare them for the racing season, which runs from August to April. Purpose-built racetracks are found in both Oman and the UAE but you may also come across an impromptu practice race on your travels: an excited, colourful gathering of owners, trainers and spectators urging on their favourites.

The camels, which can reach speeds of 60 kmph (37 mph), sometimes race until they are about 15 years old but they are at their peak at three to four years of age. Trainers pay a lot of attention to their camels' diet – which will include honey, ghee (a clarified butter), barley, alfalfa, eggs and dates – but they also place great store by secret concoctions. Family pedigree is highly respected and a well-bred camel will be trained until the age of two when it will enter its first race.

Until recently small boys, often trafficked from Pakistan or India, were employed as jockeys. Pressure from human rights organisations eventually led to the banning of this practice in both the UAE and Oman. The UAE, along with Qatar, pioneered the development of "robot" jockeys that simulate the weight and actions of young riders.

Attending a camel race remains a colourful spectacle. The camels are held down while the the robots are strapped to the backs and then, in a flurry of dust and to a volley of shouts from the crowd, the camels take off – sometimes the wrong way – with their teeth bared. They bolt down the track, often veering across the width of the course while their bobbing jockeys struggle to bring them into line.

An assortment of vehicles follows the race, each one vying for the position close to the course rails. A cacophony of noise pours from car horns and desperate spectators cling to parts

of vehicles you never knew existed. They follow as close to the race as possible, often within a whisker of the next car.

The winner of a race will normally receive a cash prize but prestigious events may award cars. However, the real money is in the selling of a successful racer, which will often attract buyers from other Gulf countries.

Races are normally held on Fridays and public holidays; local newspapers carry details of the time and place. The informal desert tracks can often provide better entertainment for the casual observer than the better-organised stadium events. As with horse racing, betting is not permitted   ❏

LEFT: robots have replaced child jockeys.
ABOVE RIGHT: a camel takes a rest.

Oman

0   50 km

0   50 miles

PLACES: OMAN

*A detailed guide to the country, with the principal sites
cross-referenced by number to the maps*

Oman's potential as a tourist destination is still unfolding, but all the right ingredients are here: unspoilt landscapes, wonderful beaches, a rich culture and dignified, friendly people. Even Muscat, the capital, is beguiling. Though mainly modern, the low-level buildings are entwined in the folds of serrated hills. The city thus reveals itself gradually and never completely. It is still "the real-isation of a pirate's lair as imagined by any schoolboy," as Cedric Belfrage, a visitor to Muscat, observed in 1936.

Oman's variety of landscapes isn't found anywhere else in the Gulf, likewise the range of climate. In summer, while temperatures in the north and interior soar to 50°C (122°F), the coastal area of Dho-far is wet and misty, the vegetation lush, with bananas and coconuts flourishing. And in spite of modernisation, you will still find perched mud villages in the mountainous interior, *barasti* (palm frond) houses on the Batinah coast, and round, thatched homes in the mountains of Dhofar, traditional modes of living not impetuously swept away as they so often were elsewhere in the region but preserved as a valuable part of the heritage.

Formidable natural barriers – the Rub al Khali (Empty Quarter), the Hajar Mountains, and the Jiddat al Harasis – mean that parts of the country are not easily accessible, at least not for humans. Remote regions of the Jebel Akhdar, southwest of Muscat, harbour the rare Arabian *tahr*, a goatlike creature unique to Oman, and an area of the Jiddat al Harasis is a sanctuary for the Arabian oryx, a creature once extinct in the wild. The Musandam Peninsula is one of the last refuges of the Arabian leopard *(see page 203)*, and over on the east coast, below Sur, are the world's largest breeding grounds for green turtles. Birdlife is also rich. The Daymaniyat Islands, north of Mus-cat, are a designated bird sanctuary. More easily seen is the beautiful birdlife of Dhofar *(see pages 178–9)*.

It is possible to sample a little of each of Oman's regions in the space of about two weeks. Muscat makes a good base for the north, offering forays along the Batinah coast to Sohar; through the Sumail Gap to Nizwa, Jabrin and Bahla; and along the rugged east coast to Sur, a boatbuilding town with the dreamy air of a 19th-century water-colour of the orient. Salalah is the obvious base for Dhofar, a region well worth making a special effort to visit, preferably by air but also possible by road. ❏

PRECEDING PAGES: sunset near Sohar; villas in Nizwa; camels in Dhofar.
ABOVE: an Arabian oryx in the Jiddat al Harasis.

MUSCAT

Until 1970 Muscat locked its gates at night and its citizens weren't allowed out without a lantern. Today its long, slender tentacles reach from the airport at Seeb to the Al Bustan Hotel

Map, page 134

he sleepy old town of Muscat, clinging to a small natural harbour, and its old port of Muttrah in the neighbouring bay are just fragments of modern Muscat. Since the 1970s, the city has blossomed with the help of oil money, and new business and office districts have sprouted in all directions. Modern highways and flyovers cut through a dramatic topography, leading from one tranquil district to the next up the coast towards Seeb International Airport and into the neighbouring valleys.

But one thing the rapidly developing city has tried to hold onto is its pride and traditions. Unlike Dubai, which has sold out to the Western way of things in many aspects of life, Oman holds on to its past with determination. Modern lifestyles are modified by the Omanis' love and respect for tradition, and past and present mingle. It is not unusual to see old women from the interior balancing bundles of alfalfa on their heads while a teenage Omani passes in the latest Mercedes sports car.

There are no skyscrapers and most of the large office blocks and ministries adhere to the traditional Gulf-Arab style of architecture, in keeping with the Muscat Municipality's book of acceptable architectural designs (pitched roofs are forbidden, satellite dishes and areas where clothes are dried must be screened from view). New buildings are either white or sand-coloured and surrounded by some of the cleanest streets you are likely to find anywhere. And presiding over it all is the image of Sultan Qaboos. Every shop and office has a picture of the Sultan hanging in its reception and many homes also get the royal touch.

Although not the wealthiest of Gulf states, Oman does have its fair share of oil money and those families who latched onto the oil boom and its ensuing riches often boast the excesses for which the region is renowned. The city is also home to a huge expatriate Indian population which, together with strong trade links with India, has resulted in a big Indian influence. The oldest buildings in Muttrah display Indian flourishes, perhaps in a window grille or ornate wooden balcony. Most restaurants can produce a fine curry, and Omani food has absorbed numerous Indian ideas. Many offices and shops are staffed by Indians. Other nationalities prominent in the city are the British, Dutch and Americans, most of whom are linked to the oil industry.

City sights

Although Muscat's foundation dates from the 1st century, the town didn't gain recognition until the 14th and 15th centuries, when it attracted traders. In the 16th century it drew the Portuguese, who developed Muscat as their principal naval base and strengthened its defences – until 1650 when they were ousted by an Omani force.

PRECEDING PAGES: Old Muscat clustered around the palace. **LEFT:** ornate doorway in Sultan Qaboos mosque. **BELOW:** coastal suburb.

Entrance of Al Alam Palace. Though listed as one of the Sultan's homes, the palace is generally used only for formal affairs.

The great **forts** which stand high above the harbour in **Old Muscat** are Portuguese, both built by Philip of Spain. The western fort, **Mirani Ⓐ**, was completed in 1587; the eastern fort, **Jalali Ⓑ**, was finished in 1588. Following two sackings of the city by the Turks, the fortifications were extended in the early 17th century. Mirani has been transformed into a museum for VIP visitors.

Old Muscat is easily viewed on foot. One of the most striking buildings in the quarter, although new, is **Al Alam Palace Ⓒ**, approached along Al Alam Street through **Kebir Gate** (Bab Kebir) Ⓓ, the main gate in the old city walls. The palace, built in 1972 to replace the simple, two-storey old palace, has a storybook facade, with towering columns in blue and gold.

Old Muscat is home to some fabulous old mosques and houses. Several fine 18th-century buildings have served as embassies and consulates, including Bait Graiza. Among those still standing is the 18th-century Bait Fransa, the residence of French consuls until 1920, which now operates as the **Omani French Museum Ⓔ** (Sat–Wed, mornings only) commemorating Oman's historical links with France. Built by Ghaliah bint Salim, a niece of Sultan Said bin Sultan, it was presented to Paul Ottavi, the first French consul in Oman, to serve as the French Consulate by Sultan Feisal bin Turki Al Said in 1894. French ships carrying spices and sugar from the Indian Ocean had called at Muscat since the 17th century, and trade links intensified in the 19th century.

Bait al Zubair (Sat–Thur 9.30am–1pm and 4–7pm; guided tours; nominal admission charge), in Al Saidiya Street in Old Muscat, has also been turned into a museum. Occupying a traditional house, it displays weapons, jewellery, costumes, household items and a collection of old photographs; the grounds contain a recreation of a typical Omani village, complete with falaj system. Next door to

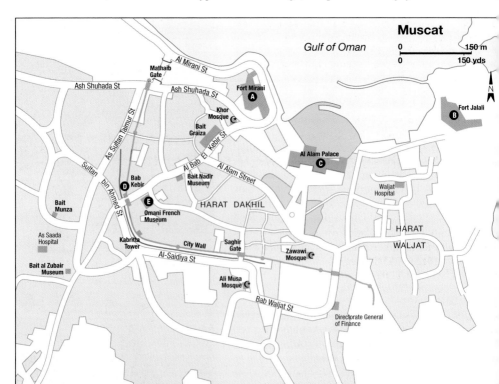

the museum is the **Bait Munza** art gallery, a former royal home that has been turned into an attractive setting for modern works by international artists.

Map, pages 136–7

Muttrah

In the neighbouring bay to Old Muscat, less than 3 km (2 miles) along the dual carriageway winding along the waterfront, is **Muttrah**. Its majestic corniche makes it more memorable than its neighbour. But although opportunities for tourism abound, it caters primarily for trade and local fishermen. But the corniche has a few hidden gems leading from it.

The **Muttrah Souq F**, accessible from two points off the Corniche, is a must. Though modern – concrete booths replaced the original palm structures in the 1970s – the narrow lanes, laced with the smell of frankincense and sandalwood, bustle with traders, money-changers and shoppers eager to do business. The souq, one of the most authentic in Arabia, is divided into various sectors, each dealing with a particular product – textiles, houseware, gold, silver, spices – punctuated by *halwa* (sweetmeat) sellers and coffee shops. The alleyways provide a glimpse of Oman's past (a palm frond roof has recently been added to recapture the mysterious fenestrated effect of a traditional souq) even though the products sold are rarely Omani. It is easy to get disorientated but one is never far away from the main thoroughfares. Two areas particularly worth exploring are the gold (22 carat) and silver souqs – the latter providing a good range of traditional items (*see pages 104–5*).

The incense burner monument above Riyam Park, Muttrah, built to celebrate Oman's 20th National Day.

On the Corniche the **Liwatiya quarter G**, houses a Shia sect of the same name who were traditionally merchants and originated from Hyderabad. Their residential area is walled and off-limits to outsiders – guards sit at the gates to make sure that only those who live there enter – but the houses back onto the Corniche, where the lattice grilles and balconies offer enticing glimpses of what lies inside. Also here is the **Bait Al Baranda museum H** (Sat–Thur 9am–1pm and 4–6pm; admission charge), the "House with a Verandah", in which interactive displays recount the history of Muscat.

BELOW: trader in the Muttrah *souq*.

South of Old Muscat and Muttrah

A highlight of the coast 6 km (4 miles) south of Old Muscat is **Al Bustan Palace Hotel I**, completed between 1983 and 1985 for a Gulf Co-operation Council summit and the recipient of a two-year renovation, completed at the end of 2008. Al Bustan is regularly voted the top hotel in the Middle East, The hotel stands majestically in its own bay, the site and design being chosen after long consideration of other possibilities. To make way for the hotel, a hill had to be blasted away and the old village of Al Bustan, which had once served as a leper colony, was moved to a new site just behind the small *jabal* (hill), on the beach. Based on an octagon, a recurring theme in Islamic architecture, the design of the hotel was intended to reflect the hierarchy of the delegates at the Gulf summit, with heads of state level at the top, then crown princes or ministers, and ordinary delegates in the bottom tiers.

The *pièce de résistance* of the hotel is the 38-metre (125-ft) high lobby, at the centre of which is a stunning crystal chandelier and fountain. The hotel is clad in Blue de France and White Dionysus marble, just some of the 800,000 tonnes of marble, from France, Greece, Italy and elsewhere, that was used in the hotel's interior alone.The building's plinth, pilasters and towers are faced in stone from Rajasthan, each piece of which was hand-chiselled on the ground in India before being shipped to Oman. Even the soil in which the luxurious gardens grow is special – it was brought here from Shinas near the border with Fujairah in the UAE.

Beyond the entrance to the hotel, a roundabout commemorates the voyage of the *Sohar*, a 1980 replica of an ocean-going Omani sailing ship which sailed to Canton to mark the historic trading links between Oman and China.

In a bay between Old Muscat and the Al Bustan Palace Hotel is the **Bander Al Rowdha ⓙ**, a marina for yachts and motor cruisers. Deep-water fishing charters and dolphin-watching trips depart from here. Don't expect too much of the **Aquarium** (Sat–Thur 7am–2pm, Mon 4–8pm, free admission). Its most interesting occupants are the sea turtles.

North of Old Muscat and Muttrah

In recent years, as wealth has filtered through the city, Muscat has spread up the coast and inland. A dual carriageway lined with monuments and rock gardens feeds in from Seeb International Airport to central Muscat. The main commercial and residential development has occurred in **Ruwi**, the Central Business District; **Qurm**, the main shopping complexes; **Medinat Qaboos**, a mainly residential area; and **Al Khuwair,** the ministry and diplomatic areas. It is worth taking a taxi-ride a round Al Khuwair to see the extravagant nouveau-Gulf-style of architecture.

BELOW: inside the Grand Mosque of Sultan Qaboos, the only mosque in Oman that is open to non-Muslims.

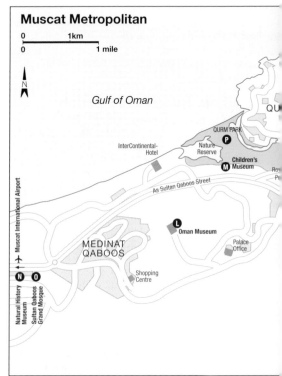

Muscat Metropolitan

0   1km

0   1 mile

N

Gulf of Oman

QU

QURM PARK

P

InterContinental-Hotel

Nature Reserve

Children's **M** Museum

As Sultan Qaboos Street

L Oman Museum

Palace Office

MEDINAT QABOOS

N **O**

Shopping Centre

← Muscat International Airport

Natural History Museum

Sultan Qaboos Grand Mosque

There are several museum in these areas, including the **Sultan's Armed Forces Museum** (Sun, Mon and Wed, am only), in the Bait al Falaj Fort in Ruwi, which gives an interesting glimpse into Oman's crucial military history and reflects the determination of the current sultan to turn the limited defence forces of Oman in 1971 into the three highly trained and equipped forces it has today; the **Oman Museum** ● (Sat–Wed, am only), dedicated to different strands of the national heritage, from seafaring to fort-building; the **Children's Museum** ● (Sat–Thur 9.30am–1.30pm; admission charge), also known as the Science Museum, off Sultan Qaboos Street in Qurm, with hands-on, educational displays; and the **Natural History Museum** ● (Sat–Thur, am only), in Al Khuwair, one of the most engaging museums of its size and kind anywhere but especially welcome in a country where good background information is still relatively hard to come by. The "Oman Through Time" exhibition traces the fossil history of Oman from the Precambrian age 800 million years ago, while "Oman – Land of Contrasts" explains the different characteristics of the six distinct physical regions: Musandam, the Northern Mountains, the Batinah, the Interior, the Dhofar Mountains and the Islands.

In the western suburb of Ghubrah, on the road to Seeb, is the **Sultan Qaboos Grand Mosque** ● (open to non-Muslims Mon–Thur 8–11am; women must dress modestly and cover their hair with a scarf), which opened in 2001. It covers 40,000 sq. metres (over 430,000 sq. ft) and its main minaret rises to a height of 91.5 metres (300 ft). A huge courtyard surrounds the inner sanctuaries, within which is the main prayer-hall with a capacity for 20,000 worshipppers. The hall is lit by 35 chandeliers made of Swarovski crystal and gold-plated metalwork: the grand chandelier weighs 8 tonnes. The vast carpet of 28 different colours was made in the eastern Iranian province of

Outside the entrance of the Natural History Museum are the fossilised remains of a 260-million-year old fir tree.

TIP

A dhow cruise is a great way to spend the early evening. Boats leave from the Al Inshirah Restaurant on Muttrah's corniche.

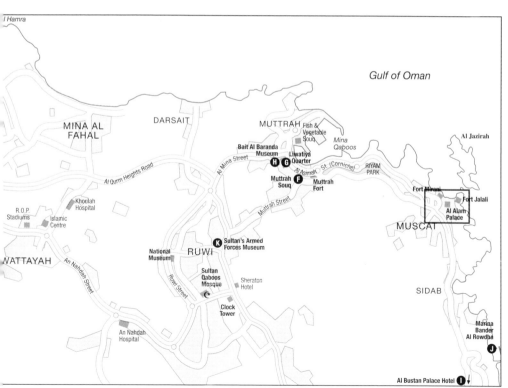

Map, pages 136–7

Café society in a Costa coffee shop, just one of many international brands in the city's numerous shopping malls.

BELOW: football on the beach at Qurm.

Khurasan by some 600 women weavers. It took four years to complete and weighs 21 tonnes.

Shopping, nightlife, beaches and excursions

With soaring summer temperatures of over 50°C (122°F) in the hottest months it is not surprising that Muscat is more lively through the night than the day.

The main **shopping** areas are in Qurm and Ruwi. Ruwi caters mainly for the Indian market (it's a good place to go for tailoring) whereas Qurm has several malls combining so-called "traditional souqs" and Western shops. The cooler night temperatures draw people to Qurm in their droves in the evenings. Apart from shopping, night-time entertainment centres on the big hotels.

One of the nicest things about Muscat is that you never have far to go to find a beach. Whether it is the long stretch of golden sand that leads from the Crowne Plaza Hotel to the Grand Hyatt or one of the secluded bays south of Al Bustan Palace Hotel, there is always a place to relax, have a barbecue and try out a watersport or two. Further out, the beautifully located Shangri-La Barr Al Jissah Resort is one of the top spots *(see page 289)*. Emphasis has been placed on recreational facilities within the city and the parks are attractive. **Qurm Park ❷** has a boating lake, fountains and a 4,000-seat amphitheatre.

Life never seems to be rushed in Muscat and its languid character makes it an ideal springboard for excursions to the wadis and forts in the interior or along the coast to Sohar or Sur and the Wahiba Sands. Muscat is now the central focus for modern Oman and the power base for government and business. Mobile phones are more in evidence than *khanjars*, but the sights and sounds of old Oman are never far away. ❑

Towering Strength

Whether you are wadi-bashing in a deserted region or sightseeing in Muscat, you can bet that a fortification stands not too far away. Wherever you go in Oman there is a constant reminder of the country's divisions and troubled past, from the massive structure of Bahla Fort in the Interior to the small watchtowers which cluster atop most jebels. Oman's topography has proved ideal for defence measures and in areas which have needed to be strong historically, forts and watchtowers, in varying states of repair, fill the skyline.

Sultan Qaboos has attempted to save as much of Oman's heritage as possible during his time in office, instigating a restoration programme that has brought many of the majestic fortifications back to life. Moroccan craftsmen were employed (the necessary skills having died out in Oman) and traditional materials used, such as mud bricks, palm fronds and limestone.

If you are staying in Muscat you don't have to travel far to see impressive examples. Oman's forts were heavily influenced by the Portuguese and Persians but Arab designs are also evident. When the Portuguese occupied Muscat in 1507, they chose the most commanding places, high above the city, to build the forts of Mirani, Jalali and Muttrah. The two great forts which sit on either side of Muscat Harbour are Portuguese, both built by Philip of Spain. The western fort, Mirani, was completed in 1587; the eastern, Jalali, in 1588. They are simple in design but very strong. Both these and Muttrah Fort are still in use, either by the military or the police.

One of the most impressive forts in Oman is the one at Jabrin, which has been restored to its former glory. Its interior, unlike the compact, basic design of a military fort such as Al Hazm, is palatial, with carved doorways and painted ceilings. Unlike military forts which were built principally for defence, castle forts were built with a bit more comfort in mind. Some castle forts, such as Jabrin and Birkat al Mauz, housed the government. Others such as Bait Na'man and Al Hobe were used as retreats and rest-houses for travellers on their way by camel from Muscat to Nizwa or Sohar.

Generally, forts protected the towns and populated areas while watchtowers were used to guard inland trade routes and water supplies. At the sight of invaders, warning shots would be fired to alert people nearby. Other watchtowers were built close to forts for obvious reasons. The highest concentrations of watchtowers are along the main mountain passes – Wadi Sumail, Wadi Jizzi, and Wadi Hawasinah.

The forts at Rustaq, Bahla, Sohar and Nizwa are considerable in size. Sohar's once required more than 1,000 men for its defence, and the great fort at Nizwa, which was built in the 17th century, took 12 years to build.

Interesting features to note when visiting any fort are its dungeons, slits above doors for channelling boiling honey, oil or water, and the well – vital in case of seige.

Forts to visit include Nizwa, Nakhl, Jabrin, Bahla, Rustaq, Al Hazm and Sohar. ❑

RIGHT: Al Mirani Fort.

SOHAR AND THE BATINAH COAST

*The flat and fertile Batinah Coast north of Muscat leads to Sohar,
once the most important trading centre on the Arabian Peninsula.
Today the region is famous for its dates*

Map, page 144

he Batinah Coast north of Muscat is said to derive its name from an Arabic root meaning "to be hidden", and from out at sea the tawny-coloured Hajar Mountains glowering over the narrow coastal plain do indeed conceal it om sight. The Batinah, accessible by a dual carriageway extending 270 km 168 miles) from Muscat to the UAE border, is completely different from the ollercoaster terrain between Muscat and Sur. Here the landscape is flat – an nbroken line of grey-sand beach is lapped by a gentle sea, and the plain, never ore than a kilometre wide, is extensively cultivated. Date plantations, some undreds of years old, line large stretches of the highway.

Modern buildings are springing up along the Batinah, but old-style *barasti* ouses made from date palms are still seen in quiet villages, and the biblical *hasha*, a canoe made from palm fronds, is still used for fishing. A drawback of he area for travellers is that the highway rarely runs alongside the sea, and ithout a detour or two the journey from Muscat to Sohar, the administrative apital of the Batinah, can be dull. By including the Rustaq loop *(see page 149)*, ou can make the journey more rewarding. Three splendid forts punctuate the ircuit and a date-processing factory in Rustaq adds urther interest.

The best way to sample the region is to drive to Sohar, tay the night, and then take the Rustaq sidetrip on your eturn. The southern Batinah, including the Rustaq circuit, can also be visited in a day trip from Muscat.

From Muscat to Sohar

Seeb ❶ is the first settlement north of Muscat. **Muscat International Airport** ❷ (35 km/22 miles from Muscat) is the official gateway to Oman. The nearby **Sultan Qaboos University** ❸, which opened in 1986, has an enrolment of nearly 15,000 students, of whom 65 percent are women, a remarkable achievement considering that just four decades or so years ago schooling for girls was officially forbidden. A fairly unremarkable own, Seeb acts as a market depot for local fishermen nd farmers with a busy souq catering to domestic eeds. Camel races are staged on National Day (18 November) and on other festive occasions.

Barka ❹ (43 km/27 miles from Muscat) is the next own of significance on the coast and the springboard or the Rustaq Loop *(see page 149)*. **Barka Fort** 7.30am–6pm; free admission), dating from the early Ya'ruba period *(see page 49)* and restored in 1985, is 100 metres/yds) west of the main crossroads in town. The former wali's quarters has a fine exhibition of mported china in the master bedroom, and a tower

PRECEDING PAGES:
sunset at A'Sawadi, a typical Batinah fishing community.
LEFT: boys on the beach at Sohar.
BELOW: taking cover.

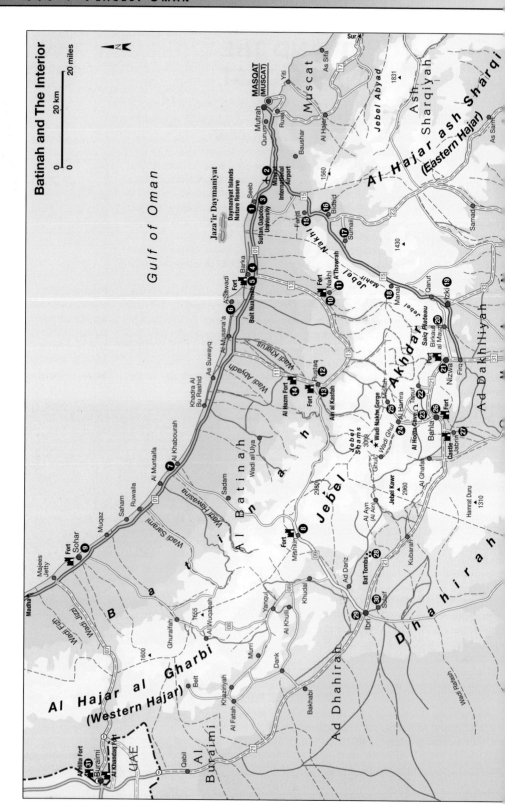

Map, page 144

gives a panoramic view of the surroundings. **Bait Nua'man ⑤** (flexible opening hours; free admission), the restored house of a wealthy merchant, is a 5-km (3-mile) drive along the highway beyond the fort plus a further 2 km (1¼ mile) left on a graded road. The house is an interesting example of old Gulf Coast architecture.

Like Fujairah in the UAE, Barka is known for its bullfights. They take place on Friday in winter (starting around 4pm; free admission). Fight rules are simple – the referee pairs animals, roughly based on equal height and weight, who are then led out and set against one another. When one bull takes a tumble in the dust the other is declared victor *(see also page 272)*. Most contests last less than five minutes but should the fight turn vicious, a rope secured to a front leg of each animal allows their owners to keep control. As with camel and horse racing, there is no betting, and the crowd, exclusively male, is content to have a jolly day out.

A'Sawadi ⑥ (63 km/39 miles from Muscat) is a large fishing community 9 km (5 miles) along a turn-off at a "prancing horses monument". The tarmac stops at the end of a long beach from where A'Sawadi, a typical Batinah town with flat-roofed houses and boats pulled up on the sand, is a 20-minute walk. As in Dhofar, a large portion of the sardine catch is dried for animal fodder. A'Sawadi Beach Resort offers modern facilities, riding and watersports *(see page 290)*.

Lying 16 km (10 miles) off the coast is the **Daymaniyat Islands Nature Reserve**, comprising nine limestone outcrops. Between April and September, thousands of migratory birds such as osprey, nest on the islands. Other species are the Common Tern, the Slender-billed Gull, Kentish Plover, Desert Wheatear and the Red-billed tropicbird, which lays its eggs on the north-facing cliffs.

My journey with Sultan was to take us through this populous province: now along the golden beaches, past little Arab ports ever associated with Sindbad the Sailor and little fishing villages whose men go forth to grope under the sea for precious pearls.
    – BERTRAM THOMAS
        Alarms and Excursions in Arabia

BELOW: Barka Fort.

*Birds to look out for:
an Indian Roller* (top)
*and a European Bee-
eater* (bottom), *both
photographed
near Sohar.*

BELOW: Sohar, the
Batinah capital.

Large numbers of endangered hawksbill turtles as well as green turtles also nes
in the sandy inlets protected by rocky overhangs. The islands can be visited b
boat (40 minutes) from the Moon Light Dive Centre at A'Sawadi Beach Hote
(see previous page), but a permit, which will be checked by the coastguard, i
required to land. The centre also runs daily diving trips to the island's extensiv
coral reefs.

Mud-brick houses in **Al Khabourah** ❼ (128 km/79 miles from Muscat) ar
dotted among the palm groves between the highway and the sea. The wives c
local fishermen and date farmers make many of the hand-woven articles on sal
in Muscat, in particular the distinctive black, brown, cream and red-patterne
mats and wall hangings. The Arab World Restaurant has a clean toilet and sell
cheap *biryani* and kebab-type meals.

Al Khabourah is built on the junction of one of several major passes throug
the Hajar Mountains to the Interior. The major part of the road is a track passin
few villages and winding in and out of dusty wadi beds. A tarmac road runs fror
Mishkin ❽ over the Western Hajar to Ibri (126 km/78 miles) *(see Nizwa and th
Interior, page 155)*.

The Batinah Coast is the food basket of Oman, and citrus fruit orchards, dat
plantations, fields of melons, aubergines, cabbages and other crops line the high
way. One of the most famous products of the region is the small round loom
lime. The British writer Ian Skeet, who spent two years in Oman during th
1960s, wrote in his book *Muscat and Oman*: "the particular tang of the Musca
lime is the *sina qua non* of local rice spicing and equally a compulsory additio
to a cup of tea". Iraq was historically a major importer of Oman's limes an
India remains an important taker today – in fact in the 1970s the export of lime

as second only to that of oil. The limes are dried before export, turning a black colour; this does not impair the flavour in any way.

Taking any right-hand turn north of Al Khabourah leads to small fishing villages. Today most fishermen own a modern boat obtained through the Fishermen's Incentive Fund, but the traditional *shasha*, a palm-frond boat, is not entirely obsolete, though these days it may have an outboard engine. Prone to capsize and becoming quickly water-logged, it has only ever been used for inshore fishing. Two people can construct a *shasha* in just two days.

Map, page 144

Sohar

The approach to **Sohar** ❾, the Batinah capital, is marked by a huge arch across the highway: a road to the right off the "date palm roundabout" cuts through a new, business district to the old centre on the sea. Sohar is a pleasant town with clean streets lined with white houses and tropical gardens. At one time it was one of the most important trading centres on the Arabian Peninsula: "Its traders and commerce cannot be enumerated. It is the most developed town in Oman," wrote Ibn Hawqal in *The Oriental Geography*, a 10th-century manual of the region. Sohar's fortunes have recently revived, thanks to the development of a major new port, factories and oil refineries, making it second only to Muscat in terms of economic importance.

Archaeological excavations date the city to the 3rd millennium BC when it was capital of the Magan Empire *(see page 22–4)* and a major exporter of copper mined in Wadi Jizzi. The fabulous Emporium Persicum near the Straits of Hormuz mentioned in a 5th-century Byzantine text is almost certainly Sohar, the home port of Sindbad the Sailor of the *Thousand and One Nights*. The city rose to prominence following the decline of the frank-incense trade in Dhofar and the weakening power of the caliphate in Baghdad, reaching its zenith in the 10th century, when it thrived on trade with Africa and Madagascar. The city was destroyed and most of its inhabitants slain by the Buyids of Baghdad in 971. Nonetheless, a description as late as the 12th century mentions 12,000 houses elaborately constructed of brick and teak and of traders from a dozen different countries rubbing shoulders in its sprawling souqs.

The seaport was absorbed into the Persian Kingdom of Hormuz in the 14th century but following capture by Portugal in 1507 its fortunes began to ebb. For the next hundred years, Portugal maintained a trade blockade which slowly choked the commercial life out of Sohar. Even after the Portuguese left Oman in the mid-16th century, the city's fate was sealed by internecine disputes. As a result, shipping from India and East Africa discharged in Sur and Aden and many local merchants and sea captains moved elsewhere.

Agriculture, fishing and commerce remain the main occupations. The town is a convenient stop-over for travellers between Oman and the UAE. Local attractions are a Handicrafts Souq, signposted, between the old and new parts of Sohar, and a seaside souq selling fish and produce from the Battinah.

The most dramatic sight is a white-washed **fort** (Sat–Wed 8am–2pm, Thur–Fri 8am–noon and 4–6pm;

BELOW: Sohar's fort now houses a museum.

free admission) at the eastern end of the corniche is its main attraction. The orig inal building, believed to date from the early 14th century and crucial to th defence of the Straits of Hormuz, is said to have been so large that it took 1,00 men to defend it – though it surrendered to Albuquerque without a single canno being fired. A Portuguese miniature shows the fort with six towers and sur rounded by palm groves but today only a single tower rises from its courtyar This has been converted into an interesting museum with exhibits on the geog raphy and geology of the region including a section on the copper-minin industry in nearby Wadi Jizzi which dates back more than 1,000 years. Also o display are handsome, brass-studded chests and fading photographs of forme rulers of Oman.

Ask a guardian to point out the **tomb of Sayyid Thuwaini bin Said bin Sul tan Al bu Said**, one of two sons of the great Sultan Said bin Sultan under who Oman regained prominence in the 19th century *(see page 50)*. On the demis of Sultan Said, Thuwaini became ruler of Oman and a colony on the Makra Coast of what is now Pakistan, while his brother was awarded Zanzibar an Omani possessions in East Africa. Sultan Thuwaini ruled for only a decade. I 1866 he was shot by his son while asleep in the fort during preparations for military expedition to recapture Buraimi Oasis.

Five km (3 miles) north of Sohar is a turn to **Majees Jetty** and an isolate strip of beach suitable for swimming. North of here, Route 07 cuts off for th Buraimi Oasis. The journey along a tarmac road takes around two hours (trav ellers to Abu Dhabi take this route). For Dubai, continue north through the tow of Liwa and Wadi Hatta *(see page 236)*. **Madha** is a tiny Omani enclave, s back from the coast 4.5 km (3 miles) south of the East Sharjah resort of Kho Fakkan and totally enclosed by the UAE. It has a hil top fort, used by the military and a couple of watc towers, but there is nothing to recommend a detour.

BELOW: exploring Wadi Bani Auf.

Hajar Mountains and Wadis

The **Hajar Mountains**, rising behind the Batina Coast, stretch from the border with the UAE for som 300 km (186 miles) to the Sumail Gap, where the become the Eastern Hajar extending into Sharqiy province. For the Western Hajar, including the 3,00 metre (9,842-ft) Jebel Akhdar (Green Mountain) massi *(see Nizwa and the Interior, page 155)*.

New tarmac roads have been laid through sever wadis leading from the coast to the interior. The moto way access is through the Sumail Gap to Nizwa, the hi toric stronghold of the Imamate *(see page 157)*. Th Rustaq Loop *(see below)* skirts the foothills of the Jeb Akhdar and rejoins the coastal highway. A third impo tant pass cuts off at Al Khabourah and winds throug **Wadi Hawasina** to Ibri, while Route 05 crosses th Northern Hajar to the UAE border.

These roads are passable in ordinary cars, but se ondary wadis cutting into the Batinah side of the Haj require four-wheel-drive. Wadi-bashing *(see page 16* is the term coined by expatriates for tackling the rough tracks to remote hamlets on the mountain te races. Wadis **Abyadh**, **Bani Auf**, **Bani Kharus**, **Mist** and the **Ghubrah Bowl**, a rocky amphitheatre beyor

Vadi Mistal containing the perched village of **Wekan**, are minor expeditions falling into the category of adventure travel.

xcursion to Rustaq

Map, page 144

The reward for making this detour off the road to Sohar is the chance to see two f Oman's finest forts, at Nakhl and Rustaq. A third smaller fort at Al Hazm can lso be visited, but the massive Qalat al Kesra, dominating Rustaq, is alone vorth the journey. To reach the turn-off, follow the coastal highway from Mus- at to the Barka roundabout and turn left onto Route 13 signposted Nakhl 32 m and Rustaq 83 km. Heading towards the Jebel Akhdar, the road crosses a mestone plain studded with low-level *saumur*, a common tree of the acacia amily with roots reaching deep into the water table.

These pots for sale near Sohar are traditionally used for storing dates.

Crowning a spur at the wadi's head, **Nakhl Fort** (Sat–Thur 9am–4pm, Fri –11am; free admission) is an awesome tribute to the skills of ancient Omani .one masons. Soaring to a height of 30 metres (98 ft) above ground level and overing an area of 3,400 sq. metres (36,597 sq. ft), it is built of limestone and vood covered with the terracotta-coloured mud and cement cladding common) more than 100 forts, palaces, watchtowers and other defences restored by •man's Ministry of National Heritage and Culture. The fort's foundations are elieved to pre-date Islam, though it was remodelled in the 9th, 16th, 19th and 0th centuries.

Nakhl was entirely self-contained with well-water and storage rooms for :ockpiling in event of a siege. The wali lived on the mezzanine level in winter nd on the breezy upper terrace during the hot summer months. His *majlis* is ned with handwoven carpets and muskets decorate the walls. The harem is

BELOW: roadside view of the Hajar Mountains.

spread with carpets and cushions while a master bedroom contains a large double bed. A sweeping panorama can be enjoyed from the top of the fort.

Nakhl ❿ is a small, nondescript village in walking distance of the fort, with several grocery shops and cafés catering to bus and taxi drivers. The main road through Nakhl continues 2.5 km (2 miles) to **A'Thowrah** ⓫, a shady oasis with a stream running under the date palms. The water here is warm enough to poach an egg. Locals picnic around the hot spring on Friday.

The fort at **Rustaq** ⓬ (51 km/32 miles from Nakhl) has stood on the site for more than 1,000 years. It looms over the date palms only to disappear from view as the road from Nakhl dips around the mosque before climbing an incline into the town. It seems curious to lose track of such a huge edifice so suddenly, but turn left at the second set of traffic lights to find it planted defiantly in front of you again. In fact, this is the rear of the fort. For the entrance, follow the dirt lane around the walls, 10 metres (33 ft) in height and decorated with more than 2,000 triangular crenellations. Access is up a ramp to a gate with the usual hole above for pouring boiling date oil or honey onto intruders.

The biggest fortification in Oman after Bahla, Rustaq is built over the site of a spring which gushes around its base – the stone structure to the left of the steps is an ablutions chamber. The ground-floor rooms were used to store dates and ammunition while the first floor appears to have been the harem with meeting rooms, a mosque, and a swimming pool supplied from the spring. The four huge towers – the Red Tower, Satan's Tower, Al Hadieth Tower and the Wind Tower – typify Omani defensive architecture.

Rustaq Fort is thought to have been founded by the Persians in the pre-Islamic period. It became the first capital of the Ya'ruba Dynasty under the Imam Nasir

Imam Nasir bin Murshid, who made Rustaq the capital of the Imamate, is reputed to have had mystical powers. As well as working miracles – such as feeding 100 men for several days on a basket of dates and rice – he is supposed to have had an aura that lit up a corner of Rustaq's mosque.

BELOW: Nakhl Fort.

Map, page 144

in Murshid (died 1649) and was rebuilt under Imam Saif bin Sultan (died 1711), who was responsible for a massive building programme all over the interior. Saif bin Sultan also repaired the *falaj* and planted more than 30,000 date palms round Rustaq. He is buried in the western corner of the Wind Tower.

The first Imam of the Al bu Said Dynasty, Ahmed bin Said (died 1783), also ruled from Rustaq, where he exercised control over the interior and coast. This broke down under his sons Said and Sultan, who split the Imamate, with Said based in Rustaq, and Sultan, the more powerful of the two brothers, ruling from Muscat.

Rustaq is a rather soulless town built on the hillside leading up from the mosque. A **date processing factory** (closes midday) near the mosque employs around 70 women responsible for washing, stoning, steaming, drying and other steps in machine-processing dates from all over Oman (except Dhofar where the date palm does not flourish), but especially Rustaq. The governorate counts more than 200 *falaj* watering its lush plantations, but bursting out of the limestone, 1.5 km (1 mile) from the town centre is **Ain al Kasfah ⓭**, a hot spring. *Biryani*-type cafés are found near the BP station from where it is a 20-km (12-mile) drive to Al Hazm.

Al Hazm ⓮ is basically a fort surrounded by a few houses to the left of Route 11 to the coastal highway. The three-storey limestone and wood structure with two cylindrical towers was built in 1708 by the Imam Sultan bin Saif II who moved here from Rustaq – an inscription on the right of two decorated wooden gates identifies him as the builder. The climb up to the bastions passes Portuguese cannons, bearing the crest of the Portuguese monarch, which were captured during sea battles in the 17th century and brought here by the Imam Azzan bin Qais. Sultan bin Saif II, who also built the fine *falaj* supplying Al Hazm, is buried in the western tower of the fort. ❑

BELOW LEFT:
a basket of fresh
dates in Rustaq.

STORY OF THE DATE

A staple food of the Bedu, a symbol of hospitality to strangers, the traditional break to the Ramadan fast, an essential ingredient at weddings, circumcisions and feasts – the date is revered throughout the Arab and Islamic world. Wilfred Thesiger, in *Arabian Sands*, recalls how when he once threw a date stone into a camp fire his Bedu companion leaned over and picked it out. In the 19th century dates were Oman's biggest export, with India and the USA its chief markets. Ships would leave Oman laden with dates and return with rice, coffee, sugar, spices, cloth, china, gunpowder and paper. Today, though date production is no longer essential to the economy, its potential is being reconsidered as part of ongoing efforts to wean the country away from oil. There are some 10 million date palms, occupying around 60 percent of cultivable land, and annual production is estimated at 280,000 tons.

NIZWA AND THE INTERIOR

Historically the power base of the Imamate, the Interior is a rich and rewarding region to visit. Nizwa and Bahla, with their impressive fortresses, are particularly interesting

Map,
page 144

The area of Oman historically known as the "Interior" refers to the region lying beyond the Hajar Mountains where, from fortified strongholds, the imams contested the authority of the sultan in Muscat. Hence the name "Muscat and Oman" to describe the country prior to 1970 – Muscat being the capital enclave and Oman what an Australian might call the Outback.

Locals continue to speak of "going into the interior", more specifically meaning **Al Jauf**, a rugged central plateau extending from the western flank of **Jebel Akhdar** (Green Mountain) to the arid expanses of Al Wusta province abutting Saudi Arabia. Counting Nizwa, capital of the illustrious Imam Sultan bin Saif Malik Al Ya'ruba, and Bahla, whose giant fort is a UNESCO World Heritage Site, Al Jauf is the kernel of traditional Oman. The new towns growing up along Highway 15 may create an illusion of the present but only a few steps off the road lie ancient villages.

The lie of the land

The "interior" is largely made up of the provinces of A'Dakhliya, A'Dhahirah and Al Wusta abutting the Arabian seaboard. Ibri, the regional capital and Buraimi (shared with Abu Dhabi) are the main towns in **A'Dhahira**, a sparsely populated area noted for agriculture and crafts. Largely waterless gravel desert, though rich in oil and gas, **Al Wusta** is also thinly populated except for small fishing communities and nomadic Bedouin living in the isolated Jiddat Al Harasis; its spectacular coastline is slowly opening up to adventure tourism. In contrast, **A'Dakhliya**, linked by motorway to Muscat is the most visited part of Oman. It includes three of the country's most famous forts – Nizwa, Bahla and Jabrin – and is reputed for handicrafts (silverware, pottery and woven items) and farming (mainly date-production and bee-keeping).

This then is the Interior, a dusty cameo of the past and present, with tourism knocking on its door in Nizwa. Still living within a tightly knit tribal society, its inhabitants wear their national costume with pride.

Sumail Gap to Nizwa

Wadi Sumail, a natural break between the Western and Eastern Hajar Mountains, has been the artery between the coast and the Interior for centuries. The broad dry valley was the obvious course for the motorway from Muscat to Nizwa, providing 166 km (103 miles) of relaxed driving

The first of the many settlements along the Gap is **Fanja** ⓫ (35 km/22 miles from Muscat). Typically, the new town lies along the road while the old town nestles against the hillside, accessible via a right-hand turn after the bridge. Fanja has a reputation for pottery, sold on

PRECEDING PAGES: pisé village. **OPPOSITE:** visiting Nizwa fort. **BELOW:** donkeys are still a common means of transport in the interior of Oman.

the edge of its souq, but some of this is, in fact, imported from Iran. Further along the highway is a turn to **Bidbid**  whose restored fort used to guard the junction of the old trade routes from Muscat, Nizwa and Sur. These now meet at a new flyover crossing the northern Sharqiya to Sur.

The town of **Sumail** ⑰ lends its name to the pass. The old town has an unusual upright rose-pink fort that stands back from the fast-flowing **A'Samdi Falaj**, the second-biggest *falaj* in Oman after the Daris Falaj in Nizwa. Ask directions to an ancient *falaj* sundial which measured the use of water by so many minutes, hours or days per week. Each plot of land would have a pre-scribed allocation of time. Generally access to the *falaj* for irrigation purposes had to be paid for and access rights were sold with the land, but drinking water (generally drawn from higher up a *falaj* system) and water for ritual ablutions and domestic purposes was available to everyone. Maintenance of a *falaj* was usually the responsibility of the landlord or main shareholders.

On either side of A'Samdi Falaj are palm groves and flourishing market gardens containing bananas, marrows and limes, among other produce. Sumail dates, renowned for their quality, were exported to California in the late 19th century where they now flourish around Palm Springs. Muezzin Ya'ruba, the first Omani to make the pilgrimage to Mecca, came from Sumail.

Manal ⑱, guarded by seven watchtowers perched on spurs in the foothills of the **Jebel Mahil**, is one of the most picturesque villages on the Sumail Gap. Between here and the poetically named **Umtydumty** are two petrol stations. The new town of **Izki** ⑲ lies on the highway 103 km (64 km) from Muscat; in the old village against the protective flank of the *jebel* are a tower, a mosque and one of the oldest *falaj* in Oman.

Many inhabitants of **Birkaut Al Mauz** ⑳ combine date farming with careers as civil servants, commuting daily to Muscat (117 km/73 miles). Their Gulf-style houses festooned with television aerials reflect their high standard of living. A right turn off the highway passes a *falaj* splashing down the hillside.

Birkaut al Mauz is the turn-off for the **Saiq Plateau**, lying at an altitude of roughly 2,000 metres (6,562 ft) beneath the summit of Jebel Akhdar (the Green Mountain). Saiq was bombed during the 1950s "Green Mountain Rebellion" and until recently it has been off-limits to visitors. You can make a fascinating road-trip up to the area of Sayh Alnuweringa, a string of rustic villages on the plateau (four-wheel-drive is essential for the winding 36-km/22-mile road journey). The 24-room Jebel Akhdar hotel makes a good base for trekking. Walks to local villages take between 2–6 hours, descending rock-cut steps and following a concrete-faced *falaj* filled with yellow frogs.

The Green Mountain is an invigorating escape from the coastal heat. The summer temperature does not exceed 30°C (86°F) and nights are pleasantly cool (in winter, the temperature drops as low as -5°C). Spring, when the orchards are covered by a canopy of peach, apricot, apple, pear, plum, almond and walnut blossom, is an enchanting time to visit. Indigenous olives, myrtles and pomegranates as well as ancient juniper trees are abundant. In June, the rose-picking season,

Water from Jebel Akhdar is collected by falaj, an ancient system of irrigation introduced by the Persians some 2,500 years ago. Underground channels transport water to villages and farmland from mother wells dug into the water table.

BELOW: view of Birkaut Al Mauz.

he air is filled with the scent of the tiny pink Jebel Akhdar roses that are used to make attar of roses.

Nizwa

Curling around a final bend, Route 15 leads to the historic town of **Nizwa** at the head of Wadi Sumail. Upon visiting Nizwa in 1350, the Moroccan geographer Ibn Battuta remarked on its massive fort, magnificent souq, redolent with smouldering incense and crowded with turbaned tribesmen, and the large number of mosques and *madrassas* (religious schools). Protected by the *jebel* and deeply conservative, it was an obvious choice as capital of the Imamate more than 300 years later.

The town of Nizwa, surrounded by square mud walls and houses entered by wooden doors and stairways, is essentially unchanged. The **Daris Falaj** irrigates its vast date plantations, each palm individually owned and providing fuel and building material as well as sustenance and a bridal dowry for poorer farmers. Around 80,000 people living in Nizwa and environs are farmers and traders with a few producing crafts and goods related to tourism. The town centre has been restored by the Ministry of National Heritage and Culture, but the result is bland, with everything – shops, banks, souq and fort – painted a uniform Revlon bronze. Nonetheless, after Muscat, Nizwa is the most popular visitor attraction in Oman. Most coach tours stay only for a day, but to see Nizwa properly and to visit other interesting places in the Interior requires two or three days. Local accommodation is limited but comfortable.

Nizwa's **fort** (daily 7.30am–4.30pm, until 5pm in summer; admission charge) was raised over a period of 12 years by Imam Sultan bin Saif in the late 17th

Map, page 144

TIP

Wednesday and Thursday are the best days to stay overnight in Nizwa. That way you can rise early to see the livestock market in full swing near the fort *(see page 159)*.

BELOW LEFT AND RIGHT: the pomegranate season.

century. According to one source it was financed by spoils from Ras al Khaimah, while a second theory claims it was financed by an Omani attack on the tiny Portuguese colony of Diu on the Malabar Coast of India. Whichever is correct, Nizwa's importance in the long struggle between Muscat and the Interior is reflected in its fort, built here to guard the Sumail Gap while also acting as a residence and administrative centre for the Imams .

Big rather than aesthetically pleasing, it consists of a massive circular tower with foundations sunk 30 metres (98 ft) deep to withstand vibrations from mortar fire. Several of more than 400 gun emplacements still have mortars in situ, one of them inscribed with the name of the Imam Sultan bin Saif and another a gift from the city of Boston to the first Omani ambassador to the USA. A narrow staircase leading up to the tower is kinked at each level, leading to a false door with gun emplacements and apertures in the ceiling to pour boiling oil onto any invader who managed to penetrate this deep inside the fort.

The easy climb opens into the drum of the tower with 120 positions for askars to stand guard on the parapets. The top – 40 metres (130 ft) above the souq – commands a panoramic view of the landmark blue-domed **mosque** next to the fort, the maze of flat-topped houses and the belt of palms surrounding Nizwa like a *cordon sanitaire*. To the northeast, the Jebel Akhdar is angled menacingly against the sky with its highest peak, Jebel Shams (3,009 metres/9,872 ft), the highest point in eastern Arabia, usually swathed in cloud.

Less than two decades ago Nizwa had one of the largest souqs in Arabia, a warren of interconnecting lanes lined with hundreds of tiny shops, some no bigger than boxes, where each trader sat like a spider in a web of paraphernalia. There was no space to squeeze inside, so customers would stand outside point-

High up in the Jebel Akhdar lives the Arabian tahr, a shy goat-like creature unique to Oman. The Wadi Sarin Nature Reserve was set up to protect and increase their numbers.

BELOW: the ramparts of Nizwa Fort.

ng out what they wanted and haggling over the price. Shafts of sunlight filtered through palm matting roofs encrusted with centuries of cooking smoke. Queen Elizabeth II, who visited Nizwa with Sultan Qaboos on her state visit to Oman in 1979, was said to have been fascinated by the souq, remarking that she could never have found her way around alone. In fact, the souq was organised as well as any supermarket, with crafts and trades grouped together for comparison and convenience. It had a street of butchers, another for incense blenders, a street for spice sellers, several streets of tailors, a corner for dates, another for gunsmiths, silversmiths and so on.

This traditional souq has now moved into a modern arcade, though the shops remain small, their owner usually found squatting behind a glass showcase containing anything from sticky sweetmeats – *halwa* is a Nizwa speciality – to silver jewellery for which the old Ya'ruba capital is equally well known. Luxury goods – rich fabrics, perfumes, embroidered hats – are found in the *kissaria* opposite the mosque.

Most silverware – the *khanjar* dagger worn by men, and the bangles, rings, anklets, necklaces and *kohl* cases – is handcrafted locally. In the old days jewellery was made from silver obtained by melting down Maria Theresa dollars, which along with the Indian rupee was used as currency. These days it is fashioned from imported ingots.

Al Akur, an authentic Omani restaurant above an interesting crafts/antiquities shop on the square off the souq, is an excellent place for lunch. Such things as fried locusts, spicy fish and goat's tripe stew are served in clean surroundings.

On Thursday and Friday, between 7am and noon, an area next to the car park becomes a livestock **market**, where traditionally attired men, many with a *khan-*

Map,
page 144

Nizwa's kissaria is the place to buy luxury goods such as a richly embroidered hat.

BELOW: the view from Nizwa Fort.

jar in their belts, a cane to hand or perhaps a rifle slung over their back, bid for goats, sheep and cattle. The market is especially busy before *Eid al Adha*, the Muslim feast of sacrifice, when every family buys an animal to slaughter.

On the edge of the market veiled women sell onions, cheese, honey, dates and woven date-palm mats. The pottery comes from Bahla, a 40-km (25-mile) drive north on the highway *(see page 161).*

Around Nizwa

Coming out of Nizwa, Route 21 passes the first of two detours to the ruined town of **Tanuf** 🎯, the former capital of the *jebali* (mountain) warlord Suleiman bin Himyar. As well as being bombed, the town had its *falaj* cut as a reprisal for supporting the Imamate revolution of 1954–59. A second sign leads to the new town (4 km/2½ miles) away, where a factory bottles Tanuf mineral water.

Near here, at the end of Wadi Tanuf is one of Oman's top tourist attractions, **Al Hoota Cave** 🎯 (Sat–Thur 9am–1pm and 2–5.15pm, Fri 9am–noon and 2–5.15pm; admission charge). Oman is peppered with sinkholes and caves, but at 4 km (2½ miles) long, this one is truly spectacular, with a forest of stalactites and stalagmites and an underground lake. A small train transports passengers from the visitors' centre to the mouth of the cave.

Al Hamra 🎯 (17 km/10 miles from Nizwa) is considered one of the most elegant and unusual towns in the interior. It has no defences and, curiously for this rugged part of Oman, it has an almost Italianate feel, with terraced gardens and a piazza, from which a flight of steps leads to a street of grand three- and four-storey houses with green wooden window shutters. The lower terrace by a gushing *falaj* makes a pleasant picnic spot beside the date plantations.

BELOW: the ruined town of Tanuf, a casualty of the 1954–59 rebellion.

The gravel road for **Wadi Ghul** is signposted 3km (2 miles) from Al Hamra. The road is well travelled through a wide gorge with Jebal Akhdar on the right and Jebel Ghul on the left. The valley is known for male weavers who make traditional red, black and brown mats on traditional horizontal looms. Beyond Wadi Ghul the road climbs a further 16 km (10 miles) towards **Jebel Shams** (the Sun Mountain: 3,009 metres/9,872 ft). The summit is closed, but a track leads out onto the plateau which affords a spectacular view of **Wadi Nakhr**, known as the Grand Canyon, an almost vertical, 1000-metre (3,280-ft) drop to the wadi below. The trek around the edge of the canyon takes about two hours. The area is a popular camping spot and has a hotel.

Misfah ㉕, accessible up a steep road from Al Hamra, is a pretty village where houses cling to the cliffside. A tank filled by a *falaj* running off the *jebel* is a favourite spot for village boys, who delight in diving in and splashing visitors. Steps beside the tank lead down to a tiny mosque with a spectacular view.

Bahla to Ibri

Bahla ㉖, 40 km (25 miles) west of Nizwa, is another town whose massive fortress fills the horizon. The Nabahina rulers of Oman from the 12th–17th century raised the **fort** on pre-Islamic foundations and also built the 12 km (7½ miles) of mud-brick surrounding walls. Covering a hilltop west of Bahla, the fort, pierced by seven gates, has been listed as a UNESCO World Heritage Site following painstaking restoration.

Bahla's once-flourishing pottery industry is reduced to only two potters working in a dusty village beyond the souq, where a sign "Pottery Made and Sold" is tacked on a date palm. One of them still throws pots on a traditional kick-wheel

On the battlements of Bahla fort, a World Heritage Site.

BELOW: a potter in Bahla.

operated by a Bangladeshi man. Its Omani owner welcomes visitors who are shown the clay pits and ovens and invited to have a glass of tea. The unglazed objects – incense burners and water jars – are mainly for local use.

Another 10 km (6 miles) west, and 4 km (2½ miles) off the highway, is **Jabrin Castle ㉗** (daily 8am–5pm; free admission), judged the finest example of residential architecture in Oman. Despite the imposing battlements, Jabrin was not a fort but a retreat for the Imams as well as a seat of learning for students of Islamic jurisprudence, medicine and astrology. Certainly its location, set back from the mountains on an open gravel plain, does not suggest that its builder, Imam Bil'arub bin Sultan Al Ya'ruba, felt under threat of attack.

Built in 1671, the three-storey rectangular building has 4-metre (13-ft) thick stone walls with north–south towers. In the high- ceilinged rooms with Moghul-style arches are traces of what must have been a sumptuously decorated palace, tastefully restored by the Ministry of National Heritage and Culture in 1983. Swirling Islamic inscriptions in the plaster walls are cut as delicately as hand-embroidered lace, rosettes cover the pine-carved ceilings while astrological designs in what is called the Sun and Moon Room have no parallel in Oman. In contrast to the splendour are the small plain cells used by students off the third-storey courtyard. Go up a final flight of steps to the top of the castle for a view of the *jebel* quivering in the heat haze.

A guide is essential if you want to see and understand everything in the castle, including Imam Bil'arub's tomb (he died in 1692) and the curious upstairs room for the Imam's horse. An interesting exhibition records the castle's impressive restoration.

In the Imam's majlis in Jabrin Castle, note the sunken recesses by the windows on the second floor. These allowed guards to fire arrows from a comfortable position and to duck any return fire.

BELOW:
the battlements of Jabrin Castle.

To Ibri

West of Jabrin, Route 21 continues to Ibri. The **Bat tombs** ❷❽ off the highway between Ibri and Kubarah are best approached from Kubarah (20 km/12 miles from Bat), with a left turn before the village of Al Ain. Linked to the Umm an-Nar civilisation (2500–2000 BC) of Abu Dhabi *(see page 216)*, the curious beehive tombs make an impressive sight perched on the stone rubble of an ancient village or necropolis (the ridge is climbed in 10 minutes from the river bed). Also here are round towers of the period, one of which is 20 metres (65 ft) high.

Ibri ❷❾, 36 km (22 miles) from Kubarah, is the heart of the Dhahira, the north-west shoulder of Oman wedged between the Western Hajar and the Empty Quarter. Historically it was a buffer against Wahhabi nationalism although many disputes were started by imams joining forces with the Saudis.

Tribalism remains strong but it does not affect travellers, who tend to pass through quickly en route to somewhere else – on their way from Nizwa to Buraimi or crossing the Hajar Mountains via Wadi Hawasina to the Batinah Coast. Petrol stations, mechanics, foodstores – all with plastic brick shopfronts – line Route 21 beside a huge new mosque. Set back off the highway is the old village with a traditional souq and a small restored fort.

Sulaif ❸⓿, a crumbling village just east of Ibri, was deserted by its inhabitants when the *falaj* dried up some 40 years ago. The old fortified town built on a rock is entered through a small black door in the city wall – note the overhead inscription – which would have been shut at nightfall. Sulaif's houses are in a ruinous state and the wooden souq is being eaten by termites, but it is worth a quick visit before rejoining Route 21 for Buraimi, 126 km (78 miles) further west.

The drive up from Ibri skirts the edge of the Empty Quarter, and sand spits

Map, page 144

A 19th-century visitor to Ibri wrote: "The neighbouring Arabs observe that to enter Ibri a man must either go armed to the teeth, or as a beggar with a cloth."

BELOW:
the landscape around Ibri.

Map, page 144

A coffee pot – a traditional symbol of hospitality all over the Middle East.

BELOW: demonstrating the traditional craft of basket weaving.

across the highway. The **Dhahira** is barren except for scattered "bag trees", so called because their thorny branches trap wind-blown plastic bags. At 46 km (28 miles) there is a Shell petrol station and a foodstore. Nearing Buraimi the road swings close to the rocky outcrop of Jebel Hafit in Abu Dhabi where archaeologists have discovered ancient tombs. A winding road up the mountain offers a view of the huge oasis, which is watered by some of the longest *fala* in Arabia. One, **Falaj Sa'ara**, is 16 km (10 miles) long.

Buraimi

The truth about **Buraimi ③**, one of several villages in the Buraimi Oasis, is that visitors to Al Ain – on the Abu Dhabi side – are excited to dip a toe into Oman while Omanis cannot wait to cross to Al Ain, which is livelier and with cheaper shopping. There are no checks at the border cutting through the centre of the oasis, but coming from the Ibri road travellers must negotiate 30 km (19 miles) of the UAE before entering Oman again.

New and sprawling, Buraimi lacks character. Its main buildings – a hotel, a mosque and Al Khandaq Fort – are linked by roundabouts where fibreglass oryx graze on real grass. A small souq supplies limes, dried fish, tobacco, canes, ropes, camel halters, paraffin and other Bedu needs.

Al-Hilla Fort, behind the souq on the edge of the oasis, is gradually being restored. The larger **Al Khandaq Fort** (Sat–Wed 8am–6pm, Thur–Fri 8am–1pm and 4–6pm; free admission), surrounded by a deep if dry moat and with crenellated battlements flying the flag of the Sultanate, makes a suitable end to a circuit of Oman's forts. There are no displays, but the dramatic architecture and a little imagination make a visit enjoyable.

Wadi-bashing

The major cities and towns of Oman and the UAE are linked by asphalt highways but to explore fully what the region's landscape has to offer, weekenders and naturalists should find themselves a seat in a 4X4 and hit the dirt and the dunes.

Wadi-bashing, as off-road driving is popularly known, is both a means to an end and an end in itself: not only will it get you from inhabited point A to isolated point B, but you'll have a lot of fun on the way.

Bouncing along a boulder-strewn wadi is like flying through bad turbulence with the "fasten seatbelt" sign on. Those who are not strapped in can become unwilling head-bangers. But those who are usually emerge from the experience unscathed with the exuberance of children after their first spin on funfair dodgem cars.

Off-road driving should not be attempted in ordinary saloon cars. The all-terrain traction provided by four-wheel-drive vehicles is essential. It's also safer if more than one vehicle takes to the wilds at a time: that way, one can tow the other out of trouble if the need arises.

The person behind the wheel needs the handling skills of a rally driver, which is why if you're a first-time wadi-basher it's a good idea to have someone else do the work. While 4X4s can be rented, less worrisome off-road tours with experienced drivers are provided by hotels and specialist tour companies.

But even those who are most adept at judging the conditions can get stuck in a sand dune. A little forethought can prevent major problems, and the experienced wadi-basher hopes for the best but prepares for the worst. A long rope, shovel, tyre jack and base (to stop the jack from sinking in the sand) are musts. A small ladder or large sheet of tarpaulin can be placed under the wheels for traction. Extra fuel, water (in the desert, one person needs 4.5 litres/1 gallon a day), a spare wheel and tyre pressure gauge are also important features of a successful trip.

Wadi-bashing depends on tyre pressure as much as skill – lower pressure for driving through sand and desert, and higher for mountain driving. When stuck in soft sand reducing the tyre pressure and reversing over your own tracks may allow your vehicle to be driven, instead of towed, out of trouble.

To avoid getting stuck, don't change gear in soft sand, as the vehicle will lose the momentum needed to pull it through. And avoid stopping where you can't start again. If engines are over-revved at the first sign of trouble, the wheels dig further into the sand.

When ascending and descending sandy slopes, the wheels should be kept straight and the most vertical route taken. Attempting to cross a slope diagonally is an invitation for disaster. When going down a slope, the vehicle should be in low gear with the engine instead of the brakes used to slow it down. That way, it's less likely that the front wheels will become stuck and that the rear end will swing around, precipitating a roll.

Wadi-bashing is a great means by which to appreciate the raw beauty of the desert and mountains. It can be done year round, as long as the bashers are mindful of wadis where winter flash floods occur regularly. ❑

RIGHT: wadi-bashing is fun and exhilarating.

SUR, THE EAST AND THE WAHIBA SANDS

Map, page 171

This region offers a beautiful coastline, the characterful old ship-building city of Sur and the dunescapes of the Wahiba Sands. It makes an ideal three- or four-day excursion from Muscat

This part of Oman combines rugged coastline, sandy plains and the spectacular Wahiba sand sea. It lies within Al Sharqiya province southeast from Muscat and is easily accessible from the capital. Sparsely populated, its main coastal towns are Quriyat, an important fishing community, and Sur, an historic boatbuilding and trading centre. Sanaw, Ibra and Al Mudaiybi are among half a dozen Bedu market depots on the edge of the sands.

A fast new road from Muscat to Sur makes the journey south considerably faster than it used to be, but it by-passes many attractive creeks and villages. The old road, Route 17, is slow but skirts fishing villages and coral-ringed bays. If you do take the slower route, perhaps returning via Route 23, a tarmac inland road, the trip can be accomplished in two days and nights, with stops in Sur and Al Qabil on the edge of the Wahiba Sands. The trip can also include a visit to the turtle-breeding headland of Ras al Hadd, the most easterly point in Arabia.

It is essential to have a four-wheel-drive vehicle for sightseeing off the main road and for Route 17, and experience of desert driving and a local Bedu guide are imperative for the Wahiba Sands. Petrol stations and foodstores are found at intervals along the inland road and in the larger coastal villages, but follow the golden rule when travelling anywhere in Oman and take extra water and petrol in case of an emergency.

PRECEDING PAGES: Wadi Tiwi. **LEFT:** dhow painting at Ras al Hadd. **BELOW:** the art of improvisation.

Quriyat

Quriyat ❶ (87 km/54 miles) on the first, tarmacked stretch of Route 17 from Muscat, is a quiet coastal town of little interest beyond its old fort. It is most animated when the fishing boats return and lay their catch out on the beach. The current sweeping around the headland off Quriyat offers one of the richest fishing grounds in Oman, and sharks, including hammerheads, are seen with other species of open-water fish. In earlier times horse-breeding on the plains between here and the Eastern Hajar was important. Affonso D'Albuquerque, who sacked Quriyat in the early 16th century, mentioned the export of horses.

At the eastern end of the beach is a rocky outcrop crowned by a watchtower which you can wade out to at low tide. A creek, today silted up, before the turn-off to Sur was in all probability Quriyat's old port.

Around 10 km (6 miles) beyond Quriyat a rough track cuts off the broad valley known as Wadi Suwayh into the Eastern Hajar. Winding through **Wadi Daiqa**, it eventually rejoins the tarmac near Hail al Ghaf. The **Daiqa Gorge ❷**, with clear pools for swimming, is a favourite wadi-bashing circuit, but the road ahead has

more interest for visitors. Stock up at the BP service station at the turn-off to Hail al Ghaf (82 km/51 miles from Muscat) before leaving for Sur, a four- to five-hour drive on a graded surface. The road crosses the dusty floor of **Wadi Suwayh** winding 36km/22 miles inland before reaching the sea again at Dibab.

The **Dibab Sinkhole**, also called the Bimmah Sinkhole, is poorly signposted but worth the effort to find. From Quriyat, head for Dagmar then continue on towards Dibab. A sign "Bama 16km" indicates the right direction. At roughly 9 km (5 miles) from Bama look out for a sign for Dibab Lake Park. Turn right here; from the carpark a faint track heads across the limestone ridge for about 700 metres/yds to the sinkhole (there are washrooms if you want to change into your swimming costume and have a dip). You cannot see the sinkhole until you are nearly in it. One of several in Oman, it is around 100 metres (330 ft) in circumference and about 20 metres (30 ft) deep. Marine life including sponges and small fish indicate a connection with the sea. Filled with blue-green water, it is a lovely place to clamber down for a swim

Dibab ❸, **Bimmah** and **Fins** are small fishing villages on the rugged coastline of A'Sharqiya. **Ash Shab** ❹ (76km/47 miles from Quriyat) is one of many pretty spots for a picnic and trekking. Nearby, **Tiwi** ❺ is another enchanting halt beside an inland creek. Date-palms hem the road winding up to mountain villages. The wadi is so narrow that it remains in shadow until midday: a 4WD is essential.

When the donkey work is over in the fishing village of Bimmah.

Qalhat

A little further down the coast is the ancient city of **Qalhat** ❻ (*see page 32*). "This city has a very good port, much frequented by merchant ships from India... since it is a centre from which spices and other goods are carried to various

BELOW: ancient Qalhat.

inland cities and towns," wrote Marco Polo, who visited **Qalhat** in the late 13th century. "Many fine war horses are exported… to the great gain of the merchants." The Moroccan explorer Ibn Battuta, who visited Qalhat some 50 years later, remarked on its splendid Persian mosque.

The city is believed to have been founded by the Persians around the 2nd century, reaching the height of prosperity under rule from Hormuz in the 13th–14th century. Damaged by an earthquake and sacked by Albuquerque in 1508 (who found "a great entrepot of shipping, which comes thither to take horses and dates to India"), Qalhat's remains are scanty. The remains of its enceinte walls run down the hillside, there are remnants of a water cistern and the headstones of a cemetery.

The most notable feature is a shrine in poor repair, named after a saintly woman known as Bibi Miriam. Ibn Battuta described it as "one of the most beautiful mosques. Its walls are tiled with qashani, which is like *zalij*, and it occupies a lofty situation from which it commands a view of the sea and the anchorage."

Qalhat's location on a narrow ridge between the mountains and the sea seems a strange choice when compared to Sur, 24 km (15 miles) further along the coast in a sheltered bay with a deepwater creek. But Qalhat probably had access to water via a *falaj* system (*see page 156*) from the mountain catchment area while Sur to this day remains short of drinking water.

Sur

From Qalhat the road descends to **Sur** ❼ (150 km/93 miles from Quriyat), a major trading port with East Africa until early in the 20th century and still the biggest wholly traditional port in Oman. Sur finally gave in to the better shipping facilities of Muscat-Muttrah, but new housing developments on the western approach to the town indicate its fortunes are again improving. Untouched by the current construction boom, old Sur and the small suburb of Aija, on the east bank of the creek, continue to provide visitors with a pastel-coloured cameo of the past.

A couple of silverware shops apart, the business district around the bus station holds few attractions but there are several cheap restaurants. Sur is renowned for fresh fish with much of the catch sold in Dubai coming from here by road.

The **dhow yards** are 4 km (2½ miles) out of town on the banks of a blue tidal creek. Access to the yards is free and the workers, mainly Indian, do not mind being photographed. The shipyards were famous throughout the ancient world, and were especially associated with the magnificent *baghala* and the smaller *ghanjah*. Both these vessels featured small windows set in a high stern designed like a Portuguese galleon. Describing the 200-tonne baghala *Hope of Compassion*, Alan Villiers who sailed on a number of Arab craft in the 1930s wrote: "Her windowed stern was especially lovely. Its elliptical area of ancient teak was covered with intricate patterns of excellent carving and her curved bow swept upwards from the sea as gracefully as the breast of a swan." The Sur craftsmen who used no drawings were renowned for carving beautifully decorated poops and sterns with only simple tools – a chisel, adze, hammer and a bow drill. Electrically powered tools have replaced traditional ones but the hulls are still sealed with shark fat and gypsum .

Map, below

TIP

The route into Sur from Qalhat passes the Sur Resort Beach Hotel, offering comfortable Western-style facilities on Sur's main beach. It is the only place in town licensed to sell alcohol.

BELOW: view across to Aija from Sur.

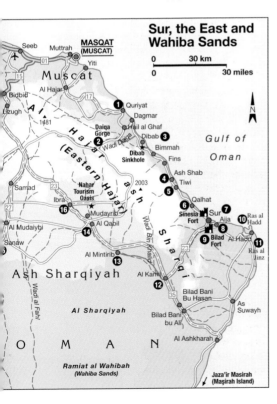

From the eight dhows built and launched in Sur in 1874 demand is down to one, or two a year. Half a dozen builders working full time take about five to six months to complete a vessel costing between OR 10,000–50,000 depending on her fittings. Around seven *sambuqs* are built each year. One or two of these and a traditional *jalibut* are usually moored in the harbour, but most craft are bum boats identified by a beaked prow and angled stern. Around 100 traditional dhows anchor in Sur harbour.

Local craftsmen have also left their mark on many fine merchant houses in the old part of Sur. Diverse patterns on green and blue wooden doors and windows reflect Indian, Persian and Zanzibari influences.

Old merchant-style houses line the creek in **Aija** , reached via a 10-km (6-mile) drive around the lagoon or in a three-minute ferry crossing (small charge) from the dhow yards. The little whitewashed community was founded in 1928 by rebellious sheikhs from the dissident Beni bu Ali, who established an independent customs post and ran up their own flag which took the sultan, aided by the British Resident in the Gulf, two years to remove. At low tide the view of Aija from Sur crosses extensive mud flats and beached bum boats, which in the evening are bathed in rose-coloured sunlight; at high tide this is one of the most charming corners of Oman.

Two forts guard Sur. The main one, **Sinesia Fort** (7.30am–6pm; free admission), with its four distinctive towers, is built on a hill overlooking the sea approaches to Sur. Inside the courtyard are a mosque and a small prison, while to the far left a wooden door gives access to the water cistern. A second defensive structure, **Bilad Fort** (7.30am–6pm; free admission) is 6 km (4 miles) from the town centre off the inland road to Al Kamil. It has a large courtyard,

The old part of Sur is known locally as "Makkah", doubtless because the wealthy owners who originally lived here were able to perform the haj *(pilgrimage).*

BELOW: the dhow yard in Sur.

lso with a small mosque, and a *mihrab* prayer niche in the western wall indi-
ating the direction of Mecca for the overflow of worshippers. Close to Bilad
ort, next to the Arobah Sports Club, is a small but interesting **marine museum**
8am–noon and 4–7pm; free admission) with early photographs of Sur, cos-
umes, traditional fishing and navigation equipment, and model boats.

Ras al Hadd

The jutting headland known as **Ras al Hadd** ❿ is the first point in Arabia
ouched by the rising sun. One of the world's largest concentrations of green
urtles (up to 13,000) nests on this 40-km (25-mile) section of coastline. To visit
Ras al Hadd, follow a section of new tarmac around to Aija. Winding inland for
ome 30 km (18 miles), a graded road then drops down to Khor Garama, a shal-
ow inlet. A score of houses around a restored fort, Ras al Hadd spreads across an
exposed headland. An airport here, its runway cracked and overgrown, was used
is a staging post by Britain's Royal Airforce during World War II.

Green turrtles are known to nest on some 250 beaches along Oman's coastline,
but **Ras al Jinz** ⓫, the main turtle-nesting beach, 23 km (14 miles) along the coast,
s a protected site (permits are available at the gate for RO 3). The turtles come
ishore at night, dig a hole in the sand and lay their eggs, covering them carefully
before returning exhausted to the sea. The eggs, which may number up to 100 per
urtle, take about 60 days to hatch, after which the tiny turtles must burrow their
vay to the surface and head as quickly as they can for the safety of the sea.

From Ras al Jinz there are two choices – either go back to Sur and return to
Muscat on Route 23 via the Wahiba Sands, or continue on to **Al Ashkharah**,
vhich is as far as the graded road currently goes.

Map, page 171

Around 20,000 green turtles lay their eggs on Oman's beaches during the summer breeding season. A female always lays her eggs on the beach where she herself hatched out.

BELOW: fun on the beach at Sur.

TIP

Oman Air operates a
service via Sur to
Masirah (50-minute
flight), but there is no
local transport, so you
will be left stranded.
The usual approach is
via the coastal road
from Al Ashkarah to
Shanah, the crossing
point to Hilf. Basic
drive-on ferries
operate during the
hour either side of high
tide so, along with
4WD, a tide timetable is
essential. The crossing
takes about 1½ hours.

BELOW: in the
Wahiba Sands.

The Beni bu Ali who installed themselves in Aija were the only tribe in Oman to subscribe to the conservative Wahhabism sect of Islam followed in Saudi Arabia. Their ancestors living in the **Bilad Beni bu Ali** (Territory of the Beni bu Ali) and Al Ashkharah remain extremely conservative. Women visitors are advised to dress very modestly if visiting either place.

Al Ashkharah has historically survived on fishing, but its future will change with the completion of the new port under construction. At present it is a quiet down-at-heel old town with a couple of foodstores, a ship's chandlers and a tackle shop. This is the end of the road for most tourists, but equipped for four to five days camping, adventurous travellers continue down the savagely beautiful Al Wusta coast to Salalah. Flamingos are among thousands of migratory birds seen on the mud flats and lagoons sheltered by Ras an-Nuqdah.

The **Masirah Island**, 18 km (11 miles) off Al Wusta coast, is a popular jaunt with local expatriates. Coral reefs, shipwrecks, marine and birdlife are some of the many reasons to visit but most visitors go there for the wind-surfing opportunities. Wind-surfers rate the east coast pounded by ocean winds – especially by the *kha reef* (see Dhofar) in June–July – as one of the best sites in the world. Dolphins and whales are frequently seen off this coast while the Masirah Channel has a population of humpbacks. The warm waters in the channel support beds of sea grasses which attract one of the world's biggest populations of loggerhead turtles, estimated at 30,000 during the nesting season between June and August.

Masirah is roughly 80 km (50 miles) long by 18 km (11 miles) wide and characterised by flat gravel plains rising to about 274 metres(900 ft) at Jebel Hamra. Hilf, the main town on the northern tip has a basic hotel and a few shops with limited supplies. Most people camp on one of the beaches and buy fresh fish

nd lobser to barbecue. About 8,000 people, mainly fishermen, live on Masirah
nd, while dependent on the sea for a living, the local Tye Hikmani tribe pro-
ibits commercial and spear-fishing on the reefs. One of the reefs off the Barr al
likman coast is the largest true coral reef in Oman. A French-led research team
as logged 60–70 different species of coral around the island, which also has
n endemic cowry shell (*Cypraea teulerej*). Being remote and undeveloped,
1asirah is also a paradise for birdlife, with 331 different species recorded.

Al Kamil , 75 km (46 miles) north of Al Ashkharah via Route 35, is a road-
ide town of traditional houses on the junction of Route 23 for Sur (63 km/29
iiles). The Muscat-Sur bus stops here for 30–40 minutes: there are petrol sta-
on, cafés and grocery shops. It is also a springboard for trips into **Wadi Bin
Khalid**, one of Oman's most spectacular wadis.

Al Mintirib ⓭ at the northeast apex of the Wahiba Sands is about 45 min-
tes' drive from Al Kamil. A market depot for local Bedouin, it sells everything
rom male stamens for pollinating female date palms to mobile phones. Enquire
ere or in Al Wasil for a Bedouin to guide you into the sands. Big dune drops
e only 2–3km (1–2 miles) distant but you must know the way or risk getting
tuck or lost. **Al Qabil** ⓮ has a comfortable hotel used by many people as a
ase for visiting the Wahiba Sands.

Wahiba Sands

unset and sunrise provide spectacular photo opportunities of this unique desert
overing 10,000 sq. km (3,860 sq. miles) of the eastern Sharqiyah, desribed by
Nigel de Winser, the project director of a British Royal Geographic Society (RGS)
xpedition to the Wahiba in 1985, as "a perfect specimen of sand sea".

Map,
page 171

*The Al Wahiba Bedu
are famous weavers,
producing fine camel
saddle bags and
superbly detailed
girdles. This black
and red design is
characteristic of
the region.*

BELOW: Wahiba
Bedu.

Map, page 171

TIP

Most women at Ibra's women's souq do not object to having their picture taken, but always ask first. "*Mumkin asawarak*" is a phonetic translation of "May I take your picture?"

BELOW AND OPPOSITE: customers and produce in Ibra's souq.

The 35 scientists in the expedition spent four months studying the ecosystem of the Wahiba Sands and discovered 150 species of plants, including woodlands of native ghaf inland from Al Ashkharah. Among the desert's most valuable trees is the *Proposis cinera,* which helps stabilise the shifting sands as well as provide fuel, shade and food for livestock. A hardy tree, it sends down an immensely long tap root to the water table, but most desert plants are sustained on dew.

A rare dew-drinking beetle was among 16,000 invertebrates collected by the RGS team. Two hundred species of mammals, birds, amphibians and reptiles were also logged. Early-risers here may see patterns made by nocturnal creatures in the sand – the swishing trail of a side-winding viper, the hip-hop footprints of a hare and the pad marks of a Rüpell's sand fox to name a few. During the day the desert is devoid of life as the creatures burrow away from the intense heat.

The dune systems of the Wahiba Sands are believed to have existed before the last pluvial period in Arabia around 4,000–6,000 years ago. Aligned mainly east–west and soaring upwards of 60–80 metres (200–260 ft), the dunes commence less than 1 km (½ mile) off the road between Al Qabil and Al Minitrib. With a four-wheel-drive vehicle, you can venture a little way into the desert. If you want more than a taste, adventure tour operators in Muscat, using Bedu guides, arrange camel treks that cross the sands in three to four days.

Around 3,000 Bedu live on the fringes of the Wahiba Sands, mostly herders of sheep, goats and a few camels. Coastal families living south of Al Ashkharah double as fishermen while men around Al Qabil and Al Mintirib act as guides for tour operators. The latter will take small parties of visitors to a Bedu encampment, where they are invited to drink coffee and perhaps buy simple crafts – *burqa* (the characteristic Bedu mask), tasselled key fobs and maybe larger woven items. Sanaw and

Ibra are the most important market towns. **Bilad Bani bu Hassan,** near Al Kamil, is a centre for pottery.

Sanaw ⓰ (171 km/106 miles from Muscat) is reached on the Route 33 via Izki. Its souq is a melting pot, as Bedu come from miles around to sell their goods and exchange news. Lining the walls around the market are shops filled with items essential to desert life, as well as silver jewellery and pottery. Before 11am on a Thursday or Friday morning are the best times to visit the souq.

Ibra ⓰ (150 km/93 miles from Muscat) has a general souq, but more interesting is the women's souq held on a Wednesday from 9am until noon. While a male relative may drive the women into Ibra, men are barred from trading on Wednesday. Run by women, the souq caters to women's needs, with as many as 60–70 Bedu selling bolts of silk and satin brocades, jewellery, *kohl*, sandalwood (*dahl oudh*), kitchen goods, spices and produce.

Times and distances

Ibra to the Nizwa–Muscat Highway is about a 70 minute drive on a low-altitude but winding road. Both Ibra and the Wahiba Sands (around 360-km/224-mile return trip) can be seen in a day's drive from Muscat. Sur is an 8–9 hour return journey via the same road (Route 23). Coming from Muscat on the Nizwa motorway (Route 15), the turn bears left off the fly-over at the Sur/Muscat sign beyond Fanja. At the road branch take the direction to Sur.

THE BIRDLIFE ALONG DHOFAR'S COAST

The special climate of coastal Dhofar in southern Oman has made its wadis, hills and creeks particularly rich in birdlife

▷ **WADING OUT**
Egrets of many kinds visit Dhofar.

Clouds in mid-summer; verdant mountain-tops; deep wooded valleys bathed in mist; freshwater creeks sheltered from the ocean swell; and all inhabited by a very special birdlife near Salalah, the capital of Oman's southwestern province of Dhofar.

From June until mid-September moisture in the southwest monsoon condenses into fog and cloud as it crosses the wind-whipped cold sea and strikes the low Dhofar Mountains, enlivening the parched vegetation and scenery to the joy of the many visitors. But this part of Dhofar has another surpise: it has a superlative variety of birds, many of them African in character, within easy reach of Salalah, and not to be seen in the north. As a bonus, if you visit in spring or autumn you can expect to find many Eurasian migrants dropping in to rest and feed on their way between winter quarters in Africa and their breeding grounds far to the northeast.

△ **A WALK IN THE HILLS**
A walk in the hills or up a valley is rewarding. From April the Didric Cuckoo (above) and the Grey-headed Kingfisher *(above left)* will be calling and nesting, while Singing Bushlark stand and buzz from any prominence and Cinnamon-breasted Rock Bunting sing in the trees. Further up you may see Arabian Red-legged Partridge.

GARDENS AND FARMS

In Salalah's gardens and farms there will be resident Rüppell's Weaver (but no House Sparrow), Abyssinian Sunbird, African Silverbill, as well as the more mundane Graceful Warbler and Yellow-vented Bulbul. Here even the widespread Palm or Laughing Dove is of a southern race, darker than the birds in the north. You may also see Black Kite and Fan-tailed Raven, the former perhaps nesting here in winter, the raven foraging from its cliff roosts and nests.

▷ **TRISTAM'S GRACKLE**
Listen for the loud fluting calls of Tristam's Grackle, a red-winged starling found only in Arabia, above Raysut's cliffs where red-billed Tropicbirds scream.

ALONG DHOFAR'S CREEKS

Good views of waterbirds are to be had at most of the fabulous creeks called *khor*. Khor Salalah is a fenced bird sanctuary and usually thronged with resting or feeding birds, but open creeks eastward to Khor Rawri (near Taqah) have their individual interest.

Visiting Greater Flamingo, egrets and herons of several kinds, Glossy Ibis (above) feeding on the grassy banks with resident moorhens and coots, gulls and terns gathering on the shore nearby – these creeks are always busy with birdlife. The many ducks in autumn will include Cotton Teal (Indian Pygmy Goose), and there may be Pheasant-tailed Jacana, occasional lapwing species, three or four species of snipe, roosting Yellow Wagtails, and a variety of waterbirds from the large visiting Eurasian Curlew and Black-tailed Godwit to the diminutive spring-nesting Kentish Plover. More birds can be scoped from a headland just east of Mirbat.

Don't neglect the surrounds of the creeks, where Little Pratincole may roost unseen, and a flock of Alpine Swift may mill over your head, or (early on a May morning) you may find the bushes bursting with fat Marsh Warblers, dawn arrivals from wintering in Africa and now on their way to nest in Europe.

◁ **SPOONBILL**
Spoonbill, identified by the spoon-shaped tip of their black bills, resting at Khor Taqah. Spoonbill may be seen in creeks all year round.

BIRDING ADVICE
Visitors wanting more information on Oman's birdlife can contact the Oman Bird Group, c/o the Natural History Museum, PO Box 668, Muscat 113, Tel: 605 400.

◁ **PINK VISITORS**
The Greater Flamingo comes to Salalah's creeks from its breeding grounds in Asia. It wanders in parties in search of invertebrate food (molluscs, crustaceans, diatoms and plants) which it filters from the water and mud through its bill.

◁ **BIRDS OF PREY**
The fish-eating osprey (left) can often be seen perched above the creeks near Salalah. Other birds of prey include eagles and harrier (autumn), Lesser Kestrel and Amur Falcon (spring and summer). A good place to see these are the fodder farms near Salalah.

شواطؤنا جميلة فلنحافظ على نظافتها وسلامتها الرجاء

DHOFAR

The only part of the Gulf that is visited by the southwest monsoon, Dhofar is a lush summer retreat for northern Omanis. Its rich history is rooted in the ancient frankincense trade

Maps
pages
184, 186

Dhofar, Oman's southern province, is a ruggedly beautiful region quite different from the rest of Oman. Its mountains attract the *khareef* (southwest monsoon) blowing off the Indian Ocean, resulting in a cool wet summer June–September) when the rest of the country is paralysingly hot. Waterfalls our off the *jebels* into coastal wadis and low-hanging mists occasionally disrupt ir services to the capital Salalah. Lush woodland is sustained by rainfall of ?7–150 mm (1–6 inches) a year, but beyond its limits you can die of thirst. "To he south, grassy downs, green jungles and shadowy gorges fell away to he...Indian Ocean...whereas immediately to the north a landscape of black rocks ind yellow sand sloped down to the Empty Quarter. I looked out over the desert. t stretched away unbroken for 1,500 miles to the orchards around Damascus," vrote Wilfred Thesiger in *Arabian Sands*.

Occupying about one-third of the total area of Oman, Dhofar adjoins the Rub l Khali (Empty Quarter), first crossed by Bertram Thomas in 1930 and then by Thesiger in the 1940s *(see pages 66–7)*. The province shares a border with Yemen o the south (Yemen and Oman completed their demarcation of the border in 1995), and in the north melts into the gravel plains of the Jiddat al Harasis. Thirty cilometres (18 miles) offshore are the five rocky Hallaniya Islands – formerly .nown as the Kuria Muria Islands – once part of British-idministered Aden but presented to the sultan of Oman n 1967. A few fishermen inhabit Helaneea, the largest of these, but none is accessible to tourists.

Dhofar has six *wilayat* (governorate), but the major-ty of its estimated population of 400,000 lives in Salalah. This figure includes many workers from the ndian subcontinent who manage shops and other small enterprises on behalf of locals. As on the Batinah Coast n northern Oman, the inhabitants of the coastal villages ire fishermen and farmers.

PRECEDING PAGES:
view over
Mughsayl.
LEFT: blowholes at
Mughsayl.
BELOW: Dhofari
woman in typically
vibrant attire.

outhern tribes

About nine mountain tribes known collectively as *Iebali* live in the coastal ranges – Jebel Qamar, Jebel Samhan and Jebel Qara – rising behind Salalah. Brown .kinned and with rounded heads, in appearance they -esemble Ethiopians more than either Omanis or the .ong-skulled Bedu of the Jiddat al Harasis and Wahiba Sands. *Jibali* dialects are related to pre-Semitic lan-guages spoken by the ancient Minaeans and Sabaeans. Short like the Yemenis, men are often bare-chested, or wear a long shirt over a sarong and carry a rifle (which nay be used should you photograph them without per-mission). Most are herdsmen running stocky mountain cattle and keeping camels for prestige. During the mon-soon, as the weather in the mountains cools down, they nove their tents to the coastal plain around Salalah.

Salalah

Most people travel to Dhofar by air, a spectacular 90-minute flight across the Wahiba Sands from Muscat. On the approach to **Salalah** ❶ the brown terrain is flecked with green and the drop down onto the coastal plain is sudden and exciting. Likewise 1,000 km (620 miles) after leaving Muscat, the highway sweeps into Salalah, flanked by lines of flame trees and coconut palms, which here replace the date palm of the north.

Salalah is the birthplace of HM Sultan Qaboos bin Said, who is said to have a special affection for it. Development has been rapid since the end of the Dhofari Rebellion in 1975 *(see page 19)* and a new container terminal and Free Zone are changing its sleepy atmosphere.

The town of white-washed, low-rise buildings covers a broad area and most visitors prefer to travel around by taxi or a rented vehicle rather than walk. The commercial centre is bounded by As-Salam Street lined with hundreds of textile and tailor's shops, but also selling every basic need. Cheap hotels surround the Bus Station and Central Market, which sells locally grown tropical fruits such as coconuts, papaws and bananas.

Al Husn Souq ❹, the incense souk on Ash-Sharooq Street just inland from the sea, is the highlight of Salalah. The best time to visit is in the soft light of dusk when the aroma of burning incense gives it a magical atmosphere. The traders, veiled but friendly women, sit outside their tiny shops mixing resins while buyers squat down to sniff and make a selection from as many as 30 different types of incense, of which the most popular are beads of frankincense, splinters of dar al *oud*, the much prized sandalwood, and the ground operculum of the tulip shell *Fascilaria trapezium*. Crumbling the incense

TIP

Although a daily bus service crosses central Oman to Salalah, the 12-hour journey is monotonous, relieved only by one or two stops at petrol stations en route. Air travel is preferable.

BELOW: pottery incense burners for sale in Al Husn Souq, Salalah.

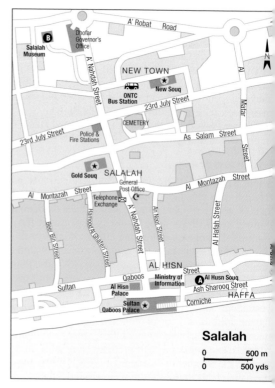

Salalah

| 0 | 500 m |
| 0 | 500 yds |

Map
page 184

between their fingers, the women fling the chips onto a pottery burner which flickers and sparkles. Bags of frankincense sell for as little as OR1 (about £2/$3) but the best quality *hujari* silver frankincense costs considerably more.

Salalah Museum ❸ (Sat–Wed 8am–2pm; free admission), in the Cultural Centre on A'Nadhah Street, is worth a visit. The ante-room contains photographs by Wilfred Thesiger, who set off on his first crossing of the Empty Quarter from Salalah in 1946. Extracts from *Arabian Sands*, Thesiger's record of his journeys caption the pictures, some of which are portraits of his Bedu travelling companions, including Bin Kabina, a young member of the Rashid tribe who faithfully followed "Umbarak" during the five years he spent travelling in southern Arabia.Other exhibits in the museum include tablets bearing Himarytic script from the ancient frankincense port of Sumhuram, model dhows, tradtional fishing tackle, regional costumes and domestic items.

[Salalah] was the Sultan's Balmoral.
— JAMES MORRIS
Sultan in Oman 1957

Salalah lies on a superb beach extending 39 km (24 miles) to Taqah *(see page 136)*, the next town along the coast. In a four-wheel-drive, you can drive along the tideline, thronged with thousands of birds, including flamingos standing in the surf. Coconut palms create a tropical impression which is all the more curious considering the desert begins only 50 km/30 miles inland. **Al Haffa** is the oldest part of Salalah but only a few of the original house with carved doors and decorative window shutters remain. The town's two most comfortable hotels, the Salalah Hilton and the Holiday Inn, have seafront locations, the latter being within walking distance of Al Balid, one of Dhofar's four UNESCO World Heritage sites.

Al Balid (site is fenced and a permit is required to enter) occupies the site

ABOVE: desert rose.
BELOW: tropical fruits, including bananas, flourish.

ARCHAEOLOGICAL EVIDENCE

Archaeologists first started excavating Al Balid in 1952, when they discovered the West Gate described by Ibn Battuta and a large mound representing the citadel. In the last 50 years, further excavations have revealed a city covering nearly 40 acres (16 hectares) on the shores of a 2,000-metre/yd long natural harbour, now silted up. The citadel is the biggest structure on the site. Walking around the ruins, you can pick out watchtowers, the pylons of a bridge, as well as the foundations of numerous houses, souqs and ablutions areas for its many mosques. The Great Mosque still has 11 of its original 148 columns still standing.

Many headstones in the graveyard, dated AD 500–600, are embellished in swirling Arabic inscriptions: one of them reads "Every soul must taste death". When trade declined towards the end of the 15th-century Al Balid was abandoned.

of ancient Zafar visited by the 14th-century traveller Ibn Batuta, who noted its many mosques and observed that its people traded in frankincense, horses and fish-oil with merchants from India. Marco Polo also commented on the "white incense", quantities of which were found packed ready for export during excavations.

Excursions from Salalah

Salalah is a comfortable springboard for a variety of mountain, desert and coastal trips. Allow one week to explore the area properly with time off for swimming and snorkelling in tranquil coastal inlets. There are food stores in larger towns such as Taqah and Thumrait, but it is prudent to pack a picnic and drinks on any trip you take. Always carry more water and petrol than you are likely to need especially on an excursion to the Empty Quarter. Most towns are linked to Salalah by tarmac roads, but four-wheel drive is essential beyond Sadih to the east and Raysut to the west. Cars can be rented locally, but most of the following excursions can also be made by taking an organised tour *(see the Travel Tips section at the end of the book, for details)*.

East to Mirbat

A half-day-trip to the old fishing community of Mirbat (74 km/46 miles from Salalah) is a pleasant drive, offering interesting diversions inland to Jebel Samhan and the Tawi Atayr sinkhole *(see page 188)* and, close to Salalah (25 km/15 miles), **Ain Razat** ❷, a lush picnic spot around a spring. There is a good road to Sadh, a tiny hamlet known for abalone diving, but four-wheel drive is essential to continue beyond.

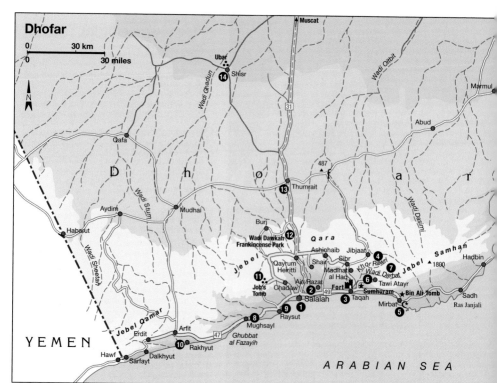

Dhofar

Map,
page 186

Taqah ❸ (36 km/22 miles from Salalah) is the second largest town in Dho-far. The majority of its 12,000 population are fishermen netting huge catches of sardines during the winter migration season beginning in December. When the vegetation dies off, dried sardines become an important food supplement for *jebali* (mountain) cattle. Where there are no roads the stinking sacks of fish are still car-ried into the mountains by camels. Plank sewn fishing boats were used in Taqah until as late as the mid-1970s, but today most fishermen share modern boats. A renovated **fort** (Sat–Wed 7.30am–4pm, small admission fee) at the entrance to the old town shows how nobles would have lived in the 19th century.

Khor Rawri ❹, 2 km (1 mile) long, is the largest of a dozen creeks between Salalah and Sadih. With a particularly low salt content, it supports freshwater fish from small guppies to ponderous milk fish of 80 cm (31 inches) in length. Pelican, stork, spoonbill and flamingo are among 186 species of birds recorded in the vicinity. Higher up in the head of the wadi is a breeding ground for Arabian Red-legged Partridge. Ruined **Sumhuram**, a beautiful site on the banks of Khor Rawri, was an important port for the export of frankincense during antiquity. A right turn off the tarmac road before Mirbat leads to an unusual white double-domed mosque enshrining **Bin Ali Al Alawi**, a 14th-century Muslim divine from Yemen. Access to the tomb is forbidden, but you may walk around the ceme-tery to see early Islamic headstones.

Mirbat ❺ is the most picturesque town on the coast of Dhofar. Its small fort with cannon emplacements pointing seawards offers good views. Beyond the headland, the old town has some fine old houses surrounding the mosque. Any-where else they would have been bought and restored by Europeans, but here they are falling into disrepair. The new part of town has a score of the usual

This inscription at Sumhuram records the foundation of the city by colonists from Shabwah.

BELOW LEFT:
Ain Razat.

SUMHURAM

Archaeologists excavating Khor Rawri in 1988 reported that soundings made on its southern perimeter confirmed the existence of a Hadrami settlement thereby dating the site to the first half of the 1st century AD. This bore out the earlier discovery of a bronze plaque bearing an inscription mentioning the name "Smhrm" which together with other inscriptions indicate that the town was founded by a king of Shabwah for the export of frankincense. Excavations have also revealed a temple in honour of the Moon God Sin, the main deity of the Hadhramaut King-dom. Khor Rawri, and its harbour known as Moscha, are also mentioned in the *Periplus of the Erythraean Sea*, a Greek manual for sea-farers written in the early first century AD.

Pits, where frankincense was stored before shipment, are seen on the hill top site above the creek and the area where the bags were weighed has been excavated. Sumhuram is the most spectacular of the four UNESCO sites in Dhofar.

shops, plus a fish market which also sells tobacco from holdings in the *jebel*

It is 64 km (40 miles) from Mirbat to **Sadh**. Known as the "Frankincense Highway", the road east crosses the rugged coastal plain with great views of Jebel Samhan. Sheltered from the monsoon, a few straggly frankincense trees grow in the wadis and stops in the shape of incense burners indicate a local bus service. On reaching Sadh, turn left at the Abalone Roundabout and drive down to a tiny harbour where a few boats are usually moored. Local women as well as men work as abalone divers wearing only goggles and diving to depths of 10 metres (30 ft) to prise the shells off the rocks. The season is short (November to December) to allow regeneration. A café in Sadh sells soft drinks and plates of *biryani*.

Historically, **Hadbin** (170 km/105 miles east of Salalah) was linked to the export of frankincense, but today, like Sadh, it relies on fishing and occasional abalone diving. It has several small foodstores, but no other facilities. Travel beyond here is strictly by four-wheel drive with a back-up vehicle.

Jebel Samhan and Tawi Atayr

Jebel Samhan, the green coastal range behind Mirbat, can be seen in a day trip from Salalah. On the main road turn left at the signpost marked Tawi Atayr, 6 km (4 miles) from Taqah, and climb. During the summer rainy season, the run-off from Jebel Samhan forms an impressive cascade down the valley into Khor Rawri which is itself occasionally broached by high seas whipped up by the strong monsoon winds.

The mountain top is lush and green with brilliantly coloured birds flitting about the woodland. Pigeons feast on wild figs and eagles soar at eye level 1,000 metres

BELOW:
Wadi Darbat.
BELOW RIGHT: water-
fall off the *jebel* in
September.

3,280 ft) above the coastal plain. Among the botanical wilderness look out for the curious *Adenium obesum* whose pink blossoms grow straight out of the trunk.

The plateau town of **Tawi Atayr** ❻ is noted for its sinkhole, signposted "Kisais Adheen", a right turn off the main road then a further 1.5 km (1 mile) to an ablutions site where you can park and ask one of the young boys to act as your guide. The enormous limestone cavity plunges more than 100 metres (328 ft). Taking care, you can scramble down a rugged path to the bottom. A subterranean stream leads out of the sinkhole, but no one has yet managed to follow it to the end. A lagoon surrounded by shady forest trees in **Wadi Darbat** ❼, a 30-minute drive from Tawi Atayr, is a popular picnic site.

West of Salalah

Leaving Salalah, the road west to Rakhyut winds through dusty wadis behind soaring cliff-tops with spectacular ocean views. Travellers currently require a pass from the military authorities to travel beyond Rakhyut, but the situation may change so it is worth checking. A four-wheel drive vehicle is essential for the trip and because of the switchback nature of the road it is sensible to return before dark.

For **Mughsayl** ❽ (45 km/28 miles from Salalah) you should follow the road to **Raysut** ❾, a modern port 10 km (6 miles) from Salalah, and bear inland at the roundabout. A rocky track on the left leads to cut-off cliffs with a view back to Raysut. Mughsayl is known for giant blowholes (signposted Kharf al Man'aif) which spurt water up to 30 metres (100 ft) high on an in-coming tide. Walking along the rock shelf you can hear the eerie sound of the sea rushing beneath your feet. Mughsayl has a good swimming beach and the creek at the southern

Map, page 186

TIP

On a clear day look out for dolphins, packs of sharks or even a whale or two off the coast at Mughsayl.

BELOW: the dramatic coastline at Mughsayl.

Map,
page 186

end is popular for birdwatching from December to February and April to June

Before 1988 the only way to visit Rakhyut was to make a 400-km (148-mile) detour inland via Thumrait and over Jebel Qamar from Salalah. Today access is by the "Furious Road", literally carved out of the cliff-face by engineers. In km (3 miles), the road rises some 400 metres (1,312 ft) in height and include eight hairpin bends at frightening gradients of between 10 and 12 percent. Some 6.4 million tonnes/tons of rock and 160,000 tonnes/tons of asphalt went into building the road which cost around £75 million (US$120 million).

Rakhyut ⑩ (148 km/92 miles from Salalah) is a small village built under the lee of the cliffs with a couple of basic foodstores and nothing else. There is a camping area behind the beach, but you should ask the wali's permission to use it; this is always granted.

Job's Tomb

Job's Tomb ⑪ (open 24 hours) lies to the north of Salalah. Famed in the Old Testament for maintaining his faith in God in spite of the sufferings sent to test him, Job (Ayoub in Arabic) is revered by Muslims as well as Jews and Christians.

To reach the site held by Muslims to be the patriarch's tomb, take the road into the *jebel* behind the Hamdan Plaza Hotel in Salalah. After about 30 km/18 miles turn left at a sign to Al Nabi Ayoub, then drive 1.5 km (1 mile) to a road fork and bear left. Enter the gate beside the mosque and walk down the path to a white shrine with a gold dome. A single long grave, the tomb is covered with a green embroidered shroud, garlands and pages from the Qur'an left by faithful pilgrims. Non-Muslims are allowed to enter the shrine, but must cover their heads and remove their shoes first.

ABOVE: Job's tomb
BELOW: the
"Furious Road".

Map,
page 186

The Empty Quarter

Frankincense trees are guaranteed on the 200-km (124-mile) round trip from Salalah to Thumrait (from which you will need a four-wheel drive to dip a toe in the Empty Quarter). The tarmac road to Thumrait, part of the Desert Highway to Muscat, starts climbing into the Jebel Qara 5 km (3 miles) outside Salalah, a gradual rise into an increasingly inhospitable landscape. The inland side of the mountains forms a plateau which dips gradually to the north, eventually giving way to gravel hills dissected by numerous wadis and the desert. The best-quality frankincense comes from this baking plateau. You may see some of the Bait Kathir Bedu, a famous tribe who own hereditary rights to the trees, either cutting or collecting the resin. Keep money handy if you wish to take their picture.

Wadi Dawkah Frankincense Park ⓬ lies on the left of the main road, 3km (1½ miles) beyond the radar station 35 km (22 miles) from Salalah (there are no restrictions to visiting: simply park your car and walk over). Extending from the Empty Quarter to the Nejd, the arid wadi contains an estimated 2,000 frankincense trees in the 9 sq. km (3½ sq. miles) listed by UNESCO as a World Heritage Site. Those attaining the maximum height of 5 metres (16 ft) are more than 200 years old. The trees are threatened by feral camels tearing off the leaves, as well as visitors making incisions in the trunks to see the sap oozing out, as the trees cannot repair such damage and eventually dry out. The Bait Kethir Bedouin, who own hereditary rights to the trees, are still allowed to collect the resin but the way they cut the trunk does no permanent damage.

About midway between Salalah and Thumrait is **Hanun**, the site of a permanent pool of water and an ancient storehouse for frankincense. The site is

Road to somewhere, on the edge of the Empty Quarter

BELOW: a frankincense tree.

Map, page 186

small and simple and consists of a building divided into a number of long narrow units which give the appearance of being store rooms, not unlike those excavated at Sumhuram (see page 187). A small detached building appears to have been a shrine or a temple dedicated to the moon god Sin.

Thumrait ⓭ is a survival post on the edge of the Empty Quarter, with foodstores and cafés, a public telephone, petrol station, mosque and two banks. From here, a graded road cuts off to the west through a featureless landscape relieved only by shimmering mirages. Follow the scores of tyre tracks, keeping a solitary rock outcrop to your right, head towards a drum on which is written "By-By". Stop here and reduce tyre pressure. Unless you have previous experience of desert driving, or a local Bedu guide, get out and walk about on foot.

The high dunes have a strong mystical appeal, especially when there is a full moon. But the "Mother of Deserts" is a threatening place if you do not obey the rules. Should it be windy, keep close to your vehicle as sand soon covers any tracks and you may not find the way back easily. If driving back to Salalah after sunset, watch out for feral camels on the Jebel Qara road.

The Lost City of Ubar

Ubar ⓮ or Wubar, is the name of the controversial city which T.E.Lawrence dubbed the "Atlantis of the Sands". The site lies close to the village of Shisr, 72 km (45 miles) northwest of Thumrait via a featureless gravel road. Despite its romantic reputation, it is not worth making the journey from Salalah. The historian Al Hamdani, writing in AD 6, described Ubar as "a city lying astride the fabled incense routes with imposing architecture, vast orchards and fabulous wealth". Other historic Arab sources claim the mysterious city was a region rather than just a single town. The Qur'an has an account of how the citizens of "Irem" (believed to be Ubar), like the biblical inhabitants of Sodom and Gomorrah, were punished for their excessive lifestyles, and how the city, which was built over the top of a huge limestone cavern, collapsed and then was buried under drifting sand dunes.

Some modern historians think that Ubar was probably only one of many *caravanserais* dotting the overland frankincense route from Southern Arabia. Others point to the evidence of infra-red aerial photography revealing miles of ancient camel tracks which suddenly disappeared beneath the desert. Still others support the theory of the sudden disappearance of a civilisation when the region caved in on the vast subterranean water table.

Artefacts discovered at Ubar include a soapstone chess set dating from AD 1000, a glass bangle from AD 700 and a frankincense burner made in around AD 300. At the site itself, there is little to see beyond the ruins of a wall, several towers and the limestone cave pierced by pipes for pumping water across the desert to Thumrait. The adjacent village of **Shisr** is inhabited by just three families, one of which runs a café. According to the village schoolteacher, it has never rained in Shisr. ❑

BELOW: girl in green.
OPPOSITE: in the Rub al Khali (the Empty Quarter).

FRANKINCENSE – THE PERFUME OF THE GODS

The fashion for frankincense is not what it was, but a new initiative has resulted in Amouage, a costly frankincense-based perfume produced in Oman

Frankincense made a considerable contribution to the wealth of southern Arabia in ancient times. Greece and Rome bought massive quantities for their religious rites, with Emperor Nero burning more than the annual harvest of Arabia at the funeral of Poppaea alone. But gradually demand dwindled and prices fell accordingly, though it remained popular in the Arab world, where it was used to create a convivial and festive atmosphere on social occasions.

A RENAISSANCE

Then in 1983 His Royal Highness Sayyid Hamad bin Hamood Al bu Said of Oman attempted to revive the tradition of perfume-making in Oman and commissioned the Parisian perfumier Guy Robert to create a new perfume that would incorporate frankincense, rosewater and myrrh. Robert, the nose behind perfumes for Chanel, Dior, Hermès and Gucci, came up with Amouage. Noted for its beautiful packaging – Aspreys of London designed and produced silver bottles plated with 24-carat gold – it is the most costly perfume in the world, more expensive than Joy by Jean Patou. Top-of-the-range products such as a silver gilt and black onyx bridal set retail for a cool US$7,360 in London. But in 1988, with an eye on the many more modest-sized pockets of ordinary mortals, the company launched its Cristal range – the Amouage fragrance in replicas of the original bottles – and in 1995 it created Ubar, named after the "lost city of Ubar", which is sold in duty-free shops worldwide for about the same price as other big name scents.

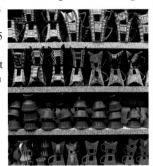

△ **A RARE TREE**
The best quality frankincense is found in the area of the Nejd in Dhofar, inland of the mountains affected by the monsoon. Some trees grow near the foothills on the seaward side of the mountains but it is probable that these were purposely planted. The tree (*Boswellia sacra*) grows in small gullies or on wadi beds to a height of up to 5 metres (16 ft), with a cluster of main branches extending from the base. Incense is first harvested when the trees are about three years old, in March, April and May before the monsoon.

△ AROMATHERAPY

Frankincense is used for many purposes apart from on religious and ceremonial occasions. On a day-to-day basis incense burners are passed around after meals and the aromatic smoke allowed to perfume the recipients' clothes, hair or beard. On other occasions clothes are arranged over burning incense to fumigate them. Frankincense is also used in culinary and medicinal recipes.

AN ANCIENT TRADE

A ruined settlement on the banks of Khor Rawri in Dhofar *(see page 187)* is believed to have been one of the main ports for exporting frankincense in ancient times. Inscriptions show that its name was Sumhuram, which archaeologists think was synonymous with Moscha mentioned in *The Periplus of the Erythraean Sea* written in the 1st century. *The Periplus* contains a description of trade between the Roman world of the east Mediter-ranean and the Red Sea, East Africa, the southern coast of Arabia and India.

Mentioned in this are the Sachalites and their frankincense country. It records how ships arrived at a port called Moscha that had been established for the receipt of Sachalitic frankincense and beyond which lay mountains, high, rocky and steep, inhabited by cave dwellers. The ships exchanged their cargoes of cloth, wheat and sesame oil for frankincense which was then shipped to the port of Cana and from there overland to Shabwah, the capital of the Hadhramaut.

The description of the country behind Moscha, inhabited by cave dwellers, is an apt description of the Dhofar Mountains. Indeed, excavations between 1952 and 1962 confirmed Dhofar as being the country of the Sachalites.

◁ PERFUMED PRESENTS

Frankincense can be bought all over Oman, but the best choice is in the incense *souq* in Salalah where women sort, weigh and package the crystals according to quality.

△ PRECIOUS DROPS

The gum resin is obtained by making an incision in the bark. The white latex-like substance that exudes is later collected and, when dried, becomes crystalline.

THE MUSANDAM PENINSULA

Map, below

Separated from the rest of Oman by part of the UAE, this rugged peninsula, with its soaring cliffs and desolate interior, has only recently opened up to the outside world

The Musandam Peninsula, the mountainous northern tip of southeast Arabia, is separated from the rest of Oman by part of the UAE. Pointing towards Iran, with which it has traded for centuries, it creates the constriction at the southern end of the Gulf that forms the Strait of Hormuz, one of the busiest sea lanes in the world. Until the early 1990s the peninsula was a strictly military zone. However, as Oman has gradually opened up to tourism, so has the Musandam. Reckoned by many to be the most beautiful region in the country, it attracts expatriates who enjoy fishing and camping in its rocky bays. There are now several hotels, including the luxurious Six Senses Hideaway *(see page 291)*.

A decade ago it was impossible to travel beyond the UAE border to Musandam except by boat. Today it can be approached from Dubai via Ras al Khaimah (the western/coastal route) about three hours' drive on a tarmac road, or via Dibba/Wadi Bih (eastern/highland route) for which a four-wheel-drive is essential (5–6 hours). The only way to explore the east coast remains by sea. Oman Air has daily flights to Khasab from Muscat, taking about 1½ hours, and there is also a catamaran ferry several times a week *(see page 285)*.

PRECEDING PAGES:
a busy day in Khasab.
LEFT: the minaret of a mosque in Khasab.

Geography

A jagged massif of dolomite, limestone and shale, Musandam has been subject to faulting and in the past 10,000 years has been forced downwards resulting in many drowned valleys. These spectacular slash–like fjords in the cliffs account for its incredibly long 600-km (370 mile) coastline. The highest summit in the peninsula, Jebel Harim (the "Woman's Mountain") peaks at 2,087 metres (6,847 ft) above sea level.

Historic battles over Musandam involved Persian, Omani, Portuguese, Dutch and British interests. There were also frequent conflicts with Ras al Khaimah, its neighbour, over everything from fishing rights to the price of dates .When the rest of the region was developed, Musandam, cut off by the mountains, dropped out of sight. Sultan Said bin Taimur (ruler 1932–1970) never set foot there. Development has remained slow, but Khasab, the capital, has a basic infrastructure.

People and culture

Musandam has an estimated population of around 27,000, many of whom still inhabit isolated mountain settlements. Unable or too poor to embrace change, some older inhabitants continue to live in caves, but one young male member of each family usually dabbles in coastal trading. The main ethnic groups, the Shihu and Kumzariah, who live on Kumzar island in the Straits of Hormuz, speak a mix of Arabic, Farsi and

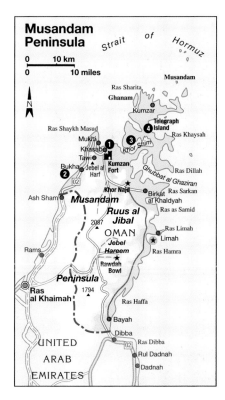

Urdu and a local dialect not understood by other Omanis. Instead of wearing the classic *khanjar* dagger, they carry an axe, or *jerz*. Many traditional items have been replaced by imports from South Asia – coffee pots by electric kettles, and woven palm frond mats by plastic tablecloths.

Places of Interest

Khasab ❶ is a typical Gulf Coast community of white, flat-roofed houses, built at the head of a steep rocky wadi with walls so steep that they block out the sun for all but one hour in the late afternoon. There is one comfortable, licensed hotel and the town can be explored on foot in 3–4 hours. **Khasab Harbour** is a 40-minute walk from the hotel through one of the oldest parts of town. In the early morning it is filled with speedboats bringing goats from Iran for an onward journey to markets in the UAE. At dusk the boats, laden with cartons of cigarettes and television sets set off on the 1½-hour trip back across the Straits of Hormuz. This thriving and legal business is the mainstay of Khasab: for Iran, of course, it is contraband.

The picturesque Portuguese **fort** overlooking Khasab Bay, has three rooms, watch-towers and cannon emplacements. A ladder leads up to the wali's former sitting room with a view of the bay, a good place for spotting waders. Other birds include kingfishers and Indian rollers, which are attracted to the the mouth of the wadi where dates and vegetables are grown on well water irrigation.

Excursion from Khasab

The 28-km (17-mile) excursion from Khasab around the northwest coast to **Bukha ❷** rates as one of the best in Oman. Running parallel with the sea, the

The winds of change blowing across Musandam have seen Khasab's ramshackle old souq replaced by a purpose-built shopping centre of around 100 shops, all selling cigarettes and electrical goods. Crafts are hard to find except for a few pottery incense burners and woven palm mats sold at Khasab Fort.

BELOW: Musandam mountains.

road is blasted through the feet of mountains, revealing vivid bands of marbling. **Quida Bay** is a spectacular place. Nearby **Wadi Quida** has petroglyphs featuring camels, sheep and hunters pecked into the rocks.

The road now climbs to **Mukhi**, an old settlement of dry-stone houses that merge into the landscape. The summit of **Al Harf**, the next mountain, offers a spectacular view over the Straits of Hormuz from a height of 400 metres (1,300 ft) above sea level. Bukha lies on the Gulf coast side of Musandam. The eastern side of the town contains Bukha Fort, which has a distinctive pear-shaped tower for deflecting cannon balls, and the ruins of the Great Mosque. Among the tailor's and grocery stores is a dusty place selling old Gulf Coast memorabilia: coins, axe-heads, boxes, sharks' jaws. From Bukha to the UAE border at Ras al Khaimah is a 30-minute drive.

Dhow excursions

A number of dhow excursions operate from Khasab, in particular around **Khor Shim ❸**, the biggest fjord in Musandam. Half a dozen villages dotted around the shore are only accessible by sea. At 6am each morning a speedboat takes children to school in Khasab, returning at noon. Shihu here lead a basic existence around fishing and goat-herding. Hardly anything grows since it rarely rains. Drinking water is brought in by barge and pumped into tanks at the foot of the mountains from where it is collected by women, who come down from the villages on the summit.

Khaysat, a good camping spot popular with expatriate visitors from the UAE, is a 15-minute boat journey from Khasab Harbour. **Qanah**, another stop-off, has a path leading up from the mosque on the beach. Many houses

Map, page 199

BELOW: the Strait of Hormuz.

Map, page 199

Life was tedious for the engineers maintaining the telegraph link. The expression "going round the bend' is said to have originated on Telegraph Island. If an engineer had to be taken off the island, it was said he was going round the bluff, back to Khasab for treatment.

BELOW: cormorants come to roost.

are padlocked, their owners having moved to Khasab, and large water-jars lie abandoned. A small cemetery counts more dead than the living. Like other villages in Khor Shim, the lofty community of **Magleb** has water delivered once a week. A steep path up to the plateau leads to a spectacular view of the fjord below. This is the narrowest part of the peninsula and you can walk from the Arabian Sea coast to the Persian Gulf in 15 minutes.

Telegraph Island ❹ is a rocky outcrop at the head of Khor Shim which was chosen as a telegraph station by the British in 1864. **Siibi**, another island at the head of Khor Shim, offers good snorkelling.

Excursion to Rawdah Bowl

The round-trip into central Musandam takes the best part of a day. The road follows the direction for Daba, signposted 110 km (68 miles) outside Khasab before climbing steeply up to the Sayh Plateau. A rare flat piece of land in the otherwise convoluted landscape, it is cultivated with wheat and onions. Jebel Hareem is the rugged roof of Musandam and with Jiddat al Harasis in the far south of Oman, is one of the last retreats of the Arabian leopard. A bar across the road prevents access to the summit and its windswept radar station. The abrupt descent from this point affords views of cavernous wadis. "Bowl" is an apt description of this valley which resembles a navel in the rocky belly of the peninsula (the park-like bowl is private property and it is polite to ask the local farmer for permission if you want to picnic here). **Wadi Bih**, the inland road to Dubai, enters the Rawdah Bowl near the junction with a pre-Islamic necropolis. It merges with a more recent cemetery whose pointed headstones are scattered on either side of the road. ☐

Arabian Leopards

Leopards in Arabia? Indeed it's true – but for how long? Persecuted by man as a threat to his domestic animals and perhaps himself, few survive in the recesses of mountain ranges in Oman, Yemen and Saudi Arabia. In the Musandam region, for instance, we know of their presence only by the reports of fresh spoor and of yet another animal shot.

More leopards (known to some as "panthers") survive in the wild and rocky gorges of Jebel Samhan in Dhofar, far from human habitation, where they live by seizing the occasional ibex, and seeking any smaller wild animals that can be overpowered, including porcupines, birds and even insects. Secretive and usually hunting at night with a combination of cunning, stealth and luck, they will hunt by day when undisturbed. Solitary animals, the females occupy smaller territories than the wide-ranging males and raise small litters of two to three cubs, the young dispersing after 18 months.

Reports of spoor and of their rasping cough indicate that leopards wander (or live) further westward along the Dhofar Mountains and foothills, and old men recall that leopards once lived in parts of the Hajar Mountains.

The leopard is now mainly distributed from Africa south of the Sahara, eastward across Arabia to southern Asia, in several geographic races, but in many areas it is threatened or already exterminated. The Arabian race is called *Panthera pardus nimr* after its Arabic name of *nimr*. Although smaller and paler than some races, the *nimr* is a large powerful cat, some males reaching 2 metres (6 ft) in total length and 60 kg (132 lbs) in weight, but its short fur is always marked with the distinctive hollow rosettes on the back and flanks. It is more sturdily built than the cheetah, which has solid black spots and a black tear-stripe from each eye, and which is thought not to occur in the Gulf.

In the UAE, where leopards live in the mountain borders with Oman, the private Arabian Leopard Trust (ALT) actively and successfully draws attention to the plight of this handsome beast. In addition to saving a caged male and arranging mating with a female from the Mammal Breeding Centre of Oman, it has raised funds, obtained sponsorship, published booklets for children and made proposals for nature reserves.

In Oman, the public's interest in these persecuted carnivores has been kept alive since 1985 by displays in the Oman Natural History Museum, where two stuffed leopards (one from Musandam and one from Dhofar, stuffed after their unfortunate deaths) are shown in a realistic diorama of their rocky habitat. The Ministerial Decision in July 1993 which forbids the "hunting, trapping and shooting of animals and birds" in the Sultanate, gave added impetus to the setting-up of nature protectorates. The rangers who patrol them will also help to increase public awareness by visiting schools. In this way it is hoped to save the leopards and their habitat in Dhofar, and later in Musandam. But it may require all the ingenuity of the conservationists to persuade the people who live and tend goats in leopard country to live and let live. ❏

RIGHT: the rare Arabian leopard.

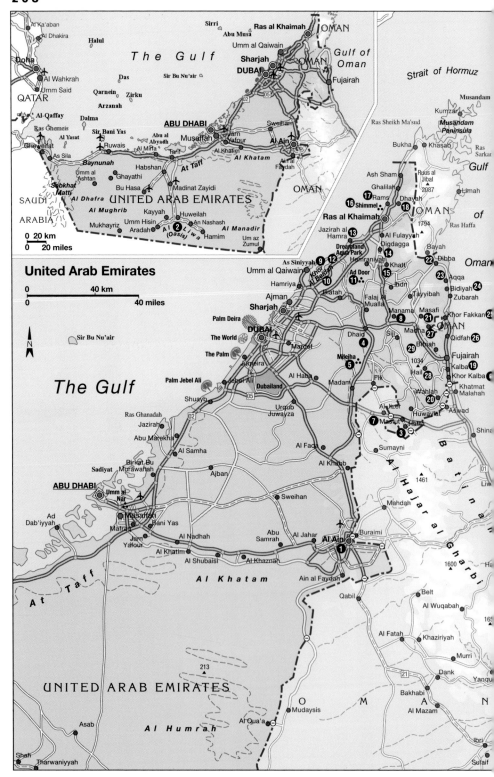

PLACES: THE UAE

Abu Dhabi and Dubai are well-known destinations. But each of the five other emirates also has something to offer visitors

The seven cities of the emirates are all on the coast – Abu Dhabi, the capital of the UAE, centres on an island; Dubai, Sharjah and Ras al Khaimah on creeks; Ajman, Umm al Qaiwain and Ras al Khaimah on sand spits curling around a lagoon. Abu Dhabi's territory is the largest (around 85 percent of the total area) and driest, a vast stretch of desert relieved only by the oases of Liwa and Al Ain. Ajman, by contrast, is so small that it is not much more than the city itself. The Places chapters of this guide begin with Abu Dhabi and work their way east to Fujairah.

Complicated tribal allegiances at the time the federation was formed mean that several states have enclaves away from their main territory. Fujairah, for example, is split by enclaves belonging to Sharjah and Oman, and on the border between Ras al Khaimah and Oman are tiny but lush parcels of Ajman and Dubai (Hatta). This pattern reflects the traditional tendency for the tribes to divide their time between two economic activities, one in the desert or the mountains and one on the coast. Herdsmen, for example, might have spent the winters in the mountains or the desert and the fiercely hot summer working the pearl banks or fishing. This economic split has a modern manifestation – it is quite common for a city civil servant also to have a country farm.

Abu Dhabi and Dubai are the richest emirates. Sharjah, at one time the main coastal city, is third in terms of wealth, while the other states are essentially subsidised by the richer members of the union. Ras al Khaimah, however, is rich in agriculture, and Fujairah is considered the most beautiful of the emirates, cut off from the rest of the UAE by the dramatic Hajar Mountains that run up from Oman.

Modern infrastructure has transformed the cities, but the stark geography of the region – sandy desert merging gradually into limpid seas scattered with islets and sandbars – is unchanging. The ring of forts and watchtowers – some ruined, some restored – are evocative reminders of a different, but not that distant, era of tribal rivalries, piracy and pearls. ❑

PRECEDING PAGES: Dhow Harbour, Abu Dhabi; ferry on Dubai Creek.

ABU DHABI

Though short on "sights", the capital of the Emirates has plenty to offer visitors, from inspiring architecture to fabulous beaches. Two hours away by car is the oasis town of Al Ain

n March 1948 Wilfred Thesiger emerged with four Bedu companions from the great golden dunes of Rub al Khali ("the Empty Quarter") at Liwa – a fertile crescent consisting of about 45–60 oases – and travelled another 240 km (150 miles) across "interminable blinding salt flats" to reach the coastal village of Abu Dhabi. Wading across the creek that separated Abu Dhabi from the mainland (now the site of the Maqta Bridge) they walked a further 16 km (10 miles) across empty desert before arriving "at a large castle that dominated a small dilapidated town along the seashore". The few palm trees offering shade near Al Hosn (the fort) have now multiplied beyond recognition, and since the discovery of enormous oil reserves during the late 1960s the town has emerged as a thriving international city.

Abu Dhabi (Father of the Gazelle) takes its name from legend. In the early 1770s, the story goes, a party of hunters from Liwa followed the tracks of a gazelle to one of the numerous coastal islands they knew in the Arabian Gulf. To their good fortune they found a freshwater spring where the animal had stopped to drink and began a settlement there in the 1790s.

Today Abu Dhabi is the capital and largest emirate of the UAE. At more than 225,330 sq. km (87,000 sq. miles) it occupies 86 percent of the country's total area. The city is the headquarters of the UAE's President and Ruler of Abu Dhabi, H.H. Sheikh Khalifa bin Zayed Al Nahyan.

The Al Nahyan, of the Al bu Falah tribe, have ruled Abu Dhabi and the Dhafrah (Liwa) since about 1690. They are a *fakhd* (sub-section) of the reputedly bellicose Bani Yas. Like most tribes of the Arabian Gulf, the Bani Yas trace their origins back to Yemen, yet unlike their coast-hugging, seafaring cousins their ancestral home is at the desert oases of the Liwa. They owned camels, some donkeys and goats and lived in rectangular palm-frond houses built into the sand dunes above carefully tended date palm groves. During the summer many of the men would go to Abu Dhabi to join the pearling fleet as divers. In 1800, under Shakbut bin Dhiyab, the Al bu Falah collectively left the Liwa to settle on Abu Dhabi island.

The first President, Sheikh Zayed, the father of the UAE *(see page 65),* was born in 1918 in eastern Al Ain – a territory fought over for centuries but finally ruled by the Al Nahyan from about 1890. He was named after his illustrious grandfather Sheikh Zayed bin Khalifa Al Nahyan (Ruler of Abu Dhabi 1855–1909) known as Zayed the Great. It is these two Zayeds who give their names to Zayed the First Street and Zayed the Second Street (otherwise referred to as Electra Street) which runs from east to west and changes name at the intersection of Sheikh Rashid bin Saeed Al Maktoum Street (Airport Road).

PRECEDING PAGES: view, Jebel Hafit. **LEFT:** banner at the Presidential Palace. **BELOW:** minaret of the mosque on Al Ittihad Square, Abu Dhabi.

In 1966 Sheikh Zayed succeeded his brother Sheikh Shakhbut bin Sultan A Nahyan as Ruler. The extreme wealth generated by the discovery of oil enable Sheikh Zayed to build first-rate public facilities for his people, but his benevo lence reached beyond the UAE and was appreciated by many international char ity programmes and Islamic communities. His son, Sheikh Khalifa, became President on Sheikh Zayed's death in November 2004.

City sights

TIP

Surrounded by a high brick wall and staffed entirely by women, the Ladies' Beach gives local ladies and visitors an opportunity to swim and enjoy the sun without being observed by men.

The ruler's enormous gold-domed residence, the **Presidential Palace**, is locate near the InterContinental Hotel, though it is strictly off limits to visitors. The nearby **Emirates Palace Hotel Ⓐ** is a magnificent site: the hotel organises tour of its 80-hectare (200-acre) landscaped property, which includes 1km (½ mile of private beach; inside it has a 42-metre (137-ft) wide grand atrium dome, and over 1,000 chandeliers. Beyond the Emirates Palace is the Ras Al Akhdar (Green headland) and the **Al Dana Ladies' Beach Ⓑ** (Wed–Fri 10am–dusk, Sat–Tues 11am–dusk; admission charge) for women and children only. Nearby is the A **Bateen Dhow Building Yard Ⓒ**, a traditional boat-building yard where visi tors are welcome to wander around.

Opposite the Hilton Hotel is the breakwater, leading to one of Abu Dhabi's top shopping malls – **Marina Mall**, a wonderful airy tent-like structure. Or the breakwater itself is the **Emirates Heritage Village Ⓓ** (Sat–Thu 9am–1pm and 5–9pm, Fri 5–9pm; free admission), displaying aspects of tra ditional life in the country, with artisans demonstrating traditional crafts, museum, and landscaped gardens leading down to the sea. There is a good view of the Abu Dhabi skyline from here.

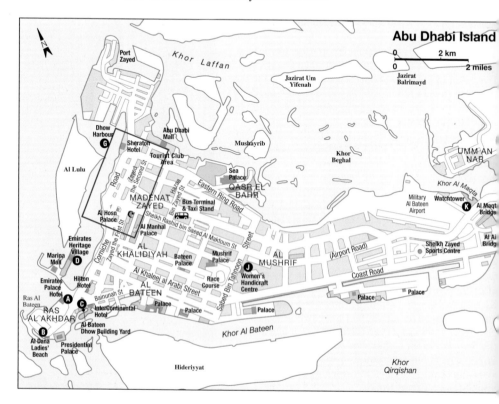

Unlike other historic cities of the UAE, Abu Dhabi has few heritage sites. **Al Hosn fort** ❺ (reopening after major renovations in 2009), the large white fort on the corner of Khalid bin Al Waleed and Al Nasr Street, was built in about 1763 (the outer wall and towers were added later), originally to protect the town's water source; at one time it was the only noteworthy building along the coast from Dubai to Doha, Qatar. Until 1972, when Sheikh Zayed moved to a new palace, it was also the ruler's residence. It's open to visitors (Sat–Wed 7.30am–1.30pm, Thur 7.30am–noon), though there is little information on site.

The **Abu Dhabi Cultural Foundation** ❻, opposite Al Hosn on the corner of Airport Road, was developed under the patronage of Sheikh Zayed. International and local exhibitions, concerts, plays and film screenings are regularly held to promote cultural development throughout the region.

The **Corniche**, stretching along the top of the island from the Sheraton to the Hilton Hotel, is a long paved walkway that comes to life every evening with joggers and families enjoying the cool sea breeze.

For a different perspective of the city's multi-storey and multicoloured skyline, try the water. **Al Dhafra Restaurant** at the **Dhow Harbour** ❼, on the city's far east side, offers evening cruises on old-fashioned wooden dhows, with traditional Arabic dinner served. **Al Safina Restaurant**, a converted wooden dhow located at the breakwater, next to the Emirates Heritage Village, is a good alternative, while Le Royal Meridien hotel runs a sunset cruise along the length of the Corniche aboard the **Shuya Yacht**, departing from the marina at the breakwater.

In a competition to build the tallest building in the Middle East, the elegant blue-glass **Hilton Baynunah Towers** ❽ added to the striking architecture of this most modern of cities in 1995. Also impressive are the folding curves of

Maps, pages 214, 216

A dhow cruise is a pleasant way to spend an evening.

BELOW: looking up into the grand atrium of the Emirates Palace Hotel.

the new ADIA building on the Corniche (opposite the British Embassy) and the two buildings of **Etisalat** (UAE's national telecommunications company) topped by giant "golf balls" that dominate Airport Road. For grand cityscape views visit the revolving restaurant on top of **Le Royal Meridien** hotel.

Until 1953, when a causeway was built across the Maqta, anyone wanting to cross to the other side had to wait for low tide and then wade through the shallow water.

The Central Souq was demolished in 2005 in favour of a new Arabian-style **Souq ❶**, filled with spices, carpets and local gifts. The **Iranian souq**, at the Dhow Harbour, has a small collection of tiles, carpets and paintings, with merchants bringing their wares across the water from Iran every few weeks.

West of the souq is **Al Ittihad Square**, also known as Cannon Square, the site not only of a sculpture of a cannon, but also of the famous coffee pot fountain.

Worth a look outside town is the **Women's Handicraft Centre ❶** (ask your taxi driver to go along Karamah Street, also called 24th Street, until it ends at a building with "Women's Union" written across it). Here you'll see women creating traditional dresses, weaving baskets and applying henna. There is also a small museum with a model of Abu Dhabi town in 1959, and a café serving Arabic fare.

The Maqta is the stretch of tidal water separating Abu Dhabi from the mainland. Coming into the city across the Maqta bridge (built in 1968) you see the **Watchtower ❶**, guarding the entrance to the city. A **Military Museum** is planned for this site, as well as a tourism information bureau.

Island attractions

Close to Abu Dhabi city is the island of **Umm an-Nar** (the site of an oil refinery). Here settlement dates to around 3000 BC. Archaeological excavations were established on the island in 1958, but it was not until 1975 that a large circular collective tomb was uncovered. The Al Ain Museum exhibits the

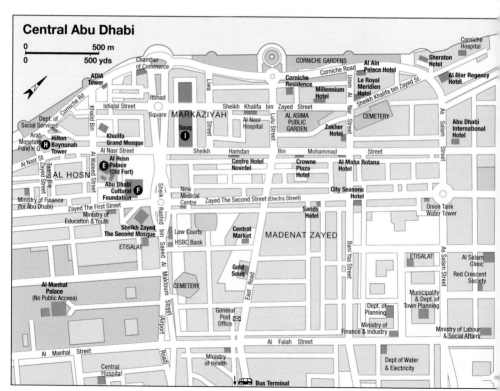

Central Abu Dhabi

results of this excavation. Inhabitants of Umm an-Nar traded with the civilisations of Mesopotamia (Iraq) and the Indian Subcontinent (*see pages 22–4*).

On nearby **Yas Island**, a Formula 1 racetrack has been designed by F1 architect Hermann Tilke and, continuing the motor-racing theme, the world's first Ferrari theme park is due to open in 2009, featuring family rides, virtual simulations and an exhibition on the history of Ferrari. A few years later, in 2012, the **Saadiyat Island Cultural District** is due to open on neighbouring Saadiyat Island. The aim of this ambitious project is to make Abu Dhabi the cultural capital of the Gulf, with a new Guggenheim museum and a branch of the Louvre topping the bill.

Al Ain

The Eastern Region of Abu Dhabi, around the oasis of Al Ain, is only two hours away from the capital by car (160 km/100 miles), but in 1958 it was still a five-day journey by camel. Dubai to Al Ain is a mere 120 km (75 miles) on a fast bump-free highway. To combat the desert and halt the ever-shifting sands, thousands of trees have been planted on either side of Abu Dhabi's major roads. About 20 million trees have been cultivated in the emirate's Western Region, covering about 100,000 hectares (247,000 acres).

Al Ain ❶ ("The Spring", previously known as Muwaiqih; www.alain.ae) is a popular destination during the hot summer months as it offers an escape from the humidity experienced on the coast. This lush oasis, the venue for the annual Al Ain Flower Festival, has been settled since about 3000 BC. A round tomb in the **Hili Archaeological Park Ⓐ** (daily 4–11pm, holidays 10am–11pm) was reconstructed by an Iraqi archaeology team in 1975 to show an important exca-

Map, pages 208, 218

Beware natural hazards of the open road.

BELOW: Hili tomb.

vation of tombs from the Jamdat Nasr Period (3200–3000 BC) at Jebel Hafit, the 1,240-metre (4,000-ft) high limestone mountain south of Al Ain. A tomb discovered in the area of Qattarah between 1973 and 1976 was re-excavated in 1988 and exposed a burial layer below the foundations. Considered to be the richest 2000 BC burial site in the UAE, its contents indicate a thriving culture that had contact with the outside world.

Driving in Al Ain can be confusing. All the streets are lined with trees and have heavily planted central reservations, and maps don't give a true scale of distances. Hili Oasis, the Hili Fun City (amusement park) and Hili Archaeological Park (Hili Gardens) are indicated by brown tourist signs, but are most easily found from the Dubai road (Rashid bin Saeed Al Maktoum Road).

Al Ain Museum is reached by driving under the flyover in the heart of the town centre, turning left at the roundabout and taking the first right towards the Coffee Pot Roundabout. The renovated mud-brick **fort** left of the roundabout is the old prison. The large walled **Livestock Market** is straight ahead, off Zayed bin Sultan Road, and the museum is on the right, across a wide gravel area. **Al Ain Museum B** (Mon–Wed 8am–1pm and 3.30–5.30pm, Thur 8am–12 noon, Fri 9–11.30am, Sun 8am–1pm, closed Sat but open on official holidays) was built during the 1970s and consists of a low flat single-storey building and the Sultan bin Zayed Fort. The exhibits offer a good introduction into the emirate's archaeological heritage, local culture and natural history. The fort has two large black cannons at its entrance, a magnificent wooden gate and photographic displays in the *majlis*. Next to the museum is an entrance into Al Ain oasis – a forest of date palms with traditional *falaj* (irrigation) channels and mud brick walls.

BELOW: mosque among the palm trees, Al Ain.

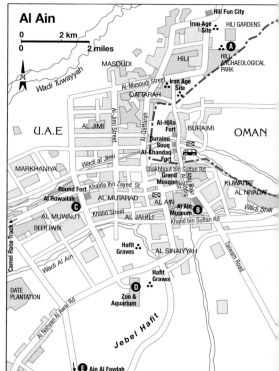

Al Ain

Scattered throughout Al Ain are a number of other forts and watchtowers. The most interesting are the Hili District defences. The two-storey **Al Ruwailah**  fortified house (off Mohammed bin Khalifa Road at the end of a small street) has an intriguing octagonal defensive wall. On the other side of Mohammed bin Khalifa Road, opposite the Al Ruwailah building, is a tower-like fort. Raised on a large mound, this circular fort provided an advanced warning post should intruders approach the palm groves from the desert. The site appears deserted, but a watchman will open a small rear door to enable exploration of the 1-metre (3-ft) thick walls and rooftop stairway. Built from *sarooj* (mud brick and straw) the foundations of the fort may be more than 500–600 years old. Directly opposite the Rotana Hotel, the recently restored Jahili fort is well worth a visit.

In the **Qattarah** district, south of Hili, are four large fortresses set amongst palm groves. One is undergoing considerable rebuilding and offers good views from its high defensive walls (to find it from Mohammed bin Khalifa Road, pass the football stadium on the right, cross the Dolphin Roundabout and turn right into 3rd Street: the rear wall faces the road, but the entrance is on the right-hand side).

Al Ain Zoo and Aquarium  (Apr–Oct: 7am–6pm; Nov–Mar: 7am–5.30pm) and **Ain Al Faydah**  (mineral springs, family swimming centre and accommodation) are in the southern part of the city. The zoo is clearly marked on Al Nahyan Al Awal Road. To reach Ain Al Faydah, turn right into Haza bin Sultan Road from Nahyan Al Awal Road and head towards Jebel Hafit. The mountain looms high on the left side of the road and is well worth a diversion, the view from the top is magnificent. The high dunes of the Empty Quarter look like a red carpet drifting off into the horizon beyond the village of **Wegan**, and the spectacular ridges of the lower rock formations below look like

Map, page 218

BELOW: keeping old skills alive.

a dragon's tail disappearing under the lush Al Ain oasis. Ain Al Faydah is about 10 km (6 miles) from Jebel Hafit Road on the left-hand side.

A dip into Oman

From Al Ain you can travel into the Omani oasis of Buraimi but a visa is required. For centuries Buraimi has been an important gateway into the desert regions of Abu Dhabi (linked to Britain by treaty from 1850–1971), Oman and Saudi Arabia. In 1952 the Saudis, supported by the American ARAMCO oil company, claimed the oasis for themselves. By 1955 all talks to expel the Saudis had foundered and a small ground-war broke out. The Saudis withdrew, but it was not until 1975 that negotiated borderlines were accepted.

Reduce your tyre pressure before venturing into the desert.

Previously you could easily drive across to Buraimi. However, in late 2005, Omanis began erecting fences and border controls. Visas for many nationalities can be issued on arrival at the border post. Check with your embassy for the latest information. Upon entering Buraimi you see the large renovated Al Hilla Fort and covered Buraimi souq. From the fort, walk down a small side road to the elegant, restored **Al Khandaq Fort** (Sat–Wed 8am–6pm, Thur–Fri 8am–1pm and 4–6pm; free admission). Built by the Al bu Shamis, a division of the local Na'im tribe, in about 1780, it was strengthened between 1808 and 1813 by Mutlaq Al Mutairi, the leader of the occupying Wahhabis (puritanical Islamists). The fort has a wonderful 7.3-metre (24-ft) moat and four decorative crenellated towers. The pristine inner courtyard is complemented by well-proportioned rooms and towers.

BELOW: one kind of desert transport.

The walled open compound beside the fort is a public prayer ground – note the *mihrab* (prayer niche) facing Mecca. The palm groves west of the souq and forts are also full of interesting old village dwellings, but respect should be shown at the public wash houses built over the area's extensive *falaj* system.

The Empty Quarter

The Western Region of Abu Dhabi encompasses the great red sand massif of the **Rub al Khali** (the Empty Quarter), the oil fields of Bu Hasa, Shah and Marzuq, and the fertile Liwa oasis. In 1948 Wilfred Thesiger was the first European to explore the Liwa's 80-km (50-mile) palm grove and scattered settlements in 60–90-metre (200–300-ft) dunes. Thesiger described what he saw in *Arabian Sands*: "The sands were like a garden. There were matted clumps of tribulus, three feet high, their dark green fronds covered with bright yellow flowers, bunches of karia, a species of heilotrope that was rated high as camel-food by the Bedu, and *qasis*, as well as numerous other plants which the camels scorned in the plenty that surrounded them."

Thesiger rode into the Liwa on a camel. Today the journey from Abu Dhabi is made easy with a tarmac road cutting through the desolate limestone ridges, drifts of white sand and stretches of gravel dotted with woody grass. It is a three-hour trip by road from Abu Dhabi to **Liwa ❷**. The Rumaitha oil-field route to Liwa passes an enormous pyramid in the desert, home to the Emirates National Auto Museum (www.enam. ae). Set up by the "rainbow sheikh", a well known motor enthusiast whose logo is a rainbow, the hangar displays oversized (some x times the original) pick-up trucks and over 30 vintage vehicles. At the time of going to press it was not open, so check with your hotel before heading there.

The Liwa crescent is well served by a four-lane highway. Passing (from west to east) the villages of **Aradah**, **Taraq**, **Al Hilah**, **Qatuf**, **Kayyah**, **Al Mariyyah**, **Dhafir**, **Huweilah**, **Qumidah**, **Shah**, **Tharwaniyyah**, **Al Nashash**, **Jarrah**, **Wedheil**, **Al Kris** and **Hamim**, it is difficult to imagine how these sparsely populated villages of *barasti* (palm frond) dwellings and carefully tended date palm groves, subsisted here for hundreds of years. The concrete houses, guesthouse and irrigated farms that you see today are a relatively recent addition, developed during the 1980s.

Any visit to the Liwa is a special experience. The effect of the remoteness and beauty of the sands is profound. Every day the dunes change and encroach on the farms nestling below. The scale of the big red dunes is best appreciated in winter, when it is possible to climb to the top of a dune without the heat burning through the soles of your shoes. Surprisingly, the Liwa has an extensive range of fauna. Hares, foxes, monitor lizards and other animals and reptiles flourish in the harsh, seemingly inhospitable desert environment.

Industrial outposts

West of Liwa are **Ruwais** and **Jebel Dhanna**. Ruwais is the site of the country's largest oil refinery, started in 1978 and still expanding, and Jebel Dhanna is an inhospitable coastal area where the export terminal for Abu Dhabi's onshore oil is sited. The oil, held in special storage tanks, is piped to tanker-mooring terminals 5km (3 miles) offshore. Further west, heading towards the Saudi border, **As Sila** is a rewarding site for ornithologists and naturalists. ❑

TIP

There are no petrol stations between leaving the Abu Dhabi highway and Hamim, so be sure to fill up in the city.

BELOW: off-road driving is not for the faint-hearted

DUBAI

*Dubai is the commercial centre of the Middle East,
but there is much more to the city than its famous duty-free
shopping, including a characterful creek and old quarters*

Maps
pages
226, 233

Abu Dhabi
UNITED ARAB
EMIRATES

Modern Dubai is characterised by the towering glass buildings that rose out of the desert sands in the 1980s and '90s, but for centuries it was known to traders of spices, gold, slaves, sandalwood and other precious cargoes as a safe haven. Dhows have moored on the shores of the Creek that runs through the city since it was first settled in the early 1800s. Archaeological sites in the areas of Jumeira, Al Qusais (15 km/9 miles from Deira) and Mina Siyahi indicate that Dubai was an important station for caravans travelling between Mesopotamia and Oman as early as 3000 BC *(see pages 22–4)*. Today, these ancient areas are joined by four-lane super highways and residential suburbs, and the city of Dubai is defined as the international commercial centre of the Middle East. But regardless of the city's obvious wealth and capacity for development, it has retained some of the atmosphere of the old trading port that existed before the 1960s.

Khor Dubai Ⓐ, or the creek, is a 300-metre (1,000-ft) wide, 10-km (6-mile) long saltwater inlet that divides the areas of Bur Dubai to the west and Deira to the east. It concludes near the Dubai Country Club with a bird sanctuary and flamingo breeding ground. Until 1963, when it was desilted and a breakwater was built at its mouth, the creek lapped the edges of the city and at high-tide often created a wading pool between the areas of Shindagha and Bur Dubai. Now the creek is a scenic thoroughfare for trading dhows, *abras* (water taxis), luxury yachts and the occasional ship.

There are three ways of crossing the creek by car from Bur Dubai to Deira – the **Maktoum Bridge** (built in 1962), **Shindagha Tunnel** (built 1975) and **Garhoud Bridge** (built 1976). Both bridges provide breathtaking views of the cityscape and, like **Jumeira Road**, to the west of the creek, and the parallel **Sheikh Zayed Road**, further inland, offer good orientation points for exploring the city.

City sights

Dubai's taste for eye-catching architecture finds expression in a number of notable structures that have made their mark on this city's increasingly spectacular skyline. Striking examples include the angular, soaring **Emirates Towers**, the office tower which, at 355 metres (1,163 ft), is the tallest building in the Middle East and Europe; the remarkable **Burj Al Arab** hotel in Jumeira; and Dubai International Airport's Terminal 1 and control tower.

However, in spite of the overwhelming impression of high-rise office towers, five-star hotels, beach world-renowned racecourses, enormous shopping centres and international-standard tennis, golf and motor-racing facilities, it is still possible to experience the atmosphere and character of old Dubai. A good place to begin is the **Dubai Museum Ⓑ** (Sat–Thur 8.30am–8.30pm; Fri

PRECEDING PAGES: Dubai's ever-changing skyline. **LEFT:** architectural reflections. **BELOW:** an *abra* (water taxi) awaits.

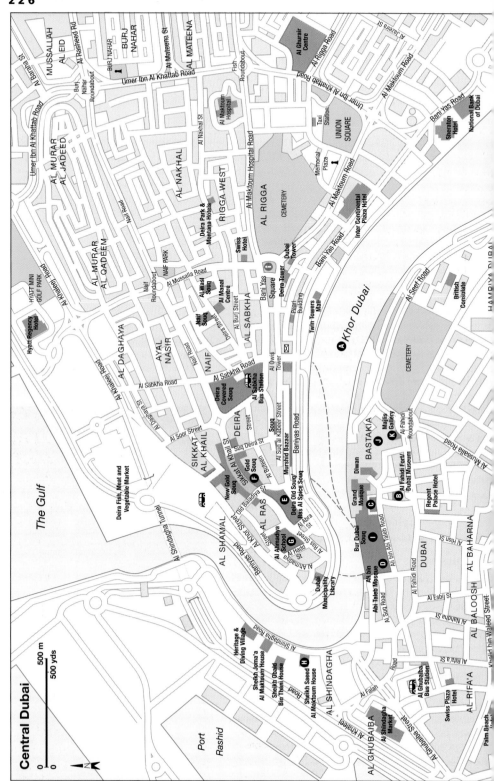

Central Dubai

The Gulf

Port Rashid

0   500 m
0   500 yds

Khor Dubai

MUSSALLAH AL EID

BURJ NAHAR

Al Baraha St

Al Rasheed Rd

Burj Nahar Roundabout

Al Khaleej Road

Umer Ibn Al Khattab Road

AL MURAR AL JADEED

AL MATEENA

Al Mateena St

BURJ NAHAR

Umer Ibn Al Khattab Road

AL MURAR AL QADEEM

AL NAKHAL

Al Nakhal St

Al Maktoum Hospital

RIGGA WEST

Al Maktoum Hospital Road

AL RIGGA

CEMETERY

Al Ghurair Centre

Al Rigga Road

Umer Ibn Al Khattab Road

Al Maktoum Road

Al Jazeera St

HAMRIYA DUBAI

Bani Yas Road

Sheraton Hotel

National Bank of Dubai

Taxi Station

UNION SQUARE

Memorial Plaza

Inter Continental Plaza Hotel

HYATT MINI GOLF PARK

Hyatt Regency Hotel

AL DAGHAYA

AL MURAR AL QADEEM

Naif Road

Naif Roundabout

NAIF PARK

Al Mussalla Road

Deira Park & Montana Hotels

Swiss Hotel

Dubai Tower

Deira Tower

Bani Yas Square

Pearl Building

Twin Towers Mall

Al Seef Road

British Consulate

Al Mussalla Road

AYAL NASIR

Naif Road

NAIF

Naif Souq

Al Wasl Souq

Al Manal Centre

Al Burj Street

Deira Street

AL SABKHA

Al Owis Tower

Al Sabkha Road

Al Soor Street

DEIRA

SIKKAT AL KHAIL

Sikkat Al Khail St

Al Sabkha Road

Deira Covered Souq

Al Sabkha Bus Station

Murshid Bazaar

Baniyas Road

CEMETERY

BASTAKIA

Majlis Gallery

Al Fahidi Roundabout

Deira Fish, Meat and Vegetable Market

Al Shindagha Tunnel

AL SHAMAL

Baniyas Road

Al Khor Street

AL RAS

New Gold Souq

Gold Souq

Al Suq al Kabeer Street

Souq

Deira Old Souq

Ras Al Spice Souq

Grand Mosque

Diwan

Al Fahidi Fort / Dubai Museum

Repent Palace Hotel

DUBAI

Al Hisn St

Al Ahmadiya School

Al Ahmadiya St

Old Baladiya St

Al Hadd St

Al Abra St

Al Ras Street

Dubai Municipality Library

Bur Dubai Souq

Ali bin Abi Taleb Road

Abi Taleb Mosque

Al Suq Road

AL BAHARNA

Al Fahidi Road

Al Esbij St

AL BALOOSH

Al Nahdra St

Banivers Road

Al Shindagha Road

Heritage & Diving Village

Sheikh Joma'a Al Maktoum House

Sheikh Obaid Bin Thani House

Sheikh Saeed Al Maktoum House

AL SHINDAGHA

Al Khaleej

Al Khaleej Road

Al Ghubaiba Road

Al Faiah

AL GHUBAIBA

Al Shindagha Market

Al Ghubaiba Bus Station

Swiss Plaza Hotel

Palm Beach

AL RIFA'A

Al Rifa'a St

Al Ghubaiba Street

Ksaid bin Waleed Street

N

1.30– 8.30pm), housed in **Al Fahidi Fort** (built *c*. 1787), which is located in the heart of Bur Dubai, on Al Fahidi Road. The museum not only displays archaeological finds dating back to the emirate's ancient past (approximately 5,000 years) but has exhibition halls that bring to life the atmosphere of the souq, traditional architecture, and the local community as it was prior to expansion in the 1960s.

Map, page 226

The fort was originally built to defend the city against foreign invasions, and was once home to approximately 100 men. Built with local materials – rectangular sea rocks, palm tree trunks, palm fronds, mud bricks and *sarooj* (mortar made from imported red clay, manure and water) – it has large towers at three corners and three vast halls facing the courtyard, which were added in about 1900. Initially built as barracks, the halls served as Dubai's jail as late as 1971. The museum has been incorporated into the fort without altering its original structure. The courtyard displays the old well, a 1785 bronze cannon, a traditional *majlis* (meeting room) and a collection of boats formerly used for fishing and pearl diving. An underground extension, completed in 1995, houses the new exhibition halls.

Al Fahidi Fort is the perfect place to begin a **Dubai Heritage Walk**. From the museum's entrance, walk towards the Diwan (Ruler's Office, not open to the public), the large white building on the opposite side of the street, facing the creek. Built in 1990, the arched windows and decorative iron screens present a sympathetic architectural addition to this historic area.

Taking an abra across the creek.

Wandering left, down Ali bin Abi Talib Road – a small but busy street lined with fabric shops – brings the Grand and Ali bin Abi Taleb mosques into view. The **Grand Mosque** ⓒ is one of the oldest in Dubai, and although photos dating from the 1950s suggest it has had a refurbishment it adds great atmosphere to the narrow street. The **Ali bin Abi Taleb Mosque** ⓓ features a towering minaret, splendid domes, gold and green mosaics and wooden screens. (Non-Muslims are requested not to enter the mosques.)

BELOW: Dubai Museum.

At the T-junction turn right and wander towards the creek. A large wooden gateway now marks the entrance to the renovated "old souq". Prior to renovation the small, colourful fabric and clothing shops opened out onto uncovered lanes. Now a wooden roof covers the narrow streets of the meandering souq, almost as far as historical Bastakia, beyond the Diwan.

The Bur Dubai *abra* (water taxi) terminal is found in the old souq, and provides one of the most authentic and inexpensive experiences available in the Emirates. Prior to 1962 *abras* provided the only means of crossing the creek. These little, open-sided, motor-powered wooden boats cross from here to two **Deira** terminals. The first terminal on Deira-side sits between the large trading dhows moored at Al Ras, on Baniyas Road – which is the best place to continue on a journey into the spice and gold souqs. The second is a larger terminal further down Baniyas Road near the intersection leading to Al Nasr Square, the main electronics souq in Dubai.

Ferry views of the buildings lining the creek expose the great contrast between old and new. The curved glass facade of the **National Bank of Dubai**, and the distant sail-like structure of the **Creek Golf Club clubhouse** are beautifully juxtaposed against the traditional windtower houses of Bastakia and two-storey mud-brick buildings on the opposite bank.

Dubai is considered the cheapest place to purchase gold in the world. Unless complex jewellery-making is involved, items can be bought at the daily gold price, displayed at the entrance to the New Gold Souq on Al Khor Street

BELOW: life on Dubai Creek.

Abra captains will negotiate a charter fee (approximately Dhs 30–50 per half hour) for journeys up and down the entire course of the Creek. Local families often hire a private *abra* to avoid the public ride. An alternative to renting an *abra* is to take a guided dhow or boat tour, some of which include options for fine dining (Bateaux Dubai and Danat Dubai Cruises operate from the British Embassy area in Bur Dubai; Al Boom Tourist Village's dhows depart from Garhoud Bridge; in Deira, Creekside Leisure operates from the Dubai Municipality waterfront, while Creek Cruises' large Malika Al Khor and Zomorrodah dhows depart from in front of the triangular blue Dubai Chamber of Commerce and Industry building. One of the most unusual ways of exploring the creek is by the Wonder Bus, an amphibious bus that departs from the BurJuman Shopping Centre on two-hour mini-tours of Dubai).

Into the souqs

Large spice-filled sacks spill out into the tiny, shop-lined, covered walkways that form **Al Ras Spice Souq** ❺ (Sat–Thur 9am–1pm and 4–8.30pm; Fri 4.30–8.30pm). Established in 1850, this souq has always been close to the dhow moorings for easy trading and unloading. Cardamom, paprika, nutmeg, cinnamon, dried limes, saffron, henna and frankincense are displayed amongst enormous cooking pots, weighing scales and tobacco. The area is always full of UAE nationals, and women should dress conservatively (permission should always be obtained before taking photographs of people).

The Al Ras area also incorporates the glittering **Gold Souq** ❻. Here the narrow, wooden-roofed streets are lined with shops dealing solely in gold, their windows hung with 24- and 22-carat bracelets, chains, tiaras, diamond rings and solid gold

wrist-watches. Designs can be intricate, with filigree work very popular locally.

At one time Dubai pearls were also bought and sold in this area. Pearling was of crucial importance to Dubai from the 1840s (*see page 35*), but the industry declined rapidly in the 1930s and 1940s with the advent of Japanese cultured pearls. Al Arsa Souq in Sharjah (*see page 242*) is one of the last places in the Emirates where elderly merchants can be seen selling the highly-prized and valuable local pearls.

Leaving the Gold Souq via Al Khor Street, turn left down Old Baladiya Street and then right into Al Ahmadiya Street to discover the Al Ahmadiya heritage building project. The **Al Ahmadiya School** was established around 1903 by a wealthy pearl merchant called Ahmed bin Delmuk. The school taught Arabic language and grammar, Islamic studies and basic mathematics to about 200 boys. Unlike pupils of the Qur'an schools, who sat on the floor, these boys sat at proper desks.

By the 1920s four main schools had been established by pearl traders, but following the 1930s depression in pearling they all closed. Al Ahmadiya was reopened in 1938, and by the 1950s approximately 500 students were enrolled. In 1965 the school was relocated elsewhere in Dubai, and the buildings were used as a religious institution until they were abandoned in the 1970s.

Great care has been taken to restore Al Ahmadiya School, Ahmed bin Delmuk's house (situated directly in front of the school), surrounding houses and the mosque. A merchant's house further along Al Ahmadiya Street shows how decorative the houses used to be in this area. Stucco panels, detailed window screens and finely carved wooden doors were largely the result of stylistic influences from India.

Al Ahmadiya Street joins Baniyas Road, which runs parallel to the creek, at the **Dubai Municipality Library**. This modern institution conveniently divides

Map, page 226

Al Ahmadiya School's most distinguished student was Sheikh Rashid bin Saeed Al Maktoum, Ruler of Dubai 1958–90 and regent for his ailing father, Sheikh Saeed, from 1939.

BELOW: shopping in the Gold Souq.

the books into Arabic and English language sections. Although it is not possible to remove books, it offers an alternative to the British Council Library near Rashid Hospital and the Maktoum Bridge.

Return to Bur Dubai by *abra* and walk to **Sheikh Saeed Al Maktoum House** ⒣ (Sat–Thur 8.30am–9pm; Fri 3pm–8pm) on the sandy promontory of **Shindagha**. Born in 1878, Sheikh Saeed bin Maktoum ruled Dubai from 1912 until his death in 1958. The Shindagha house was originally built by Sheikh Maktoum bin Hasher Al Maktoum, Sheikh Saeed's father, in 1896, and served as home to his extended family. The house was abandoned in 1958, and became so derelict by the 1980s that it has been rebuilt next to the original site.

Photographs in the museum vividly illustrate many aspects of the social, cultural, educational and religious life of old Dubai. The nomadic lifestyle of the Bedu, well digging, date harvesting, falconry and camel racing illustrate the richness of the desert and its oases. Letters, treaties, maps, coins and stamp collections focus on the development of the emirate through official documentation dating back to 1822. The square-shaped building itself, with four fine examples of the traditional *barjeel* (windtower) and square shaped, is a vanishing symbol of Arab architecture.

The renovation of Sheikh Saeed's house has led to the reconstruction of two other heritage houses further along the promontory. The first, **Sheikh Obaid Bin Thani House** (hours vary; free admission), dates from 1916 and stages exhibitions; the second, the adjacent **Sheikh Joma'a Al Maktoum House** (Sun–Thur 8am–8.30pm, Fri 3–8.30pm; admission charge) dates from 1928 andcontains historical photographs, stamps, and coins. Just beyond is the **Heritage** and **Diving Village** (Sat–Thur 8am–10pm, Fri 8–11am and 4–10pm; free) where various aspects of architecture, agriculture and the traditions of the UAE are recreated.

BELOW: Dubai Municipality.

The return walk from Shindagha to the Al Fahidi Fort includes the core of the **Bur Dubai Souq** on Al Suq Road, bustling Cosmos Lane and Al Fahidi Street. Electronic goods, fabulous fabrics and vibrant Indian saris are all good buys here, although the constant harassment from the sellers can be wearing.

Map, page 226

Continue along Al Fahidi Road to the historical area of **Bastakia** ①. Once the homes of wealthy merchant families, the windtower houses that line the small paved streets were occupied by expatriate taxi drivers and their families until the mid-1990s, when Dubai Municipality began to restore the area. Today, it's developing into an atmospheric arts quarter, with several galleries, cafés, and the Sheikh Mohammed Centre for Cultural Understanding, which can arrange mosque visits.

The **Majlis Gallery** ⓚ (Sat– Thur 9.30am–1.30pm and 4–7.30pm; closed Fri), located near the Al Fahidi Roundabout, is a commercial art gallery based in a converted windtower house in the heart of Bastakia. Enter through a low, decorative doorway into a cool, airy courtyard. All the rooms open onto the courtyard, although in the larger houses of Bastakia the courtyard is given more shade by a loggia running around three sides. The rear room, entered from a small verandah, houses the windtower. Windtowers became popular throughout the Arabian Gulf during the 1890s. They rise 15 metres (49 ft) above ground level and open into the main sitting room, or *majlis*. Built with X-shaped cross walls, providing an opening on all four sides, the tower catches the wind and channels it down an opening into the *majlis* below. The tower stops about 2 metres (6 ft) above floor level, creating a cool place underneath for sitting or sleeping.

Windtower in restoration. The ingenious cooling device was introduced to the region from Persia.

The Majlis Gallery also sells traditional artefacts such as the *khanjar* (curved dagger traditionally worn by UAE nationals until the 1970s and still common in Oman). In the alleyways behind the Majlis Gallery, the **XVA Gallery** has a relax-

BELOW: carpets, cushions and camel saddles.

ing courtyard coffee shop and offers accommodation in the heart of old Dubai.

To complete the Heritage Walk leave the Majlis Gallery, turn left at the round-about, and continue straight towards the creek. **Al Seef Road** runs along the side of the creek, past the British Embassy, and ends at the Umm Hureir Roundabout not far from the Maktoum Bridge. It offers a scenic stroll, and uninterrupted views of Deira's interesting modern buildings across the creek.

Dubai's outskirts

Today, Jumeira/Umm Suqeim is a world-renowned destination for holiday-mak-ers. The most striking landmark on the coast is the 321-metre (1,053-ft) **Burj Al Arab**, which stands on its own island. **Wild Wadi Water Park** opposite, alongside the wave-shaped Jumeirah Beach Hotel, has 23 rides, including the Jumeirah Sceirah, the tallest freefall slide outside North America.

Just along the coast, the fabulous **Madinat Jumeirah**, completed in 2004 and built around a network of canals, is home to an Arabian souq, two luxury hotels, Dubai's first purpose-built theatre and a number of cafés and restaurants in a delightful re-imagining of old Arabia, complete with windtowers and *abras*.

Further west, along Al Sufouh Road, are the towering high-rises of **Dubai Marina**, which also has cafés and restaurants on its pleasant waterfront.

Located on Jumeira Road, between the city and its coastal resorts are Jumeira Mosque, the Italianate Mercato Mall and an interesting open-air museum, **Majlis Ghorfat Um Al Sheef ❶** (Al Ghureifa Majlis; Sat–Thur 9am–1pm), which has been created at the summer house of Sheikh Rashid bin Saeed Al Maktoum. To get there, from Jumeira Road heading out of the city, turn left at the first U-turn after the **Jumeirah Beach Park ⓜ**. It is well sign-posted, in a small street

BELOW:
Dubai Duty Free.

TAX-FREE BONANZA

Once an insignificant airport on the edge of the desert, Dubai's International Airport is today one of the most famous in the world, renowned for its huge choice of tax-free goods. Growth has increased steadily since 1983 – sevenfold in the first 10 years alone, as travellers flying between Europe and the Far East have found it worthwhile to route their journeys through Dubai. By the end of 2005 Dubai will have three terminals.

Abu Dhabi gradually joined the tax-free bandwagon and has now approached Dubai's reputation in the tax-free stakes. Alongside the usual duty-free items such as cig-arettes, perfume and spirits, the biggest attractions are the latest electronic goods, designer fashions, classic Swiss watches and gold jewellery at rock-bottom prices. Prize draws for luxury cars and vast sums of cash are commonplace. Dubai's duty-free complex is seen more as a lure to attract visitors than as a money-making oper-ation for the authorities, who waive concession fees, a factor that elsewhere can add 50–60 percent to prices charged to travellers.

Tax-free does not only apply to the great array of shops at Dubai and Abu Dhabi airports. The UAE levies no income tax, purchase tax or value-added tax. It is a tax-free country.

ear a branch of HSBC. The two-storey *sarooj* structure was built in 1955 to serve s a *majlis* and residence. The sea breezes at Jumeira offered relief from the heat f Dubai. Majlis Ghorfat Um Al Sheef was also a date palm farm that supplied s residents with a healthy food supply. The *falaj* system and *barasti* coffee shop re recent additions, and were incorporated to educate visitors on the broader spects of the local culture.

Map, below

hopping in Dubai

anian silk carpets, Bedu kilims and Kashmiri rugs are available throughout Dubai nd, due to the wide range and competitive prices, are affordable even to those on ie lowest budget. Rug shops are scattered throughout the city. The ground floor f Deira Tower on Deira's **Al Nasr Square**, the **BurJurman Shopping Centre** corner of Khalid bin Waleed Street and Trade Centre Road in Bur Dubai), **Markaz Al Jumeira** shopping complex on the Jumeira (Beach) Road, Mehreen arpets on **Al Diyafah Street** in Satwa, and the neighbouring emirate's Sharjah ouq, are all reputable carpet-trading establishments.

Like most modern cities, Dubai has several large, air-conditioned shopping malls. mong the more interesting are the Egypt-inspired **Wafi Centre**, **BurJuman** and s imposing new extension, **Mercato Mall**, **Ibn Battuta Mall** in Jebel Ali, and ie vast **Mall of the Emirates**, completed in 2005 and one of the largest in the orld – it even has an indoor ski slope. **Deira City Centre** is a perennial favourite.

There is a huge range of goods on sale from boxes inlaid with mother of pearl to electronics. For many people shopping is a major reason for visiting Dubai.

porting Dubai

amel racing is one of the most interesting local sports (*see* Camel Racing, *page 21*), and from October to May races are held on Thursday and Friday afternoons

BELOW: textile merchant.

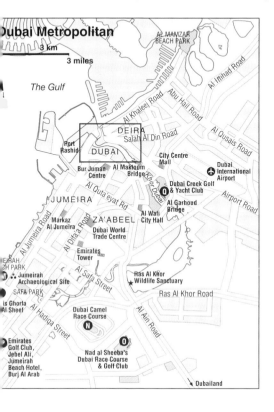

Dubai Metropolitan
3 km
3 miles

The Gulf

AL MAMZAR BEACH PARK
Al Ittihad Road
Abu Hail Road
Al Khaleej Road
DEIRA
Salah Al Din Road
Al Qusais Road
Port Rashid
DUBAI
City Centre Mall
Bur Juman Centre
Al Maktoum Bridge
Dubai International Airport
Khor Dubai
Dubai Creek Golf & Yacht Club
Airport Road
JUMEIRA
Al Quta eyat Rd
Al Garhoud Bridge
Markaz Al Jumeira
ZA'ABEEL
Al Wafi City Hall
Dubai World Trade Centre
Emirates Tower
JEIRAH CH PARK
Jumeirah Archaeological Site
Al Safa Street
Ras Al Khor Wildlife Sanctuary
SAFA PARK
Ras Al Khor Road
is Ghorfa Al Sheef
Al Hadiqa Street
Dubai Camel Race Course
Al Ain Road
Emirates Golf Club, Jebel Ali, Jumeirah Beach Hotel, Burj Al Arab
Nad al Sheeba's Dubai Race Course & Golf Club
Dubailand

from 2pm (free admission). Early morning races start just after 7am. The **Camel Race Course** is located on the southern section of Al Hadiqa Street (Safa Park exit from Sheikh Zayed Road – the tent-like roof of the grandstand is immediately visible). Also worth visiting is the camel auction yard adjacent to the track, where Bedu trainers and herdsmen wander around looking at the camels and goods on sale. If you are here around sunset, jockeys can be seen meandering across the tarmac on their camels to the pens and farms in the distant desert.

Nad Al Sheba Club ⓞ is on the same road as the Camel Race Course. Every Thursday evening in the cool winter months Dubai hosts a six-race meeting at the home of the prestigious US$6 million World Cup (*see* Kings of the Turf, *page 119*). The atmosphere is electric and the crowd a colourful, multi-cultural mixture.

Dubai Race Course and Golf Club, **Emirates Golf Club** ⓟ, and the **Dubai Creek Golf and Yacht Club** ⓠ are all international, 18-hole, grass golf courses created by American golf-course designer Karl Litten. They all boast distinguished architectural features, including the Emirates clubhouse, which is shaped like a Bedu tent. The annual Dubai Desert Classic, the first Middle East tournament on the PGA European circuit, is held at the Emirates Golf Club or at the Dubai Creek Golf and Yacht Club. **The Montgomerie** at Emirates Hills, designed by Colin Montgomerie, is one of the city's most popular courses. For an authentic desert course however, try **The Desert Course** at Arabian Ranches, designed by Ian Baker-Finch.

Dubai is also home to the annual Dubai Tennis Championships, featuring back-to-back men's ATP and women's WTA tournaments, held every February/March. The highlight of the sporting calendar is the world famous Dubai Rugby Sevens tournament, held in December at the Dubai Exiles ground in Ras Al Khor.

TIP

Betting on the horses at Nad Al Sheba Club is illegal but punters can enter the free "Pick Six" competition to win a new Mercedes, Rolls Royce or Range Rover.

BELOW: the Camel Race Course.

Dubailand

Enormous resources have gone into creating ever larger and grander leisure facilities, the most ambitious of which is **Dubailand**, a theme park near the airport that will be bigger than Disneyland and Disneyworld combined when it is finished in around 2018. It will comprise thrill rides, hotels, spas, sports facilities and malls. Some of these have already opened, including the Al Sahra Desert Resort, and Dubai Autodrome, a venue for racing, go-karting and rock concerts.

In the meantime, Dubai has a wealth of wonderful parks. Creekside Park, Al Mamzar Beach Park (on the north side of Al Hamriya Port), Jumeira Beach Park, Safa Park, Mushrif Park (turn right off Al Khawaneej Road, about 10 km/6 miles past Dubai International Airport) and Umm Suqeim Park have playground facilities, picnic areas and lush garden settings. Little expense has been spared. The beautifully landscaped Creekside Park, for example, has its own cable car system.

A trip to Hatta

An hour away by road to the east, but within Dubai emirate, is Hatta, a recommended excursion from Dubai city. The journey there cuts through wide gravel plains, high red sand dunes, date palm oases and the rugged Hajar Mountains. From Dubai, set out from the roundabout near the bird sanctuary at the end of the creek and take the road signposted to Al Awir. At Hebeb the mountains come into view and the colour of the sand begins to change. After a few kilometres, Margum oil field will appear on the right, and shortly after that a large dune, known as Big Red, looms on the left.

From the village of **Madam** the landscape flattens out into a gravel plain, and a wide wadi runs parallel to the road. Watch for camels during the next 30 km (18

Map, pages 208, 233

Ras Al Khor Sanctuary (Sat–Thur 9am–4pm; free) is Dubai's only nature reserve. A tidal lagoon that can host up to 15,000 birds on a single day, it lies at the southern end of the Creek, off Route E66 from Wafi City Mall to Al Ain. Permits are needed for groups of 6 or more (tel: 04-206 4240).

BELOW: aerial view showing Creek Golf Club.

Map, page 208

ABOVE: wading in the water, Hatta Pools, a cool escape from Dubai city.
BELOW: Hatta Heritage Village.

miles) as there is no fence to keep them off the tarmac. The road from Madam to Hatta passes through Omani territory – in fact, Hatta is surrounded by territory belonging to Oman, Ras al-Khaimah and Ajman. No visas are required, for this is simply an anomaly that occurred when the borders were drawn: the borderpost for Oman is about 5 km (3 miles) east of Hatta.

The approach to Hatta highlights the enormous contrasts in habitat that exist in Dubai. Beautiful beaches and open desert country give way to rocky mountain ranges. At Hatta the air is cooler and the lifestyle less arduous than in the hot desert or along the humid coast.

The Hajar Mountains were formed over 90 million years ago beneath the Tethys Sea. Their rugged shapes are seen to best advantage on the road to the village of **Huwaylat**. Go straight on from the Fort Roundabout in front of the entrance to the Hatta Fort Hotel, and turn left at the signpost. The winding road is 10 km (6 miles) long and shows how undeveloped much of the mountain region has remained.

Return to the Fort Roundabout and turn left to the old village of **Hatta ❸**. A municipality sign marks the left turn to the **Hatta Heritage Village**. The square fort, several houses, a farm fed by a *falaj* , and hilltop watchtowers give visitors a closer look at life in the UAE before modernisation. Burial tombs found close to the village revealed that settlement in Hatta dates back to 3000 BC.

Beyond the residential area of new Hatta is a gravel road that continues to the **Hatta Pools** (water catchment areas in the wadis) and the Omani villages of **Al Fay** and **Rayy**. This is four-wheel-drive terrain that is best explored with assistance. The luxurious **Hatta Fort Hotel**, with its lovely gardens, offers tours with experienced drivers and guides. It is also a good place to lunch and swim after an adventure into the mountains and wadis. ❑

A Taste for Grand Designs

Just as Dubai is ambitious to overtake Hong Kong as a centre of trade, so Dubai's citizens like to think big when it comes to building projects. Until recently, the most famous of these was the magnificent, sail-shaped Burj al-Arab, the only seven-star hotel on the planet, whose lobby is high enough to accommodate the Eiffel Tower.

Now, 6 km (4 miles) off the Emirates coast, two artificial islands have been built, each in the shape of a palm tree. They are so large that they are one of only two man-made structures in the world that can be seen from space with the naked eye (the other, of course, being the Great Wall of China). Some 100 million cubic metres of sand and stone were required to create just one of the islands, enough to build a 2-metre high wall around the globe three times.

The two artificial islands, Palm Jumeirah and Palm Jebel Ali, give Dubai an additional 120 km (75 miles) of sandy beach. This was one of the major reasons for creating the palm-shaped islands, which are dotted with super-deluxe hotels, around 4,000 exclusive villas (each with its own private stretch of beach), plus water parks, marinas, shopping malls, health spas, entertainment complexes, etc. Palm Jebel Jumeirah, the smaller of the two islands, has 17 fronds, a 2-km (1¼-mile) trunk and an arc-like breakwater measuring 11 km (7 miles) from end to end, which offers a sheltered habitat for tropical fish. It incorporates its own underwater dive site, comprising copies of the world's most famous reef habitats. The "Lost City", inspired by the mythical city of Atlantis, incorporates ruined temples and an underwater Pyramid.

Palm Jebel Ali features a ring of water homes on stilts, arranged in such a fashion as to spell out a verse from a poem ("Take wisdom from the wise people – not everyone who rides is a jockey") by Sheikh Mohammed, the original driving force behind the Palm developments. A third palm-shaped island, The Palm Deira is also underway. This will be the largest of the palm tree developments, measuring 14 km (8½ miles) in length and 8.5 km (5 miles) wide, with 41 fronds, on which will stand some 8,000 two-storey villas, plus high-profile offices, leisure amenities, etc.

Nakheel, the property developer in charge of the Palms, is pushing the land reclamation concept further. Its latest grand project is "The World", a mini-archipelago of 250–300 islands, some intended for private ownership, others housing small, exclusive communities, arranged in the shape of a world map.

On a more practical level, work is pressing ahead on a new light railway, the Dubai Metro, comprising 70 km (44 miles) of track and some 47 stations on two lines (Red and Green). Parts of the Red Line are due to open in September 2009 and the whole system should be completed in 2012. It is hoped that the Metro will entice Dubai residents out of their cars by offering an efficient service with stations strategically sited and linked. The carriages will be stylish and comfortable, with two classes – gold and silver – as well as carriages exclusively for women and children.   ❑

Right: the magnificent Burj al-Arab hotel.

SHARJAH

*In the shadow of Dubai, Sharjah is often overlooked
by visitors, but it has some fine old architecture and
atmospheric souqs. At one time it was the leading Trucial State*

t's Sharjah's good fortune to have been included in Sir Wilfred Thesiger's 1959 book *Arabian Sands*. It's just a shame that Thesiger, respected chronicler of the Arab world, didn't like it. "We approached a small Arab town on an open beach," he wrote, "it was as Arab and tumble-down as Abu Dhabi, but infinitely more squalid, for it was littered with discarded rubbish which had been mass-produced elsewhere."

It's indicative of the amazing pace of change in the UAE that less than 50 years later "drab", "tumble-down", "squalid" Sharjah is regarded as the UAE's heritage centre, famed for its architecture and souqs.

Its ruler, Sheikh Dr Sultan bin Mohammed Al Qasimi, instigated the restoration and reconstruction of buildings in the Al Marija and Al Souq Al Shuheen districts in the early 1990s. The resulting clusters of coral-stone museums, with their cool, high-sided alleyways and attractive windtowers, offer glimpses of what life was like here 100 years before Thesiger arrived.

Although the city, capital of the country's third largest emirate, is now overshadowed by Abu Dhabi and Dubai, it's older than both. Recorded references to Sharjah, which means "Eastern" in Arabic, date back to at least 1490, when the Arab navigator Ahmad ibn Majid wrote that ships could find it if they followed the stars from the island of Tunb. On a map of 1669, the city is called Quiximi, after the Qasimi family, ancestors of the present ruler. In the 18th century, the Dutch knew Sharjah as Scharge.

By the time British interests developed in the late 18th century, the city was a stronghold from which the seafaring Qasimis, known as the Qawasim or Joasmees, dominated the Arabian Gulf. In 1819 the British, alarmed by the power of the Qawasim, attacked and destroyed its fleet and bases at Sharjah and Ras Al Khaimah. Sharjah's standing did not diminish, however. Throughout the 19th century it remained the leading city on the Trucial Coast and the second most important port in the Gulf after Kuwait. The Sheikh of the Qawasim, Sultan bin Saqr – great-great grandfather to the present ruler – chose Sharjah as his headquarters. From 1823, Britain's resident political agent for the Trucial States and Oman lived here (the political agency didn't move to Dubai until 1954).

The British built the Trucial States' first airport on Sharjah's outskirts in 1932 and maintained a military presence there until independence in 1971. Sharjah was the headquarters of the British-sponsored Trucial Oman Scouts and in 1970 the staging post for Special Air Service (SAS) operations in Oman.

The city's fortunes waned in the 1940s when Khalid Creek silted up and sea trade was diverted to Dubai. Fortunes improved with the discovery of offshore oil in 1972 and the dredging of the creek, but the oil price

PRECEDING PAGES:
Sharjah's Central
Souq, depicted on
the Dhs5 banknote.
LEFT: by the Book.
BELOW: modern
communication.

crash of 1985 left Sharjah in debt. In 1992, major new natural gas and condensate discoveries improved the economy to the extent that the city's motto: "Smile You Are In Sharjah" has never seemed more appropriate.

City sights

Al Arsa Souq, a good place to browse for antique daggers.

UNESCO awarded Sharjah the Cultural Capital of the Arab World title in 1998 and evidence of this can still be seen in the beautifully restored Heritage Area between Hisn Avenue and Corniche Road.

Most sights are within walking distance of **Arouba Road**, Sharjah's main street which runs northeast from Khalid Lagoon through the city centre. The surrounding streets, crammed with textile and perfume shops, come alive after dark. To the west of the road lie the old districts of Al Marija and Al Souq Al Shuheen, with **Al Borj Avenue** (Bank Street) cutting between them. **Al Marija**, south of Al Borj, is a delight to explore. **Al Arsa Souq Ⓐ** (daily 9am–1pm and 4.30–10.30pm), made from coral-stone, lime and plaster and topped with palm fronds, is lined with small antique and souvenir shops. Here a few pearl traders still buy and sell, the last participants in an industry that in the 19th century sent more boats to the pearl banks than Dubai. In the evening the souq's coffee house is where elderly local men, dressed in traditional robes, while away the hours between prayers at one of the district's three mosques.

The rooftops are dotted with minarets and windtowers, early forms of air-conditioning designed to catch and circulate breezes *(see page 231)*. The most distinctive tower is the round one above **Majlis of Ibrahim Mohammed Al Madfa Ⓑ** (Sat–Thur 8.30am–1pm and 5–8pm, Fri 5–8pm), the only one of its kind in the Trucial States. In addition to founding the region's first newspaper, *Oman*, in 1927,

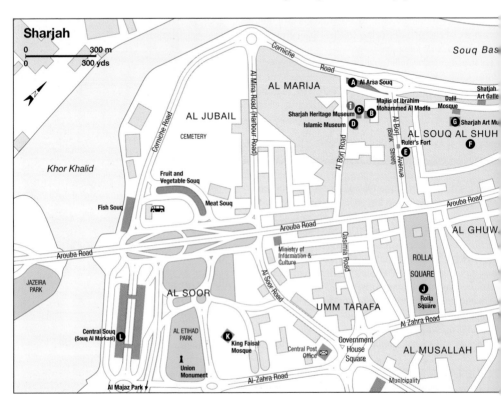

Ibrahim Mohammed Al Madfa acted as adviser to the ruling Al Qasimi family. His *majlis*, where he would receive business guests, is now a small **museum** (open daily; Friday, evening only) housing some of his personal effects.

The nearby home of wealthy trading family Al Naboodah, an atmospheric two-storey collection of rooms around a colonnaded courtyard, has become **Sharjah Heritage Museum ●** (Sat–Thur 9am–1pm and 5–8pm, Fri 5–8pm). A tour of its colourful displays of regional costumes, jewellery and restored bedrooms is invariably followed by an invitation to recline on Bedu cushions and enjoy a cardamom-flavoured coffee with one of the guides.

Behind the Naboodah residence, a splendid building formerly housing a souq is now the **Sharjah Museum of Islamic Civilization ●** (Sat–Thur 8am–8pm, Fri 4–8pm). A showcase for artefacts from Islamic countries, the museum aims to stimulate knowledge and appreciation of Islamic art, science, history and culture.

On Al Borj Avenue (known as Bank Street), the **Ruler's Fort ●** (9am–1pm and 5–8pm; Mon and Fri am), demolished before the possibilities of tourism were envisaged, has been painstakingly rebuilt as another heritage museum. To the west of it, on the far side of **Khalid Creek**, the skeletal frames of oil rigs in **Port Khalid** contrast with the masts of more traditional wooden vessels moored at the **dhow wharf** parallel to **Corniche Road**. The Corniche, a short walk from the fort, is a hive of activity in the cooler mornings and evenings, when goods from Iran, India and Pakistan are unloaded onto the quayside.

Inland from the Corniche, north of Al Borj Avenue, is **Al Souq Al Shuheen ●** district, the trading centre of old Sharjah, where women dressed in flowing black robes and wearing traditional *burqa* face masks are still a common sight. Several old storefronts on the Corniche mark the beginning of the souq, but in the main it

Map, pages 242–3

Following Dubai's success in attracting international sporting events, Sharjah has become a venue for world-class cricket and now hosts the Sharjah Cup.

BELOW: in the Sharjah sun.

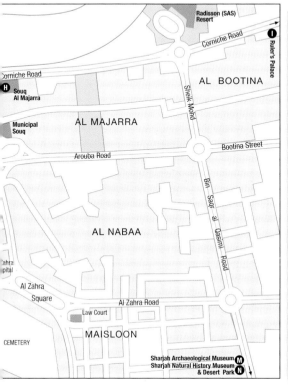

is now a jumble of fluorescent lighting and plastic, topped with corrugated zinc

Narrow alleyways connect the souq with the former home of Eisa bin Abdu Letif Al Rurkai, British resident agent from 1919–1935. In the 1960s the 150-year old building became an American missionary hospital specialising in gynaecol ogy. Across the road is the purpose-built **Sharjah Art Museum G** (Sat–Thu 9am–1pm and 5–8pm, Fri 5–8pm) in the newly declared Arts Area. An imposing modern building, it nonetheless remains in keeping with others in the area, one c which is the restored **Ad Dalil Mosque**, next to the museum and said to be the old est mosque in Sharjah. Between the mosque and Al Borj Avenue is **The Collec tion of H.H. Sheikh Sultan bin Mohammed Al-Qasimi**, a building that houses the ruler's private collection of 300 artworks by the likes of 18th-century orientalis David Roberts, as well as other oils, watercolours and lithographs. Fronting the Corniche is Bait Obaid Al Shamsi, which houses **Sharjah Art Galleries**, one c the venues for the Sharjah Biennial art exhibition.

Further north along Corniche Road is **Souq Al Majarra H**. Golden-dome with an attractive terracotta and grey stone finish, it opened in 1987. To the north the imposing **Radisson SAS Resort, Sharjah**, dominates the entrance to the cree and has its own sandy beach. Behind it stands the modern **Ruler's Palace I**.

To the east of Arouba Road is **Rolla Square J**, such a popular meeting plac for the large Indian Keralite community that each village has its own particula banyan tree. The original banyan is remembered by a sculpture with a hollow centre in the shape of a tree. Fountains at each end of the park are guarded by cannons. Stone columns brought from India in 1926 are dotted around the edges

Rolla is a popular meeting place on Thursday evenings, Fridays and on National Day (2 December), but Emiratis prefer to picnic in **Al Majaz Park**

TIP

In an impressive building on the water-front is the new **Sharjah Aquarium**. Opened in June 2008, its displays of colourful and dramatic marine life are great for adults and kids alike. For opening times, visit www.sharjah aquarium.ae.

BELOW: Rolla Square.

near the banks of **Khalid Lagoon**, in the newer Buhaira district to the south. The lagoon has the world's third-largest water fountain, after Geneva and Jeddah. The 100-metre (330-ft) fountain can be best enjoyed at sunset from the lagoon's northeastern shore. South-west of the lagoon, a man-made canal feeds into Al Khan Lagoon at the attractive **Qanat Al Qasba** development, a venue for cultural events and the **'Eye of the Emirates'** observation wheel.

At the eastern end of Rolla Park lies Al Zahra Road, which connects the Al Zahra Roundabout (**Clocktower Roundabout**) with **Government House Square**. Despite the grand title, the square, which also has Sharjah's main post office, is bland.

Al Ittihad Square is verdant in comparison. At the lagoon end of Arouba Road, it boasts **Al Ittihad Monument**, unveiled in 1989, whose seven pearl branches symbolise the unity of the seven emirates. **King Faisal Mosque** , with room for 3,000 worshippers and one of the largest mosques in the UAE, is on one side of the square in what was once the turning circle for aircraft using the original Sharjah airport. The runway is now King Abd Al Aziz Street and the original fortress-resthouse, built in 1932 when Sharjah was a stopover on Imperial Airways' London to India and Australia routes, can still be seen to the north of the road. Housing the aviation-themed **Al Mahattah Museum** (9am–1pm and 5–8pm; closed Mon and Fri am), the fort was the UAE's first hotel and cinema. Among the aircraft on display are a World War II-era Avro Anson and a Douglas DC3, which belonged to the Gulf Aviation Co., the forerunner of Gulf Air.

At the lagoon end of Al Ittihad Square is the superb **Central Souq** (Souq Al Markasi or Blue Souk), a landmark building depicted on the country's Dhs5 banknote (*pictured on pages 238–9 of this book*). The first floor antique and

Map, pages 242–3

TIP

In 1985 Sharjah's Sheikh banned the sale of alcohol. To offset a subsequent loss of business among expats, restaurateurs have kept prices much lower than their counterparts in Dubai, a short distance away.

BELOW: Khalid Lagoon at dusk.

Maps, pp 242–3, 208

Songbirds, a popular home accessory, for sale in Sharjah's animal market

BELOW: Khor Kalba.
OPPOSITE: Sharjah's fish market.

carpet shops are particularly interesting and attract souvenir-hunting visitors staying in other emirates. Persian carpets are a speciality.

Nearby, water taxis *(abra)* offer enjoyable excursions around the lagoon and to the mouth of the creek. The 10-sq. km (4-sq. mile) **Jazeira Park**, on an island but connected to the city centre by Sharjah Bridge, is just a short walk away.

On the lagoon-end of Al Arouba, but on the opposite side of a road flyover from Central Souq, is the **fish market**. The best time to watch restaurateurs bidding for sharks' fins and the like is early morning. The nearby **fruit and vegetable market** is a riot of colour, especially pleasant to visit in the evening, when its outdoor stalls are lit by hissing kerosene lamps. The **meat market** next to it is not for the squeamish. A live **animal market**, selling everything from falcons to cows, is tucked behind shops and restaurants on the south side of nearby Al Mina Road. Most of the falcons are imported from India or Pakistan.

Sharjah Archaeology Museum ⓜ (Sat–Thur 9am–1pm and 5–8pm, Fri 5–8pm) stands in the northern suburbs near the Ruler's Office and close to an impressive Qur'an monument at Cultural Roundabout (on the road to the international airport and the town of Dhaid). Completed in 1992, the purpose-built museum has two storeys of exhibition rooms showcasing objects from Sharjah's past – from finds at the ancient town of Mileiha *(see below)* to the 1930s and more recent times, as well as Islamic antiquities.

Sharjah Natural History Museum and Desert Park ⓝ (Sat–Wed 9am–7pm, Thur noon–7pm, Fri 2–8pm), the headquarters for the Arabian Leopard Trust, which is dedicated to saving the animal from extinction *(see page 203)*, is beyond the airport on the left side of the Sharjah-Dhaid highway. The museum has five exhibition halls featuring displays on UAE geology (including a section documenting the story of oil), ecology, flora and fauna and marine life. The site also houses the Arabian Wildlife centre and a children's farm.

Outside the city

Dhaid ❹ an ancient inland oasis 50 km (30 miles) east of the city and roughly halfway between Sharjah's Arabian Gulf coast and Gulf of Oman coast (it's the only emirate to have two such coasts) is worth visiting if only to see that parts of Arabia can be incredibly fertile. Irrigation in Dhaid is based on ancient *falaj* water courses *(see page 156)* that run from the foot of the Hajar Mountains, but the supply is now a trickle and is topped up with mains water.

To the south of Dhaid are the 4th-century BC ruins at **Mileiha** ❺, where excavations have revealed a necropolis of large, monumental tombs, a fort and graves containing sacrificed camels and horses *(see page 25)*, while on the Gulf of Oman coast, **Khor Kalba** ❻ is home to a 2,000-year-old mangrove swamp and one of the world's most famous shell beaches. Such sites were attractive to early settlers, as the mangrove swamps were a rich source of easily obtainable food such as shellfish and birds.

In 1936 Britain recognised Kalba as independent from Sharjah in an attempt to persuade the local sheikh, Said bin Hamad, to grant landing rights for British planes. However, Kalba eventually rejoined the state of Sharjah in 1951. ❑

AJMAN

The smallest of the seven emirates, Ajman is almost a suburb of Sharjah. Its chief attraction for visitors is its traditional dhow-building yards

Map, page 252

Abu Dhabi
UNITED ARAB EMIRATES

At 259 sq. km (100 sq. miles), Ajman is the smallest of the UAE's seven emirates. Its main territory, surrounded by Sharjah, basks along the sunscorched beaches of the Arabian Gulf coast. But there are also two inland enclaves, the fertile mountain villages of Masfut and Manama, to the southeast and east of the modest port town that passes for the emirate's capital.

Ajman town, 8 km (5 miles) north of Sharjah, is known for its dhow-building heritage. Pearling dhows sailed from its shores from the 3rd century BC until the 1930s, when the stiff easterly winds of competition, from Japanese cultured pearls, swept them – and the men who worked on them – into the history books. Fishing dhows are still made on Ajman's sheltered creek, though today most are made of fibreglass.

Ajman hasn't experienced the oil and gas bonanzas enjoyed by other emirates, but it has cashed in on them by updating its boatyard tradition: its port now houses one of the UAE's largest ship repair companies, which maintains oilfield supply boats along more than 5 km (3 miles) of creekside wharfage.

The town has a proud media heritage, too. In 1961, the Public Radio Station, the UAE's first, was established here by Rashid Abdullah Ali bin Hamdha. Powered with dry batteries and supported by public donations, the station broadcast readings from the Qur'an, speeches of the Prophet Mohammed, poems and songs until it closed in 1965. Today, Ajman's television channel, Channel 4, competes for viewers with global satellite networks. But it still maintains its predecessor's tradition of readings from the holy book.

Apart from Ajman's dhow-building yards, the biggest draw for visitors is its excellent fortress museum, which, with its sand-plastered round-towers, deliberate parapets and lack of windows, looks like a magnificent sandcastle.

Ajman's sights

It's possible to see Ajman in a day; at the widest point of its tapered north-facing promontory, just 2.5 km (1½ miles) of streets and sandy lanes separate the Gulf from the creek.

For visitors arriving from Sharjah on the coastal Arabian Gulf Street, the first of the town's rather limited number of sights is a crumbling **watchtower** that stands guard over a long sandy beach. Most of the UAE's defensive watchtowers are round, but, unusually, this one is square. Created from dirt, sand and stone, it looks as if it was constructed by a colony of African ants working from a blueprint of the squat parapeted tower of an English Norman church.

For visitors in the summer, when the temperatures soar into the high 40°s C (over 110–120°F) with high

PRECEDING PAGES: shadows in the boatyards. **LEFT:** the fortress housing Ajman Museum. **BELOW:** a school girl caught by a camera.

humidity, nearby **juice shops** offer a variety of thirst-quenching fruit concoctions which will reinvigorate them for the 3-km (2-mile) walk through the town centre to the fort.

From the coast road, Khalid bin Al Waleed Street leads to the **Ruler's Palace Ⓐ**, which stands on the south side of the junction with Kasr Az Zahr Street and Sheikh Rashid Street. The palace, home to Sheikh Humaid bin Rashid Al Nuaimi, who succeeded his father in 1981, is not open to the public, but it's possible to peer into the leafy compound from its main gate.

Sheikh Rashid Street, a tree-lined road of carpet and tricycle shops, runs north from the palace. Together with **Hamad bin Abdul Aziz Street**, a street of banks and ubiquitous camera shops that continues northwards, it forms Ajman's main thoroughfare. A new shopping centre, Ajman City Centre, offers a Continent hypermarket, Magic Planet amusement centre and other outlets.

The must-see fortress, which has housed **Ajman Museum Ⓑ** (Sun–Wed 9am–1pm and 4–7pm, Thur 9am–noon, Fri 4–7pm) since the 1980s, is just off Clocktower Roundabout and Central Square. Built around 1775, this building was the ruler's residence until 1970 and the police headquarters from 1970–78. The museum showcases life in the region from ancient times to the modern era with *barasti* houses and dhows just beyond the entrance and, in the old fort proper, displays on policing (practised since the days of the Prophet Mohammed in the 7th century), the bedroom of Sheikh Rashid bin Humaid Al Nuaimi (1928–81), and a market tableau.

The museum's Traditional Medicine Hall has bottles of medicinal red mud, mercury and coconut oil, amongst others, and a fascinating section on Qur'anic treatments. In one, a pious elder would write verses from the holy book on a

Windtower at Ajman Museum

BELOW: a dhow and a traditional palm-frond canoe at Ajman Museum.

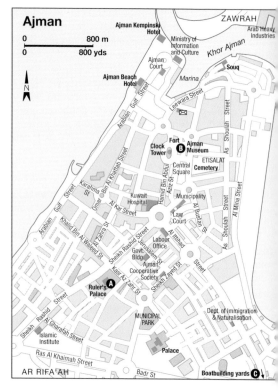

white china bowl using a mix of saffron and rose water for ink. The inscription was then washed with rosewater and the collected solution given to the patient to drink or rub on the affected part of his body.

The museum also has an excellent example of a windtower *(barjeel)* open on four sides to catch breezes and disperse rising hot air. Benches have been placed under it for visitors to sit in the *majlis* with the cooing pigeons that congregate in its rafters. Beyond the fort, off Leewara Street and alongside a marina where wooden dhows jostle with modern leisure craft, are Ajman's bustling **souqs**, selling bric-a-brac, vegetables, meat and fish.

On the other side of the marina, at the northern end of Arabian Gulf Street, hotels will let you soak up the sun on their **beaches** for a small fee. They also serve alcohol to non-Muslims, except during Ramadan. The five-star Ajman Kempinski Hotel and Resort has a beautiful beach, luxurious rooms and many recreational facilities, along with several good restaurants and bars.

Ajman's **boatbuilding yards ⑥** are on the creek, a taxi ride from the town centre. Two of the most accessible are on **Tareq bin Ziyad Street** in the Mushairef district. Typically, a primitive production line of fishing dhow hulls are propped up on oil drums. Although most boats are made of fibreglass now, the deck rails that rise toward the stern are still made of wood.

Away from the coast, **Masfut ⑦** is at the foot of the Hajar Mountains near the Dubai enclave of Hatta, 100 km (62 miles) southeast of Ajman town. It's known for its tobacco.

The date palms, citrus trees and reputedly haunted fort of more accessible **Manama ⑧**, "the sleeping place", are near Dhaid, 60 km (37 miles) east of Ajman town. ❑

Maps, pages 252, 208

BELOW: building boats.

UMM AL QAIWAIN

The second-smallest emirate and the least populated, UAQ is something of a backwater. Its main activity is fishing, and there is a strong flavour of the Subcontinent

Maps, 208 & below

U mm Al Qaiwain may be known locally as UAQ, after the letters on its car licence plates, but it's no LA or KL – initials do not a city make. The north-ern Emirates town is a sleepy backwater of low buildings and backyard palm trees on a sandy spit well off the main highway that links Ajman, some 20 km (12 miles) southwest, with Ras Al Khaimah.

It may not be the smallest Emirate in terms of land area (Ajman is) but it's the least populous. UAQ's 40,000 residents would be pushed to fill Abu Dhabi's Sheikh Zayed sports stadium, and in the heat of the day there are more animals than people on its streets: scrawny cats that dart down back alleys in big-eyed alarm; goats that munch discarded tea bags at its roadsides; and cows that graze on patchy scrub around three defensive watchtowers that stand at the neck of the old town promontory like fortified links in a chain.

The emirate belongs as much to animals as anything. The island of **As Siniyyah ⑨**, visible from the old town's Corniche Road and site of the origi-nal settlement until sweetwater supplies ran out, is a wildlife haven. Herons nest among the mangrove trees at the water's edge; cormorants, turtles and sea-snakes are not uncommon; dugong, or sea cows, swim in its shallows. With an estimated dugong population of 1,000, the UAE is the world's second-largest sanctuary for the curious-looking mammal, known in Arabic as *arus al bahar* (sea-bride). Archaeological excavations on the island of Akab revealed that inhabi-tants were hunting dugong 5,000 years ago.

Permission is needed to visit As Siniyyah, but along the coast to the south and east of UAQ town, **Khor Al Beidah ⑩** holds further delights for naturalists – bird-watchers, in particular. It hosts the country's largest wintering flock of Crab Plover, the rare Great Knot (pre-viously thought to winter only in the Far East and Aus-tralasia), the Greater Sand Plover, Whimbrel and Terek Sandpiper. Its intertidal mudflats, islands and man-groves are bounded inland by *sabkha* (salt flats) and dunes that host breeding larks. In winter Isabelline and Desert Wheatear, Desert Warbler and Tawny Pipit are as common in these parts as coffee and dates.

City sights

It takes little more than a day to see Umm Al Qaiwain. Its name means, in Arabic, "mother of the powers", reflect-ing a long seafaring tradition that is today maintained by Indian and Bangladeshi fishermen and, by those who take to its warm coastal waters in rental motor boats.

The three defensive **watchtowers ⓐ** off Al Soor Road, to the west of King Faisal Road, are a good place to begin a walking tour of the old town. Round and of differing sizes, they were once joined together by a sturdy protective wall which has been partially rebuilt.

United Arab Emirates

Abu Dhabi

UAQ 9003

PRECEDING PAGES: abstract pattern on a gate, Umm al Qaiwan. **LEFT:** the fishing industry is still important in UAQ.

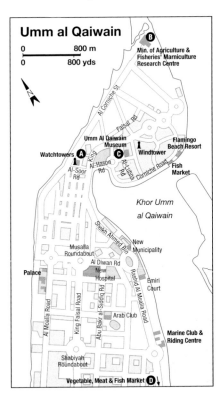

Umm al Qaiwain

0   800 m
0   800 yds

Min. of Agriculture & Fisheries' Marniculture Research Centre

Al Corniche St.

Faisal Rd.

Umm Al Qaiwain Museum
Watchtowers ⓐ

Al King
Al-Soor Rd.
Al-Hason Rd.

Al Corniche Road
Al Ubba Rd.

Flamingo Beach Resort
Windtower

Fish Market

Khor Umm al Qaiwain

Sheikh Ahmed Bin
Musalla Roundabout
New Municipality

Al Diwan Rd
Palace
New Hospital

Rashid Al Moalla Road
Emiri Court

Al Moalla Road
King Faisal Road
Abu Bakr al-Siddiq Rd
Arab Club

Marine Club & Riding Centre

Shabiyah Roundabout
Vegetable, Meat & Fish Market ⓓ

The Ministry of Agriculture and Fisheries' **Marniculture and Research Centre** ❸ (Sat–Wed 7.30am–1.30pm, Thur 7.30am–noon) can be reached by following Al Soor Road west, to the Arabian Gulf, and then turning right. The centre is working to increase sea-based food production and has an aquarium and research laboratory devoted to marine fauna.

On the creek side of Al Soor Road, Al Hason Road passes a small but surprisingly lush public park on its way to UAQ's fortress, which stands at the junction with Al Lubna Road. Established by Sheikh Rashid bin Majid Al Mualla in 1768 as a residence, and a seat of government until 1969 after which it served as a police station, the fort is now home to **Umm Al Qaiwain Museum** ❻ (Sat–Sun, Tues–Thur 8am–1pm and 5–8pm, Fri 5–8pm). A tumbledown coral-stone merchant's house behind it provides an interesting dissection of traditional architecture.

South along Al Lubna Road lies Corniche Road, where UAQ's main activity, fishing, is much in evidence. The **Flamingo Beach Resort**, formerly the Umm Al Qaiwain Tourist Centre, has good rooms, a pleasant atmosphere and an attractive, safe beach for swimming or sunbathing. Among the sea-based activities on offer here are sport fishing charters in search of blue marlin, and night-time crab-hunting expeditions in the mangroves.

There is a strong Subcontinental feel to the old town: posters for Bollywood movies are plastered on walls, its restaurants sell *biriyani*, its pavements are stained red with beteljuice, and its dusty roads are home to boxy Padmini cars, imported from India.

Corniche Road loops around the old town to become King Faisal Road. In the streets in the centre of the loop are flour mills, small general stores and textile

TIP

The Flamingo Resort boasts one of the capital's four bars (the others are in the Ciaq Beach Hotel, the Barracuda Resort and the Pearl Hotel).

BELOW: a cruise ship docks.

traders. Minarets are taller than the houses here, and cast long shadows in the sandy back lanes. On the rooftops, three old windtowers *(see page 231)* mingle with the satellite dishes.

On Al Moalla Road you will find the emirate's most ostentatious buildings, the beachside homes of UAQ ruler Sheikh Rashid bin Ahmad Al Mualla's family. From the junction of Al Moalla Road and Aqba bin Nafa Road, it is a short walk to the modest vegetable, meat and fish **market ⑩** on Sheikh Ahmed bin Rashid Al Moalla Road.

Outside the city

The archaeological site of **Ad Door ⑪** is opposite Khor Al Beidah, off the coastal highway that passes about 10 km (6 miles) south of the town centre. The 2,000-year-old remains of the settlement, which means "the houses" in Arabic, were exposed by archaeologists from Belgium, France, Australia and Britain. Ad Door, separated from the road by undulating dunes, is thought to have been "Omana", noted by classical geographers as an important trading emporium and one of the largest towns in Arabia. *The Periplus of the Erythraean Sea*, a description of trade around the coast of the Indian Ocean written by a Greek sailor in the employ of the Roman navy in the 1st century AD, mentions Omana. Archaeological evidence confirms that Ad Door had commercial links with India and the eastern Mediterranean.

One of the UAE's best water parks is 17 km (10½ miles) north of the Umm Al Qaiwain turn-off, on the way to Ras Al Khaimah. **Dreamland Aqua Park ⑫** (daily: Mar–May 10am–7pm; June–Oct 10am–9pm; Nov–Feb 10am–6pm; www.dreamlanduae.com) has 25 water rides, as well as go-karting. ❑

Maps, pages 257, 208

Smart address, Al Moalla Road

BELOW: the fortress.

RAS AL KHAIMAH

Map, below

*The base of the Qawasim "pirates" in the 19th century,
Ras al Khaimah was once a powerful maritime state.
Today RAK is known for its restful beauty*

For centuries **Ras al Khaimah** has been renowned as a place "where dwell persons of great wealth, great navigators and traders" (Duarte Barbosa, *c.* 1510). It is a fertile area rich in resources with extensive date palm groves, grazing plains for sheep and cattle, and abundant sea life. The natural beauty of the high mountains, coastal sand dunes and native plants and animals have made it a favoured place for both residents and visitors to the UAE.

The ruling family of Ras Al Khaimah are Al Qawasim (plural of Qasimi), who claim to be *sharifs*, descendants of the Prophet Mohammed. In 711 the General Mohammed (born Al Qasim Al Thaqafi) laid the foundations of the Muslim colony of Sind by converting all who lived between Fars Province, Persia and the mouth of Indus south of Karachi. The Hawala, the parent clan of the Qawasim, have inhabited both sides of the Arabian Gulf for millennia.

During maritime conflicts with the British in the early 1800s the Qawasim were referred to as "pirates" *(see page 34)*. At the time the British had aligned themselves with the sultan of Oman and disliked the trading strength of the Qawasim in India. The Qasimi considered the British intrusion unsustainable and a fierce naval campaign resulted. In 1806 Sheikh Sultan bin Saqr signed a treaty with the British agreeing "not to molest English ships in the future". The piratical reputation of the people of Ras al Khaimah has been corrected by recent history books.

PRECEDING PAGES AND LEFT: the waterfront in Ras al Khaimah.

City sights

The Old Town of Ras al Khaimah, first settled in around 1500, is right on the sea, bordering the mouth of the *khor* (creek) and is easily discovered on foot. From Ras al Khaimah Museum, on Al Hosn Road, walk along the small street lined with tailors and fabric shops, with the long, white-sand beach and the Corniche straight ahead. Turn right at the Corniche and walk towards the boat-building yards at the far end. A beautiful crenellated mud-brick mosque stands out on a small rise overlooking the sea. The road continues around to the right and follows the shore of the *khor*. The shops here have quaint wooden shutters and sell grain, fabric, household items and camel sticks.

Take the first left-hand turn to visit **Al Abrah Market**, a small group of stalls set up on the shore of the creek. On a gravel area opposite this market fish nets are prepared daily by local fishermen, and large rolls of *barasti* (palm fronds) are stored for sale to local farmers. On the same road, under the impressively long Khor Bridge, is Ras al Khaimah's colourful fruit and vegetable market, with its extensive range of fresh produce.

The **National Museum of Ras al Khaimah** Ⓐ (Wed–Mon 8am–12 noon and 4–7pm, closed Fri during Ramadan) is housed in a 19th-century fort. Until the

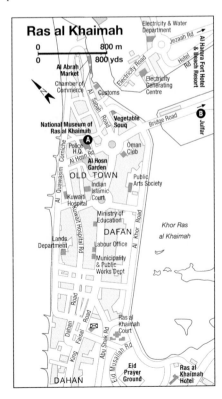

Ras al Khaimah

0 — 800 m
0 — 800 yds

Electricity & Water Department
Jezaah Rd
Al Hamra Fort Hotel & Beach Resort
Hotel Rd
Al Abrah Market
Chamber of Commerce
Electricity Road
Customs
Electricity Generating Centre
Bridge Road
Al Sabah Road
National Museum of Ras al Khaimah Ⓐ
Vegetable Souq
Ⓑ Julfar
Police H.Q.
Corniche
Al Hosn Rd
Oman Club
Al Quawasim
Al Hosn Garden
OLD TOWN
Indian Islamic Court
Public Arts Society
Al Kuwaiti Hospital
Ministry of Education
Al Khor Road
Khor Ras al Khaimah
Lands Department
Al Kuwait Hospital Rd
DAFAN
Labour Office
Municipality & Public Works Dept
Dahan Road
Ras al Khaimah Court
King Faisal Road
Abu Shak Rd
Eid Musallah Rd
Eid Prayer Ground
Ras al Khaimah Hotel
DAHAN

early 1960s it was the home of Sheikh Saqr bin Mohammed Al Qasimi, Ruler of the emirate since 1948, and then used as a prison until it was developed as a museum in the 1980s. The impressive building includes several styles of construction, a defensive staggered entrance and a magnificent windtower. Inside, displays include ancient manuscripts, coins minted in Samarkand, Tashkent, Baghdad and Sohar during the 10th century, finds made by archaeologists in the region, local jewellery, costumes, furniture and natural history displays.

Beyond the Old Town, modern Ras al Khaimah expands. Houses and commercial buildings spread from the shore of the creek to the edge of the majestic Hajar Mountains, a range formed about 200 million years ago and running from the Musandam into northern Oman. The Hajar are Eastern Arabia's oldest mountain group. Great for a weekend stay is the luxurious new **Al Hamra Fort Hotel and Beach Resort** between the sea and lagoon on the way to Ras al Khaimah. The hotel has a long stretch of beach, offers many leisure activities and has excellent restaurants.

Ancient Julfar

The predecessor of modern-day Ras al Khaimah was **Julfar** , a flourishing trading port dating back to around AD 200 but which had disappeared by the mid-1600s. Streets, houses, a fort and a mosque of the city were excavated during the 1980s, but evidence pre-AD 300 has yet to be found. Like Ubar in the Dhofar, ancient Julfar was always considered a mythical place, but archaeological evidence and records show that it is located north of Ras al Khaimah.

To reach Julfar from Ras al Khaimah, cross the bridge to Al Nakheel and turn left at the first set of traffic lights. After two more sets of lights turn right at the T-junction, and take the U-turn back to the left. Take the first right, continue for about 2 km (1 mile), then turn left about 50 metres/yds after the only service station on this road, with the sea directly ahead. An abandoned house standing alone marks the entrance to the site.

From about 900 Julfar was a rival to Sohar in Oman, reputedly the home of Sindbad the Sailor and cornerstone of trade from Asia into medieval Europe. Arab geographers such as Al Idrisi (writing in 1154) and a Yaqut Al Hamawi (c. 1250) described how fertile the region was, how at Sharm there was "a sizeable river that flowed out to the sea close to Julfar". It is believed that Ahmed bin Majid, one of the great Arab navigators, was born in Julfar during the 1430s.

Sited so close to the Strait of Hormuz, this prosperous city inevitably attracted unwelcome attention. From about 1400 much of Julfar was controlled by the island of Hormuz. The Arab dynasty that controlled the island also mastered the pearl trade stretching from Julfar to Bahrain. By 1500 the Portuguese coveted this Arabian jewel, and for almost a century they occupied the coastal city.

In 1621 the Portuguese lost Hormuz to the Persians and British, the new force in the region. In retaliation a Portuguese captain set up his cannons in a local mosque and bombarded the seized fort. The Portuguese continued their hold on Julfar until 1633, when they were eventually overthrown by local forces.

TIP

The Musandam Peninsula (Ruus al Jebel – the Mountain Peaks), an Omani enclave north of Ras al Khaimah, is easily reached by road, but an Omani visa is required at the Ash Sham border post.

BELOW: in Ras al Khaimah museum.

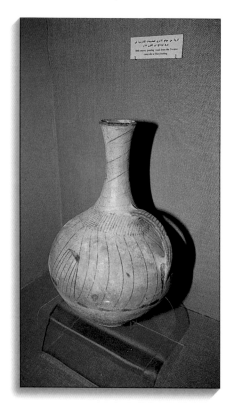

Map, page 208

Around Ras al Khaimah

There are a number of interesting places to visit around Ras al Khaimah. The coastal village of **Jazirah Al Hamra** ⑬ (The Red Island) was originally built on a small promontory which at high tide became an island (it is also believed that the earliest Julfar settlement was on this site). The old village and fort still stand but are abandoned, for the new village is on the mainland.

Travelling along the coast by road from Sharjah, you will see two large watchtowers set high on a right-hand sand dune. These mark the entrance to Jazirat Al Hamra, even thought the village is another 2 km (1 mile) away. The towers gave advanced warning of intruders approaching the village from the desert.

The **Ras al Khaimah Camel Racing Track** is about 10 km (6 miles) out of town in the village of **Digdagga** ⑭. Claimed to be the most exciting venue for camel racing in the UAE it offers an entertaining way to spend a Friday morning in winter. Locals enjoy the excitement and thrill of following the camels in four-wheel-drives, so watch out for vehicles as well as unwieldly camels.

The village of **Khatt** ⑮ is about 800 metres/yds away from the **Khatt Hot Springs** (5am–11pm). From Ras al Khaimah drive towards the airport and take an easy-to-miss left turn to the village about 10 km (6 miles) from the *khor* (creek) bridge. Since 1985 the bathing areas have been developed into segregated enclosures that provide both privacy and comfort. Prior to this development the bathing area was open and shaded by a palm tree oasis.

Shimmel ⑯ is the site of an archaeological dig that has discovered remnants of a settlement dating from about 3000 BC. Located in the foothills north of Wadi Bih, about 5 km (3 miles) north of Ras al Khaimah, Shimmel has extensive palm groves that once fed the entire region. A large circular, divided burial tomb, like

BELOW: Ras al Khaimah's Friday market.

the one discovered at Umm an-Nar island in Abu Dhabi and dating to about 2500 BC was excavated here during the late 1980s. Prior to 1986 it was believed that the Umm an-Nar-type tomb was restricted to the Abu Dhabi region but a similar find in Ajman altered archaeological perceptions of the Emirates. The Shimmel tomb is one of the largest of its type to be found to date and has the most northerly location.

At Shimmel too is the famed **Queen of Sheba's Palace**, or *Hisn Shimmel*. The stony ruins of the "palace" are believed to have been part of a large fortified hill settlement that existed from about 1300–1800, and have little connection with the 10th-century Yemeni queen. The view towards Ras al Khaimah and the sea is wonderful. To reach this unaltered, ancient place turn right about 4.5 km (3 miles) out of RAK on the Oman Road heading towards Rams, and after 1.5 km (1 mile) take the first right turn off the roundabout and continue for about 2.5 km (1½ miles). Turn left at a fort-like building, continue straight ahead on a dirt track and take the right track at a fork just after a small mosque. A hill surrounded by a fence appears straight ahead. Keep the hill to the right and after less than 1 km park. Continue on foot through a hole in the fence and climb the hill via a rough track. The villagers are not fond of visitors so the site must be approached with care.

The small, quiet villages of **Rams** ⓱ and **Dhayah** ⓲, north of Ras al Khaimah, are worth exploring on foot. Old watchtowers, Dhayah Fort and other coral and mudbrick buildings nestle amongst palm groves. British forces chose Rams as a stategic landing site for their invasion of the southern Gulf in 1819. The people of Rams fled to Dhayah fort, where they surrendered after four days of intensive fighting.

Ras al Khaimah is able to supply fresh milk daily to its citizens thanks to air-conditioned barns and a constantly watered green pasture that its herd of specially imported Friesians enjoy

BELOW: fresh milk supplied at Digdagga.

Wadi Bih

One of the most thrilling adventures in the UAE is to cross the Hajar Mountains from Ras al Khaimah to Dibba via the Wadi Bih. In the past, to avoid the treacherous waters of the Strait of Hormuz, **Wadi Bih** was used as a trade route linking the Arabian Gulf with the Gulf of Oman, a journey that would take up to three weeks to complete.

Today this journey can be achieved in a day with a four-wheel-drive. To find Wadi Bih cross the Khor Bridge in Ras al Khaimah, turn right at the second set of lights, and then turn left at the lights after the Emirates petrol station. Go straight over the Palm Tree and Coffee Pot roundabouts and continue to a group of small shops on the right. At this junction turn right, keeping the shops on the left. Continue straight on, then turn left after the military camp. Take the first road on the right, then go straight towards a T-intersection and turn right again. Follow the tarmac road as it sweeps back towards the left around the back of Wadi Bih's large dam wall.

The road climbs into the mountains through a natural cut and ends in a stony wadi (from here it is impossible to continue without a four-wheel-drive). After a further 20 minutes' driving the track forks on a gravel plain. Keep right as the heavily used track on the left goes into Wadi Khab Shamsi. At the Omani Police Post, more than an hour into the journey, turn right along the fenceline and begin the 1,500-metre (4,900-ft) climb to the "top of the world". The track to Dibba is often impassable after heavy rains as the road becomes dangerous and covered with boulders from landslides.

As with all wadi trips, extra caution should be taken during the winter months as flash floods are a hazard and can occur with frightening speed. ❏

Map, page 208

BELOW: Dhayah Fort.

FUJAIRAH AND THE EAST COAST

Map, page 272

Hemmed in by the Hajar Mountains, Fujairah is a beautiful emirate, with deserted beaches and dramatic wadis. Within this region are several enclaves belonging to Sharjah

The pace of life in Fujairah is relaxed. The city faces the Indian Ocean and is protected from the rest of the Arabian Peninsula by the Hajar mountain range. It is the only emirate of the UAE not located on the Arabian Gulf.

The Arabs of the east coast are Sharqiyyin, who trace their origins back to Yemen, and the great Hinawi-Ghafiri tribes that divided southeastern Arabia during the 17th century. They are of the Azdite group of Arab tribes, descended from Fahm bin Malik. Their arrival in the area around 570, followed the collapse of Saba's Great Dam of Marib. Their cousins are the Shihuh, an important tribe that continues to populate the Musandam Peninsula north of Dibba and Ras Al Khaimah.

The strength of the Sharqiyyin lay in their control of Wadi Ham, which runs from Fujairah past Bitnah and Masafi to link with Wadi Siji where it continues out onto desert plains. Wadi Ham has been the site of many battles down the centuries. Apart from the trade route from Ras Al Khaimah to Dibba it was the only means of access to the Gulf of Oman from the western regions.

Although the Persians, Portuguese and Dutch had a presence on the east coast, the remoteness of the mountains has enabled the people of Fujairah to protect themselves against foreign rule and outside tribal influences. Sheikh Abdulla bin Mohammed Al Sharqi is considered to be the emirate's founder. He united the four sub-tribes of the Sharqiyyin in their fight to maintain independence during the 19th century. In 1888 he was succeeded by his son Sheikh Hamad, grandfather of today's ruler Sheikh Hamad bin Mohammed Al Sharqi.

Until his death in 1932, Sheikh Hamad struggled for recognition of Fujairah's independence from Sharjah (the British maintained the area was part of the Trucial State of Sharjah). In a clash with the British Royal Navy on 20 April 1925, the ruler refused to comply with the terms of the ultimatum from the Political Resident, Lt Colonel Prideaux, and British ships were ordered to bombard Fujairah castle for 90 minutes, resulting in damage to the towers and walls that can still be seen today. It was not until 1952 that Fujairah was acknowledged by Britain as the seventh Trucial State.

Fujairah city

Fujairah is a small city. A large green belt of date palms separates the old fort and town from the coast. The easiest route to the old town is from Al Njaimat Road in the Al Mudhannab area – turn right at Madab Road and follow the signs to the Fujairah Museum; the fort and low mudbrick houses of the old town

PRECEDING PAGES: Asian workers dry sardines for winter feeding of livestock. **LEFT:** Masafi road from Dibba. **BELOW:** bringing it all back home.

Date palms flourish.

come into view on the left. To reach the designated heritage area continue straight ahead to the Coffee Pot Roundabout, make a U-turn back down the opposite side of the road and, leaving the bitumen road, turn right onto a sandy track leading to the old village.

The **fort** , also the location of the Heritage Village that opened in 1996, stands majestically on a rocky hill with the Hajar Mountains looming in the background. Although in disrepair, with both square and round towers awkwardly repaired with concrete bricks, the high solid walls give the impression of a once impenetrable structure. Built in the late 18th century, the fort was the residence of Fujairah's ruler and his extended family.

Many of the mudbrick village houses that surrounded the fort still stand. Some have been reduced to low walls, but others show signs of being inhabited – air-conditioners protrude from windows and old cars are parked in make-shift carports. A mosque below the fort has been well maintained. It has small, decorative wooden windows and doors typical of the area.

Fujairah Museum **B** (Sun–Thur 9am–1pm and 4.30–6.30pm, Fri 2–6pm) is at the intersection of Al Nakheel and Sheikh Zayed bin Sultan roads, in a low, walled building. Enlarged in 1998, it houses archaeological and ethnographic exhibits from the area, mostly from sites discovered at Bitnah, Qidfah and Bidiyah, presenting 4,500 years of local history.

The **Corniche** is a short paved walking area beginning at the Fujairah Hilton, across from the Al Nakheel Road/Coffee Pot Roundabout. It is possible to walk along the beach from Fujairah to Kalba, but the five-minute taxi ride is more relaxing. **Kalba** **⑲** (part of Sharjah emirate) is a long and narrow fishing village. Large holiday homes dominate its Corniche, but many small older build-

BULLFIGHTING

Traditional Arab sports such as falconry and camel racing are not suited to the terrain of the east coast. As a result, the large Brahmin bull, which has worked for centuries in the area's palm groves, is bred to compete in a contest of strength. The contest is between two large, pampered bulls, each weighing a tonne (ton) or more and fed on a diet of milk, honey and meal. The bulls try to force each other to the ground. Winners are also declared if an opposing bull turns and flees. The sport was possibly introduced in the 16th century by the Portuguese. An almost identical competition between bulls take place in parts of western India, and Barka and Seeb in Oman, both under Portuguese influence from 1500–1650. However, the sport may pre-date Islam with its source in Persia, where the bull was once worshipped. The Fujairah contests are held on Friday in winter from 4–5.30pm, near the palm groves off the Kalba/Oman road.

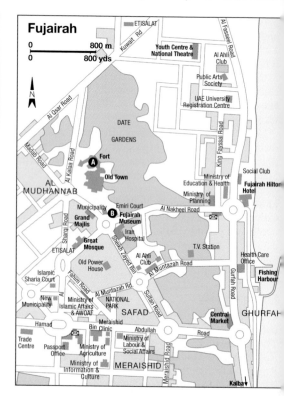

ings show that it hasn't changed that much since the 1960s. Halfway along the Corniche several old buildings have been incorporated into a roundabout, and a renovated fort with cream stone walls is visible on the right. Fifty metres/yards further down the road is the colourful Kalba fish and vegetable souq.

Continue the drive out of Kalba towards **Khor Kalba** to see the mangroves at the *khor* (creek) entrance (*also see page 246*). At sunset the blue water of the Gulf highlights their rich green, emphasising the natural beauty of this region.

From Khor Kalba the road leads into Oman at the **Khatmat Malahah** checkpoint, where visas are issued for the journey along the Batinah Coast to Muscat, but the view along the Batinah Coast makes it worth the effort. **Wahlah ㉑** (Awhalla), a one-hour drive on a rough track southwest of Khatmat Malahah, is the site of an on-going archaeological dig. A 4WD is imperative for this journey, especially if the track is followed all the way to Hatta, a mountain oasis in Dubai (*see page 235*).

Outside Fujairah city

The two main routes to Fujairah from the western emirates begin at Masafi, where the roads divides at a large roundabout. **Masafi ㉑** itself is a small rural village surrounded by deep wadis and the Hajar Mountains. A water-bottling factory has made the town a familiar place name throughout the Emirates. The **Friday Market**, 5 km (3 miles) outside Masafi on the road leading to Dhaid and Sharjah, is a wonderful place to browse for local pottery, inexpensive machine-made carpets, fruit and vegetables.

The left-hand route to Fujairah quickly ascends into the mountains, passes the Masafi Water Factory, then plunges down through the wadis towards the coastal city of Dibba. **Dibba ㉒** divides into three sections, each governed by

**Maps,
pages
208, 272**

BELOW: locking horns at a bullfight.

Clocktower in Dibba.
Clocktowers have
become popular
city decorations
throughout the
UAE and Oman.

Fujairah, Sharjah and Oman respectively. It is a beautiful coastal place untouched by tourism. Located on a wide bay it is home to families of fishermen and farmers. From the main road from Masafi, turn left at the Dolphin Roundabout, continue straight through the Tower Roundabout and turn right at the small Sharjah Police Box. From here the road goes into the old village then curves left along the Corniche. A small **fort** (closed to visitors) and harbour souq are part of Sharjah emirate. Omani Dibba is marked by a sign saying Welcome to Oman, but there is no border post, and no visa is required unless travel to Khasab in the Musandam is intended. The further north the village spreads along the coast the stronger the Omani influence becomes. Houses are mostly one-storey with colourful gates, and the men who can often be seen playing cards on the white sandy beach, wear typical Omani dress. A distinguishing feature of Dibba is the magnificent backdrop created by the Musandam mountains.

From Dibba the main road follows the coastline. The impressive view is often interrupted by sudden and dramatic passes that have been cut through the mountains running parallel to the sea. Fishermen can be spotted on the beaches in this area hauling large nets full of sardines onto the shore. The fish are left to dry and the catch is later bagged as fertiliser.

Aqqa ㉓ near Sharm is best known for the five-star Le Meridien Al Aqah Beach Resort and the Sandy Beach Motel. "Snoopy Rock", named after a small off-shore island that looks like the well-known cartoon character lying on his kennel, has become a renowned snorkelling and diving site. The Dive Centre provides good hire equipment and organises one-day and weekend diving trips. Many colourful and exotic fish feed from the coral reef that surrounds the island. At low tide you can walk across a sand bar to the island. The luxurious

BELOW: snorkelling among the coral off Sandy Beach Motel.

Map, page 208

Meridien or the individual chalets at the Sandy Beach make comfortable and convenient bases for exploring the east coast.

Five minutes drive from **Sharm** is the tiny village of **Bidiyah** ㉔. Two small **watchtowers**, that may have been Portuguese fortifications, mark the entrance. Below them is the small white **Ottoman Mosque**, named after its architect Othman, not the empire. The mosque is built from alabaster and stone, has two flattened cupolas supported by a single internal pillar and has no minaret. It is the oldest mosque still in use in the UAE, and possibly dates to a time when Islam had not yet been fully accepted in the area. As it continues to be used for prayers non-Muslims are asked not to enter.

The walk up the hill to the watchtowers is recommended, especially at sunset when the elevation presents a glorious view across to the mountains and the reds and purples of the sky are beautifully juxtaposed against a floor of green date palms. The opposite view is also worth the climb – hundreds of banana trees and date palms set against a blue sea.

Behind the row of shops opposite Bidiyah's colourful fruit and vegetable souq are the foundations of a stone-built round tower that archaeologists believe is almost identical to the plan and construction of the one at Hili, in Al Ain (*see page 217*). This tower dates settlement in Bidiyah to well over 4,000 years. Another important archaeological site in the area includes a massive 30-metre (98-ft) long covered tomb similar to the type excavated at Shimmel in Ras Al Khaimah, and dating to approximately 1000 BC.

Fifteen kilometres (9 miles) south of Bidiyah and 20 km (12 miles) away from Fujairah, is the Sharjah enclave of **Khor Fakkan** ㉕. A spur of the Hajar Mountains sweeps down onto the coast and forms a natural defence for the picturesque

BELOW: roundabout in Dibba.

township. The defences are reinforced by a watchtower perched high on the spur. Khor Fakkan's horseshoe-shaped harbour is constantly busy with trading dhows and tankers. To reach the small fish souq and the port follow the Corniche to the far right-hand side: the road gets a bit rough, but once there the area offers myriad sights, smells and sounds.

The **Oceanic Hotel** is an architectural landmark of Khor Fakkan. It is the town's tallest building and the rooms feature a porthole effect with enormous round windows. The hotel's white sandy beach is ideal for swimming, wind surfing, sailing and snorkelling. A dive centre provides tuition and regular diving trips into the Gulf of Oman.

In 1985 an archaeologist's dream came true when an untouched ancient burial was discovered in the palm groves of the village of **Qidfah 26**, 5 km (3 miles) south of Khor Fakkan. The 3,000-year-old horseshoe-shaped tomb was uncovered by a local farmer while he was using a bulldozer to level a mound of earth. The site yielded an enormous collection of different artefacts, including bronze vessels, swords, daggers, axes, bracelets and pottery, and is believed to be the most important Iron Age (1500–500 BC) burial to be found in the whole Arabian Peninsula.

A small Omani neutral zone can be visited inland from the villages of **Qidfah** and **Murbah**. The main village is **Madha 27**, which is well known for its mineral spring (*ain*). The village's small hilltop fort is not open to the public but the two watchtowers highlight the Omani architectural style.

BELOW: the oldest mosque in the UAE at Khor Fakkan.

From Murbah the coastal road leads back into Fujairah. To complete the loop back to Masafi turn right at Al Nakheel Road (Coffee Pot Roundabout in front of the Fujairah Hilton) and travel inland through the mountains along Wadi Ham.

About 2 km (1 mile) after Fujairah's last roundabout there is a left turn, opposite a small police post, into **Wadi Hail**, a rough four-wheel-drive trip to the site of the summer palace of the Fujairah sheikhs. The old village of **Hail** ㉘ was for centuries a summer retreat enjoyed for its cool altitude and lush fertility. From the new village of Hail a rough stony track rises into the mountains and ends at an impressive fortified castle and large square watchtower. The buildings are in good repair and clearly demonstrate how important this mountain oasis was to the ruling family. An abundance of flora and fauna can be seen on any one of the many mountain and wadi walks in the area.

Bitnah ㉙ is about 12 km (7 miles) from Fujairah on the right-hand side of the Wadi Ham road, approximately 30 km (19 miles) from Masafi. Nestled amongst a series of lush palm groves, and high above the water course of Wadi Ham is the village **fort**. Look for the UAE flag that proudly flies from the top of the round tower. The best way to explore the oasis and fort is to walk along the wadi, and follow the *falaj* high on the left wall. By car, from the main road turn right onto the tarmac side road leading to the Etisalat communications tower, after about 500 metres/yards turn left onto a gravel track, then keep right where the track forks. Head towards an unused bridge, leave the car under a tree for shade and walk down into the wadi.

Bitnah has been settled since about 1000 BC, and is the site of a massive T-shaped burial tomb. This tomb and others in the area were used over successive centuries and have yielded finds showing Greek influence in the Gulf from about 325 BC. A Greek designed ceramic glazed vessel from the Hellenistic period (300 BC–AD 200) found at Bitnah in the early 1990s shows that the Greek world influenced the Shumayliyah coast before the acceptance of Islam. ❑

Map, page 208

BELOW: Friday drumming near Dibba.

INSIGHT GUIDES

TRAVEL TIPS

OMAN & THE UAE

TRAVEL TIPS

OMAN

A – Z

Accommodation

Eating Out

Activities

THE UAE

A – Z

Accommodation

Eating Out

Activities

Language

Further Reading

A – Z

A HANDY SUMMARY OF PRACTICAL INFORMATION, ARRANGED ALPHABETICALLY

A dmission Charges

Museums range in price from 500 baisa to RO3 or US$1.30 to US$7.80, and galleries are free. **Al Hoota Cave** is RO5.500 (US$14) for adults and RO3 (US$8) for children aged 6–11; free for the under-6s.

Beaches are free to use. In general, **hotels** do not allow non-guests to use their facilities. Exceptions are the Grand Hyatt, which charges RO12 (US$31) per day for adults to use the pool and gym, and RO4 (US$10) for children to use the pool; the Radisson SAS, which has adult pool and gym day passes for RO6 (US$15) and children's pool passes for RO3 (US$8). The Al Bustan does not even allow non-guests to use their restaurants if the hotel is full.

B udgeting for Your Trip

Oman is not a cheap destination, and certainly not promoted to budget travellers. **Tours** are fairly expensive (between RO50/US$140 for a half-day city tour to over RO200/US$500 for a full-day wadi tour. Overnight tours can cost more than RO250 (US$650). Be sure to establish

whether the charge you are quoted is per person or per vehicle. **Hotels** are also fairly expensive. Expect to pay RO27–70 (US$70–180) for a double room per night in a three-star hotel. A good **dinner** at a mid-range restaurant is likely to cost RO10–20 (US$13–40) per person without wine.

Car rental costs range from RO12–15 (US$31–40) per day and from RO25–65 (US$65–170) per day for a 4WD. Most car rental companies include insurance but do double check exclusions.

Business Hours

Bear in mind there are no standard opening times and that the following are a guideline only. **Government offices** are open 8am–2.30pm Sat–Thur. Hours of **private sector businesses** vary widely. Most open 8am–1pm and 4–7pm, though not all open in the afternoon. The majority of businesses are closed on Friday. Most **large malls** open 10am–10pm Sat–Thur and 2–10pm Fri. Smaller shops and supermarkets are open 8am–1pm and 4–7pm.

Markets are open 8am–1pm and 4–9pm except **Muttrah souq**, which closes at 7.30pm.

Banks are open 8am–2pm Sun–Thur, although it is worth checking with your branch as some have later opening hours.

The Weekend

Banks have recently changed to a Fri–Sat weekend; the rest of the country is still accustomed to the Thur–Fri weekend but will follow suit in the near future.

Business Travellers

Many of the five-star hotels contain **business centres**. The Grand Hyatt's is open 24 hours as the majority of their guests are on business. Al Bustan's business centre is open 7am–11pm, Shangri La's 8am–7pm, and Radisson SAS offers a 24-hour business centre as well as business-class rooms. The Chedi does not have a business centre, as most of its guests are tourists.

C hildren

Attractions specifically aimed at families include **amusement parks** (Funworld at Qurum, Riyam Park on Muttrah Corniche, Naseem Gardens in Seeb), the **Children's Museum** and games arcades in shopping malls.

Most of the five-star hotels offer **babysitting services** and many have separate children's areas, although some limit the number of children staying at any one time. Most can provide cribs or children's beds but these should be requested when booking. The **Al Bustan hotel** does not allow children to stay in their Lagoon rooms for safety reasons.

Major supermarkets carry **baby and children's products**. Almost everything is available although sometimes a particular brand will be out of stock for many months.

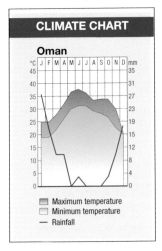

CLIMATE CHART

Oman

Legend:
- ☐ Maximum temperature
- ☐ Minimum temperature
- — Rainfall

Climate

The best time to visit Oman is from **October to March**. The coolest months in Muscat are **December and January** when nights are cool and daytime temperatures rarely go above 30˚C (86˚F). **May to September** is the "off season", when it is hot and humid except in Dhofar where it rains during the monsoon. **July and August** are the hottest months, with temperatures sometimes hitting 50˚C (122˚F). Rainfall in the Muscat region is rare, but torrential when it does occur, often causing flash floods.

Crime and Safety

Oman is one of the safest tourist destinations in the world. Crime is rare and rape is unknown. That said, theft is not unknown and it is sensible to observe the same sort of precautions as you would at home; in particular lock your vehicle and never leave valuables in view of passers by.

For up-to-date advice on security in the region, see www.fco.gov.uk or call:

0845 850 2829 (UK); US citizens see http://travel.state.gov.

Traffic laws in Oman are strictly upheld and the legal blood-alcohol level for driving is close to zero.

Emergency Services

Fire and Police, tel: 9999
Muscat Royal Oman Police, tel: 456 0021
Salalah Royal Oman Police, tel: 2329 0099

Customs Regulations

Oman is a Muslim state and Islamic customs are strictly observed. Non-Muslims can import alcohol, to a maximum of 2 litres per family.

Do not bring narcotics or obscene materials into Oman. There are severe penalties even for so-called soft drugs. Possession of cannabis, even in very small quantities, will incur a minimum 12-month prison sentence followed by deportation.

D isabled Travellers

Most malls and parking areas have wheelchair access, but not all public toilets are wheelchair-accessible. Al Hoota Cave has limited access for disabled people.

E conomy

Oman's economy is oil-based and since 1970 the country has blossomed into a modern state with an impressive infrastructure.

The country is also encouraging tourism and, together with the booming construction industry, this is reducing Oman's economic dependence on oil.

Electricity

220/240 volts AC with three-pin plugs. Many appliances have two-pin plugs so adaptors are used.

Embassies and Consulates

In the event of an emergency, contact your embassy or consulate.
Consulate of Canada
Tel: 2478 8890; www.international.gc.ca
Honorary Consulate of Ireland
Tel: 2470 1282; www.foriegnaffairs.gov.ie
Embassy of United Arab Emirates
Tel: 2460 0302; email:
uaeoman@omantel.net.com
Embassy of the UK
Tel: 2460 9000;
www.ukinoman.fco.gov.uk
Embassy of USA
Tel: 2464 3400;
www.oman.usembassy.gov

Entry Requirements

A valid passport is required to enter Oman, plus a visa. The type of visa issued depends, in part, on your nationality, as does its cost.

Visitors from the UK, USA, Ireland, Australia and New Zealand (and many other countries: see www.omanairports.com/visaonarivals.asp) arriving at Muscat International Airport can obtain a **tourist visa** upon arrival. This can be purchased at the Travelex Foreign Exchange bureau in the immigration arrivals hall. The desk is directly in front of you as you enter the terminal. Most currencies are accepted for payment, or you can pay by credit card. Once you have paid the RO6 (around US$16) an automatic receipt will be issued; this must be presented at the immigration desk.

The tourist visa is a single entry visa valid for one month. However, your passport must have a validity period of not less than six months after your arrival.

Residents and their Families

Most people residing in a GCC (Gulf Cooperation Council) country, relatives and those travelling with them, do not need to obtain a visa to enter Oman. However, if you have members of your family travelling at a separate time, written authorisation and identification documents must be submitted.

Arriving from Dubai

Oman and Dubai operate a common visa facility. This means visitors who already have a valid visa for Dubai do not need to get a separate visa for Oman. See www.omanairports.com/visaonarivals.asp.

BELOW: signs in Arabic and English.

OMAN

THE UAE

LANGUAGE

Etiquette

Generally, Oman remains very traditional. It's fine to wear shorts on the beach, but not in the shops. Women should wear garments that cover their upper arms and their legs down to the knee. Displaying the soles of the feet is seen as insulting.

When taking photographs of local people, especially women, always ask permission first. Taking photographs of military establishments and ministry and government buildings is not allowed.

Non-Muslims are not allowed to enter mosques (with the exception of the Sultan Qaboos Mosque in Muscat). During Ramadan do not eat, smoke or drink in public.

G ay and Lesbian Travellers

Homosexuality is illegal. Although there is a large underground gay community, nobody discusses it or even admits it exists. Any display of public affection, such as hand holding is frowned upon, even between heterosexual couples.

Getting Around

On Arrival

Muscat International Airport (www.omanairports.com) is 30 km (19 miles) from the old town of Muscat. Car hire is available from the airport or you can take a taxi. Taxis are priced at RO8–20 depending on the distance from the airport to your hotel. The drive to Qurum takes about 20 minutes; it takes around 40 minutes to get to Al Bustan Hotel, depending on traffic. **Muscat International Airport** Tel: 2451 9210 **Salalah International Airport** Tel: 2329 1016

Taxis from the Airport

Private taxis (orange and white) are available outside the arrivals hall in the terminal building. Although they are not metered, they have fixed rates both from Muscat International Airport and most of the large hotels in Muscat. Fares range in price from RO7 to 13 (US $18–35).

See Muscat International Airport website for information on rates (www.omanairports.com/transport.asp).

Public Transport

Bus services operate between the major towns and there is also a service between Dubai and Muscat. But generally, if you have not hired a car, you will opt to use taxis (see below). They are numerous and

should not be too expensive once you have perfected your haggling technique.

A cheaper alternative to car-taxis are **bus-taxis** – 12-seater buses which swarm all over the country picking people up from the side of the roads. The bus-taxi follows designated routes. When you board, tell the driver where you wish to go, and he will let you know if he is heading there. The cost is 200–600 baisa. Muscat's main bus terminal is in Ruwi, just down from the Sheraton Hotel.

There is no **railway** in Oman.

Street Taxis

These taxis are hailed on the street. They do not have fixed rates, so it is recommended that you haggle with the driver or he will quote you an over-inflated price. The concierge in your hotel should be able to advise you on what would be a reasonable amount to pay for your journey.

Beware of taking a street taxi directly from your hotel: these drivers operate flat rates, which means you will be charged at least 200 percent more than the fare should be.

Metered Taxis

Muscat's metered taxi service is more reliable than the street taxis. However, if you want to be somewhere at a specific time, it is best to book the taxi in advance. It is also advisable to keep small notes on hand, as the drivers often claim to have no change.
Hello Taxi, tel: 2460 7011
This taxi company is reliable, but more expensive than Swift (below).
Swift Taxi, tel: 8007 7779
Not as reliable as Hello and City, but it can offer women a female driver if so desired.

City Taxi, tel: 2460 2211
These taxis do not actually have meters; instead the drivers set the odometer to 0 and then manually calculate the number of kilometres by 200 baisa (US$0.52). This service is the cheapest in Muscat.

Driving

Omanis drive on the right-hand side of the road. Watch out for the bus-taxis which stop or pull out with little notice. Driving standards generally are not as good as in the West, so be on your guard for some bizarre manoeuvres. You should avoid offending local cultural norms when driving, eg through abusive gestures or language.

Traffic in Muscat can become very congested, especially during rush hour, which occurs between 7–9am and 1.30–3.30pm. The construction of a new highway through Muscat also causes delays and traffic jams. In Dhofar, in particular, be wary of **wandering camels**. If an approaching vehicle displays hazard lights, this indicates camels ahead. Adopt the same procedure.

If you have an **accident**, you must not move the vehicles involved until a policeman arrives (unless it is only a minor accident: in this case, get the other driver's name, vehicle registration number and insurance details; if you do not agree whose fault it is, then go to the police station to report it).

Speed limits go up to 120 kmph (75 mph) on the dual carriageways (in Muscat and between Muscat and Dubai, and Muscat and Nizwa).Other speed limits vary from 60–100 kmph depending on the type of road and where it is. **Signs** are in Arabic and English.

BELOW: taxi sign at night, Muscat.

Off-road Driving

To really appreciate the country you need to go off-road in a four-wheel-drive, but this is not for the inexperienced as you will have to navigate steep and dangerous roads.

If you do decide to drive yourself, make sure that you go with another vehicle driven by someone with experience because it is very easy to find yourself in difficulties. You must be properly prepared before you head off into the Interior. Alternatively, tour companies can organise wadi-bashing (driving in river beds) trips for you.

Car Hire

Hiring either saloon cars or four-wheel-drive vehicles is not too expensive – one bonus of driving in Oman is the low cost of petrol. Most hotels have a car-hire desk.

Car Hire Firms

Avis, tel: 2440 0888; www.avisoman.com
Budget, tel: 2479 4721; www.budget.com
Europcar, tel: 2470 0190; www.europcar.com
Global Car Rental, tel: 2469 7140; www.alhashotelargroup.com
Hertz, tel: 2456 6208; www.nttoman.com
Mark Rent-a-Car, tel: 2456 2444; www.marktoursoman.com
Sixt, tel: 2448 9082
Suwatco, tel: 2470 7840
Thrifty Car Rental, tel: 2448 9248; www.thriftyoman.com
Value Plus, tel: 2481 7964; www.valueoman.com

Ferry between Muscat and Khasab

A new **catamaran service** (four times a week) operates from Muscat to Khasab on the Musandam peninsula, dispensing with the need for travellers to pass through UAE territory. The journey takes about six hours, but passengers must arrive at the terminal an hour beforehand. They must be pre-book. All seats must be reserved in advance through the **National Ferry Company** (SAOC): nfo.reservations@gmail.com, tel: 800 72000 (toll free). Vehicles are not permitted at present.

Getting There

By Air

Many major airlines operate direct flights to Oman; for some, it is used as a stop-over on flights to and from the Far East. The national carrier, Oman Air, is expanding its network.

For a payment of £5–10 you can make your flight carbon-neutral at

either www.climatecare.org or www.carbonneutral.com.

Flight Information

24-hour information, tel: 2451 9223
Air Arabia, tel: 2470 0828
Air Canada, tel: 2456 6046
Air India, tel: 2481 8666
American Airlines, tel: 2481 2952
British Airways, tel: 2456 8777
Cathay Pacific, tel: 2478 9818
Emirates Airlines, tel: 2478 6700
Gulf Air, tel: 2470 3222
Oman Air, tel: 2451 9416
United Airlines, tel: 2478 9852

By Car

If you are driving from the UAE your passport will be checked at the border crossing in both Oman and the UAE; a road permit is no longer required. Road development is taking place all the time, and roads linking major towns are excellent.

By Ship

There are no scheduled passenger services into Oman, but some cruise ships visit Muscat and Salalah.

Government

The ruler, Sultan Qaboos bin Said, has total control of the running of the country. In 1992, a consultative council was set up and the council members discuss topics put forward to them by the Sultan. There is no heir to the Sultan, although measures are in place in case of any eventuality.

ealth and Medical Care

Make sure you have full medical insurance. No specific vaccinations are required for Oman except a compulsory certificate against yellow fever if coming from an infected area. However, typhoid and hepatitis A vaccinations are recommended and you should ensure your tetanus and polio jabs are up to date. It is advisable to seek medical advice as requirements do change. Tap water is safe to drink in urban areas; mineral water is available everywhere.

Medical Services

There are good hospitals in major towns and clinics elsewhere. Pharmacies are mainly open 9am–1pm and 4–9pm, and some open 24 hours.

Hospitals in Muscat

Muscat Private Hospital, www.muscatprivatehospital.com tel: 24583600
Royal Hospital, tel: 2459 9525
Khoula Hospital, tel: 2456 3625

Outside Muscat

Nizwa Hospital, tel: 2544 9361
Sur Hospital, tel: 2556 1373
Sohar Hospital, tel: 2684 0399
Sultan Qaboos Hospital, Salalah, tel: 2321 1151
These all have English-speaking members of staff. For a list of all 25 hospitals in Oman, as well as pharmacies, see www.omantribune.com.

nternet

There are plenty of internet shops and cafés in Muscat, especially in the shopping malls, but you will also find facilities in other towns.

edia

Print

All media is government-controlled and censored, as are books and magazines entering the country. There are three daily English language newspapers – the *Oman Daily Observer*, the *Times of Oman* and the *Oman Tribune*. They contain good local news and sports results and their international news coverage has improved, too. Gulf papers such as the *Khaleej Times* and *Gulf News* are also available. *The Week* is a weekly newspaper distributed free each Wednesday; it can be downloaded from www.freetheweek.com.

Oman2day, a monthly English-language leisure magazine aimed at expats and visitors, is worth buying. Along with feature articles (often including some on exploring Oman independently), it contains a comprehensive dining guide and information on the latest happenings and events. If there isn't a complimentary copy in your hotel room, ask for it at the bookshop. The same publishing house also produces the monthly *Business Today*. For back issues of both see www.apexstuff.com.

A press act allows the government to censor publications for political or cultural reasons.

Newspapers from other countries are sold at shops and hotels about two days after publication, but expect higher than normal prices.

Broadcast Media

Oman TV has an English news segment but generally there is nothing worth watching. Satellite TV is widely available featuring BBC and CNN reports. Nilesat is a free satellite service, which airs most of the popular American programmes and films.

State-run Oman FM is at 90.4, 91.3. A new radio station in English

(95.5 FM) plays a good mix of music and (mainly local) news.

Money

Credit cards are accepted in the major hotels, but in smaller hotels and restaurants, it is advisable to check first. The best rates are from foreign exchange dealers.
Currency: Rial (OMR/RO) divided into 1000 baizas. 1 RO = US$ 2.60 approximately at time of going to press.

Photography

You should always ask permission before taking photographs of people. Film and digital imaging services are available at photo shops around the city.

Postal and Courier Services

Post Offices are dotted all over towns but the most central one in Muscat is at Al Harthy Shopping Complex. Post offices are usually open from 8am–1.30pm Saturday to Wednesday and 8–11am Thursday.

Couriers

ATS Worldwide Express
Stars Cinema Complex, Ruwi.
Tel: 2470 3342
DHL Express
Sultan Qaboos Street
Wallayah
Tel: 8007 7008
Fedex
Sinaw House, Hamriya (opposite Al Nahda hospital)
Tel: 2483 3311
TNT International Express
GAC Building, Al Khuwair
Tel: 2447 7870

Public Holidays

For most people Friday is a weekly holiday. The date of the National Day holiday in November is decided by the Sultan each year.
Religious holidays, the dates of which are governed by the lunar cycle, and are therefore moveable, are the **Islamic New Year**, the **Prophet Mohammed's birthday**, **Ascension of the Prophet**, **Eid Al Fitr** (four days at the end of Ramadan), and **Eid Al Adha** (five days at the end of the month of the pilgrimage to Mecca, or Haj). Christian expatriates are usually allowed Christmas Day off.

Religious Services

Catholic Church of St Peter and St Paul, Darsait, tel: 2470 1893.

The Protestant Church in Oman, Darsait, tel: 2479 9475.
Salalah Christian Centre, Salalah, tel: 2323 5677/5727.

Taxes

The Oman tax rate is 17 percent, which consists of municipality and tourism tax and service charge. This is charged even in fast food restaurants.

Telecommunications

Calling from your hotel room is likely to be expensive. It is considerably cheaper to make calls home from public phone booths. **Phone cards** are available from supermarkets for both local and international calls.
For directory assistance in Oman call 1318. Alternatively, look online at www.businessdirectoryoman.com or www.omantel-yellowpages.com
Oman telephone numbers are all eight digits, with no area codes. Muscat numbers begin with 24, Salalah with 23.

Useful Numbers

International Dialling Code: 00 968.

Time Zone

GMT + 4 hours, BST + 3 hours.

Tipping

A tip of 10 percent is considered the norm in hotels and restaurants. Some restaurants add a service charge to the bill. It is not usual to tip custodians of museums, forts and such like, who are usually Omani citizens rather than immigrant workers. Fares for taxis should be agreed before you get into the car – always haggle, it's expected!

Toilets

Public bathrooms in malls are usually clean. Some tourist sites have no toilets at present, but 48 new ones are planned for these sites and 17 have been approved so far.

Tourist Information Offices

Tourist Information Offices do not exist in Oman. It is best to try the nearest tour operator (see next column). For advance information, contact:
Ministry of Tourism: tel: 2458 8700; www.omantourism.gov.om
Ministry of Information, PO Box 600, Muscat 100, tel: 2460 3222; www.omanet.om

You can also try contacting the **Omani Embassy** before leaving for Oman. They can provide basic brochures:
London: tel: 020- 8877 4524 (tourism) or 020-7225 0001 (Embassy).
Washington: tel: 202-387 1980.
Other useful websites are:
www.destinationoman.com
www.holiday-in-oman.com
www.timesofoman.com

Tour Operators

A number of companies operating from the UK arrange holidays, tours and activities.
Abercrombie & Kent, tel: 020-7190 7750; www.abercrobiekent.co.uk
Cox & Kings, tel: 020-7873 5000; www.coxandkings.co.uk; for USA tel: 1-800 999 1758; www.coxandkings.com
Destination Oman, tel: 0870-413 3355; www.destoman.com
Gane & Marshall, tel: 020-8445 6000; www.ganeandmarshall.co.uk
Hebridean Island Cruises Ltd, tel: 01756-704 704; for USA tel: 1-800 659 2648; www.hebridean.co.uk
Indian Ocean & Arabian Getaways, tel: 0161-437 4371; www.gateways.co.uk
Kuoni Travel Limited, tel: 020-7589 8958; www.kuoni.co.uk
Odyssey Experience, tel: 01242-224 482; www.odysseyexperience.co.uk
Regaldive, tel: 0870-2201 777; www.regal-diving.co.uk
The Shaw Travel Company, tel: 01635-47055; www.shawtravel.co.uk
Steppes East Travel, tel: 01285-880 980; www.steppestravel.co.uk
Tropical Sky, tel: 0870-9079 605; www.tropicalsky.co.uk

Specialist Tours

Oman offers a wide variety of exciting tours, including wadi-bashing, dhow trips, diving courses, camping in the desert, wildlife safaris and visits to historic sites. Tours should be booked a few days in advance, although some companies will cater for late bookings. Tour prices are usually per vehicle and most companies will ask you to pay a 50 percent deposit when you book, and the remainder when the tour begins. Check the company's cancellation policy, as this varies. Tours generally leave from the hotel or a designated meeting point.
Arabian Sea Safaris
Next to OC Centre, Ruwi
Tel: 2469 3223;
www.arabianseasafaris.com
Offers marine tours, fishing, sailing, kayaking with dolphins and aqua bike rentals.

OMAN

Desert Discovery Tours
Azaiba
Tel: 2449 3232
www.desert-discovery.com
Tours range from a half-day city tour to a 12-day geology tour, plus standard range of adventure tours.

Elite Travel and Tourism
Mina Al Fahal
Tel: 2448 5020
www.eliteoman.com
Offers camel and mountain trekking, cave exploration, geology and marine-life tours, scuba diving and snorkelling, and a range of deep-sea adventures. Dinner cruises on an authentic Omani dhow available.

Empty Quarter Tours
Madinat Al Sultan Qaboos
Tel: 9938 7654
www.emptyquartertours.com
Various city tours and desert camping trips available.

Holiday-In-Oman
Tel: 2448 5663
www.holiday-in-oman.com
Run by Muscat Diving and Adventure Centre. A range of water and land activities including climbing, abseiling, archery, trekking, and caving in the second biggest cave chamber in the world. Their website has good background information on Oman.

Khasab Travel and Tours
PO Box 50, Khasab
Musandam 811
Tel/fax: 2683 0464
Four-wheel-drive mountain safaris, dhow cruises in the spectacular Musandam fjords, camping trips.

Majan Tours
Ruwi
Tel: 2470 0900;
www.muscatoverseas.com
Runs similar tours to other operators but also offers fly/drive packages, shopping tours and a host of client services.

Mark Tours
Rex Road (Al Iskan Street)
Tel: 2456 7996
www.marktoursoman.com
Wide choice of tours includes dhow cruises, dolphin- and turtle-watching trips, city tours, safaris, wadi-bashing, and self-drive tours.

Muscat Diving and Adventure Centre
Al Khuwair
Tel: 2448 5663
www.holiday-in-oman.com
This organisation runs the same tours as Holiday-in-Oman.

Musandam Sea Adventure Tourism,
Khasab
Tel: 2673 0424
www.msaoman.com
One- and two-day dhow cruises, as well as desert/mountain safaris.

ABOVE: the ubiquitous mobile phone.

Oman World Tourism
Madinat al Sultan Qaboos
Tel: 9943 1333
www.omanworldtourism.com
Offers many of the standard one- and two-day tours, with camping, diving or fishing, and kite boarding.

Sun & Sand Tours
Azaiba
Tel: 9937 3928
www.sunsandtour.com
This company specialises in adventurous land tours. Some of the tours on offer cover mountain trekking, crossing Oman's "Grand Canyon", and desert camping in a spot known only to a few.

Zahara Tours
Al Khuwair
Tel: 2440 0844
www.zaharatours.com
Offers all the standard tours, plus rejuvenation therapy, dhow cruises and trips on the frankincense trail.

W ebsites

Muscat International Airport
www.omanairports.com
Omantel Yellow Pages
www.omantel-yellowpages.com
Tourist Information
www.destinationoman.com
Oman National Transport Co
www.ontcoman.com

Weights and Measures

Oman employs the metric system.
1 inch = 2.54 centimetres (cm)
1 foot = 0.30 metres (m)
1 mile = 1.61 kilometres (km)
1 pound = 0.45 kilograms (kg)
1 American gallon = 3.79 litres (l)
1 British gallon = 4.5 litres.

What to Wear

For most of the year loose-fitting cotton or linen clothes are ideal to cope with the heat. From November to March a light jacket or jumper may be needed in the evening. Swimwear or revealing clothing should only be worn on the beach. Err on the conservative side for swimwear.

Visitors are expected to cover upper arms and legs. Capri pants, shirts and skirts or shorts below the knee are all acceptable. Sunglasses, sun cream and a hat are essential, as are boots if you want to explore.

Women Travellers

Supermarkets only carry one brand of sanitary towels and tampons so bring supplies if you have a preferred brand. The Sultan Centre has a limited but sometimes better selection.

Oman is a pretty safe place for women travelling alone but you should still observe normal precautions. Have your shoulders and knees covered at all times. This is not law but it shows respect and as women are stared at all the time, it makes sense to avoid unwanted attention by leaving tight-fitting or revealing clothing behind. Women do wear sleeveless tops in bars and clubs but wear a pashmina or shawl around your shoulders until you are inside. Women get honked at when walking around, which should just be ignored.

THE UAE

LANGUAGE

A CCOMMODATION

HOTELS, APARTMENTS AND CAMPSITES

Booking a Hotel

During the main tourist season (between October and March) it is wise to **reserve** your accommodation several weeks in advance, as hotels become fully booked during the winter. However, if you are able to travel during the summer months, you'll find many great deals being offered by hotels across the country, and cheap packages can easily be negotiated.

Although Oman has never been promoted as a destination for budget travellers, the number of two- and three-star hotels popping up in the city has increased over the past two years and there are now more hotels and guesthouses available for under $100 for a double room.

Camping

A few **campsites** exist in Oman and as camping is a favourite with many of the expatriates living here, camping equipment is readily available to buy if you decide to save money and rough it for a few nights. Also, while it is still quite common to pitch a tent in a wadi or on a beach, the government recently set up several dedicated campsites where visitors can camp or stay in a hut with basic facilities such as running water and toilets.

Unless otherwise stated, all hotel prices are subject to an additional 17 percent tax. When booking your accommodation check the hotel's cancellation policy, as it varies between establishments.

ACCOMMODATION LISTINGS

MUSCAT AND AROUND

HOTELS

Al Bustan Palace Hotel
Tel: 2479 9666
Fax: 2479 9600
www.albustanpalace.com
The Al Bustan, which has been refurbished, is regularly voted one of the top hotels in the Middle East. Set on its own bay just outside Muscat, it has a resort feel. Tennis village, 7 restaurants, pool, squash courts, gym, diving and water-sports. **££££**

Al Falaj Hotel
Tel: 2470 2311
Fax: 2479 5853
Ruwi
www.omanhotels.com
One of the oldest hotels in the country with good sporting facilities (two pools, excellent gymn and tennis and squash courts). **£££–££££**

Barasti Bungalow
Oman Dive Center
Bar Al Jissah
Tel: 2482 4240
www.omandivecenter.com
Set in a cove not far from the Shangri-La Barr Al Jissah Resort, these rustic-looking huts are a unique way to experience Oman. During winter you need to book at least one month in advance. Price includes breakfast, dinner and taxes. **£££**

The Chedi
North Ghubra 232
Way 3215 Street No. 46
Tel: 2452 4400
www.chedimuscat.com
This hotel is an oasis of peace and tranquillity. A blending of Arabian architecture with Asian design (it has a sister hotel in Singapore) gives it a simple elegance that is incredibly calming. The muted tones and subtle bursts of colour are in keeping with this mood. To maintain the sense of harmony, children under 12 are only allowed to use one of the hotel's two pools. The hotel also has a policy that restricts the number of children in the resort to 20 at any one time. **££££**

Crowne Plaza, Muscat
Tel: 2466 0660
Fax: 2456 0650
www.cpmuscat.com
Perched on a cliff overlooking Qurum beach, this hotel has the best views in the city. **££££**

Dream Resort
Seeb (across from the beach)
Tel: 2445 3399
Fax: 2445 7030
Single and duplex chalets available. **££–£££**

Golden Tulip Seeb
Tel: 2451 0300
Fax: 2451 0055
www.goldentulipseeb.com
Large, recently-renovated hotel (formerly Seeb Novotel) near the airport. Twenty minutes' drive from the city. Pool and fitness facilities. **£££**

Grand Hyatt, Muscat
Tel: 2464 1234
Fax: 2460 5282
www.muscat.grand.hyatt.com
Lavish, 5-star hotel with excellent amenities, including gym, beauty salon, water sports, and excellent beachside location. **££££**

OMAN

THE UAE

LANGUAGE

Haffa House Hotel
Tel: 2470 7207
Fax: 2470 7208
Ruwi
This hotel was created with business people in mind. Facilities include a pool, a corporate centre with private, furnished offices, conference rooms, secretarial services, fax and copier machines. An Arabic and English translation service is available and can be hired on a daily, weekly or hourly basis. £££

Majan Continental Hotel
Tel: 2459 2900
Fax: 2459 2979
www.majanhotel.com
Medium-sized hotel with a range of rooms, including 10 family apartments with cooking facilities, several restaurants, swimming pool and pool-hall, in the Al Khuwair area of the city. Rates include breakfast. £££–££££

Midan Hotel Suites
Al Ghubra (near the Ghubra roundabout), off Al Marefah Street
Tel: 2449 9565
Fax: 2449 9575
The Midan offers modern one-, two- and three-bedroom suites fully fitted with all the amenities you might expect to find in a furnished apartment. There is also a great Thai restaurant next to the lobby. Price includes a continental buffet breakfast. £££–££££

Mina Hotel
Tel: 2471 1828
Fax: 2471 4981
Great location on the Muttrah Corniche but fairly basic. ££

Muscat Holiday Inn
Tel: 2448 7123
Fax: 2448 0986
www.ichotelsgroup.com
In the Al Khuwair area, providing the usual Holiday Inn standards, including outdoor pool and tennis courts, at reasonable prices. £££–££££

Muscat Inter-Continental Hotel
Tel: 2468 0000 (UK reservations: 0870 400 9650)
Fax: 2460 0012
www.ichotelsgroup.com

ABOVE: the elegant lobby of The Chedi hotel.

Next to the beach in the Shati Al Qurm district of the city, this large resort hotel attracts both businesspeople and holidaymakers. High standards of food and accommodation. Executive floor. ££££

Qurm Beach House
Tel: 2456 4070
Fax: 2456 0761
Small hotel tucked away at the bottom of a hill close to Qurum beach. Unlicensed. ££–£££

Radisson SAS
Tel: 2468 7777
Fax: 2468 7778
www.radisson.com/muscatom
Located halfway between the airport and the central business district, this establishment caters primarily for the business traveller. Executive floor available. ££££

Ramada Muscat
Shatti Al Qurum
Tel: 2460 3555
Fax: 2469 4500
Rates include breakfast, but are not inclusive of the 17 percent tax. Facilities include a health club with sauna, steam room and swimming pool and 24-hour access to the business centre. ££££

Ruwi Hotel
Tel: 2470 4244
Fax: 2470 4248
www.ruwihotel.com
Hotel in the Ruwi district offering standard accommodation. Men-only gym available. £££

Safeer Hotel Suites
Madinat Qaboos
Tel: 2469 1200
Fax: 2469 2227
www.safeerintll.com
Furnished suites, designed for long-stay business travellers and families. Both standard rooms and apartments are available. £££–££££

Shangri-La's Barr Al Jissah Resort and Spa
Tel: 2477 6666
Fax: 2477 6677
www.shangri-la.com/muscat/
Spectacularly situated on the bay at Barr Al Jissah, this large new resort comprises three hotels (**Al Waha**, designed with families in mind, **Al Bandar**, and, the most luxurious of the three, **Al Husn**, where the rate includes a butler). There is a choice of eight restaurants in all, plus cafés, bars, a nightclub, a spa and three private beaches. ££££

Asas Oman Hotel Apartments
Qurum Heights
Tel: 2456 8555
Fax: 2456 0018
These furnished two- and three-bedroom suites are located in the prestigious area of Qurum heights. £££

Nuzha Hotel Apartments
Al Mujamma Street, Darsait
Tel: 2478 9199
Fax: 2478 4144
www.safeerintll.com
Good-value option in Ruwi area. ££–£££

Al Khuwair Hotel Apartments
Al Kuleiah Street, Al Khuwair
Tel: 2447 8171
Fax: 2448 9060
www.safeerintll.com
These apartments offer good-value and a central location. ££–£££

BATINAH REGION (MUSCAT TO SOHAR)

Buraimi

Al Buraimi Hotel
Tel: 2564 2010
Fax: 2565 2011
In Buraimi Oasis on the UAE/Oman border. Not particularly good (quite shabby and signs of lack of maintenance), but the only half-way decent option in the area. You would probably do better to stay in nearby Al Ain. **£££**

Barka

Al Nahda Resort & Spa
Barka, turn left at Barka

Roundabout
Tel: 2688 3710
Fax: 2688 3175
www.alnahdaresort.com
A family-oriented resort, with spacious grounds and pool, as well as an eclectic range of spa and health treatments (the resident Ayurvedic doctor can test your well-being). Also offers diving trips to the Dimaniyat islands. **££££**

Al Sawadi

Al Sawadi Beach Resort
Tel: 2679 5545
Fax: 2679 5535

www.alsawadibeach.com
About 45 minutes north of Muscat. Well-managed hotel with large rooms and good facilities, including diving and horse-riding. Rates include breakfast. **££££**

Sohar

Al Wadi Hotel, Sohar
Tel: 2684 0058
Fax: 2684 1997
www.omanhotels.com
Long-established medium-sized hotel in the centre of Sohar, with a pool and comfortable rooms. **£££**

Sohar Beach Hotel
Tel: 2684 1111
Fax: 2684 3766
www.soharbeach.com
A good resort hotel belonging to the Taj International chain. Convenient if travelling by car between the UAE and Oman. **£££–££££**

Suwaiq

Suwaiq Motel
Tel: 2686 2241
Fax: 2686 2242
A small and inexpensive motel. Little English spoken. **££**

DHAKILIYA REGION (NIZWA, BAHLA AREA)

Nizwa

Al Dyar Hotel
Tel: 2541 2402
Fax: 2541 2405
About 1 km (½ mile) from Nizwa Fort. The staff's English is not very good, so patience is needed to get information.
££–£££
Falaj Daris Hotel
Tel: 2541 0500
Fax: 2541 0537
www.falajdarishotel.com
Pleasant, long-established hotel, recently refurbished, with two pools, and a reasonably good restaurant. The pool at the back of the hotel has a small bar. **£££**

Golden Tulip Nizwa
Tel: 2543 1616
www.goldentulipnizwa.com
Quiet, modern hotel about 10 minutes' drive from Nizwa. Pleasant rooms, high standards, good value. **£££–££££**
Majan Guest House
Tel: 2543 1910
Fax: 2543 1911
www.majangh.com
Clean and spacious guesthouse offering a range of rooms, convenient to Nizwa. Relatively inexpensive with breakfast included in the rates. **££**
Tanuf Guest House
Nizwa
Tel: 2541 1601

Fax: 2541 1059
Clean, reasonably comfortable and inexpensive, but the staff here speak little English. **££**

Jabel Akhdar

Jebel Al Akhdar Hotel
Tel: 2542 9009
Fax: 2542 9119
Email: jakhotel@omantel.net.com
Situated high up in the Jebel Akhdar, 160 km (100 miles) from Muscat. Clean and pleasant hotel with a bistro-style unlicensed restaurant. Hotel staff suggest you book one month in advance during the winter season. **££–£££**

CAMPSITE

Jebel Shams Travelling and Camping Centre
Faris Al Khatri
Tel: 2463 5222 (landline) 9938 2639 (mobile)
www.rahaloman.com
In the northwest part of the Jebel Akhdar, the peak of Jebel Shams soars to 3,000 metres (9,840 ft). Oman's own Grand Canyon, Wadi Nakhr, is nearby. Accommodation is available in one-room villas with hot water and bathrooms, or a Bedouin-style tent. Trekking and camping tours can be arranged. **££**

SHARQIYA REGION (SUR AREA)

Ras Al Hadd

Turtle Beach Camp
Ras Al Hadd
Tel: 2554 0068
Fax: 2554 3900
Located on the beach, these small huts are ideal for viewing the turtles. Some of the huts have air conditioning and bathrooms, while others have only air con. However, if you do not wish to sleep

inside, you can pitch a tent or sleep under the stars. Price includes breakfast and dinner.
££–£££
Ras Al Hadd Beach Hotel
Tel: 9937 6989
Fax: 2554 2228
www.surhotels.com
Mid-price hotel that is part of Sur International hotels. Remote location 60 km (37 miles) east of Sur. Beachside

location and a good base for turtle-watching.
££–£££

Ras Al Jinz

Ras Al Jinz Sea Turtle and Nature Reserve
Tel: 9655 0606
Fax: 9985 1594
www.rasaljinz.org
This eco-tourism project provides the best turtle-watching experience. Included in the price is a

room at the Carapace Lodge, a guided tour with an eco-guide for night and early morning turtle observation, as well as

PRICE CATEGORIES

Price categories are for a standard double room in high season:
£ = under OR15
££ = OR15–40
£££ = OR40–100
££££ = more than OR100

breakfast and dinner.
£££

Sharqiyah Sands

Nomadic Desert Camp
Tel: 9933 6273
Fax: 2550 4507
www.nomadicdesertcamp.com
Accommodation is
provided in small
huts 20 km (12 miles)
south of the village
of Al Wasil. The price
includes breakfast,
dinner and a camel
ride. The camp has no
generator, so candles
and paraffin lamps
provide lighting at night.
££

Sur

Sur Beach Hotel
Tel: 2554 2031/32/33
Fax: 2554 2228
www.surhotels.com
Located a 12-minute
taxi ride from Sur. Com-
fortable rooms with sea
views. Choice of four
themed bars; nice pool
and tennis courts.
££–££££

Sur Plaza Hotel
Tel: 2554 3777
Fax: 2544 2626
www.omanhotels.com
Medium-level and medium-
sized hotel with swimming
pool but an unattractive
location. **££**

ABOVE: Kargeen Café, Muscat.

DHOFAR/THE SOUTH

Salalah

Arabian Sea Villas
www.arabian-sea-villas.com
Well-run small hotel with
a restaurant. Right on
the beach. **££**

Crowne Plaza Resort
Tel: 2323 5333 (UK reservations:
0870 400 9093)
Fax: 2323 5137
www.ichotelsgroup.com
Re-branded from Holiday
Inn Salalah after a
multi-million-dollar
renovation, and in a
superb beachfront
location. **£££–££££**

Haffa House
Tel: 2329 5444
Fax: 2329 4873
www.haffahouse.com

Large, clean hotel in
commercial block off the
clock-tower roundabout
from Salalah Airport. **££**

Hamilton Plaza Hotel,
Tel: 2321 1025
Fax: 2321 1187
In a large commercial
complex in uptown Salalah.
Pool and gym. **££–£££**

Hilton Salalah
Tel: 2321 1234
Fax: 2321 0084
www.hilton.co.uk
Beautiful beach location.
Excellent reception.
Popular with locals.
£££–££££

Safeer Residence Salalah
Al Dahreej North, about 8 km
(5 miles) from Salalah
Tel: 2323 5639

This three-bedroom villa is
ideal for families or a
group of people. **£££**

Salalah Tourist Hotel
Tel: 2329 5332
Fax: 2329 2145
Opposite the ONTC
bus-stop and Central
Market in uptown Salalah.
Best local value. **£**

Elsewhere in Dhofar

**Arabian Oryx Nature
Reserve**
Jaaluni, off the Muscat to
Salalah highway towards
Hayma
Tel: 2469 3537
Fax: 2469 3883
www.oryxoman.com

This sanctuary was
developed to protect the
Omani Oryx. Visitors are
welcome to stay in the
nature reserve, but
permission must be
granted beforehand from
the Office of the Adviser
for the Conservation of
the Environment in the
Diwan Royal Court,
Muscat. See website for
details. Bring your own
camping supplies.

Thumrait Tourist Hotel
Tel: 2327 9371
Fax: 2327 9373
About two hours' drive
north of Salalah on the
road to Muscat. Very basic,
and the staff barely speak
English. **£**

MUSANDAM PENINSULA

Golden Tulip Dibba
Dibba
Tel: 2673 0777
Fax: 2673 0888
www.goldentulipdibba.com
Medium-sized modern
hotel set on the northern
tip of the peninsula.
£££

**Golden Tulip Khasab
Hotel Resort**
Tel: 2673 0777
www.goldentulipkhasab.com
Sixty rooms with sea
and mountain views.
The remote location is

great for relaxation
and diving with the
hotel scuba diving centre.
£££

Khasab Hotel
Tel: 2683 0267
Fax: 830 989
www.dolphintourism.net
Pleasant small hotel with
pool in Khasab. Organises
boat and diving trips. **£**

Six Senses Hideaway
Zighy Bay, Musandam
Tel: 2673 5555
Fax: 2673 5556
www.sixsenses.com

In keeping with its
name, this luxury
resort is very secluded,
with a location in the
northernmost part of
the Musandam Peninsula.
££££

CAMPSITE

**The Golden Tulip Beach
Campsite**
This is a free camp site
located 200 metres/yds

east of the hotel of the
same name, situated
on a beautiful beach.
Picnic tables are provided.
Toilets and shower facilities
are basic.

PRICE CATEGORIES

Price categories are for a
standard double room in
high season:
£ = under OR15
££ = OR15–40
£££ = OR40–100
££££ = more than OR100

OMAN

THE UAE

LANGUAGE

E ATING OUT

RECOMMENDED RESTAURANTS, CAFÉS AND BARS

Places to Eat

Not long ago almost all the decent restaurants in Oman were found in the five-star hotels, but that is no longer the case. New restaurants offering cuisines from around the globe are opening weekly, and it is now possible to get almost any kind of food you desire, from fast food to fine dining. What's more, these places will often offer better food at cheaper prices.

That said, the larger hotels still draw many diners. Hotel restaurants that are recommended are **Shiraz Persian** restaurant in the Crowne Plaza, **Vue** French restaurant at Al Bustan Palace, **Trader Vic's** (www.tradervics.com) seafood at the Intercontinental, and for excellent Indian cuisine in beautiful surroundings visit the **Passage to India** in the Hatat House Compound, Muscat.

There are also Western-style cafés and eateries in Muscat's **shopping malls**, such as the Sultan Center, the Al-Zakher Center, the SABCO Centre (Qurm), the Carrefour (Seeb and Qurm) and the LuLu Hypermarket. The **Muscat Bakery** (numerous branches) is recommended for snacks and many shops sell take-away samosas, etc. McDonald's, Hardee's and Pizza Hut are among the many fast-food outlets.

For a comprehensive list of the restaurants available in the capital pick up a copy of the useful *Oman2day*, on sale in supermarkets and bookstores. Sometimes there are complimentary copies in hotel rooms.

Reservations

During the winter months it is always best to make a reservation for the more expensive or popular restaurants as they become very busy. The peak times for most restaurants in the capital are between 7pm and 9pm, so before and after those times restaurants can usually cater to those without reservations. In Omani homes, lunch is usually the main meal of the day, with a lighter meal in the evening.

Children in Restaurants

Most restaurants are very tolerant of children, but few provide special seating or child-friendly menus, so if these are needed it is best to enquire in advance.

Alcohol and Other Restrictions

Having wine with lunch or dinner is generally not a problem, as all the larger and more expensive restaurants have liquor licences. However, many of the smaller, cheaper places do not. Eating out during the month of Ramadan can be problematic for visitors, as all food and drink establishments in Oman are then closed until after sunset, and no alcohol is sold at all during this time. Having said that, there are some hotels that will sell alcohol to their guests, as long as it is consumed in their rooms.

Tax and Tipping

It should be noted that the suggested cost of meals does not include the 17 percent tourist tax that is added to most hotel and restaurant bills. (Breakdown of tax: 5 percent municipality tax, 4 percent tourism tax, 8 percent service charge.) The service charge element does not go to the waiters, so many people leave an additional cash tip – anything from 10 percent to a few baisa – if they are happy with the service.

Traditional Omani Dishes

In addition to the dishes listed below, you will find many Indian and Pakistani dishes, reflecting historical and contemporary links between Oman and the Indian sub-continent.
Aursia Mashed rice and spices, made for special occasions.
Bapaloo Slightly sour-tasting curried fish.
Halwa This is a generic name for dessert or sweetmeats, but it also refers to a special Omani dessert made from sugar, nuts, rosewater, cardamom, cornflour and ghee. It is often served with coffee.
Harees Meat (usually lamb) cooked slowly with whole wheat.
Khawa Roasted ground coffee beans mixed with cardamom powder.

Laban Salty buttermilk.
Maqbous Rice with saffron, cooked over a spicy meat.
Marak Vegetable curry.
Mashuai A whole spit-roasted kingfish with lemon rice.
Mishkak Skewered meat grilled on charcoal.
Qabooli Similar to Indian Biryani.
Rukhal Thin, round bread served with Omani honey or crumbled over curry.
Ruz al Mudhroub A dish made with cooked rice and fried fish.
Sakhana A thick, sweet soup made of wheat, date, molasses and milk.
Shuwa Meat cooked slowly (up to two days) in a pit dug in the ground. This is a special meal most often prepared during Eid Al Fitr and Eid Al Adha.

MUSCAT

OMAN

HOTEL RESTAURANTS

Al Bustan

Al Khiran Terrace
Al Bustan Palace Hotel
Tel: 2479 9666
Terrace dining with theme nights. Very popular. Restaurant moves indoors during summer. **££**

China Mood
Tel: 2479 9666
Recruited from China, the chefs in this restaurant prepare an array of fresh authentic cuisine that is the best Chinese food in Oman. **£££**.

Seblat Al Bustan
Tel: 2479 9666
(Sunday and Wednesday evening only)
For those who want to sample the best in traditional Omani cuisine, the Seblat Al Bustan recreates the traditional surroundings of a Bedouin village. **£££**

Vue
Tel: 2479 9666
Showcases the contemporary French cuisine of Australian Chef Shannon Bennett in a chic ambience. Extensive wine list. **£££**

Chedi Muscat

Arabic Courtyard
Tel: 2452 4400
Outdoor buffet-style restaurant. Dinner is a traditional Arab feast, with fantastic food prepared on an outside grill. Enjoy a traditional shisha pipe in the adjacent courtyard. **£££**

The Beach Restaurant
Tel: 2452 4400
On the beach, overlooking the Gulf of Oman, the hotel's newest eatery offers a huge selection of seafood in an open-air setting. During summer the restaurant is enclosed with glass. **£££**

The Restaurant
Tel: 2452 4343
This is The Chedi's premier restaurant. It has four kitchens, serving Middle Eastern, European, Indian and Asian cuisine. **£££**

Crowne Plaza

Shiraz
Crowne Plaza Hotel
Tel: 2466 0660
A tented ceiling, combined with good Persian cuisine create a reasonably authentic Middle Eastern experience. **£££**

Grand Hyatt Muscat

Safari Grill House
Tel: 2464 1231
On the roof-top terrace of the hotel, this restaurant is only open during the cooler months. The excellent set meals, combined with the copious wine that is included in the price, makes the Safari Terrace very popular with local people. **£££**

Tuscany
Tel: 2464 1234
Highly regarded restaurant with an extensive menu offering many classic Italian dishes. It is very popular, so it is wise to make a reservation. **£££**

Intercontinental

Señor Pico
Tel: 2468 0000
Great Mexican food and a nice ambience.

Trader Vic's Restaurant and Mai Tai Lounge
(Adjacent to the hotel)
Tel: 2468 0000
Polynesian-style restaurant with live Cuban music (Sat–Tues). A popular choice among locals. The cuisine on offer is an eclectic mix of international fare. **£££**

Rassison SAS Hotel

Al Tajin Grill
Tel: 2448 7777
Radisson SAS Hotel

This all-inclusive buffet-style meal, with house beverages thrown in, is a fantastic offer in a city where a single glass of wine can cost more than a meal. **£££**

Olivo
Tel: 2487 7777
Offers daily buffets for breakfast and lunch, and a seafood and BBQ Bazaar dinner. Definitely one of the best buffets in town, but à la carte is also available. **££**

Shangri-La's Barr Al Jissah Resort & Spa

Al Tanoor
Tel: 2477 6565
(Al Bandar Hotel)
Diners can choose to sit on the beachside terrace or inside the souq-like restaurant with its Arabian tents and traditional Omani crafts. Dinner is served buffet style, but à la carte dining is also available. The menu is international fare, with Middle Eastern, Turkish, Greek Lebanese, Persian and Indian cuisine. **£££**

Bait Al Bahar
Tel: 2477 6565
(Al Waha Hotel)
Located on the beach between Al Waha and Al Bandar hotels, this restaurant offers a selection of fresh seafood. The floor-to-ceiling windows give wonderful sea views and a large rooftop terrace serves pre- and post-dinner cocktails (only in cooler months). **£££**

Capri Court
Tel: 2477 6565
(Al Bandar Hotel)
Provides both indoor and outdoor dining, and serves contemporary Italian cuisine. There's a large selection of fine wines. **£££**

Circles
Tel: 2177 6565
(Al Bandar Hotel)
A great feature is

excellent pizza cooked in a wood-fired oven, but a tapas menu is also available. **£££**

Samba
Tel: 2477 6677
(Al Waha Hotel)
South American-Argentinian inspired restaurant offering inside and outside dining. Great buffet. **££**

Shahrazad
(Al Husn Hotel)
Tel: 2477 6565
Hailed as Shangri La's premier restaurant. Lavish setting, fantastic views and top-notch Moroccan cuisine. Dinner only. **£££**.

Sultanah
Tel: 2477 6565
(A1 Husn Hotel)
This upscale restaurant was named after the first Omani ship to sail to America, and the decor suggests a luxury cruise ship. An impressive international menu is complemented by stunning views of the resort's spectacular grounds. **£££**

Surf Café
(al Waha Hotel)
Tel: 2477 6565
This upmarket café was designed with a younger clientele in mind. Great place if you are looking for a quick bite. With its own internet access, pool tables, and several flat screen televisions. **£**

Tapas and Sablah
(Al Bandar Hotel)
Tel: 2477 6565
Features hot and cold tapas with a Mediterranean and Asian bent, as well as Middle Eastern mezze. Serves late into the night. **£££**.

THE UAE

LANGUAGE

OTHER RESTAURANTS

Automatic Café
AlKhuwair.
Tel: 2448 7200
Fresh juices and an array of Arabic food. **£**

D' Arcy's Kitchen
Tel: 2460 0234
JawaratA' Shati Complex
Madinat Sultan Qaboos
Tel: 2469 9119
Designed to give the impression of a country kitchen. Serves hearty portions of standard British/American cuisine. **£**

Bin Ateeq
Al Khuwair (behind the Shell station on the slip road)
Tel: 2447 8225

Bedouin-style eatery, which means there are no tables. You sit on a carpet in a private room. **£**

Café Vergnano 1882
Madinat Al-Sultan Qaboos
Tel: 2469 2370
This chain of Italian cafés has been in the Vergnano family for four generations. Voted as the best coffee shop in *Oman2day*'s restaurant awards. **£**

Copper Chimney
Opposite British Bank in Muscat Business District
Tel: 2470 6420
Reasonably priced Indian dishes. **££**

Curry House
Opposite car showroom in Wattayah
Tel: 2456 4033
Simple restaurant serving a vast array of Indian dishes

at good prices. **£**

Golden Dragon
Behind Al Fair Supermarket in Medinat Qaboos
Tel: 2469 7374
Chinese and Thai food attracts a good mix of customers. **££**

Lai Thai
Al Khuwair
(Between the Safeer International Hotel and the Safeer Plaza Hotel)
Tel: 9802 5189
Thai restaurant serving great food at reasonable prices. **£**

Mumtaz Mahal
Tel: 2460 5907
Near Qurum Natural Park backing onto the prestigious Left Bank bar Perched on a hilltop over-looking Qurum Natural Park this restaurant creates some of the best Indian food in the city. Wonderful views

of the surrounding area, and serenades by musicians playing traditional Indian instruments. Voted best Indian restaurant in the *Oman2day* restaurant awards. **£££**

Ofair Public Food Restaurant
Al Khuwair, behind the Shell station on the slip road.
Tel: 2448 2965
Popular Bedouin-style restaurant. **£**

Passage to India
Tel: 2456 84820
Behind Hatat House, Wattayah
Very good North Indian food and nice ambience. **££**

Pane Caldo
Tel: 2469 8697
JawharatA'Shati Complex
Shatti Al Qurum
A good Italian bistro. **££**

OUTSIDE MUSCAT

Barka

Khalab
Al Nahda Resort and Spa,
Tel: 2688 3710
Has an international buffet with different themes every night. A la carte menu is also available. **£–££**

Jasmine Garden Restaurant
Tel: 2688 6064
When heading towards Sohar from Muscat, turn left from the Barka roundabout, and Jasmine is on the right. You can get a great lunch platter for just RO 1.500. **£**

Coral Reef Café
Al Sawadi Beach Resort
Tel: 2689 5545
Buffets, theme nights and fisherman's catch every Thursday night. **£–££**

Bidiya

Traveller"s Oasis
Tel: 2558 3235
On the main road from Muscat to Sur. Serves Arabic and Asian food. **£–££**

Buraimi

Tropicana, Buraimi
Buraimi Hotel
Tel: 2565 2010
Continental buffets. **££**

Ibra

Penguin
Tel: 2557 0694
Fast-food chain selling pizzas, burgers and kebabs. **£**

Skyline Coffee Shop
Tel: 9951 4456
Alayat, Ibra, opposite Omanoil filling station.
A choice of 42 juices. **£**

Nizwa

Bin Ateeq
Tel: 2541 0466
Serves traditional Omani cuisine. **£–££**

Birkat Al Mauz, Nizwa
Nizwa Hotel
Tel: 2543 1616
Quiet, pleasant restaurant. **££**

Nizwa Catering Restaurant
Tel: 2541 0000
On the road into Nizwa (coming from Muscat) just before the roundabout sign to Bahla, this restaurant has bright green, plastic date palms outside. **£–££**

Safari Hotel Restaurant and Coffee Shop
Tel: 2543 2150
The coffee shop is located outdoors.Both the café and restaurant offer fusion cuisine. **£–££**

Spicy Village
Tel: 2543 1694
Branch of a small chain specialising in Indian and Chinese food. On the highway before you enter Nizwa. **£–££**

Ras Al Hadd

Ras Al Hadd Beach Hotel Restaurant
Tel: 9937 6989
International à la carte and buffet-style breakfast, lunch and dinner. **£–££**

Salalah

Al Maha
Hilton Resort
Tel: 2321 1234
Has a reasonably priced buffet every night.

Bin Ateeq, Salalah
23rd July Street
Tel: 2329 2384
Simple, inexpensive Arabic food. **£**

Darbat Restaurant
Crowne Plaza Resort
Tel: 2323 5333
Great views. Buffets and à

la carte menu. Open all day. **£–££**

Palm Grove
Hilton Resort
Tel: 2321 1234
This open-air beachside restaurant offers seafood, and Asian and Mediterra-nean cuisine for lunch and dinner. **£–££**

Woodlands
Salalah Airport
Tel: 2320 4280
One of the best Indian res-taurants in the sultanate. Won *Oman2day*'s award vote for best service. **£££**

Sohar

Al Zafran
Sohar Beach Hotel
Tel: 2684 3701
Seafood grill. Good stop-off when travelling between Dubai and Muscat. **££**

Sur

Al Rasagh
Sur Beach Hotel
Tel: 2554 2031
A la carte and buffet-style breakfast, lunch and dinner. **£–££**

Oyster Restaurant
Sur Plaza Hotel
Tel: 2554 3777
Continental, Indian, Chinese and Arabic food. **£–££**

ACTIVITIES

THE ARTS, FESTIVALS, NIGHTLIFE, SPORTS AND SHOPPING

THE ARTS

Theatre, Music and Dance

Muscat is not a destination where you will find an abundance of cultural activities, but it is due to have a new **Opera house and cultural centre** (scheduled to open in 2009).
The **Muscat Amateur Theatre** group and the **Muscat Singers** occasionally put on performances, but there is no official website, so it is difficult to know when and where events are happening. Sometimes local newspapers announce upcoming events, but more often than not you will read about them afterwards. Word of mouth is still the most reliable source of information.

Royal Oman Symphony Concert Series
Tel: 2479 9666
www.albustanpalace.com
A series of concerts held during the winter, usually in the Al Bustan Palace Hotel's Auditorium. Enquire at the hotel for the concert schedule.

Fête de la Musique
Tel: 2468 1800
www.ambafrance-om.org
This is organised by the French Embassy every year, normally on 21 June. The embassy and the Omani-French Centre also arrange an annual film festival.

Art Galleries

Al Tarhal Gallery
Way 3048, Villa 3927
(near the Grand Hyatt)
Tel: 9660 3296 (or by appointment, tel: 9915 4545)

www.altarhalgallery.com
A contemporary gallery that exhibits work by artists from around the world.

Bait Munza Gallery
Tel: 2473 9204
Old Muscat, next to Bait Al Zubair
Located in a traditional Omani house, it displays oil paintings, mixed media and prints by international artists.

Al Madina Art Gallery
Tel: 2469 1380
Al Inshirah Street
Medinat Sultan Qaboos
More of a shop than a gallery, selling furniture, gift items and paintings.

Yiti Art Gallery
Tel: 2456 4297
Al Khamis Plaza, Qurum

Omani Society for Fine Arts
Tel: 2469 4969
Near Al Sarooj roundabout
Muttrah
www.omanartsociety.org
Stages exhibitions, performances and meetings.

Cinemas

Cinema information lines do not usually open until after 2pm. Children under 3 years of age are not permitted, and credit card purchases must be over RO5 (US$13). A mix of English, Arabic and Hindi films are shown. For current listings see the theatre website or a local newspaper.

Muscat Area

Al Bahja Cinema
Seeb, Markaz Al Bahji Mall
Tel: 2454 0856
www.albahjacinema.com
Three screens.

Al Shatti Plaza
Shatti Al Qurum (near Ramada Hotel)
Tel: 2469 2656
www.filmcityoman.com
Three screens.

Ruwi Cinema
Tel: 2478 0380
www.ruwicinema.com
Four screens.

Star Cinema
Ruwi
Tel: 2479 1641
www.omanaccess.com
Five screens.

Al Nasr Cinema
Ruwi
Tel: 2483 1358
www.filmcityoman.com
Four screens.

Sur

Al Wafi Plaza
Tel: 2554 5544
www.filmcityoman.com
Two screens.

Sohar

Sohar Plaza
Al Waqaibah Street (next to Bank Muscat)
www.filmcityoman.com
Four screens.

FESTIVALS

Muscat Festival
This 22-day event, held in January and February, celebrates Oman's culture and history. It includes a wide range of shopping opportunities, and activities such as dance, magic shows, music and craft demonstrations. For more details, visit www.muscat-festival.com.

Khareef Festival, Salalah

This festival (15 July–end of August) celebrates the monsoon season when the southernmost tip of Oman transforms from a dry desert to a lush green carpet. Events include sport, dance, music and handicrafts sale.

National Day Celebration

National Day is officially 18 November, Sultan Qaboos's birthday. However, the celebrations rarely take place on the actual day. Various events are held around Muscat and coloured lights are strung along the main highway for the celebrations.

NIGHTLIFE

Muscat is not bursting with options for after-hours entertainment, but there are some decent clubs if you don't mind a lot of smoke, late-night crowds and very loud music. There are some great piano bars in some of the five-star hotels.

Al Ghazal Pub

Intercontinental Hotel, Upper level
Tel: 2460 0500
Very popular with both Omanis and expats. Some of the best live bands in the city, and great for dancing, decent food, playing pool or watching a match on big screen televisions.

Club Safari

Tel: 2464 1234
Grand Hyatt Hotel
(no access from the hotel; entry is outside to the left)
This African-themed club with faux animal skins, African masks and bamboo adorning the walls offers a fun and friendly atmosphere. Great for live music and dancing, but can get smoky and over-crowded.

Copacabana

Tel: 2464 1234
Grand Hyatt Hotel
(no access from the hotel; entry is on the lower level across from the car park)
Although this club does not have live bands, it is often very crowded. The resident DJ plays an eclectic mix of music.

John Barry Bar

Tel: 2464 1234
Grand Hyatt Hotel
(accessed from the lobby)
Nautically-themed piano bar, with large porthole lights and ship paraphernalia. Extensive menu with an impressive, but expensive, wine list. Live music nightly.

The Cellar Bar

Tel: 2448 7777
Radisson SAS Hotel
(access behind the hotel)
Filipino cover band, and a largely male clientele.

The Coral Bar

Tel: 2448 7777
Radisson SAS Hotel
(accessed from the lobby)
Small, smoky and predominantly male. The large underwater mural in this piano bar has remained the same for years. In fact, the only thing that really changes here is the piano player (every few months).

Left Bank

Tel: 2469 3699
(Behind the Mumtaz Mahal Restaurant)
Muscat's hottest new nightspot has an extensive and appealing menu and chic décor, as well as great views from its hilltop location. Caters to a largely expat clientele.

Long Bar & Zyro

Tel: 2477 6666
Shangri La's Barr Al Jissah Resort & Spa, Al Bandar Hotel (beachside)
A comprehensive list of cocktails, beer and spirits. Rarely crowded.

Pavo Real

Tel: 2460 2603
A restaurant during the day and a dance club at night, this Mexican-inspired place serves great margaritas and has a live band.

Piano Bar

Tel: 2477 6666
Shangri La's Barr Al Jissah Resort & Spa, Al Bandar Hotel (lobby level)
This chic and luxurious piano bar is the perfect place to relax and listen to live music.

Rock Bottom Café

Tel: 2456 4443
Ramee Guestline Hotel, Al Qurum Street
Although not a particularly popular café during the day, in the evening it transforms into the most happening place in Muscat. Crowds flock to this club to rock the night away. Has a live band and/or a DJ.

The Chedi Poolside Cabana

Tel: 2452 4400
Chedi Hotel (by the adult-only pool on the beach)
Live jazz, buffet and barbecue set-up at the Chedi Poolside Cabana every Saturday, Sunday, Wednesday and Thursday. Reservations essential.

SPORTS

Participant Sports

Watersports

The long coastline offers excellent opportunities for watersports. There are lengthy stretches of public beachfront between the Hyatt and Crowne Plaza hotels in Muscat, but the best beaches are in Salalah, Dhofar. Good watersports facilities are available at the Al Bustan Palace, Hyatt Regency, Muscat Inter-Continental, The Chedi hotels and Al Jissah Resort and Spa. Other hotels have arrangements for guests to use these hotels' beach clubs.

Diving

The relatively untouched waters off Oman offer some of the best diving in the Middle East, with warm, clear water and excellent underwater flora and fauna. Nearby locations include Bandar Jussa, Bandar Khairan (where, a 3,000-tonne vessel sunk in 2003 is developing into a good dive site), Fahal Island, the Damaniyat Islands, and Ras Abu Daoud.

Snorkelling and scuba-diving are available from PADI instructors at:

Blue Zone Watersports

Marina Bandar al-Rowdha, Muscat, Tel: 2473 7293
www.bluzonediving.com
Offers diving and snorkelling, PADI courses, live-aboard and a dive shop, dolphin- and whale-watching, game fishing and boat charters.

Moonlight Dive Centre

Tel: 9931 7700
www.moonlightdive.com
Attached to the A'Suwaidi Hotel (45 minutes north of Muscat)
Variety of dive packages and courses.

Muscat Diving and Adventure Centre

Tel: 2448 5663
www.omandiving.com
Scuba, snorkelling, sea-kayaking, fishing, dolphin- and whale-watching.

Oman Dive Centre

Qantab Beach, south of Muscat
Tel: 2482 4240
ww.diveoman.com.om
See also:
www.musandamdiving.com
www.alsawadibeach.com

Golf

Muscat area

Ghallah Wentworth Golf Club

Tel: 2459 1248
http://ghallahwentworthgolfclub.com

An 18-hole par 72 sand course surrounded by dramatic mountains. Cost for non-members: 18 holes-Brown fees RO5 (US$13); 9 holes-Brown fees RO3 (US$8).

Green Links Golf Course
Seeb
Designed by Greg Norman, and part of a new seaside development called The Wave, Green Links will be Oman's first PGA standard 18-hole golf course when it opens in 2009,

Salalah
Marco Polo Golf Course
Tel: 2323 5333
www.crowneplaza.com
Crowne Plaza Hotel, Salalah

Spectator Sports

Although Oman features a number of sports stadia, there are few high-profile events. The national football team normally plays at the stadium in Wattayeh. Powerboat racing takes place at the marina.

Traditional spectator sports are horse-racing and, on the southern Batinah coast, **bullfighting** (bloodless, bull-versus-bull contests of strength). Matches start around 4pm during the winter in Barka and Seeb. Free.

Rally Oman
www.omanrally.com
Oman's biggest motorsport event takes place in March or April. The freestyle competition is held over three days, and includes concerts and other activities. Free.

Camel Racing
Held at tracks in Seeb, Salalah, the Interior and Batinal regions. Usually take place during public holidays and National Day celebrations. Free.

SHOPPING

There are many Western-style shopping malls in Muscat. Qurum is particularly well-endowed with malls. For a list of malls and the shops they contain see www.muscatmall.com.

Muttrah Souq in Muscat, and **Nizwa Souq** in the interior, offer a vast array of traditional goods and crafts plus attractive Indian-made artefacts – silver vases, incense holders and boxes. **Salalah** is renowned for its incense souq and hundreds of textile shops and cheap tailors. Rasool Buksh Bin Osman Al-Balushi in Muttrah Souq is recommended for traditional antique weaponry, jewellery and coins.

Art and Antiques

Jabreen Art Gallery at the Al Araimi Shopping Complex, and **Yiti Art Gallery**, close to the Sheraton Hotel in the Muscat Business District, are commercial galleries that stock the work of local artists.

Bait Muzna Gallery (opposite the Bait Al Zubair Museum in Muscat; tel: 2473 9204) displays artworks, jewellery and furniture.

L-Majlis Gallery (Villa 57, Street 44, North Azaiba; tel: 501 057) specialises in Arab and colonial antiques and artworks.

Khanjars

These are the curved daggers worn by Omani men. They have intricate designs and the handles can be made from a variety of materials. The scabbard is made of silver. Styles vary, depending on the region in which they are made. The best places to get these are Muttrah or Nizwa souqs.

Silver

Oman is famous for its silver and you can find both old and new items in the shopping malls and Muttrah Souq. But buying antique silverware is not for the inexperienced and you may be taken for a ride by the vendor. Omani silversmiths can be seen at work in Nizwa souq.

Gold

Oman is one of the cheapest places to buy gold. The price is determined by the weight of the article. Muttrah Souq has a huge section of gold outlets and all the shopping centres contain specialist gold stores.

Pottery

Bahla is the best place to buy typical Omani pots. If you're travelling on the road to Nizwa you will see pottery for sale at the roadside in Fanja.

Carpets and Handicrafts

Expensive Persian carpets are available from the large shopping centres. In the same shops you'll see chests and tables with brass detail from Pakistan and India.

Oman Heritage Shop, in the commercial block to the left of the entrance to the Muscat Inter-Continental hotel, is a non-profit enterprise selling traditional arts and crafts. **Village Arts and Crafts** (Majid Trading Enterprises LLC) has several locations around the city. For beautiful carpets and unique hand-made Sheesham wood furniture (similar to ebony or walnut in terms of strength and durability) this is the place to shop. Pashminas and handicrafts are also available.

Taalali Oman (www.taalalioman.biz) om Mutrah Corniche (next to the Mosque and Rainbow Café on the first floor of the Gold Souq Building) sells traditional Omani clothes (for men, women and children) with a Western twist, designed by a French woman, Florence Rusconi. Also sells handmade sandals and jewellery featuring beautiful Arabic calligraphy.

Frankincense

There are hundreds of blends and mixtures, including substances such as sandalwood. Make sure you buy a burner as well as the frankincense. The powdered blends are available in the souqs and malls.

BELOW: looking for bargains in Muttrah Souq.

OMAN

THE UAE

LANGUAGE

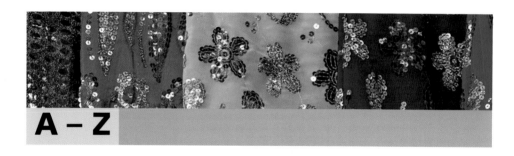

A – Z

A HANDY SUMMARY OF PRACTICAL INFORMATION, ARRANGED ALPHABETICALLY

A ge restrictions

Car-rental agencies require drivers to be at least 21 or 22 years old. This rises to 25 and 30 depending on the vehicle. Children under 10 are not allowed to sit in the front passenger seat of cars. The minimum age for entry to bars and nightclubs varies between 18 and 21. On the water, the minimum age for activities such as water-skiing and parasailing is seven or eight, but it also depends on the child's weight (minimum 40kg/88lb). For diving lessons, the minimum age for junior open water training is 10, but children can begin learning in a pool from the age of eight.

B udgeting for Your Trip

The cost for a standard double room ranges from around Dhs350 per night in a one-star city centre hotel to Dhs575-1,000 at a four-star hotel and Dhs1,000-3,500 at a five-star hotel. Sandwiches and curries from street-level restaurants can be bought for as little as Dhs15. Main courses in most decent Western-style, non-hotel retsaurants are between Dhs25-45. For fine dining,

allow upwards of Dhs55 per person for mains. Soft drinks start at Dhs1 in shops but are heavily marked up in restaurants. Imported alcoholic drinks tend to be more expensive than in the West.

Generally taxis are cheaper than those in Western cities, but the taxi fare from airports is higher than that from elsewhere in cities. Package deals arranged from your home country are likely to be cheaper than separately arranged air travel and accommodation. The best prices occur in low season (July–Sept) when the UAE is at its hottest. Bus tickets offer good value, costing between Dhs1-3, while a creek crossing on a water taxi is Dhs1.

Business Hours

Government offices work 7/7.30am–1.30pm Saturday to Wednesday. On Thursday offices are either closed or open only until noon.

Banks are generally open from 8am–1pm Sunday to Wednesday, closing at noon on Thursdays in preparation for the weekend. Some private companies either work in the evening after taking a long lunch break, or work 8am–5pm. Some take

a two-day weekend, others only close on Fridays. Times vary, so do check.

Shops are usually open 9am–1pm and 4–9pm, while some supermarkets open for 24 hours. Shops in Abu Dhabi and Dubai also tend to be open all day. Shopping malls can be open 10am–10pm, some even until midnight, Saturday to Thursday. Those that open on Friday close for prayers 11.30am–1.30pm due to it being the Islamic day of rest. All shops in Ras Al Khaimah close at prayer times.

Prayer times usually only mean a delay of about half an hour while the proprietor goes to pray. Most shops are closed during religious holidays.

C hildren

Childcare facilities are on a par with those in the West. Most malls have changing facilities in the women's public toilets; some also have supervised indoor play areas.

Climate

Summers are very hot. From **May to September** daytime temperatures are rarely below 40°C (104°F), with humidity up to 90 percent.

CLIMATE CHART

UAE

- ▦ Maximum temperature
- ☐ Minimum temperature
- — Rainfall

From **October to April** there is very good weather (sunny and warm) with temperatures ranging from as low as 10°C (50°F) inland to 30°C (mid-80°sF), with little or no humidity. However, strong winds sometimes bring sandstorms, and it occasionally rains very heavily. The rain usually comes sometime from **January to March**, and can result in large areas of flooding. The desert inland gets much colder than the coastal regions at night and during the winter months.

What to Bring

In the summer months it is extremely hot, so bring a sun hat, sunblock and wear cool cotton clothes. A jumper or jacket is needed at night in the cooler winter months. Women are advised to wear modest clothes in the streets, particularly in the souqs, so avoid short shorts and skirts and keep your shoulders covered to avoid unwanted attention and risk offending anyone. Men should not bare their torsos for the same reason. On the beaches swimsuits, shorts or bikinis are fine. In Sharjah, women are only allowed to wear swimwear on private beaches. For business a light suit is useful, and men are expected to wear a jacket and tie in some hotel restaurants.

Crime and Safety

The UAE is generally a safe country for both men and women. The crime rate is low, and although petty theft is as common as in most countries, major crimes are relatively rare. The level of personal security is also high: for women to avoid personal harassment not walking around alone at night is recommended, but there is no real physical danger.

Taxis are safe to take during the day, or at night within towns as long as a woman is wearing demure clothing and knows her route so that she can avoid being taken on a "detour". Fares, except in metered taxis, should be agreed in advance, to avoid arguments at the end of the journey. Inter-emirate registered taxis are fine and taxi shares are safe for women in the day. At night, lone women are advised not to get a taxi out of town into desert areas, or for a long inter-emirate drive.

Customs Regulations

Duty-free goods can be brought into the country:
- 400 cigarettes or 2 kg loose tobacco.
- A reasonable amount of perfume.
- Non-Muslims can bring in 4 litres of wine, beer or spirits, unless you are arriving in Sharjah where alcohol is prohibited. You are not allowed to bring in alcohol if arriving overland. Check these allowances have not changed when you travel.

Books and magazines are expensive so it's wise to bring some paperbacks to read, avoiding any that may cause offence. The same applies to DVDs and videos – though customs checks are far less stringent than they used to be. However, pirated video and audiotapes, CDs and DVDs will be confiscated due to the strict enforcement of copyright laws. There are also severe penalties if you are found carrying drugs.

D isabled Travellers

Dubai Simply Accessible, a special guide for travellers with disabilities, is published by the Dubai Department of Tourism and Commerce Marketing (DTCM) and is available at tourist information centres in most malls. An online version can be seen at www.dubai tourism.ae (click on "Special Needs Tourism" on the home page). Subjects covered include specialist taxi transport, access to hotels, heritage sites, desert tours, cinemas, parks and malls, and specialist medical facilities. Most hotels have ramps for wheelchair access while malls tend to have lifts as well as escalators. Most toilets in the UAE have enlarged cubicles for wheelchair access.

E conomy

The UAE's economy is based on oil and gas extraction, which brings in the vast majority of the government's revenue and forms about 40 percent of GDP. Abu Dhabi generates about two-thirds of the total GDP and Dubai, the main port of the UAE, about a quarter. Over the past 10 years non-oil industries have begun to play a more substantial part in the economy, and in Dubai trade and tourism are now significant contributers to GDP.

Electricity

220/240 volts. The majority of sockets accept three pin 13-amp British-style plugs. Adaptors for two pin appliances can be bought in supermarkets.

Embassies and Consulates

As Abu Dhabi, not Dubai, is the federal capital of the UAE, Dubai tends to have foreign consulates rather than embassies. Embassies are usually open 8.30am–1.30pm, with all closing on Friday and some closing on Saturday.

Abu Dhabi

Australia, Al Muhairy Centre, Sheikh Zayed the First Street, tel: 02-634 6100
Canada, Abu Dhabi Trade Towers (Abu Dhabi Mall) West Tower, tel: 02-694 0300
UK, near the Corniche, tel: 02-610 1100
US, off Airport Road, tel: 02-414 2200

Dubai (Consulates)

Australia, Consulate-General, BurJuman Business Tower, Khalifa Bin Zayed Road, tel: 04-508 7100.
Canada, Bank Street building, Khalid bin Waleed Street, tel: 04-314 5555.
UK, Al Seef Road (Dubai side of creek), tel: 04-309 4444.
US, World Trade Centre, Sheikh Zayed Road, tel: 04-311 6000.

Entry Requirements

Visas are required by all nationalities except Gulf Co-operation Council members. Citizens of Australia, Canada, New Zealand, the US, all EU countries and some Asian countries

Emergency Numbers

Police: tel: 999
Fire: tel: 997
Ambulance: tel: 998
Dubai Police Headquarters: tel: 04 229 2222.
Dubai Police Tourist Security Department: tel: 800 4438.

including Singapore, Malaysia and Japan, get an automatic single visit visa upon entry – valid for up to 60 days. This visa (free to UK citizens) does not permit the holder to work.

Other nationalities visiting the UAE must be sponsored by the company they are seeing on business, by friends or family resident in the UAE or by the hotel they are staying at in the UAE. These 30-day, non-renewable tourist visas should be arranged before entry to the UAE and cost Dhs120. If a hotel obtains a tourist visa for you, you enter the country on their sponsorship for the duration of your stay. You generally have to stay with them for a few nights and you can then travel freely within the UAE for the rest of your stay. It is very important to keep copies of all paperwork, and of your visa, and useful to carry a photocopy of your passport with you. Entry regulations change from time to time so check before your trip.

UAE Embassy in London
30 Princes Gate, London SW7 1PT, tel: 020 7581 1281 (9am–3pm); www.unitedarabemirates.embassy homepage.com
UAE Embassy in Washington
3522 International Court, NW Washington DC 20008, tel: 202-243 2400; fax: 202-243 2432 (9am–4pm); www.uae-embassy.org

Etiquette

Although the UAE is a very liberal country compared with other states in the Gulf region, it is still a conservative Muslim country and visitors should respect this. Women especially should remember that clothing that is acceptable in a nightclub or on the beach is not appropriate to wear on the street during the day.

Outside the cities, dress more conservatively. Everyone should cover their upper arms and women should wear longer skirts or trousers. Men should not wear shorts in a business situation.

During the holy month of Ramadan don't eat, smoke or drink in public. Never drink and drive as you could end up in jail for a month, and don't offer alcohol to Muslims.

If visiting the home of a UAE citizen it is customary to remove shoes before venturing on the carpets (a measure originally introduced when conditions were considerably dustier than they are today), though increasingly, many local families no longer follow this custom. Avoid showing the soles of

your feet when sitting down. If you wish to take a present, a box of pastries or sweetmeats is a safe option.

G ay and Lesbian Travellers

Homosexuality is not tolerated in the UAE and is officially illegal, so discretion is strongly advised.

Getting Around

Public Transport

The Dubai Metro light rail project is being phased in and will consist of three routes connecting Dubai International Airport with Deira, Bur Dubai and Jebel Ali, but there are currently no trains in the UAE. Details of bus services are available from all main bus stations. For journeys from one emirate to another, service (shared) taxis provide a frequent and cheap service.

Generally, taxis are cheap and metered. There are taxi companies which can be pre-booked by telephone to collect you, as well as metered taxis on the street. Women should always sit in the back of a taxi.

Abu Dhabi

Bus The main bus terminal is on East Road. It is often easier to get a taxi than a bus for local trips, as the bus routes cater for those living in outer suburbs and workers' camps outside the city. It is not a particularly recommended mode of transport in Abu Dhabi city.
Service Taxi This is located adjacent to the main bus station on East Road. From here you can get to Dubai, Sharjah and Al Ain.
Taxi Taxis have meters but it is still wise to agree the fare before setting off. You can phone **Al Ghazal Taxi Service**, tel: 02-444 7787 or **National Taxi**: 02-555 2212. The minimum fare is Dhs3, with Dhs0.75 added for every kilometre.

Al Ain

Bus Buses run regularly to Abu Dhabi from the bus station behind the Al Ain souk. ONAT bus company also runs a service to Ruwi bus station in Muscat from outside Hotel Al Buraimi. Visitors must have an Omani visa before setting off. Expatriates resident in Oman need a road permit.
Service Taxi These are located in the large parking area behind the Grand Mosque near to Abu Baker Al Siddiq Street, near the Coffeepot Roundabout. Service taxis are easy to get to Dubai and Abu Dhabi.
Taxi Taxis have meters, although it is

always best to agree a fare before setting off. The number for Al Ghazal Taxis in Al Ain is tel: 03-751 6565.

Dubai

Bus Used mainly by lower-income workers, Dubai's bus service has undergone vast improvements and is a cheaper option for longer journeys than a hire car. However, it is not really a convenient alternative to taxis for trips within the city. The service operates in Deira from Al Sabkha bus station between the Gold Souk and Beniyas Square, and in Bur Dubai from Al Ghubaiba Street. The bus for Hatta is the no.16, which departs from the Gold Souk. The bus for Abu Dhabi is E1, which leaves from Bur Dubai bus station on the Creek. Routes and numbers are in Arabic and English.
Taxi The best way to get around the city. Cabs are metered, air-conditioned, mostly reliable and can be flagged down on the street or pre-booked. Taxis from the airport start with the meter at Dhs20, though in the city, meters start at around Dhs3. The main operators are Dubai Transport Corporation or DTC (tel: 04-208 0808), Cars Taxis (tel: 04-269 2900), Metro Taxi (tel: 04-267 3222) and National Taxis (tel: 04-339 0002).

If you use a non-metered taxi, agree the fare before getting in, which should start at Dhs5 for short local journeys and Dhs10-15 if you cross the Creek. Hotel taxis are more expensive but are reliable.
Water Taxi or Abra Dubai is split in two by the creek, use an abra or water taxi to get across. This is an atmospheric short journey of about five minutes. The abra stands on the Deira side are opposite the Gold Souq. Fares are only Dhs1 for trips from Deira to Bur Dubai and vice versa, while for Dhs100, an abra captain can take you on a one-hour tour up and down the creek.
Water Bus Introduced in 2007, the air-conditioned water bus serves commuters and tourists from the Creekside water taxi stations in Deira and Bur Dubai. Journeys on the tourist route cost around Dhs25 per person and run between 8am and midnight.

Sharjah

Bus After a trial run, a public bus service has just been launched, which covers 18 routes.
Service Taxi There are two stations. From Al Arouba Road in Rolla opposite Al Hamra Cinema they go to Umm Al Qaiwain and Ras Al Khaimah. The other station is next to

ABOVE: the cost of hiring a car is relatively low.

the vegetable souq near Khalid Lagoon, by the amusement park. To reach the nearby emirates of Ajman or Dubai it is often easier to get an ordinary taxi.

Taxi Non-metered taxis are gradually being phased out. Metered taxi companies are Emirates Taxis, tel: 06-539 6666, Citi Taxis, tel: 06-533 4444 and Delta Taxis, tel: 06-559 8598.

Ajman
There is no bus service or taxi stand. It is easy to get a Sharjah taxi to or from here.

Umm Al Qaiwain
Taxis only, from the stand on King Faisal Street across from Al Salam Hotel.

Ras Al Khaimah
Bus No bus service.
Service taxi The station is located on King Faisal Street near the Bin Majid Beach Hotel. Taxis go from here to Dubai, passing Umm Al Qaiwain, Ajman and Sharjah on the way. Change in Dubai for Abu Dhabi, Al Ain and the east coast.
Taxi Non-metered taxis only.

Fujairah
Bus No bus service.
Service taxi The stand is on the edge of town, west of the airport on the road to Sharjahi.
Taxi Non-metered taxis only.

Private Transport
The UAE has very efficient traffic systems, but the general standard of driving is poor and characterised by impatience and carelessness. Lane discipline is bad and reckless driving common. Once out on the

main highways cars travel fast. Roads are mainly dual-carriageway, well-signposted and in good condition. Authorities are trying to improve road safety through the use of traffic cameras monitoring speed offences.

Be aware that the penalty for drink-driving is a month in jail. It is illegal to use a mobile phone when driving and seatbelts are compulsory for drivers and front seat passengers. Any accident, however minor, must be reported to the police. In most of the emirates you must not move the car until the police arrive. In Dubai, cars can be moved to the side of the road if they are blocking traffic and if the accident is not serious. Always wait with the car for the police.

Inter-emirate Travel
This is unrestricted and easy by road. It is advisable to carry your papers on you while travelling in the UAE: there are no check-points or passport controls to go through between emirates, but occasionally the police do spot checks on the road for illegal immigrants or alcohol, although this is rare. Inter-emirate buses provide another option.

Car Hire
Hiring a car makes travelling around much easier, especially in the very hot summer months. Most car-hire companies will accept foreign licences if you have a visit or transit visa. You will also need your passport and two photos. Hire costs are relatively low, and there is fierce competition between companies so a good bargain can usually be found. For insurance reasons, visitors can only drive rental cars; a temporary

licence from the police is needed if you wish to drive a privately-owned vehicle.

Abu Dhabi
Avis, Abu Dhabi New International airport - arrivals terminal, tel: 02-575 7180.
Budget Abu Dhabi International airport, tel: 02-575 8808.
Thrifty, Al Nasr Street, tel: 02-634 5663.

Dubai
Avis, Dubai International airport - terminal 2, tel: 04-299 5465.
Budget, Emirates Towers Hotel, Sheikh Zayed Road, tel: 04-319 8733.
Europcar, Dubai International airport - terminal 3, tel: 04-295 1812.
Hertz, Dubai airport terminal 1 (tel: 04-224 5222) and terminal 3 (tel: 04-220 3013).

Sharjah
Avis, King Faisal Road, tel: 06-559 5925.
Budget, 56 Al Wasl Road, Al Khazamiya, tel: 06-544 1888.

Ras Al Khaimah
Budget, Al Hamra Hotel & Beach Resort, tel: 07-244 6666.
Sixt, tel: 07-235 5888.

Fujairah
Avis, tel: 09-222 5384.

Rules of the Road
● Drive on the right-hand side of the road.
● No right turns at lights.
● Speed limits are normally 60 kph in town and 120 kph on highways.
● Speeding tickets are often issued automatically by camera, without the driver knowing. Car rental agencies claim these from you.
● Always carry your driving licence and car registration card with you.

Getting There

By Air
Most major airlines operate in and out of the main airports, and smaller airlines and charter flights are also available. Dubai offers the largest choice of airlines operating in and out of the country. The main international airports are:
Abu Dhabi, tel: 02-575 7500.
Dubai, tel: 04-216 2525.
Sharjah, tel: 06-558 1111.

There are smaller airports at:
Al Ain, tel: 03-785 5555.
Fujairah, tel: 09-222 6222.
Ras Al Khaimah, tel: 07-244 8111.

Airlines
Abu Dhabi
Air India, tel: 02-633 4766
British Airways, tel: 02-622 5777
Emirates, tel:02-575 7474
Etihad Airways, tel: 02-505 8000;
call Centre: 800 2277 (24 hours).
Singapore Airlines, tel: 02-622 1110

Dubai
Air India, tel: 04-227 6747
British Airways, tel: 04-307 5555
Cathay Pacific, tel: 04-204 2888
Emirates, tel: 04-214 4444
Gulf Air, tel: 04-271 3111
KLM, tel: 04-335 5777

Emirates Airlines
London: First Floor, Gloucester Park,
95 Cromwell Road, SW7 4DL;
tel: 0844 800 2777.
New York: 55 East 59th Street,
NY 10022; tel: 1-800 777 3999;
www.emirates.com
Etihad Airways
London: 200 Hammersmith Road,
W6 7DL; tel: 0870 241 7121;
Toronto: 5000 Yonge Street, Suite
1706, Toronto, Ontario, M2N 7E9;
tel: 1-416-221 4744
www.etihadairways.com.

By Ship
Arrival by ship is not as common as
by plane. Make sure you have the
correct paperwork for port entry: it is
essential to have the paperwork
clarified before leaving your own
country and to check these
procedures carefully. Visas can be
obtained from some entry ports on
arrival in the country. Dubai's Cruise
Terminal is located at Port Rashid.

By Train or Bus
There are no trains in the UAE but
there are bus services from Oman in

the form of a daily service from
Muscat to Abu Dhabi via Al Ain and a
twice daily service to Dubai via Hatta.

By Car
The city and inter-emirate roads are
well-planned and well-maintained,
and are mainly dual carriageways. As
with other means of entry, if you are
arriving by road from outside the
UAE, you will need to obtain a visa
beforehand.

On Arrival
There are buses and taxis available
from the airports, or you can hire a
car. If you are with a tour group or
being met by a hotel, they will provide
a free bus to your hotel.
Abu Dhabi Bus No. 901 runs
between the airport and the main
bus station, 24 hours, costs Dhs3.
Airport and ordinary taxis are also
available. Check the fare in advance.
The airport is located on the
mainland, approx 40 mins drive from
the city centre.
Al Ain The airport is on the Abu
Dhabi Road, approximately 20 km
(12½ miles) from the centre. Bus
No. 500 runs every 30 minutes, 24
hours a day. Bus No. 130 is another
option. Both take approximately one
hour. Airport taxis are more expensive than ordinary metered taxis.
Dubai The airport is approximately 20
minutes from the city centre. Buses
No. 401 and 402 run between the
airport, Deira and Bur Dubai. Airport
taxis are more expensive than ordinary
metered taxis, and taxi fares are
higher to Bur Dubai across the creek.
Sharjah The airport is approximately
15 km (9 miles) from the centre.
There are no buses, so get a
metered taxi to the town centre or to
nearby Dubai.

Ras Al Khaimah The airport is
23 km (14 miles) from the centre.
Take a taxi.
Fujairah The airport is located south
of the city. Metered taxis only.

On Departure
There is no airport departure tax
and the UAE's duty-free shops are
some of the best in the world, so
it's worth getting to the airport
early. The UAE is an excellent point
of transit for other destinations.
Many airlines and tour operators
transit through Dubai.
   Many cargo ships leave the main
ports and some take passengers.
Phone an agent and ask for details.

Abu Dhabi
**Mazroui International Cargo
Company (MICCO)**
Tel: 02-677 6096
National Shipping Gulf Agency
Tel: 02-673 0500

Dubai
Inchcape Shipping Services
Tel: 04-303 8500
The Kanoo Group
Tel: 04-393 3633
Linkage International
Tel: 04-227 0309
Orient Shipping Services
Tel: 04-396 0888

Sharjah
Oasis Freight Company
Tel: 06-559 6325

Fujairah
Fujairah National Shipping Company
Tel: 09-222 8151

To Oman You can fly to Muscat, or
go by bus or car from Dubai. You
must have a visa but this is
relatively easy to obtain through a
hotel, directly from the Omani
Consulate in Bur Dubai (behind the
Indian Consulate, tel: 04-397 1000)
or, for most western citizens, on
arrival at Muscat airport or the
various border crossings at ports
from the UAE – at Hatta, Buraimi
and Jebel Hafit.

Government
The UAE is a federation of seven
emirates, all of which are ruled by
sheikhs. The president of the UAE
is the Sheikh of Abu Dhabi, the
largest and richest emirate. The
federal government runs a major
part of the country's infrastructure
and affairs, while the individual
emirates retain considerable
autonomy which they exercise to a
greater or lesser degree.

BELOW: if arriving by boat, you need the correct paperwork on arrival.

H ealth and Medical Care

Travel insurance is advisable as healthcare can be expensive, although there are good government hospitals as well as numerous private clinics.

No special injections are required for the UAE. Cholera and yellow fever certificates are only necessary if you arrive from an infected area. It is wise to drink bottled water. The drinking water is safe but your system may not have time to acclimatise.

You can buy most items in the UAE but if you're taking certain medicines then you should bring a supply with you. Just make sure you have a prescription with you, as certain drugs that are readily available in the west are prohibited in the UAE without one.

Medical Services

There are good government hospitals where treatment is free to health-card holders (only available with residence visas).

Emergency treatment is available to everyone but it is often easier for visitors to visit a private clinic and make a health insurance claim rather than spend time queueing in the government hospitals.

Hospitals
Abu Dhabi
Al Noor Hospital, Khalifa Street, tel: 02-626 5265.
Central Hospital, Al Manhal Street, tel: 02-671 1000. 24-hour emergency.

Dubai
Al Wasl Hospital, Oud Metha Road (opposite Wafi Shopping Mall), tel: 04-219 3000. Primarily paediatric.
American Hospital Dubai (In front of Al Nasr Leisureland), tel: 04-336 7777. Private hospital operating to American standards.
Rashid Hospital (Bur Dubai side of Al Maktoum Bridge near the British Council), tel: 04-219 2000. 24-hour casualty.
Welcare Hospital in Garhoud, tel: 04-282 7788. Modern private hospital.

Sharjah
Al Zahra Private Hospital, Al Zahra Square (Clocktower Roundabout), tel: 06-561 9999. Private general hospital. All medical, surgical and dental specialities. 24-hour emergency. Takes insurance plans.

Private Clinics
Abu Dhabi
Gulf Diagnostic Centre, 30th Street

(Khaleej Al Arabi Street), tel: 02-665 8090.
New National Medical Centre, Electra Street (Hamad Centre Building), tel: 02-633 2255.

Dubai
Al Borj Medical Centre, Al Diyafah Street, Satwa, tel: 04-345 4666.
Dubai London Clinic, Al Wasl Road, Jumeirah, tel: 04-344 6663.
General Medical Centre, Beach Road, Jumeirah, Magrudy Centre, tel: 04-349 5959.
Manchester Clinic, Beach Road, Jumeirah, tel: 04-344 0300.

Dentists
Abu Dhabi
Advanced Dental Clinic, above Spinneys in Khalidiya, tel: 02-681 2921.
Advanced American Dental Centre, behind BMW showroom in Khalidiya, tel: 02-681 2921.
British Dental Clinic, Hamdan Street (Bin Ham Building), tel: 02-677 3308.

Dubai
American Dental Clinic, Villa 54, next to Dubai Zoo, Beach Road, Jumeirah, tel: 04-344 0668.
Swedish Dental Clinic, Al Maktoum Street, (Nasr Building), tel: 04-223 1297

Sharjah
Al Zahra Private Hospital, Al Zahra Square (Clocktower Roundabout), tel: 06-561 9999.

I nternet

Emirates Internet & Media (EIM), a part of the national telecommunications company Etisalat, is the main provider of internet services. Access to certain websites may be blocked. The internet can usually be accessed in the guest rooms and business centres of larger hotels. In Dubai internet cafes can be found at various locations, including the Dune Centre, Satwa (tel: 04-345 3390; www.internetcafe.ae) and the F1 Net Cafe (tel: 04-345 1232; www.f1netcafe-dubai.com) in the Palm Strip Mall, Jumeirah. The charges are Dhs12 per hour. There are also an increasing number of hot spots offering free wireless connectivity for those with laptops, such as Coffee Bean & Tea Leaf on Jumeirah Road in Dubai.

L ost Property

If you lose your property, call the relevant authority or organisation in the general area where you believe

you lost your belongings. This might be the local police station, mall management office, taxi company, hotel or bar. The number for lost property at Dubai International Airport is 04-224 5383.

M aps

Hotel shops, bookshops and super-markets are all good sources of city street maps and road maps. Do be aware that official names of roads are used on signs but people may refer to them by unofficial or older names. Dubai in particular is changing so rapidly that city maps quickly become out of date. Try Dubai Municipality's Dubai Tourist Map. GEOprojects also produces a 1:750,000 scale map of the UAE with city maps of Dubai and other key cities: www.geoprojects.net/uae.htm.

Media
Print

The main English-language newspapers in the UAE are: *Gulf News*, *Khaleej Times* and the tabloid *7 Days*, based in Dubai; and *Gulf Today*, produced in Sharjah. The broadsheets have a daily tabloid section, film and TV listings, and a features magazine published once a week. Most British newspapers arrive a day late, excluding *The Times* and *The Sunday Times*, which are printed in Dubai.

The main sources of information on events, concerts and hotel functions in the UAE are *What's On*, *Time Out Abu Dhabi* (monthly) and *Time Out Dubai* (weekly), listings magazines available at most bookshops and hotel newsagents. A good women's magazine is *Emirates Woman*. A useful local guide aimed at the expatriate is *Connector* magazine, free in shops.

Broadcast Media

The main English-language TV stations are Abu Dhabi channel 2, Dubai's One TV, the Sharjah channel and Ajman TV. These show imported serials and English-language films, and most have news in English.

The international satellite TV stations available include CNN, SKY and BBC. Listings are in the local English press.

Dubai Eye, the UAE's first English-language "talk radio" station on 103.8FM covers current affairs, sport and general lifestyle, with panel discussions and phone-ins. Music stations broadcasting in English include Dubai 92 (92FM), Channel 4 (104.8FM), Emirates Radio 1

(99.3FM and 100.5FM) and Emirates Radio 2 (90.5FM and 98.5FM). In Abu Dhabi, Capital Radio is at 100.5 on the dial.

The BBC and Voice of America are also available on short- and medium-wave radio, and through PAS4 satellite service.

Money

Any currency can be exchanged at one of the many banks or at money exchanges in all major malls. Money changers offer varying rates and are sometimes better value than banks. Among them is Thomas Cook Al Rostamani (tel: 04-227 3690).

Travellers' cheques are sometimes accepted in major shops and are easily exchanged at banks. It is best to have the purchase receipt with you. Credit cards are accepted in hotels but anywhere else, check first. Smaller shops may add 5 percent to your bill if you pay by credit card. Banks also have globally linked ATM points and money transfers can be made through any bank.

If you plan to bargain, you'll need cash.
Currency 1 UAE Dirham (Dh) = 100 fils. Value is linked with the US$.

P hotography

Don't photograph men without asking permission first and never photograph or stare at women. The best place to photograph local people is at the Heritage and Diving Village in Dubai or Hatta Heritage Village where they are more used to the attentions of camera-toting tourists. Never take photos of government or military buildings or airports.

Postal Services

Poste restante facilities are not available in the UAE. The American Express office will hold mail for card holders, or you can receive it at your hotel. Mail is usually delivered to a PO Box number, not directly to a residence. The main **Abu Dhabi Post Office** is located on East Road, between Al Falah Street and Zayed the Second Street. The main **Dubai Post Office** is located on Zabeel Road, Al Karama (Sat–Thurs 8am–8pm). Mail is collected morning and evening.

Public Holidays

Religious holidays follow the Islamic calendar and are not fixed dates due to being timed according to the moon's phases. The main holidays are the Eid Al Fitr (the end of Ramadan) in October, Eid Al Adha (during the month of the Haj, or pilgrimage to Mecca) in December, the Islamic New Year in January, the Prophet's birthday in March, and the ascension of the Prophet in August/September. Other holidays include New Year's Day (1 January) and National Day (2 December). Some emirates honour their rulers, as in Abu Dhabi where 6 August is a holiday to mark the accession of former president HH Sheikh Zayed.

R eligious Services

Islam is the official religion of the UAE, with nationals being mostly Sunni Muslims; however, there is freedom of worship for Christians in church compounds. The main services are held on Friday – the local weekend.

Abu Dhabi

St Andrew's Church
Tel: 02-446 1631. In between Al Khubairat School and Sheikh Mohammed Bin Zayed Mosque, off Airport Road.
St George Orthodox Church
Tel: 02-446 4565. Behind the Immigration Office, off Airport Road.
St Joseph's Catholic Church
Tel: 02-446 1929. Between Karamah Street and Airport Road, close to Al Khubairat school.

Al Ain

St Mary's Catholic Church
Tel: 03-721 4417

Dubai

A Hindu temple is located in the souq area of Bur Dubai, near the abra station. The Christian churches are in two main areas, along Oud Metha Road in Bur Dubai, and in a compound near Jebel Ali village.
Dubai Evangelical Church Centre (DECC)
Tel: 04-884 6630
Holy Trinity Church
Tel: 04-337 4947.
United Christian Church of Dubai (UCCD)
Tel: 04-884 6623.
St Mary's Church (Roman Catholic)
Tel: 04-337 0087.

Sharjah

St Gregorios Orthodox Church
Tel: 06-566 9622.
St Martin's Church
Tel: 06-566 3388.
St Michael's Catholic Church
Tel: 06-566 2424.

S moking

In general, the attitude to smoking is similar to that in Western countries. In 2005 the UAE ratified the World Health Organisation Framework Convention on Tobacco Control, under which it must adhere to internatioal standards on tobacco-control measures, such as reducing exposure to passive smoking in public places. Anti-tobacco laws came into effect in two phases in May and September 2007. Now smoking in malls is only allowed in designated areas. During Ramadan, smoking anywhere in public is forbidden during daylight hours.

T elecommunications

Direct international telephone dialling is available from all phones. Local calls within the same city are free from a subscriber's phone. There are coin- and card-operated public phones on the streets and in shopping malls. Pre-paid phone cards can be purchased from local shops and supermarkets and cost Dhs30. Some phones also use credit cards, and in many hotels you can make a call and pay for it at the reception desk. Cheap rates for international calls exist between 9pm–7am and all day on Friday.

Activate the roaming function on your mobile phone if it has one. If not, you can buy a new SIM card. Mobile phone numbers are identified by the prefix 050.

Faxes can also be sent from many shops, offices or the main ETISALAT offices. The big hotels can usually send a fax for you.

Useful Numbers

International Dialling Code 00 971 followed by city code and number.
City Codes Abu Dhabi: 02; Al Ain: 03; Dubai: 04; Fujairah: 09; Ras Al Khaimah: 07; Sharjah, Ajman and Umm al Quwain: 06. There is no need to use the access code when dialling within an emirate.
Directory enquiries 181

Time Zone

GMT + 4 hours, BST + 3 hours.

Tipping

It is not compulsory to tip, but most people do. It is usual to tip waiters in restaurants, although service charges are also added to your bill. Supermarket employees who carry bags to your car are usually tipped,

ABOVE: fiery flavours to tempt the palate.

as are petrol attendants who wash your windscreens.

Toilets

Hotels and restaurants have western-style toilets. In malls and other public places there's usually a mix of western-style and squat toilets.

Tourist Information Offices

There are no actual tourist offices in the UAE. Hotels or travel agents can give you advice, and in Dubai there is the **Dubai Department of Tourism and Commerce Marketing**, PO Box 594, on Baniyas Road, Deira, tel: 04-223 0000.

There is a growing number of websites covering the UAE. Visit www.uaeinteract.com, www.dubai.com, www.godubai.com, www.sharjah-welcome.com, www.visitabudhabi.ae and follow links from there.

Tour Operators

Most tourists come to the UAE to explore the glorious emptiness of the desert, the wadis and the mountains. The romance of the idea should not blind you to the risks involved. It is dangerous to go off-road with only one vehicle, or in a group with no desert experience. You will be safer with one of the tour operators. Tours on offer range from day trips to overnight stays, and tour operators will collect from hotel.

Abu Dhabi
Al Ain Camel Safari, tel: 03-768 6666, Hilton hotel. Camel safaris with overnight stays in the desert.
Arabian Adventures, tel: 02-691 1711, On Corniche; www.arabian-

adventures.com. Organises desert safaris, city tours, camel trekking.
Blue Dolphin Company, tel: 02-666 6888/626 2200, Hotel Intercontinental. Fishing, BBQ and diving trips to islands off Abu Dhabi.
Falcon Tours, tel: 02-634 8000, Khalidiya Street; email: faltours@net.ae. Four-wheel drive excursions, sunset desert trips.
Net Tours, tel: 02-679 4656, Khalifa St, near Sheraton Hotel; www.nettoursdubai.com. Large tour operator offering BBQ in the desert, trips on dhows.
Off Road Emirates, tel: 02-633 3232, Hamdan St, near BHS; www.offroademirates.com. Specialising in tailor made tours in the desert region, and Abu Dhabi's islands.
Sunshine Tours, tel: 02-444 9914 Airport Rd, nr Carrefour. Wide range of trips and safaris into the desert.

Dubai
Arabian Adventures, tel: 04-303 4888, www.arabianadventures.com Emirates Holidays Building, Sheikh Zayed Road. City tours, east coast safaris, desert dinners.
The Big Bus Company, tel: 04-340 7709, www.bigbustours.com. Wafi City, Umm Hurair. Double-decker bus tours of the major sights. Hop-on, hop-off open-top buses.
Desert Rangers, tel: 04-422 0044, www.desertrangers.com. Dubai Garden Centre, Sheikh Zayed Road. Canoe, mountain bikes, outward bound.
Net Tours, tel: 04-266 6655, www.nettoursdubai.com. Deira, near DNATA centre. Dhow trips, desert barbecues and trips to the other emirates.
Voyagers Xtreme, tel: 04-345 4505, www.turnertraveldubai.com. Dune Centre, Al Satwa. Dune driving, dive charters,

sailing, rock climbing, hot air ballooning, sky diving.
Wonder Bus Tours, tel: 04-359 5656, http://wonderbusdubai.net. Bur Juman Centre, Bur Dubai. Land and water tours in an amphibious vehicle.

Sharjah
Orient Tours, tel: 06-568 2323, www.fanoos.com. Al Aruba Street. Dune surfing and a wide variety of other excursions and desert safaris.
SNTTA, tel: 06-554 5296, email: sntta@emirates.net.ae. Al Aruba Street, opposite Sharjah Cinema. All types of tours.

Weights and Meaures

The metric system is used.

Women Travellers

Unlike in neighbouring Saudi Arabia, in the UAE women are not expected to cover up in public (except when visiting mosques), and they are allowed to drive. One of the very few restrictions is at Dubai Youth Hostel (tel: 04-298 8151), part of the UAE Youth Hostel Association (www.uaeyha.com), where women travelling solo may be refused a booking. However, Dubai in particualr is one of the easiest places in the Middle East for lone women to travel around, and many feel comfortable on their own in the evening.

In terms of personal security, women are generally safe, but reports of rape have been carried in the local press; exercise standard precautions and never accept lifts from men met in bars and nightclubs. Dressing modestly will help women avoid unwanted attention.

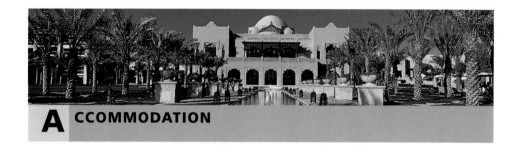

A CCOMMODATION

HOTELS, APARTMENTS AND CAMPSITES

Accommodation

All the emirates now have international standard hotels ranging from two to five stars, but there are few quality cheap hotels. Most cater for business travellers and MICE delegates, or offer rates linked to package holidays. Apartments and self-service flats can also be rented for longer stays, usually of a month or more. There are beach chalets available in some emirates, for rent on a nightly or daily basis. These often offer weekend packages.

Booking a Hotel

Generally, hotels in the UAE are not cheap and cater for business travellers and tour groups rather than individual budget travellers. If you are travelling independently, it is possible to find cheaper hotels, although they are still expensive compared with comparative accommodation in other countries.

Single women cannot book a hotel room unless they are part of a group or on business and can produce a company letter to prove it. Women would be advised to check on this before arrival as it is subject to change.

The price guide in this section gives an indication of the rates per night charged for two people sharing a standard double room. However, these prices do vary according to season and length of stay. An extra charge of 15–20 percent (tax and service) is usually added, so it's worth checking whether this has been included in the price you are quoted. Peak season is November to April. Note that Dhs (Dirhams) and AED (Arab Emirate Dirhams) are the same currency.

Holiday Apartments

Many hotels offer apartments for short-term lets.

Al Diar Mina Hotel
Tel: 02-678 1000, fax: 02-679 1000, www.aldiarhotels.com
Located next to the Regency hotel, each room has a kitchenette, and shares recreational facilities with the Regency.

Hilton Corniche Hotel Apartments
Tel: 02-627 6000, fax: 02-627 0099, email: corniche@hilton.com.
Facing onto the gardens of the Corniche, the suites have kitchenettes, balconies and separate working and dining areas. Rooms have kitchenettes and marble bathrooms.

Shangri-La Hotel
Tel: 04-343 8888, fax: 04-343 7232, www.shangri-la.com
Offers 126 serviced apartments for longer-stay visitors. Good location; facilities include spa, health club, pool and restaurants. One-, 2- and 3-bed rooms and suites available.

Camping

There are no official campsites in the UAE, but it's possible to camp almost anywhere in the desert and mountain areas. It's better not to camp too close to a village or town, and to beware of camping or driving in wadi beds during the rainy season.

You can hire a four-wheel-drive but it's safer not to go alone. Tell someone where you're going and when you're planning to come back, and take lots of water, spare petrol and a map. Larger supermarkets sell books advising routes to follow.

Camping equipment is widely available, and it's sensible to add a rope and a shovel to the usual list – to get you out of deep sand should you suddenly sink up to your axles!

BELOW: in the grounds of the opulent Emirates Palace Hotel.

ABU DHABI

Al Ain Palace Hotel
Tel: 02-679 4777
Fax: 02-679 5713
www.alainpalacehotel.com
The first hotel to be built in Abu Dhabi on the Corniche. Has a pool, health and fitness centre, squash courts and beauty salon. **£££**

Al Diar Regency
Tel: 02-676 5000
Fax: 02-677 7446
www.aldiarhotels.com
Email: regencyh@emirates.net.ae
Modern 193-room tower block, next to Sheraton Hotel, with gym and business centre. **£££**

Al Diar Sands Hotel
Tel: 02-615 6666
Fax: 02-633 5766
www.aldiarhotels.com
Email: sandshot@emirates.net.ae
Centrally located hotel with executive suites and business centre, Oriental massage centre and rooftop pool. Good Lebanese restaurant. **££**

Al Maha Arjaan Hotel
Tel: 02-610 6666
Fax: 02-610 6777
www.rotana.com
Email: almaha.arjaan@rotana.com
Centrally located business hotel, newly built, with fitness centre and pool. **£££**

Beach Rotana Hotel
Tel: 02-697 9000
Fax: 02-644 2111
www.rotana.com
Email: beach.hotel@rotana.com
New 5-star hotel, located next to Abu Dhabi Mall. Set on its own beach with superb restaurants, and comprehensive conference and business facilities. **£££**

City Seasons Hotel
Tel: 02-672 5000
Fax: 02-676 6338
www.cityseasonsabudhabi.com
On Electra Street, in town centre, offers standard rooms, plus suites and 2- and 3-bedroom apartments. **££**

Crowne Plaza
Tel: 02-621 0000
Fax: 02-621 7444

www.ichotelsgroup.com
Email: cpauh@cpabudhabi.ae
In the middle of town, on Hamdan Street, offers rooms for non-smokers and people with disabilities. It has a business conference centre and rooftop pool, and a well-reputed bar and restaurants. **£££**

Emirates Palace Hotel
Tel: 02-690 9000
Fax: 02-690 9999
www.emiratespalace.com
Email:reservation.emiratespalace@kempinski.com
Opulent palatial hotel, with private beach and extensive gardens. The top hotel in town. **£££**

Hilton Baynunah Towers
Tel: 02-632 7777
Fax: 02-621 6777
Email: baynunah-towers@hilton.com
Soaring blue-glass tower offers hotel rooms, and apartments for long-term stay. Good business and fitness centres, and great sea-view rooms overlooking the Corniche. **£££**

Hilton International Hotel
Tel: 02-681 1900
Fax: 02-681 1696
Email: abudhabi@hilton.com
One of Abu Dhabi's finest and largest hotels, and much improved after a dramatic expansion a few years ago. Hemingway's bar is a popular gathering spot in town. The hotel has its own health and fitness club with four pools and a beach and is accessible to non-hotel guests. **£££**

Intercontinental Abu Dhabi
Tel: 02-666 6888
Fax: 02-666 9153
www.ichotelsgroup.com
Located at the western edge of the Corniche with its own marina, this well-established hotel has many top restaurants and extensive gardens. **£££**

Le Méridien
Tel: 02-644 6666
Fax: 02-644 0348
www.starwoodhotels.com
Email: lemeridien.abudhabi@lemeridien.com
Near Abu Dhabi Mall, old

style hotel which has undergone extensive renovations. It has its own beach and leisure resort and 15 restaurants/cafés set in luscious gardens. **£££**

Le Royal Méridien
Tel: 02-674 2020
Fax: 02-695 0434
www.starwoodhotels.com
Email: info.lrmad@lemeridien.com
Smart 275-room tower hotel, overlooking the Corniche, with wonderful views from the revolving restaurant, Al Fanar. It has indoor and outdoor pools, good conference facilities, and gym, Jacuzzi, sauna and steam room. **£££**

Millennium Hotel
Tel: 02-626 2700
Fax: 02-626 0333
www.millenniumhotels.com
Email: sales@mill-abudhabi.com
Comfortable, modern hotel with champagne and cigar bar. **£££**

Novotel Centre Hotel
Tel: 02-633 3555
Fax: 02-634 3633
www.accorhotels.com
Email: reservation@novotel-abudhabi.ae
Well-established hotel on Hamdan Street in the middle of town, it has a French feel, with bars and bistros. Outdoor pool and fitness centre. **£££**

Sheraton Hotel and Resort
Tel: 02-677 3333
Fax: 02-672 5149
www.starwoodhotels.com/sheraton
Email: sheraton.abudhabi@sheraton.com
On the Corniche, with its own beach and lagoon, this 272-room hotel has a good business centre and several quality restaurants to choose from, including the well-established Tavern pub. **£££**

Al Ain

Al Ain Rotana Hotel
Tel: 03-754 5111
Fax: 03-754 5444
www.rotana.com
Email: alain.hotel@rotana.com
Comprises 198 rooms, suites, villas and chalets

ABOVE: tea at the Emirates.

and the Polynesian Trader Vic's restaurant in the heart of the oasis city. **£££**

Hilton Al Ain
Tel: 03-768 6666
Fax: 03-768 6888
www.hilton.co.uk/alain
Email: mohamed.fathi@hilton.com
Al Sarooj Street, near the Museum. A luxury hotel in an oasis of lush gardens with a backdrop of mountains. All sports facilities. Ideal base for exploring the area. Tour groups operate from this hotel for desert safari trips. **£££**

InterContinental Al Ain Resort
Tel: 03-768 6686
Fax: 03-768 6766
www.ichotelsgroup.com/intercontinental
Niadat Street, near the Mazeed Roundabout. Luxury hotel with huge landscaped gardens and all sports facilities. **£££**

Mercure Grand Jebel Hafeet
Tel: 03-783 8888
Fax: 03-783 9000
Email: resa@mercure-alain.ae
Perched on the side of the mountain – or *Jebel* – from which it takes its name, this 124-room hotel offers stunning views of the desert and mountains. **££**

PRICE CATEGORIES

Price categories are for a standard double room in high season:
£ = less than Dhs 500
££ = Dhs 500–800
£££ = more than Dhs 800

OMAN

THE UAE

LANGUAGE

DUBAI

Al Bustan Rotana
Tel: 04-282 0000
Fax: 04-282 8100
Email: albustan.hotel@rotana.com
Five-star hotel well-located
for the airport and Dubai
Tennis Stadium. Several
good restaurants. **£££**

Al Khaleej Hotel
Tel: 04-221 1144
Fax: 04-223 7140
www.alkhaleejhotels.com
On Al Nasser Square
beside Emirates Bank
International, Deira. **££**

Al Maha Desert Resort
Tel: 04-303 4222
Fax: 04-343 9696
www.al-maha.com
The world's first Arabian
eco-tourism resort, in an
exclusive oasis set within a
desert conservation
reserve. Built in the style of
a traditional Bedouin
encampment, Al Maha
combines pure luxury with
the wonders of the desert.
£££+

Ambassador Hotel
Tel: 04-393 9444
Fax: 04-393 9193
www.astmb.com
Al Falah Street, Bur Dubai.
Right in the heart of Dubai,
near the souqs and
convenient for the *abras*
(water taxis). **££**

Ascot Hotel
Tel: 04-352 0900
Fax: 04-352 1035
www.ascothoteldubai.com
Bur Dubai, next to Royal
Ascot hotel on Khalid bin
Waleed Road. Central
location and transfers to
the hotel's beach facilities.
Russian, Thai, Japanese
and Irish cuisine. **££**

Astoria
Tel: 04-353 4300
Fax: 04-353 5665
In the middle of the Bur
Dubai souq area. Lively
nightlife at Pancho Villa's, a
Tex-Mex restaurant and
club. **££**

**Bab Al Shams Desert
Resort and Spa**
Tel: 04-809 6100
Fax: 04-832 6698
www.jumeirahbabalshams.com
Translated as "the gateway
to the sun", this hotel is
set in a recreated Arabian
fort, luxuriously appointed.
£££

Burj Al Arab
Tel: 04-301 7777
Fax: 04-301 7000
www.burj-al-arab.com
Iconic, ultra-luxurious, sail-
shaped hotel – the tallest
all-suite hotel in the world –
built on a man-made island.
Private beach exclusively
for guests. Extravagant
decor, superb cuisine,
lavish spa. **£££+**

Carlton Tower Hotel
Tel: 04-222 7111
Fax: 04-222 8249
www.carltontower.net
On Baniyas Road, Deira,
past the Dubai
InterContinental Hotel. **££**

**Dubai Marine Beach
Resort & Spa**
Tel: 04-346 1111
Fax: 04-346 0234
www.dxbmarine.com
The closest Jumeirah
beach resort to the city, it
lies opposite Jumeira
mosque on the Beach
Road. Private beach, good
restaurants. Price includes
breakfast. **£££**

Dusit Thani Dubai
Tel: 04-343 3333
Fax: 04-343 4222
www.dusit.com
The design of this Thai-
owned hotel represents two
hands pressed together in
the traditional Thai
greeting. Luxurious rooms,
suites and furnished
apartments. **£££**

Fairmont Hotel
Tel: 04-332 5555
Fax: 04-332 4555
www.fairmont.com
On Sheikh Zayed Road,
opposite the Dubai
International Exhibition
Centre. Space-age atrium,
excellent restaurants. **£££**

Golden Sands
Tel: 04-355 5553
Fax: 04-352 6903
www.goldensandsdubai.com
Eleven apartment buildings
offer a self-catering option
in Bur Dubai. Ideal for
large groups as the more
people sharing, the lower
the cost. **£**

Grand Hyatt Dubai
Tel: 04-317 1234
Fax: 04-317 1235
www.dubai.grand.hyatt.com
Imposing landmark hotel
between Garhoud Bridge

and Creekside Park.
Stunning city views. **£££**

Hilton Dubai Creek
Tel: 04-227 1111
Fax: 04-227 1131
Email: sales.dubai@hilton.com
Trendy hotel in Deira,
though not actually located
on the creek. Its
restaurants include Gordon
Ramsey's Verre. **£££**

Hilton Dubai Jumeirah
Tel: 04-399 1111
Fax: 04-399 1112
Email: reservations.jumeirah@hilton.com
Family-friendly beachfront
hotel on the world-famous
Jumeirah strip. **£££**

Holiday Inn Downtown
Tel: 04-228 8889
Fax: 04-228 0033
www.ichotelsgroup.com
Conveniently located in
Deira, close to the lively Al
Riqqa Road. **££**

Hyatt Regency Hotel
Tel: 04-209 1234
Fax: 04-209 1235
www.dubai.regency.hyatt.com
On the Corniche Road,
Deira. Pitch and putt
course, ice rink and spa.
Lively, with revolving rooftop
restaurant and a popular
bar. **£££**

Ibis World Trade Centre
Tel: 04-332 4444
Fax: 04-331 1220
www.ibishotel.com
Conveniently located next
to the Exhibition Centre on
Sheikh Zayed Road. Good
value for money. **££**

**InterContinental Dubai
Festival City**
Tel: 04-701 1111
Fax: 04-232 9098
www.ichotelsgroup.com/intercontinental
In Deira, on Baniyas Street.
Top suites have 180º views
of the creek. The French
restaurant's menu was
created by a three-Michelin-
starred chef. **£££**

Jebel Ali Hotel
Tel: 04-883 6000
Fax: 04-883 5543
www.jebelali-international.com
Beyond Jebel Ali freezone
area, within Jebel Ali Golf
Resort. Spectacular hotel
next to the sea. Enormous
gardens, palm trees on the
beach, marina and
wonderful restaurants. One
of the most attractive
hotels in Dubai, 40

minutes' drive from the city
centre. **£££**

Jumeirah Beach Hotel
Tel: 04-348 0000
Fax: 04-301 6800
Email: JBHinfo@jumeirah.com
Beach Road, Umm
Sequiem. Spectacular
building designed to look
like a wave, with wonderful
location on a private beach.
PADI-accredited dive centre,
complimentary access to
Wild Wadi waterpark. **£££**

**Jumeirah Emirates
Towers**
Tel: 04-330 0000
Fax: 04-330 3030
Email: JETinfo@jumeirah.com
One of the world's tallest
hotels, located next to the
Dubai Exhibition Centre.
Beach access, 400 rooms
and suites, male spa and
ladies-only floor. **£££**

J.W. Marriott
Tel: 04-262 4444
Fax: 04-262 6264
www.marriott.com
Abu Baker Al Siddiq Road in
Deira, next to Hamarain
shopping centre. Ten
restaurants and bars
include a good American
bar and steak house.
Rooftop pool and squash
court. **£££**

Le Méridien Dubai
Tel: 04-217 0000
Fax: 04-282 1650
www.starwoodhotels.com/lemeridien
Opposite Dubai
International Airport. Lush
gardens, three pools, spa
and tennis courts. A choice
of 16 restaurants. **£££**

**Le Méridien Mina Seyahi
Beach Resort**
Tel: 04-399 3333
Fax: 04-399 3111
Email: guestservices@lemeridien-
minaseyahi.com
Located in the Jumeira
area, it has the largest
marina in Dubai, and lies
opposite Montgomerie golf
course. **£££**

**Le Royal Méridien Beach
Resort & Spa**
Tel: 04-399 5555
Fax: 04-317 6980
Email: reservations@lrm-gh-dubai.com
Situated in the Jumeira
area away from the city
centre. Private beach,
gardens and two outdoor
pools. **£££**

Madinat Jumeirah Resort Al Qasr Hotel and Mina A' Salam
Tel: 04-366 8888
Fax: 04-366 7788
www.madinatjumeirah.com
Two luxury hotels in a fabulous Arabian-themed resort that manages to avoid being tacky. A wonderful destination in its own right. £££

Metropolitan Hotel
Tel: 04-343 0000
Fax: 04-343 1146
www.metropolitandubai.habtoorhotels.com
On Sheikh Zayed Road past the Exhibition Centre. Business hotel with eight-screen cinema and good restaurants. £££

Millennium Airport Hotel
Tel: 04-282 3464
Fax: 04-282 0627
Email: sales.airdxb@mill-cop.com
Near the airport, with sound-insulated rooms. Excellent value; popular Italian restaurant with terrace, lively English pub and good health club facilities. £££

Mövenpick Hotel Bur Dubai
Tel: 04-336 6000
Fax: 04-336 6626
Email: hotel.burdubai@moevenpick.com
Between Wafi City and Lancy Plaza Malls. Has 255 rooms and an excellent Lebanese restaurant. £££

Novotel World Trade Centre
Tel: 04-332 0000
Fax: 04-332 0001
www.novotel.com

Ideal for business travellers as it forms part of the Exhibition Centre and is 10 minutes' drive from the airport. Two pools. £££

One & Only Royal Mirage
Tel: 04-399 9999
Fax: 04-399 9998
www.oneandonlyresorts.com
Four hotel buildings spread over one spectacular resort facing Palm Island Bay. Luxurious rooms, magnificent gardens and pools, fine dining. £££

Palm Beach Hotel
Tel: 04-393 1999
Fax: 04-393 3111
Khalid bin Waleed Street in Bur Dubai. Good value for money. £

Ramada Hotel
Tel: 04-351 9999
Fax: 04-352 1033
www.ramadadubai.com
Near BurJuman mall in Bur Dubai. Particularly convenient for the souq. Has one of the largest stained glass murals in the world as a design feature in the lobby. Nightclub and pool. £££

Rimal Rotana Suites
Tel: 04-268 8000
Fax: 04-268 8777
www.rotana.com
On Murraqabat Road. Has a bus shuttle service into town. It doesn't serve alcohol but has a restaurant and self-catering facilities. Gym and rooftop pool. Recommended. £££

Ritz-Carlton Dubai
Tel: 04-399 4000
Fax: 04-399 4001

www.ritzcarlton.com
Luxury hotel with integrated Arabic and Mediterranean design in the Jumeirah area. Ideal retreat as it lacks the crowds found in larger resorts. Excellent restaurants and spa. Adjoins the beach. £££+

Shangri-La Hotel
Tel: 04-343 8888
Fax: 04-343 8886
www.shangri-la.com
Towering Gotham-esque hotel on Sheikh Zayed Road offering superb views of the Jumeirah coast. *Syriana* film scenes were shot here. £££

Sheraton Dubai Creek Hotel & Towers
Tel: 04-228 1111
Fax: 04-221 3468
www.starwoodhotels.com/sheraton
Located on Deira creekside. Interesting building with uninterrupted creek views from the 262 rooms and suites. The dhows are moored close by. £££

Taj Palace
Tel: 04-223 2222
Fax: 04-227 8222
www.tajhotels.com
Large luxury rooms and apartments in the heart of Deira. Operates a no-alcohol policy. £££

The Palm Hotel
Tel: 04-399 2222
Fax: 04-399 2111
www.thepalmhoteldubai.com
Off Sheikh Zayed Road opposite Emirates Golf Club. Fairly good value. Has a popular Irish pub. £££

UAE Youth Hostel Association
Tel: 04-298 8161
Fax: 04-298 8141
www.hihostels.com/www.uaeyha.com
Located on Al Nahda Road in Qusais area, near the Al Bustan Centre. Clean singles, doubles and dorms. Cheapest accommodation in Dubai. £

XVA Art Hotel
Tel: 04-353 5383
Fax: 04-3353 5988
www.xvagallery.com
An authentic Arabian boutique guesthouse with six designer-decorated rooms. The XVA is first and foremost an art gallery set around the inner courtyard of a restored home in the historic Bastakiya district. ££

Hatta

Hatta Fort Hotel
Tel: 04-852 3211
Fax: 04-852 3561
www.hattaforthotel.com
Hatta is in Dubai Emirate 105 km (65 miles) from Dubai city, near the Hajar Mountains. It is clearly signposted at the town's main roundabout. A wonderful resort hotel offering peace and quiet. Bar and dining area overlook the pool, with spectacular views of the surrounding mountains. Chalet-style rooms with huge views. Many sports including archery, golf and 4WD safaris. £££

SHARJAH

There are many reasonably priced beachside hotels in Sharjah. The city is only 30 minutes' drive from Dubai and it is well-located for the northern and eastern emirates. Alcohol is not sold in any hotels.

Beach Hotel
Tel: 06-528 1311
Fax: 06-528 5422
www.beachhotel-sharjah.com
Port Road, Al Khan area. £

Coral Beach Resort
Tel: 06-522 1011
Fax: 06-527 4101
Corniche Road towards

Ajman. Beside Ajman Roundabout. ££

Hotel Holiday International
Tel: 06-573 6666
Fax: 06-572 5060
www.holidayinternational.com
Located on Al Buhaira Corniche on the edge of Khalid Lagoon. ££

Radisson SAS Resort Sharjah
Tel: 06-565 7777
Fax: 06-565 0090
www.sharjah.radissonsas.com
On the Corniche. One of the best hotels in town. Near the dhows and the

souq area. Good coffee house. £££

Sharjah Carlton Hotel
Tel: 06-528 3711
Fax: 06-528 4962
www.sharjahcarlton.com
On Port Road, Al Khan. Accommodation also in chalets next to main hotel. Recently refurbished. ££

Sharjah Rotana Hotel
Tel: 06-563 7777
Fax: 06-563 5000
Email: sharjah.hotel@rotana.com
Excellent business hotel on Al Arouba Street, a block or so from Sharjah Creek.

Breakfast included. ££

Summerland Motel
Tel: 06-528 1321
Fax: 06-528 0745
On Port Road, Al Khan area. It has hotel rooms and holiday apartments. A long-stay option. £

PRICE CATEGORIES

Price categories are for a standard double room in high season:
£ = less than Dhs 500
££ = Dhs 500–800
£££ = more than Dhs 800

OMAN

THE UAE

LANGUAGE

FUJAIRAH

The east coast, with its beautiful beaches and mountainous backdrop, is a wonderful place to spend a few quiet, relaxing days beside the sea.

Hilton International Fujairah
Tel: 09-222 2411
Fax: 09-222 6541
www.hilton.co.uk/Fujairah
This hotel has a good position right on its own private beach; there are also bungalows in the grounds. Excellent open-fronted seafood restaurant right by the sea; fitness centre. **££**

Le Méridien Al Aqah Beach Resort
Tel: 09-244 9000
Fax: 09-244 9001
www.starwoodhotels.com/lemeridien
Resort hotel with Hajar mountains backdrop. **£££**

Oceanic Hotel, Khor Fakkan
Tel: 09-238 5111
Fax: 09-238 7716
www.oceanichotel.com/khorfakkan
Corniche Road, Khor Fakkan. PADI-accredited dive centre and extensive range of water sports. The price includes breakfast. **££**

Sandy Beach Hotel
Tel: 09-244 5555
Fax: 09-244 5200
www.sandybm.com
Between Dibba and Khor Fakkan. Quiet, un-glitzy rooms and chalets on a private beach facing an island you can walk to at low tide, and with a mountain backdrop. Chalets are self-catering but there's a good restaurant and bar. PADI-accredited dive centre. **££**

AJMAN

Kempinski Hotel Ajman
Tel: 06-714 5555
Fax: 06-745 1222
www.ajmankempinski.com
Located on the 500-metre private beach a few minutes' drive from Sharjah and 25 km (15 miles) from Dubai International Airport. Luxury modern rooms, cabanas around the pool, good restaurants, relaxing gardens, excellent facilities including spa and fitness centre, water sports and children's club. **£££**

UMM AL QAIWAIN

Flamingo Beach Resort
Tel: 06-765 0000
Fax: 06-765 0001
www.flamingoresort.ae
Pleasant resort in the old town that's popular with water sport enthusiasts. Offers the more unusual activities of crab hunting and mangrove boating. Has an Ayurvedic spa and various dining options. **££**

UAQ Beach Hotel
Tel: 06-766 6647
Fax: 06-766 2778
www.uaqbeachotel.com
This hotel comprises 38 villas spread throughout immaculate grounds, with a beach that's a haven from the crowds. Has a Lebanese restaurant and a coffee shop serving buffet breakfasts. **££**

RAS AL KHAIMAH

Al Hamra Fort Hotel
Tel: 07-244 6666
Fax: 07-244 6677
www.alhamrafort.com
Located on the main road to Ras Al Khaimah, about 40 minutes' drive from Sharjah. There are 83 rooms in the main hotel, and villas in the grounds offer a further 183 bedrooms. Long stretch of pristine beach, many sporting and other activities, five restaurants and a coffee shop. Also has a business centre, two bars and a nightclub. **£££**

Hilton Ras Al Khaimah
Tel: 07-228 8888
Fax: 07-228 8889
www.hiltonworldresorts.com
Located on the creekside in the Nakheel area, close to the city centre and old town; 151 villas and facilities that include an on-site dive centre. **£££**

Ras Al Khaimah Hotel
Tel: 07-236 2999
Fax: 07-236 2990
www.rak-hotel.co.ae
Located in the Khozan area, close to the Corniche. 4 km (2½ miles) from Clocktower Roundabout. 100 rooms with sea or mountain views. Restaurant and coffee shop. **££**

PRICE CATEGORIES

Price categories are for a standard double room in high season:
£ = less than Dhs 500
££ = Dhs 500–800
£££ = more than Dhs 800

BELOW: enjoy barbecued fish from one of many seafood restaurants along the beach.

E ATING OUT

RECOMMENDED RESTAURANTS, CAFÉS AND BARS

What to Eat

The choice of places to eat out in the UAE is huge. You can find dishes from almost anywhere in the world, either in small, sometimes quite basic, unlicensed eating houses or in larger, more lavish, licensed hotel restaurants. Standards of hygiene are high: even simple restaurants are clean, as inspections are frequent and the penalties for poor cleanliness severe.

The Arabic convenience foods such as *shawarmas* (what we know in the West as kebabs – meat cooked on a vertical spit, then sliced, topped with tahini or yogurt and salad, served in pitta bread and eaten like a sandwich), or *falafel* (deep-fried chick-pea balls, served in paper bags from street vendors), make cheap and tasty snacks on the move.

Lebanese and Arabic food is delicious. Meals usually begin with an array of small dishes, the mezze, followed by a main course of grilled meat or fish. Puddings often include nuts, syrup and fresh cream. Finish with Arabic coffee or peppermint tea. These restaurants often offer good-value lunchtime specials, and the quantities are usually very generous.

Freshly squeezed fruit and vegetable juices or sodas accompany meals in unlicensed premises. If you do want to drink alcohol with your meal, there are plenty of hotel restaurants to choose from but the prices are higher. These restaurants are often luxuriously decorated and have first-class chefs. There are often "specials" on for a short while, which can offer memorable tastes and sometimes include entertainment. Look for details in the local press.

ABOVE: mint tea in style at the Grand Hyatt Hotel.

When to Eat

Residents tend to dine late at night, so for a good atmosphere plan to have dinner from around 9pm. If you're heading for a hotel venue, book in advance. Wherever you eat, major credit and debit cards are widely accepted.

Whatever your religion, it is illegal to eat or drink in public in daylight during the holy month of Ramadan, when Muslims abstain from food and drink from sunrise to sunset. Some restaurants open for lunch but screen off their eating areas; however, alcohol will not be served until the evening. Although pork and alcohol are not consumed by Muslims, most hotel restaurants use them as ingredients in certain dishes. These will be highlighted with a symbol on the menu.

Alcohol

Local restaurants tend to be unlicensed. If you want to drink alcohol with your meal, head for a hotel; all the main hotels in Abu Dhabi and Dubai are licensed.

Note also that Dubai has a zero-tolerance approach to drink driving. The penalty for being found with the smallest amount of alcohol in your bloodstream can be a month in jail. If you're going to drink, take a taxi.

Code to Symbols

L after the price code (eg **££L**) indicates that the restaurant is licensed to sell alcohol; **U** denotes unlicensed premises; **CU** refers to an unlicensed café.

A Note on Drinking

You cannot buy alcohol for home consumption in the UAE unless you hold an alcohol licence, which are only issued to non-Muslims with residence visas. However, alcohol is served in hotel bars and restaurants in most of the emirates, apart from Sharjah. There are many excellent pubs, bars and discos (see Nightlife, page 304).

OMAN

THE UAE

LANGUAGE

ABU DHABI

Alamo Bar and Restaurant
Abu Dhabi Marina Club
Tel: 02-644 0300
Very popular Tex-Mex; live Cuban music while you eat. **£££L**

Al Atlal
Al Diar Sands Hotel
Tel: 02-615 6666
Authentic Lebanese with quick, friendly service. **££L**

Al Majlis & Caviar Bar
Emirates Palace Hotel,
West End Corniche
Tel: 02-690 9000
This opulent hotel, an Abu Dhabi landmark, is a fine setting for a memorable, if expensive, high tea or sampling of gold-dipped chocolates. Situated in the lobby, with a champagne menu and caviar selection also available. **£££L**

**Al Arish Restaurant,
Al Dhafra**
Port area
Tel: 02-673 2266
Dhow restaurant serving traditional Gulf cuisine. Good grilled fish and meats. **££U**

Al Fanar
Le Royal Méridien
Tel: 02-674 2020
A revolving rooftop restaurant with good views. Seafood and grills. Open lunch and dinner. **£££L**

Al Safina Dhow Restaurant
Anchored at the Corniche breakwater
Tel: 02-681 6085
Good Lebanese food and atmosphere. **££U**

Amalfi
Le Royal Méridien Hotel
Tel: 02-674 2020
Good but expensive Italian food. **£££L**

BiCE
Hilton International Hotel
Tel: 02-681 1900
Elegant and sophisticated with floor-to-ceiling windows; specialises in Italian cuisine. **£££L**

Café Firenze
Corner of Al Nasr and Tariq Ziyad Streets, Al Hosn
Tel: 02-666 0955
European-style café, with

terrace overlooking the park of the Corniche. **££U**

Fishmarket
Intercontinental
Tel: 02-666 6888
Fresh seafood cooked Thai-style and served indoors or on the terrace overlooking the beach. Select your fish and specify how you want it cooked. **££L**

Finz
Beach Rotana Hotel
Tel: 02-644 3000
Exquisite seafood restaurant built on stilts over the sea. **£££L**

Havana Café
Near Marina Mall, on the breakwater
Tel: 02-681 0044
The mainly Arabic menu includes international fare such as sandwiches and pizza. Excellent views across the waterfront to the high rises lining the Corniche. Patio and rooftop seating available in the cooler months.

Hemingway's
Hilton International
Tel: 02-681 1900
Named after the famous writer, with a suitably Cuban-American theme and menu. **££L**

India Palace
On Salam Street
Tel: 02-644 8777
Good quality Indian food, from an extensive menu. **£££L**

La Mamma
Sheraton Abu Dhabi Hotel
Tel: 02-677 3333
Typical Italian; comprehensive menu. **£££L**

Mawal
Hilton International Hotel
Tel: 02-681 1900
Highly regarded, award-winning Lebanese restaurant. Offers mezze, grills and seafood in an unpretentious atmosphere. Live music and belly-dancing in the evenings. **££L**

Nihal Restaurant
Next to the Al Diar Sands Hotel on Sheikh Zayed 2nd Street
Tel: 02-631 8088

One of the best restaurants serving Indian and Chinese food. Some continental dishes. **£L**

Pappagallo
Le Méridien Abu Dhabi
Tel: 02-644 6666
Authentic Italian in atmospheric setting with live strolling music. **££L**

Prego's
Beach Rotana Hotel
Tel: 02-644 3000
Stylish contemporary Italian with theatre-style kitchen. **£££L**

Rodeo Grill
Beach Rotana Hotel
Tel: 02-644 3000
Meat and fish dishes, speciality grills. **£££L**

Royal Orchid
Hilton International Hotel
Tel: 02-681 1900
Thai décor restaurant serving Thai, Chinese and Mongolian dishes with attentive service. **£££U**

Sayad
Emirates Palace Hotel,
West End Corniche
Tel: 02-690 9000
State-of-the-art seafood restaurant with low lighting and high prices. **£££L**

Sevilo's
Millennium Hotel
Tel: 02-614 6000
Italian restaurant overlooking the Capital Gardens, with a pizza and pasta night on Monday and seafood buffet on Wednesday. **££L**

Shuja Yacht
Le Royal Méridien
Tel: 02-674 2020
A romantic dinner cruise. **£££L**

The Garden Restaurant
Crowne Plaza Hotel,
Hamdan Street
Tel: 02-621 0000
Ideal for a more relaxed meal out. Seafood buffet on Tuesday and champagne brunch on Friday. **££L**

The Yacht Club
Intercontinental Hotel
Tel: 02-666 6888
A nautically-themed restaurant and bar, the

best seating being on the outside decking facing directly onto the marina. Pacific Rim food. **£££L**

Trader Vic's
Beach Rotana Hotel
Tel: 02-644 3000
French Polynesian. One of the city's favourite places. Exotic menu with oriental and South-Sea-Island specialities. **£££L**

Vasco's
Hilton International Hotel
Tel: 02-681 1900
Set in lush greenery overlooking the sea, this is one of the best outdoor locations in town. International cuisine and fine service. **£££L**

Waka Taua
Le Méridien
Tel: 02-644 6666
Polynesian cuisine. Beside the sea. Outside terrace as well as inside. Excellent cocktails. **£££L**

Al Ain

Al Khayam Persian Restaurant
Hilton Al Ain
Tel: 03-768 6666
Iranian cuisine in a room featuring decorative wooden screens and traditional cushions. **££L**

Golden Gate Restaurant
Al Ain Street
Tel: 03-766 2467
Chinese and Filipino cuisine. **£U**

The Wok
InterContinental Al Ain Resort
Tel: 03-768 6686
Oriental dishes dominate the menu, but a seafood buffet and separate sushi bar also feature. **££L**

PRICE CATEGORIES

Price categories are per meal per person. *See page 311* for code to symbols.

£U = Dhs40–60
££U = Dhs60–110
££L = Dhs80–110
£££L = more than Dhs110

DUBAI

Al Bandar
Heritage Village, Shindagha
Tel: 04-393 9001
This unlicensed restaurant in the Heritage Area is an ideal place to sit outside and watch the *abras* on the Creek. Emphasis on international seafood, but there are also meat and vegetarian choices. Large buffets at weekends. **££U**

Al Dawaar
Hyatt Regency Hotel
Tel: 04-317 2222
Revolving restaurant with amazing views and mix of European, local, Asian and Japanese food. **£££L**

Al Mahara
Tel: 04-301 7600
The luxury Burj Al Arab hotel's seafood restaurant. The aquarium alone is a reason to visit. **£££**

Al Makan
Souk Madinat Jumeirah
Tel: 04-368 6593
Located in an atmospheric souk, this is one of the few restaurants in Dubai serving authentic Emirati cuisine. Lebanese mezze also available. Outdoor terrace seating overlooks the Burj Al Arab hotel.

Al Muntaha Skyview Restaurant
Tel: 04-301 7600
Located in the Burj Al Arab, 200 metres above the Arabian Gulf, with fantastic views; excellent modern European cuisine. **£££L**

Al Nafoorah
Jumeirah Emirates Towers Boulevard
Tel: 02-330 0000
Dubai's best Lebanese restaurant for lunch or dinner. Surprisingly good value. **££L**

Blue Elephant
Al Bustan Rotana
Tel: 04-282 0000
Superb Thai curries in a Thai village setting, complete with streams and traditional huts. **££L**

Cactus Cantina
Rydges Plaza Hotel, Al Diyafal Street, Satwa Roundabout
Tel: 04-398 2222
Hearty Mexican cuisine in a relaxed atmosphere. Salsa dancing on Saturday and Sunday from 8pm. **£–££L**

Café Arabesque
Park Hyatt Dubai
Tel: 04-602 1234
A mixture of flavours from Lebanon and Syria are ensconced in the regional specialities served here. Choose from the menu, the mezze selection or five different buffets. **£££L**

Café Ceramique
On 26th Street
Tel: 02-666 4412
Stylish café serving light snacks and salads; you can also use your creative talent and paint plates, cups and pots. **££U**

Café Chic
Le Méridien
Tel: 04-217 0000
Excellent, unpretentious French restaurant. **£££L**

Capanna Nuova
Dubai Marina Beach Resort & Spa
Tel: 04-346 1111
Superb Italian restaurant with elegant terrace overlooking the sea. **£££L**

Century Village
At the Dubai Tennis Stadium, part of the Aviation Club
Tel: 04-282 4122
Comprises a number of restaurants serving Portuguese, Italian, Japanese, French and Persian food, and more, in a courtyard setting. **££L**

Coconut Grove
Rydges Plaza Hotel
Tel: 04-398 2222
Delicious food in a room full of Indian artefacts.

Deliciously spicy south Indian curries, with Goan influences. **££L**

Da Vinci's
Millennium Airport Hotel
Tel: 04-282 3464
Homely Italian restaurant. Very popular. Reasonable prices and friendly staff. Trattoria decor. Has an outside patio which is enclosed in the summer. **££L**

Dynasty
Ramada Hotel
Tel: 04-506 1148
Quality Chinese restaurant. Cantonese and Szechuan food. **£££L**

Fish Bazaar
Metropolitan Hotel
Tel: 04-343 0000
Choose your fish and have it cooked to your taste. Thai seafood market-themed room, with windows overlooking the main highway to Abu Dhabi and further across Al Safa Park. **££L**

Gerard Patisserie
Tel: 04-222 8637 (Al Ghurair City)
Very popular café to stop at for a croissant and a cappuccino.

Japengo Café
At Palm Strip Mall, Jumeira, with four other outlets in Dubai, the newest one in Wafi Mall
Tel: 04-343 5028
Understandably popular Asian/international menu. Haunt for Dubai's in-crowd. **£U**

Johnny Rockets
Juma al Majid Centre, Jumeirah Beach Road
Tel: 04-344 7859
1950s-style American diner. Rock'n'roll and hamburgers. **£U**

JW's Steakhouse
J.W. Marriott
Tel: 04-607 7977
Grills with an American slant. Cooked under a flame and prepared exactly as you like. Very good wine list. Clubby decor: lots of panelled wood and huge deep leather chairs. **£££L**

Kan Zaman
Creekside, Shindagha Heritage Village
Tel: 04-393 9913
Meaning "once upon a time", this huge Arabic restaurant with outdoor seating has a pleasant creekside setting. Lebanese mezze, Turkish coffee and shisha available. **£U**

Kiku
Le Méridien Dubai
Tel: 04-217 0000
For a taste of Japan, try the sushi and teppanyaki. Also features a sake bar. **££L**

La Baie
Ritz-Carlton Hotel
Tel: 04-399 4000
French restaurant specialising in seafood and offering Gulf views. **£££L**

Le Notre Paris
Spinney Centre, Jumeirah Road
Tel: 04-349 4433

BELOW: baklava filled with pistachios.

Chic and elegant French restaurant with intimate atmosphere. Cheaper café downstairs with upscale restaurant above. **££–£££L**

Lime Tree Café
Jumeirah Beach Road, near Spinneys
Tel: 04-349 8498
Spread over two floors of a villa, this is the ultimate expat café. Funky decor and music; healthy menu. **£U**

More
Near Welcare Hospital, Garhoud
Tel: 04-283 0224
Funky café serving a wide menu of savoury and sweet treats. Great for lunch. Not to be missed. **£U**

Noodle House
Jumeirah Emirates Towers
Tel: 04-319 8088
Bustling Asian restaurant that's especially popular among business execs at lunchtime. Delicious fare. **££L**

Pars Iranian Kitchen
Al Dhiyafa Road, Satwa

Roundabout
Tel: 04-398 4000
Excellent choice of authentic Iranian dishes. **££U**

Pierchic
Al Qasr, Madinat Jumeirah
Tel: 04-366 8888
Wonderfully romantic seafood restaurant at the end of a wooden pier. **£££L**

Ravi Restaurant
Satwa
Tel: 04-331 5353
Delicious *dal*, *chapattis* and tandoori chicken. Excellent value. **£U**

Shakespeare & Co
Al Attar Business Tower, Sheikh Zayed Road
Tel: 04-331 1757
Extensive menu, shabby chic decor with a tilt towards Victoriana. Very popular. **£U**

Shu
Jumeirah Road, opposite Jumeirah Beach Park
Tel: 04-349 1303
Trendy Lebanese restaurant with a nightclub vibe inside

but a more relaxed atmosphere on the outside terrace. Try the house speciality if you're feeling adventurous: fried sparrow with pomegranate syrup.

Spectrum on One
The Fairmont, Sheikh Zayed Road
Tel: 04-332 5555
Award-winning international restaurant. Super cool venue. **££L**

Sushi Sushi
Century Village, Dubai Tennis Stadium
Tel: 04-282 9908
Trendy Japanese with food displayed on conveyor belt. Eat inside or outside. **££L**

Tagine
The Palace, One & Only Royal Mirage Hotel
Tel: 04-399 9999
Intimate Moroccan restaurant with excellent selection of North African dishes. Dinner only. **£££L**

Teatro
Towers Rotana, Sheikh Zayed Road
Tel: 04-343 8000
Five different types of

international cuisine in a theatre-themed setting. **££L**

Thai Bistro
Dubai Marine Beach Resort
Tel: 04-346 1111
Excellent Thai food in a poolside setting. **££L**

The Boardwalk
Dubai Creek Golf & Yacht Club, on the Creek
Tel: 04-295 6000
Sit outside under an umbrella and watch the yachts, dhows and *abras* go by. Salads and oriental dishes, Mexican tastes and toasted sandwiches. **££L**

Verre
Hilton Dubai Creek
Tel: 04-212 7551
Gordon Ramsey's Dubai restaurant. Highly recommended if you want to splash out. **£££L**

Vu's
Jumeirah Emirates Towers
Tel: 04-319 8088
50th-floor fine dining with superb views. European menu. **££L**

SHARJAH

Al Arsah Public Coffee Shop
Courtyard Souq
Tel: 06-554 0903
Authentic Arabian coffee shop. Great location. **CU**

Al Fawar
King Faisal Street
Tel: 06-559 4662
Excellent Lebanese restaurant with good mezze. Has a good-value buffet on Friday. **££U**

Al Gahwa Al Shaabiya
Khalid Lagoon
Tel: 06-554 7788
Barasti (palm-frond) setting

with open section on waterfront. No sign at the front. Soak up the traditional atmosphere and sample the local dishes. **CU**

Chillout Café
Radisson SAS Hotel, Old Corniche
Tel: 06-565 7777
Pleasant café in the leafy atrium of Sharjah's grandest hotel. Menu offers salads and sandwiches that can be packed up to take away. **CU**

Danial
Crystal Plaza Mall, Buheirah Corniche

Tel: 06-574 4668
Iranian restaurant serving good value buffet meals. During the cooler months, it's a great place from which to enjoy the view of nearby Sharjah souk and Khalid Lagoon. **CU**

Fish Corner
Block C, Al Qasba
Tel: 06-556 8884
Greek-influenced fish tavern. **£U**

Gerard Patisserie
Khalid Lagoon
Tel: 06-556 0425
Come here in the morning for delicious croissants

and fresh coffee. **CU**

Little Hut
Old Spinney's roundabout
Tel: 06-566 4421
Good Indian and Chinese food, friendly service. **£U**

Shababeek
Block B, Al Qasba
Tel: 06-554 0444
Great Lebanese food with a separate children's menu. **£U**

Peking Chinese
Al Qassimia Roundabout
Tel: 06-567 3666
An intimate candle-lit restaurant serving excellent seafood specialities. **££U**

EAST COAST

Al Gargour rooftop restaurant
Oceanic Hotel
Khor Fakkan
Tel: 09-238 5111
This hotel has an international buffet restaurant with wonderful sea views. Themed nights at weekends. **£££L**

Neptunia
Hilton Fujairah Resort
Fujairah
Tel: 09-222 2411
Terraced restaurant overlooking gardens and serving Mediterranean dishes alongside local delicacies. Excellent value lunch buffets. The beach

café offers a pleasant alternative. **£££L**

The Views
Le Meridien Al Aqah Beach Resort
Al Aqah
Tel: 09-244 9000
As the name suggests, fabulous views over the Arabian Sea. Lunch buffet served daily. **££–£££L**

A CTIVITIES

THE ARTS, NIGHTLIFE, CHILDREN'S ACTIVITIES, SPORTS AND SHOPPING

THE ARTS

Music and Dance

There are not many concerts or dance performances in the UAE although performers do come and give concerts in the larger hotels. Also, many bands and groups perform in nightclubs and bars. Ask at your hotel, or see local press and local radio for details.

Art Galleries

Abu Dhabi

The Cultural Foundation
Tel: 02-621 5300, www.adach.ae
The compound contains the National Library as well as an exhibition hall, four lecture halls, an auditorium and an open-air amphitheatre.
Hemisphere Design Studio and Gallery
Tel: 02-676 8614, www.hemisphere.ae.
Supports local artists and designers, displaying their photography, prints and handcrafted gifts.

Dubai

Al Abbar Art Galleries
Tel: 04-337 5537/04-344 9207.
Main gallery at Gulf Towers with second one in Jumeirah Beach Centre. Prints, paintings and sculpture.
Dubai International Arts Centre
Tel: 04-344 4398, off Jumeira Road.
Runs professionally-taught art and craft workshops and courses.
Green Art Gallery
Tel: 04-344 9888. Near Dubai Zoo, off Jumeirah Beach Road. Exhibits and sells quality paintings.
Majlis Gallery
Tel: 04-353 6233. Bastakiya area

in Bur Dubai. Original art by well-known artists for sale in old Arab windtower.
The Courtyard
Tel: 04-347 5050. Al Quoz, off the Sheikh Zayed Road.
The Third Line
Tel: 04-341 1367. Al Quoz, next to The Courtyard. Displays work by contemporary Middle Eastern artists.
XVA Gallery
Tel: 04-353 5383. Bastakiya district. Galleries, courtyard coffee-shop and accommodation. Lovely old building.

Sharjah

Sharjah Art Museum
Tel: 06-567 1116. Holds exhibitions.
Sharjah Museum for Contemporary Arab Art
Tel: 06-569 5050. The Arts Area, Al Shuwaiheen.
Sharjah Ladies Club Art Centre
Tel: 06-506 7777. Art classes and exhibitions.

Theatre

Seasonal travelling groups put on dinner theatre in the major hotels (see local press). Active amateur dramatic groups also stage productions. The world-class Madinat Theatre (tel: 04-366 6546, Madinat Juneirah) is Dubai's first purpose-built theatre.

Cinema

Films in English (censored) can be seen. See the English press.

Abu Dhabi

Century Cinemas, tel: 02-645 9499. Grand Abu Dhabi Mall. Multi-screen.
CineStar Cinema, tel: 02-681 8484. Marina Mall. Multi-screen.

Dubai

Century Cinemas, tel: 04-349 9713. Mercato Mall, Jumeira. Italian-look multi-screen.
CineStar Cinemas, tel: 04-29 49000. Deira City Centre. Multi-screen near Virgin store.
Grand Cineplex, tel: 04-324 2000. Near to the Grand Hyatt. Multi-screen with food court.
Grand Megaplex, tel: 04-366 9898. Ibn Battuta Mall, Jebel Ali. 21 screens and IMAX theatre.

Sharjah

Al Hamra, tel: 06-565 0953. Al Arouba Street.

NIGHTLIFE

The UAE has a lively nightlife. Dubai is the clubbing capital, followed by Abu Dhabi. Except in Sharjah, all the main hotels have bars and some have entertainment. There are no bars outside hotels. See current listings in *What's On* magazine.

Pubs and Bars

Abu Dhabi

49ers, Al Diar Dana Hotel, tel: 02-645 6000. Relaxed American bar and restaurant on the penthouse level specialising in BBQ dishes.
Ally Pally, Al Ain Palace Hotel, tel: 02-679 4777. Long-established English pub; holds quiz nights.
Café Columbia, Beach Rotana Hotel, tel: 02-644 3000. Pianist.
Captain's Arms, Le Méridien Hotel, tel: 02-644 6666. British-style pub with garden.
Cristal Cigar & Champagne Bar, Millennium Hotel, tel: 02-626 2700. Jazz music.

OMAN

THE UAE

LANGUAGE

Jazz Bar, Hilton Hotel, tel: 02-681 1900. Great ambiance.

PJ O'Reilly's, Le Royal Méridien, tel: 02-674 2020. Lively Irish pub.

Rock Bottom Café, Al Diar Capital Hotel, tel: 02-678 7700. Buzzing with life til the wee hours.

Tavern Pub, Sheraton Hotel, tel: 02-677 3333. Popular pub, good food and theme nights.

Al Ain

Horse and Jockey, InterContinental Hotel, tel: 03-768 6686. Lively English-style pub. Holds quiz nights.

Paco's Bar, Hilton Hotel, tel: 03-768 6666. Pub with Tex-Mex food. Special nights with music, as advertised on the noticeboard.

Dubai

Bahri Bar, Mina A' Salam, tel: 04-366 8888. Charming Arabian decor yet manages to be hip too. Live jazz. Not to be missed.

Barasti, Le Méridien Mina Seyahi, tel: 04-399 3333. Popular hang-out, especially for Friday sundowners.

Biggles, Millennium Airport Hotel, tel: 04-282 3464. English-style pub decorated with aviation memorabilia. Good food and a popular meeting place.

Billy Blues, Rydges Plaza Hotel, tel: 04-398 2222. A cowboy bar, very lively, fun and young with rhythm-and-blues music. Barbeque food. Open late.

Chelsea Arms, Sheraton Dubai Creek Hotel, tel: 04-207 1721. Pleasant English-style pub. Dark panelled room with stained glass. Jazz and blues appeal to the slightly older crowd.

Crossroads Cocktail Bar & Terrace, Raffles Hotel, Wafi City, tel: 04-314 9888. Upmarket Balinese-inspired bar with attractive outside terrace. Good menu and cocktails.

The Dubliner's, Le Méridien. tel: 04-217 0000. Irish pub. Excellent music and food. Tables outside and inside.

Fibber Magee's, Sheikh Zayed Road, tel: 04-332 2400. Lively Irish bar with live sports TV.

The Irish Village, Aviation Club Tennis Stadium, tel: 04-282 4750. One of the most popular drinking holes in Dubai, with large outside area. Traditional Irish food and music.

Long's, Towers Rotana Hotel. Sheikh Zayed Road, tel: 04-343 8000. Boasts the longest bar in the Middle East.

Qd's, Dubai Creek Yacht Club, tel: 04-295 6000. Outdoor venue on the waterfront. Wonderful in winter.

Scarlett's, Emirates Towers Hotel, tel: 04-319 8088. Large flair bar and restaurant with an American Deep South theme.

Sho Cho, Dubai Marine Beach Resort, tel: 04-346 1111. Japanese seafood restaurant and lounge. Supremely friendly. A nightlife hotspot.

Nightclubs and Discos

Abu Dhabi

Colosseum, Abu Dhabi Marina, tel: 02-644 0300. Roman-themed club and bar.

G Club, Le Méridien Hotel, tel: 02-644 6666. Relaxed atmosphere, with cocktails and regular salsa nights.

Zenith, Sheraton Hotel, tel: 02-677 3333. Two DJs nightly selecting good tunes.

Al Ain

LUCE Ristorante Italiano & Club, InterContinental Al Ain Resort, Resort Garden entrance, tel: 03-768 6686. Listen to a live Colombian band as you dine, then dance until the small hours when the DJ takes over at midnight.

Dubai

Amnesia, Palm Hotel on Sheikh Zayed Road, on the tower of the Hard Rock Café, tel: 04-399 2222. Multi-level dance floors and mix of chart, Arabic, Latin and R&B.

Kasbar, The Palace at the One & Only Royal Mirage Hotel, tel: 04-399 9999. Upscale playground for Dubai residents and visiting VIPs: three-level venue features live music till midnight, then DJs hit the decks with a mix of Arabic and western music.

New Asia Bar and Club, Raffles Hotel at Wafi City, tel: 04-314 9888. 110 cocktails available. Smart-elegant dress code.

Rumours, Ramada Hotel, tel: 04-506 1169. Atmospheric and friendly.

Tehran by Night, St George Hotel, tel: 04-225 1122. Iranian restaurant and club. Excellent late-night downtown feel. Strict door code is enforced.

Serai has resident DJs, **Malecon** is a Cuban restaurant and club and **Boudoir** is a French-themed club offering house music. All at Dubai Marine Beach Resort, Jumeirah, tel: 04-346 1111.

Zinc, Crowne Plaza Dubai, Sheihk Zayed Road, tel: 04-331 1111. Live bands and resident and guest DJs. Very popular.

CHILDREN'S ACTIVITIES

Abu Dhabi

Abu Dhabi Ice Rink
Tel: 02-44 48458. Off Airport Road near Zayed Sports City Stadium. Olympic-size rink with teachers on hand plus ice hockey lessons at the weekend.

Al Ain

Al Ain Zoo and Aquarium
Tel: 03-782 8188. South of town at the foot of Jebel Hafeet. Open Sunday to Friday.

Dubai

Al Nasr Leisureland
Tel: 04-337 1234. Near Zabeel Road. Ice rink, bowling, pool with water slides and wave machine.
Dubai Zoo
Tel: 04-349 6444. On Beach Road in Jumeirah, but due to move to a new location later in 2009.

BELOW: kids paddling on the beach in Ajman.

Galleria Ice Skating Rink
Tel: 04-209 6000. Hyatt Hotel Mall.
Magic Planet
Tel: 04-341 4444. Mall of the
Emirates. Huge indoor area filled with
rides, bumper cars and 10-pin
bowling. Many fast-food restaurants
around the perimeter. Childcare
service.
Sega Republic
Tel: 04-362 7500. Dubai Mall. Sega
indoor theme park due to open mid-
2009.
Wild Wadi Water Park
Tel: 04-348 4444. Next to the
Jumeira Beach Hotel. Unique water
theme park for big and small, based
on an Arabian legend.
WonderLand Theme & Water Park
Tel: 04-324 1222. Next to Al
Garhoud Bridge adjoining the Creek
Park. Rides and amusements for
children including Splashland, a
fantastic area of water rides and
pools next to the creek.

Umm Al Qaiwain

Dreamland Aqua Park
Ras Al Khaimah Road, 17 km (10½
miles) past Umm Al Qaiwain. One of
the largest water parks in the world.
Fantastic rides and scenic walks for
all ages. Cafés and shops.

Cruises

There are many dhow cruises
available. Details from hotels or tour
operators.

SPORTS

The UAE offers numerous choices for
summer sports: there are long,
deserted beaches open to the public,
desert and mountains to explore,
and pools, sports facilities and clubs
in the cities. Many independent
sports clubs and hotels have
gymnasiums, swimming pools and
tennis courts where daily entrance
rates are usually available.

Other sports available include
abseiling, aquabiking, deep-sea
fishing, dune-buggy driving, fishing,
golf, polo, ice skating, go-karting,
sailing, sand skiing, skiing, water
sports of all kinds and more. Horse
and camel races usually take place
on Thursday and Friday during the
cooler winter months, and are open
to everyone. Dhow sailing and racing
are memorable sights – see press.

Major tournaments that attract
world-class players, including golf,
tennis, powerboat racing and horse
racing, are also held throughout the

winter. Details of these events are
advertised in the local press.

Sports Facilities
Abu Dhabi
Beach Rotana Hotel
Tel: 02-697 9000. Floodlit tennis,
swimming pools, water-skiing and
PADI-qualified instructors at the
ocean diving centre.
Al Ain Palace Hotel
Tel: 02-679 4777. Health club,
swimming pool and squash courts.
Hilton Hotel, Hiltonia Club
Tel: 02-681 1900. Beach setting.
Three interconnecting pools, water-
skiing, wind surfing and fitness
centre.
InterContinental
Tel: 02-666 6888. Wonderful beach,
water sports and all facilities.
Le Royal Méridien
Tel: 02-674 2020. Indoor and
outdoor pools, gym and squash
court.
Sheraton Hotel and Resort
Tel: 02-677 3333. Lovely beach.
Water-skiing and beach volleyball.
Boat excursions, fishing trips and
sand boarding can all be arranged.
The Club
Tel: 02-673 1111. Private members'
leisure club for UAE residents and
their guests. Sailing and sub aqua
clubs, kayaking, climbing wall,
swimming pool, tennis, squash and
adults-only beach.

Dubai
Dubai Country Club
Tel: 04-333 1155. Golf, pool, gym.
Jumeirah Beach Hotel
Tel: 04-348 0000. Beach with all
water sports. Tennis courts,
children's club.
**Le Méridien Mina Seyahi Beach
Resort and Marina**
Tel: 04-399 3333. Waterskiing,
kayaking, windsurfing, sailing and
swimming pools.
Le Royal Méridien Beach Resort
Tel: 04-399 5555. Kayaking,
windsurfing, deep sea fishing, tennis
and squash courts.
Ski Dubai
www.skidubai.com. The first indoor ski
resort in the Middle East, with real
snow and five runs.

Al Ain
Contact the **Al Ain Hilton** (tel: 03-768
6666) or the **InterContinental Al Ain
Resort** (tel: 03-768 6686) or Al Ain
Rotana (tel: 03-754 5111).

Fujairah
Hilton Fujairah Resort
Tel: 09-222 2411. Gym, water sports
and beach.

Sandy Beach Hotel and Resort
Tel: 09-244 5555. Beach, diving
centre and watersports.

Sharjah
Sharjah Carlton
Tel: 06-528 3711. Gym, beach and
swimming pools.

Sports Clubs
Abu Dhabi
AD Chess Club
www.abudhabichess.com.
AD Equestrian and Golf Club
Tel: 02-445 5500, www.adec-web.com.
AD Golf Club
Tel: 02-558 8990, www.adgolfclub.com.
AD Health and Fitness Club
Tel: 02-443 6333, www.adhfc.com.
AD Netball League
www.abnetball.com.
AD Rugby Union Football Club
Tel: +971 50 562 1738,
www.abudhabiquins.com.
AD Sailing Club
Tel: 02-673 1111,
www.abudhabisailing.com.
AD Sub Aqua Club
Tel: 02-673 1111,
www.abudhabisubaqua.com.
AD Tennis
Tel: 02-673 1111,
www.abudhabitennis.com.
Al Ghazal Golf Club
Tel: 02-575 8040, www.alghazalgolf.ae.
The Club
Tel: 02-673 1111, www.the-club.com.

Dubai
Desert Sport Diving Club
Tel: 050-853 8652
Dubai Archers
Tel: 050-881 7366
Dubai Flying Association (for qualified
pilots with a minimum of 100 hours
and a valid medical licence)
Tel: 050-625 8440
Dubai International Marine Club
(includes parasailing and sailing)
Tel: 04-399 5777
Dubai Polo and Equestrian Club
Tel: 04-361 8111
Dubai Racing Club, Nad Al Sheba
Racecourse
Tel: 04-327 0077
Dubai Tri Club
www.dubaitriclub.net
Emirates Golf Club
Tel: 04-380 2222
Jebel Ali Equestrian Club
Tel: 04-884 5101
Jebel Ali Shooting Club
Tel: 04-883 6000
Rugby – Dubai Exiles RFC
Tel: 04-832 6728
Umm Al Quwain Skydiving Club
Tel: 06-768 1447
UAE Squash Rackets Association
Tel: 04-824 122, www.dubaisquash.org.

OMAN

THE UAE

LANGUAGE

ABOVE: you can even learn to ski in Dubai, as shown here at Ski Dubai.

SHOPPING

Where to Shop

Many people come to the UAE solely to shop. Goods from all over the world come here, so the choice is huge, and prices are very competitive. You can go to the souqs full of small shops packed to the roof with general goods and electronics, or shop in the huge shopping malls for designer clothing or antiques. Bargaining is expected in the souqs, but in the shopping malls prices are usually fixed. The cities of Abu Dhabi, Dubai and Sharjah are the best for shopping malls and high-quality goods. Ajman and Ras Al Khaimah are unlikely to have anything you can't get in the major centres.

The Dubai Shopping Festival, introduced in 1996, has provided an added draw-card for bargain hunters early each year. More discounts are to be had in the stores and hotels in Dubai Summer Surprises, which attracts visitors to Dubai during the hottest summer months.

The duty-free complexes at the airports are some of the best in the world. The selection is huge and there are discounts, so if you cannot find a gift in town, you will probably find something there. The largest are Dubai, Abu Dhabi and Al Ain.

Export Procedures

If you want to export your purchases, there are hundreds of companies who will advise on procedures and arrange for your goods to be sent anywhere in the world. It is best to seek advice from your hotel or a tour operator who will tell you a reliable company to use.

Complaints

Shopkeepers are generally very keen to have happy customers, and faulty bought goods are usually easily exchanged at the shop of purchase: always keep receipts and ask to see the manager if there is a problem.

Abu Dhabi

Souqs

The traditional souqs with winding bustling alleyways, famed in Oman and Morocco, no longer exist in Abu Dhabi. They have been replaced with modern air-conditioned centres.
The central souq (at Khalifa Street) was demolished in 2005, and will be replaced with a recreation of a traditional souq selling spices, gold and handicrafts at the junction of Khalifa and Hamdan Streets, which is due to open in 2011.
Madinat Zayed (on East Road, near Post Office) is a shopping centre with clothing, perfume and jewellery. The gold souq is located within.
The small Iranian souq (at the Dhow harbour) is probably the closest match to an old style outdoor souq; you can haggle for pottery, paintings and carpets, brought over weekly by boat from Iran.
At the **Emirates Heritage Village**, you can see craftsmen making carpets, glassware, leather goods and silverware, and buy the items.

Perfume

Paris Gallery and Grand Stores (located in Abu Dhabi and Marina malls) sell brand-name perfumes. There are local perfumeries located in Hamdan Centre and Liwa Centre on Hamdan Street.

Jewellery

Al Manara Jewellery, tel: 02-626 8000. On Hamdan St.
Al Masaood Jewellery, tel: 02-633 7800. Khalid Bin Al Walid Street in Khalidiya.
Damas Jewellery, tel: 02-631 6022. Delma centre on Hamdan Street. Twelve other branches in town, each specialising in diamonds, gold or pearl jewellery.
The gold souq, within Madinat Zayed, has a good selection of all types of jewellery.

Antiques, Carpets and Gifts

Many of the 5-star hotels in town have shops selling good quality gift items. Other options are:
Centre of Original Iranian Carpets, tel: 02-681 1156. On 30th Street, at the Corniche.
Gulf Antiques and Carpet Exhibition, tel: 02-645 9956. Khalifa Compound Market.
Handmade Carpet House and Antiques, tel: 02-634 6633. Next to Chamber of Commerce Building, on Corniche.
Persian House of Carpets, tel: 02-645 2115. In Abu Dhabi Mall.
Red Sea Handmade Carpets, tel: 02-626 6145. Khalifa Street, next to Al Noor Hospital.

Shopping Malls

Abu Dhabi Mall, near the Beach Rotana Hotel, in Al Meena.
Marina Mall, on the Breakwater, opposite the Corniche near Emirates Palace.

Dubai

Dubai is world-famous for shopping, and hosts an annual Shopping Festival early in the year, when people visit from around the world to pick up bargains.

Souqs

Old Souq
Lying across the Creek from Deira, this Bur Dubai souq is devoted to textiles, with handicrafts, carpets and silver carvings also available. Mornings are the best time to browse; note also that sales are sometimes held around holidays such as Eid and Diwali.
Deira Gold Souq
Located on 45 Street, off Al Khor Street, is the famous covered gold souq, the main part of which runs along Sikkat Al Khail Street.
Deira Old Souq
Occupying a warren of lanes and

alleyways at the bottom of Old Baladiya Street, this souq sells everything from rice to textiles to stationery. The spice souq, where stallholders display sacks of nutmeg, frankincense and saffron, is also located here, but is shrinking due to competition from hypermarkets.

Fish Souq

The fish market is on the Gulf side of Al Khaleej Road. This is huge and well worth a visit early in the morning. You will find a vast variety of fish and a wonderful bustling atmosphere. Women sell local handicrafts (baskets, incense burners and woven mats) towards the outer edge of the souq area.

Meat and Fruit-and-Vegetable Souqs

Next to the main fish market. Skinned goat, lamb and cow hangs at the smaller meat souq, while the fruit and vegetable souq displays piles of fresh produce.

Shopping Areas

Deira's Al Riqqa Road is a pleasant avenue of boutiques, while the parallel Maktoum Road's boutiques include Versace, Dolce & Gabbana and Cartier.

Al Dhiyafah Road in Satwa also has boutiques dotted along it.

Al Faheidi Road, Bur Dubai, is the centre of electronics and very lively in the evenings. Good prices.

If you want silks or textiles visit the many small shops to the rear of Dubai Museum in Bur Dubai, or Karama for cheap clothes and tailors.

Dubai Marina hosts an open-air craft market on Friday and Saturday between October and April.

Shopping Malls

Al Ghurair City, Al Riqqa Road, Deira.

Al Mulla Plaza, Sharjah Road.

Beach Centre, Jumeirah Beach Road.

BurJuman Centre, Trade Centre Road, Bur Dubai.

Deira City Centre, opposite Dubai Creek Golf and Yacht Club.

Ibn Battuta Mall, Jebel Ali, on Sheikh Zayed Road.

Jumeirah Plaza, pink mall on the Jumeirah Beach Road.

Lamcy Plaza, Oud Metha. Complete with a replica of London's Tower Bridge.

Mall of the Emirates, near Interchange 4, Sheikh Zayed Road.

Mercato Mall, Jumeirah Beach Road.

Oasis Centre, Sheikh Zayed Road.

Souk Madinat Jumeirah, in the eponymous resort.

Town Centre Jumeirah, Jumeirah Beach Road.

Wafi City Mall lies west across the Creek from Dubai Creek Golf Club.

Antiques, Carpets and Gifts

Afghan Carpet Palace. On the Airport Road (tel: 04-286 9661) and in the Oasis Centre, Jumeira (tel: 04-339 5786).

Creative Art Centre. Tel: 04-344 4394. Jumeirah Beach Road. Sells fine art, heritage items and old maps of the region.

Kashmir Craft Corner. Tel: 04-349 7492. Jumeirah Plaza, Jumeirah Beach Road. Sells walnut and rosewood furniture, rugs, wall hangings and much else.

Tehran Persian Carpet. Tel: 04-344 4384. Part of the Persian Carpet House company, in Mercato Mall. Handmade carpets, handicrafts and antiques.

The Camel Company (tel: 04-340 2670) offers souvenirs, and Asala Antiques (tel: 04-341 1993) sells wooden carvings, embroidered clothes and hangings. Both can be found on the first floor of Mall of the Emirates, Sheikh Zayed Road.

Sharjah

Famous for its two main souqs and a good place to buy Persian carpets.

Blue or Central Souq

Next to Sharjah Creek. Two huge blue-domed buildings full of mainly ordinary shops on the ground floor, but a treasure trove of antique furniture, carpets and Gulf mementos awaits upstairs.

Souq Al Arsah (Old Souq)

Behind Bank Street (Al Borj Avenue). Restored area near the Corniche. Old trading houses full of small antique shops selling artefacts and Indian furniture from Rajasthan. Excellent coffee house.

East Coast

Just outside Masafi is an open-air pottery market. This makes a pleasant stopping point on the road to Fujairah and the east coast.

What to Buy

Carpets are brought here from all over Asia, and vary in price from reasonable to very expensive. It is wise not to pay a lot without some knowledge, or having someone along who understands about carpets. There are good selections in Abu Dhabi, Dubai and especially in Sharjah.

Old silver jewellery is becoming hard to find. Omani and heavy Indian Rajasthani silver is available but it isn't cheap.

Gold is good value. The selection is enormous, especially in Dubai, which has the largest gold souq. If you do want to treat yourself (or someone else), this is the place to come. The souq is very well regulated and standards are high. All gold is genuine, and not much is sold below 18 carat. The local tastes are for 22 and 24 carat gold. Old gold can be traded for new, but no consideration of workmanship is made. A cheaper rate is paid for secondhand goods.

Saffron is cheap in the spice souqs, and comes in many qualities. Many other spices are sold from sacks; shops are lined with jars of exotic ingredients.

Perfume, famous throughout Arabia, is worth buying just to visit the perfume shops, sit on cushions and smell the scents from all the decanters. A unique purchase is the scented wood or *oud* for incense burners.

Dried nuts and fruits are cheap and make good presents.

Arabic coffee is sold everywhere in many varieties, including cardamom-flavoured coffee, as well as the uniquely shaped coffee pots which make good souvenirs.

BELOW: shopping for gold in the gold souq.

OMAN

THE UAE

LANGUAGE

LANGUAGE

UNDERSTANDING THE **L**ANGUAGE

Greetings

Hello or **Welcome**/*Márhaba, ahlan*
(reply)/*áhlayn*
Greetings/*As-salám aláykum* (peace be with you)
(reply)/*Waláykum as-salám* (and to you peace)
Good morning/Sabáh al-kháyr
(reply)/*Sabáh an-núr* (a morning of light)
Good evening/*Misá al-kháyr*
(reply)/*Misá an núr*
Good night/*Tisbáh al-kháyr* (wake up well)
(reply)/*Wa ínta min áhlu* (and you are from His people)
Good bye/*Máa Saláma*
How are you?/*Káyf hálak?* (to a man)/*Káyf hálik?* (to a woman)
Fine, thank you/*Zayn, al-hámdu, li-la*
Please/*min fádlak* (to a man)/*min fádlik* (to a woman)
Thank you/*Shúkran*
Thanks be to God/*Al-hámdu li-llá*
God willing (hopefully)/*Inshá allá*
Yes/*Náam* or *áiwa*
No/*La*

Useful Phrases

What is your name?/*Shú ismak?* (to a man)/*Shú ismik?* (to a woman)
My name is.../*Ismi...*
Where are you from?/*Min wáyn inta?* (for a man)/*Min wáyn inti?* (for a woman)
I am from: England/*Ána min Ingíltra*
the United States/*Ána min Amérika*
Australia/*Ána min Ustrália*
Do you speak English?/*Btíhki inglízi?*
I speak English/*Bíhki inglízi*
I do not speak Arabic/*Ma bíhki árabi*
I do not understand/*Ma báfham*
Repeat, once more/*Kamán márra*
Do you have...?/*Ándkum...?*
Is there any...?/*Fí...?*
There isn't any.../*Ma fí...*

Never mind/*Ma'alésh*
It is forbidden.../*Mamnú'a*
What is this?/*Shú hádha?*
I want/*Uríd*
I do not want/*Mauríd*
Hurry up/*Yalla/bi súra'a*
Slow down/*Shwáyya*
Go away!/*Imshi!*
What time is it?/*Adáysh as-sáa?/kam as-sáa?*
How long, how many hours?/*Kam sáa?*

Vocabulary

General

embassy/*safára*
post office/*máktab al-baríd*
stamps/*tawábi'a*
bank/*bank*
hotel/*otél/fúnduq*
museum/*máthaf*
ticket/*tádhkara*
passport/*jiwáz as-sáfar*
good/*kuwáys*
not good, bad/*mish kuways*
open/*maftúh*
closed/*musákkar/múghlik*
today/*al-yáum*
tonight/*allaylah*
tomorrow/*baachir*

Eating Out/Drinking

restaurant/*máta'am*
food/*ákl*
fish/*simich*
meat/*láhm*
milk/*halíb*
bread/*khúbz*
salad/*saláta*
delicious/*ladhidh*
coffee/*káhwa*
tea/*chai*
cup/*finján*
with sugar/*bi súkkar*
without sugar/*bidún súkkar*
mineral water/*mái ma'adaniya*
glass/*gelaas*

bottle/*zajaja/botel*
I am a vegetarian/*Ána nabbáti* (for a man)/*nabbátiya* (for a woman)
the bill/*al-hisáb*

Getting Around

Where...?/*Wáyn...?*
downtown/*wást al bálad*
street/*shária*
car/*sayára*
taxi/*táxi*
shared taxi/*servís*
bus/*bas*
aeroplane/*tayára*
airport/*matár*
to/*íla*
from/*min*
right/*yamín*
left/*yassar*
straight/*gida*
petrol, super/*benzín*

Numbers

zero/*sifir*
one/*wáhad*
two/*ithnayn*
three/*taláta*
four/*árba'a*
five/*khámsa*
six/*sítta*
seven/*sába'a*
eight/*tamánia*
nine/*tísa'a*
ten/*áshara*
eleven/*hidáshar*
twelve/*itnáshar*

Shopping

market/*souq*
shop/*dukkán*
money/*fulús*
cheap/*rakhís*
expensive (very)/*gháli (jídan)*
receipt, invoice/*fatúra, wásl*
How much does it cost?/*Adáysh?/bi-kam?*
I like this/*Buhíbb hádha*
I do not like this/*Ma buhíbb hádha*

FURTHER READING

History and Reference

A History of the Arab Peoples, A. Hourani. Excellent introduction to the peoples of the region.
Arabia, The Gulf and the West, J.B. Kelly. A long history of the dealings between the West and the Gulf.
The Arabs, Peter Mansfield. Broad history of the Middle East, and look at its current politics.
Inside the Arab World, Michael Field. One of the best analyses of the politics of the Arab world.

The UAE

From Rags to Riches: A Story of Abu Dhabi, Mohammed Al Fahim. Reminiscence by one of the UAE's leading businessmen of how he started as a small boy with no education or wealth.
From Trucial States to United Arab Emirates, Frauke Heard-Bey. Covers all aspects of the UAE.
Myth of Arab Piracy in the Gulf, Sultan Muhammed Al Qasimi, Ruler of Sharjah. A detailed account of how the UAE Arabs met and skirmished with the British and India in the 18th and 19th centuries.
Rashid's Legacy: The Genesis of the Maktoum Family, Graeme Wilson. Depicts the family's history and approach to transforming Dubai.
Sheikh Zayed Life and Times 1918–2004, through the lens of Noor Ali Rashid. The history of a nation personified in its founder. Published by Motivate.
Telling Tales: An Oral History of Dubai, Julia Wheeler. Photographs accompany insights from some of Dubai's founding citizens. Written by a BBC Gulf correspondent.
The Trucial States, Donald Hawley. Historical perspective written by a British ex-diplomat.
This Strange Eventful History: Memoirs of earlier days in the UAE and Oman, Edward Henderson. A good account of how the country evolved.
The Wind of Morning, Colonel Sir Hugh Boustead. An autobiography of a British soldier who served in Abu Dhabi, and retired to run the stables belonging to the ruler of Abu Dhabi.

Oman

Forts of Oman, Walter Dinteman, published by Motivate. Pictorial account of the role of the fort in Oman's history.
Oman and Its Renaissance, Donald Hawley, published by Stacey International.
Oman and Muscat, An Early Modern History, Patricia Risso, published by Croom Helm.
Oman: A Seafaring Nation, William Facey, Ministry of Heritage and Culture.
Seafarers of the Gulf, Shirley Kay, published by Motivate. A chronicle of the importance of the sea in the history of the Gulf.
Travels to Oman, Ronald Codrai, published by Motivate. Diary extracts and photographs of Oman before the boom.
Wings Over the Gulf, Shirley Kay. A history of civil aviation in the Gulf from the early 1920s.

Business

Don't They Know It's Friday? Jeremy Williams, published by Motivate. Comprehensive guide on doing business in the Middle East.
Dubai Property Investment Guide. The ins and outs of buying freehold in the emirate. Published by Cross Border Legal Publishing.
Dubai Red-Tape, Explorer Publishing. Covers everything from business to communicating to housing.
Living and Working in Dubai, Pippa Sanderson. An ex-resident highlights the pros and cons.
Setting up in Dubai, Essam Al Tamimi. Covers the process and legal procedures involved in starting up a business.
The Arab Way: How to Work More Effectively with Arab Cultures, Dr J. Al-Omari. Guide to developing successful business relationships in the Middle East.

People and Society

The Bedouin, Shirley Kay. Traditions surrounding marriage and childbirth, tribal and social structures in the UAE.

Culture Shock – UAE, Gina L. Crocetti. Useful guide to customs and etiquette.
Explorers of Arabia, Zahra Freeth and Victor Winstone. Profiles of important early travellers.
Heart-beguiling Araby – The English Romance with Arabia, Kathryn Tidrick. Account of travels in Arabia by various literary figures in the 19th century and up until World War I.
The Merchants, Michael Field. Focusing on nine of the Gulf's prominent families, gives a good impression of how society has changed since oil.
The New Arabians, Peter Mansfield. A wide-ranging look at post-oil Gulf society by one of the most respected writers on the region. Sadly, it stops in the early 1980s.
Oman Before 1970, Ian Skeet. A sympathetic portrait of pre-oil Oman, giving a wealth of social detail which is still relevant today.
Travelling the Sands, Andrew Taylor, published by Motivate. Explorers of the Arabian Peninsula.
Understanding Arabs: A Guide for Westerners, M. K. Nydell. Accessible guide to the cultures and customs of the Arab world.

Women

Arab Women: Old Boundaries, New Frontiers, Judith E. Tucker. Collection of women's writing on the changing lives of Arab women.
Mother Without a Mask, Patricia Holton. A personal account from a Western woman who lived with a UAE family.
Behind the Veil in Arabia: Women in Oman, Unni Wikan. Fairly academic, but a good book on Gulf customs and traditions, and women's role in rural society.
Women of Sand & Myrrh, Hanan Al Shaykh. Collection of women's stories.
The Women of the United Arab Emirates, Linda U. Soffan.

Falconry

Falconry and Birds of Prey in the Gulf, Dr David Remple and Christian

Gross, published by Motivate. Good photographs and excellent insight.
Falconry in Arabia, Mark Allen. Well-written and all-embracing.

Horses

Dubai Millennium: A Vision Realised, a Dream Lost, Rachel Pagones. The life of Sheikh Mohammed's horse, from winning the world's richest horse race to his tragic end.

Coffee-table Books

Abu Dhabi – An Arabian Album, Ronald Codrai, published by Motivate. Diary extracts and mid-20th-century photographs.
Al Ain – Oasis City, Peter Hellyer and R. Buckton, published by Motivate.
Bedouin, Alan Keohane. Photographs of Bedouin tribes.
Crossing the Sands, Wilfred Thesiger, published by Motivate. Chronicles the five years the writer spent with the Bedu.
A Day Above Oman, John Nowell, published by Motivate. Stunning aerial photography of Oman.
A Day Above the Emirates, John Nowell, published by Motivate. Aerial photography of the UAE.
Dubai: A City Portrait, Patrick Lichfield. Lavish coffee-table book.
Dubai – An Arabian Album, Ronald Codrai, published by Motivate. Diary extracts and collection of mid-20th-century photographs.
Dubai 24 Hours, by Michael Tobias, published by Motivate. The city as experienced by a team of Dubai's leading photographers during the course of a single day.
Dubai: The Arabian Dream, David Saunders, published by IB Tauris & Co. Account of Dubai's rapid development, illustrated with many stunning photographs.
Emirates, Helene Rogers and Kevin Higgins. The seven emirates' natural and man-made wonders.
The Emirates by The First Photographers, William Facey and Gillian Grant.
Fujairah – An Arabian Jewel, Peter Hellyer, published by Motivate. Portrait of the east coast.
Images of Dubai, by Explorer Publishing. Inspiring visual guide to Dubai by various photographers
images of Women – The Portrayal of Women in Photography of the Middle East 1860–1950, Sarah Graham-Brown.
Now and Then Dubai, Robert Nowell. Comparison pictures of past and present, published by Zodiac Publishing.
Oman: A Pictorial Tour, Jaap Croese.

One Second in the Arab World, 50 years of Photographic Memoirs, Ronald Codrai. Photographic history.
Photography of Kamil Chadirji 1920–1940. Social photographs.
Portrait of Ras Al Khaimah, Shirley Kay, published by Motivate. Interesting account of the history and progress of this emirate.
Sharjah and the North-East Sheikhdoms – An Arabian Album, Ronald Codrai, published by Motivate. Interesting old photographs of the area.
The UAE Formative Years, 1965–75. A Collection of Historical Photographs, Ramesh Shukla.
The UAE: Visions of Change, Noor Ali Rashid. Photographs from 1958 to 1997.
The United Arab Emirates and Oman, W. Weiss and K. Westermann, published by Motivate.
Visions of a Nomad, Wilfred Thesiger. Thesiger's photographs taken over 50 years cover the Arab world as well as Asia and Africa.

Food

The Complete Middle East Cookbook, Tess Mallos. Contains etiquette and customs.
The Complete UAE Cookbook, Celia Ann Brock-Al Ansari. Recipes, customs and traditions from the area alongside glossy photographs.
The New Book of Middle Eastern Food, Claudia Roden. Interesting and easy-to-use recipe book.
Vegetarian Dishes from the Middle East, Arto Der Haroutunian. Stories introduce many of the recipes.

Archaeology

Atlantis of the Sands: The Search for the Lost City of Ubar, Ranulph Fiennes. Archaeological discovery in southern Oman.
Filling in the Blanks, Peter Hellyer, published by Motivate. Recent discoveries made in Abu Dhabi and on the island of Umm Al Nar.

Islam

A New Introduction to Islam, Daniel W. Brown. A clear and well-organised look at Muslim beliefs as well as the development of Islamic studies.
Islam and the West, Bernard Lewis. A view on the East–West relationship by the Professor of Arabic at Edinburgh University.
Nine Parts of Desire – The Hidden World of Islamic Women, Geraldine Brooks. Based on the author's personal experiences of talking to women in the Gulf.

The Caged Virgin – A Muslim Woman's Cry for Reason, Ayaan Hirsi Ali. Controversial attempts to free women from oppressive Islamic practices.
The Koran (with parallel Arabic text), N.J. Dawood. An invaluable translation.
The Koran Interpreted, A.J. Arberry. Insights into the holy book of Islam.

Travel Writing/Novels

Among the Believers - An Islamist Journey, V.S. Naipaul. Analysis of Islamic fundamentalism as Naipaul journeys through Iran and Pakistan.
Arabian Destiny, Edward Henderson, published by Motivate Publishing. Autobiography.
Arabian Sands, Wilfred Thesiger. Journeys made from 1945–1950 in and around the Empty Quarter of Oman, Saudi Arabia and the UAE.
Arabia Through the Looking Glass, Jonathan Raban. An excellent and amusing overview of the different Gulf and Middle Eastern countries.
Dubai Tales, Muhammed Al Murr. Short stories set in Dubai and area.
Freya Stark in Persia, South Arabia, Iraq and Kuwait, Malise Ruthven. A biography of one of the greatest British travellers in the remote parts of 20th-century Arabia.
Sandstorms – Days and Nights in Arabia, Peter Theroux. Amusing observations of expatriate life.
The Son of a Duck is a Floater, Primrose Arnander and Ashkhain Skipwith. A collection of Arab proverbs and sayings.
The Wink of the Mona Lisa, Mohammad Al Murr. Short stories by a leading UAE writer.

Poetry

Soul of Sea: A Journey to the Coastal Waters of the Emirates and Oman, written and published by Gloria Kifayeh and Toni Briegel.
The Prophet, Kahlil Gibran. The world-renowned collection of 26 poetic essays that have never been out of print since first published in 1923.

Art and Architecture

Architectural Heritage of the Gulf, Shirley Kay and Dariush Zandi, published by Motivate. Traditional architectural styles of the UAE.
Islamic Art, David Talbot Rice. The definitive general study of the subject. Rather academic but packed with information.
The Mosque, Martin Frishman and Hasan-Uddin Khan. Glossy

photographic book on the historical and architectural diversity in mosques.
Omani Silver, Ruth Hawley. A great book for professional and amateur collectors of Gulf silver.

Arabic Language

Berlitz Arabic Guaranteed, an all-audio course comprising simple lessons on four audio CDs. A free downloadable audioscript is available.
Berlitz Arabic in 60 Minutes, all-audio course with more than 250 words and phrases. Audioscript provided.
Berlitz Arabic Phrase Book & Dictionary, a two-way dictionary of useful words accompanies language on new technologies, business and general conversation.
Very Simple Arabic Script, James Peters. The title says it all.

Wildlife and Flora

Arabia: Sand, Sea, Sky, Michael McKinnon, published by BBC Books. Natural history of the peninsula's land and shore.
Beachcombers' Guide to the Gulf, Tony Woodward, published by Motivate. Useful for anyone interested in knowing more about what they see on the Gulf beaches.
The Birds of Oman, M. Gallagher and M. Woodcock, published by Quartet Books. The book's large size makes it impractical as a field guide but it is an attractive volume.
Birds of Southern Arabia, Dave Robinson and Adrian Chapman, published by Motivate. Photographs and anecdotes.
Birds of the Middle East, R.F. Porter, S. Christensen and P. Schiermacker-Hansen. Excellent field guide.
Butterflies of Oman, T.B. Larsen, published by Bartholomew Books. A 1984 reprint of a first edition, with descriptions and colour illustrations of more than 70 species.
The Green Guide to the Emirates, Marycke Jongbloed. Invaluable information about the relationship of man and nature in the desert, as well as details on the country's conservation policies.
The Living Seas, Frances Dipper and Tony Woodward, published by Motivate. Interesting text and brilliant underwater photographs.
Mammals of the Southern Gulf, Christian Gross, published by Motivate. Photographic account of the amazing variety of sea life.
Natural Emirates – Wildlife and Environment of the UAE, Peter Vine

et al. Includes coverage of mammals, fossils, conservation and the Bedouins' relationship with nature.
Seashells of Eastern Arabia, edited by S. Peter Dance. One thousand photographs and drawings, featuring more than 1,270 species.
Snorkelling and Diving in Oman, Robert Baldwin and Rod Salm, published by Motivate. Maps and descriptions of the best places to enjoy Oman's ocean life.

Off-Road Driving

Oman Off-Road and **UAE Off-Road**, published by Explorer Publishing. Excellent guides featuring satellite imaging and GPS co-ordinates for 20 routes.
The Off-Roader's Manual, J. Ali Khan, published by Motivate.
Off-Road in the Emirates, Dariush Zandi, published by Motivate. An indispensable spiral-bound guide to 15 routes. The definitive work.

Golf

On Course in the Gulf, Adrian Flaherty. Guide to the game on grass and sand. Includes GCC directory of golf courses.

Books published by Motivate Publishing can be found on the website www.booksarabia.com.

Send Us Your Thoughts

We do our best to ensure the information in our books is as accurate and up-to-date as possible. The books are updated on a regular basis using local contacts, who painstakingly add, amend and correct as required. However, some details (such as telephone numbers and opening times) are liable to change, and we are ultimately reliant on our readers to put us in the picture.

We welcome your feedback, especially your experience of using the book "on the road". Maybe we recommended a hotel that you liked (or another that you didn't), or you came across a great bar or new attraction we missed.

We will acknowledge all contributions, and we'll offer an Insight Guide to the best letters received.

Please write to us at:
Insight Guides
PO Box 7910
London SE1 1WE
Or email us at:
insight@apaguide.co.uk

Other Insight Guides

With their expert text and stunning images, the classic Insight Guides inspire and motivate, help with advance planning and provide a great souvenir of your trip. Titles in this region include: Egypt, Gambia & Senegal, Jordan, Kenya, Morocco, Namibia and Tanzania & Zanzibar.

Insight **Step by Step Guides** are a stylish series of self-guided walks and tours, written by local experts and designed to help travellers get the most out of a destination. Titles include Dubai and Marrakesh.

Insight **Smart Guides** are a new series which will satisfy independent travellers looking for comprehensive listings presented in a snappy, easy-to-find way. The listings provide all the information needed to keep foodies, clubbers, culture vultures and keen shoppers busy. Titles include Dubai and Marrakesh.

ART AND PHOTO CREDITS

⚜ **INSIGHT GUIDE**

OMAN & THE UAE

Cartographic Editor **Zoë Goodwin**
Production **Linton Donaldson**
Design Consultants
Carlotta Junger, Graham Mitchener
Picture Research **Hilary Genin**

INDEX

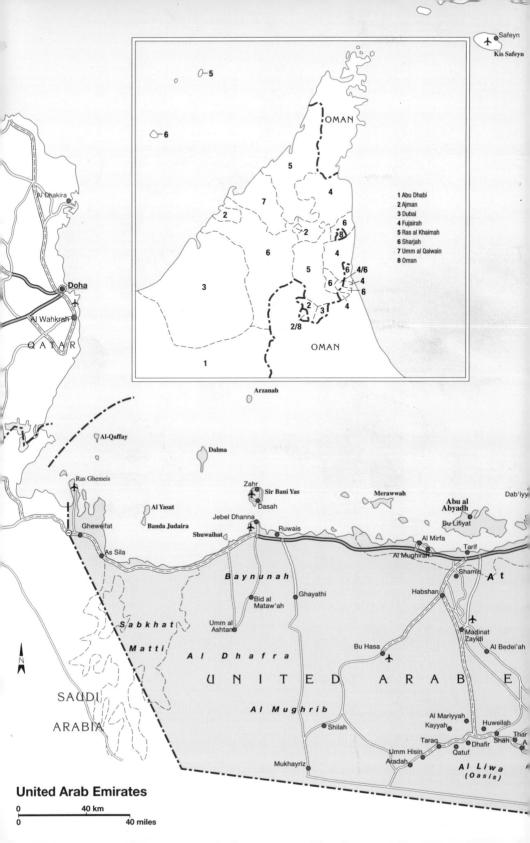

OMAN

1 Abu Dhabi
2 Ajman
3 Dubai
4 Fujairah
5 Ras al Khaimah
6 Sharjah
7 Umm al Qaiwain
8 Oman

5

6

5

7

4

2

6

6

4

3

6

5

6

4/6
4
6
4

2
3
2/8

1

OMAN

Arzanah

Safeyn
Kis Safeyn

Al Dhakira

Doha

Al Wahkrah

QATAR

Al-Qaffay

Dalma

Zahr
Sir Bani Yas
Dasah

Merawwah

Dab'iyy

Abu al Abyadh

Al Yasat

Banda Judaira

Jebel Dhanna

Shuwaihat

Ruwais

Bu Lifiyat

Al Mirfa

Tarif

Ras Ghemeis

Gheweifat

Al Mughirah

Shamis

A t

As Sila

B a y n u n a h

Habshan

S a b k h a t

Bid al Mataw'ah

Ghayathi

Umm al Ashtan

M a t t i

A l   D h a f r a

Bu Hasa

Madinat Zayidi

Al Bedei'ah

N

U N I T E D   A R A B   E

SAUDI

ARABIA

A l   M u g h r i b

Shilah

Al Mariyyah
Kayyah

Huweilah

Shah
Thar
A

Taraq

Dhafir

Umm Hisin
Aradah

Qatuf

*A l   L i w a
(O a s i s)*

Mukhayriz

United Arab Emirates

0   40 km

0   40 miles